To JOE —

A longtime fan and
student of the game!
Go giants!

Dan Font

the GIANTS

BASEBALL EXPERIENCE

A YEAR-BY-YEAR CHRONICLE

FROM NEW YORK TO SAN FRANCISCO

Dan Fost

MVP
BOOKS

First published in 2014 by MVP Books, an imprint of Quayside Publishing Group, Inc.
400 First Avenue North, Suite 400, Minneapolis, MN 55401 USA

MVP Books titles are also available at discounts in bulk quantity for industrial or
sales-promotional use. For details write to Special Sales Manager at Quayside
Publishing Group, Inc. 400 First Avenue North, Suite 400, Minneapolis, MN 55401 USA.

To find out more about our books, visit us online at www.mvpbooks.com.

Library of Congress Cataloging-in-Publication Data

ISBN-13: 978-0-7603-4572-6

On the front cover: Willie Mays, circa 1970. *Focus on Sport/Getty Images*
On the previous page: AT&T Park, 2010. *Eric Broder Van Dyke/Shutterstock.com*
On the following pages: AT&T Park, 2011. *Marcio Jose Sanchez/Getty Images*

Text compiled, edited, and fact-checked by Facts That Matter, Inc.
Contributing writer and editor: David Aretha
Contributing writer: Eric Short
Acquiring editor: Josh Leventhal
Design manager: James Kegley
Designer: Kim Winscher

Printed in China

CONTENTS

Introduction: Heartache and Happiness 4

The Nineteenth Century: Growing Into Giants. 6

The 1900–1909: Big Six and Big Brawls 12

The 1910s: No Cigars, Only Heartache 30

The 1920s: A New Dynasty 48

The 1930s: Passing the Torch. 66

The 1940s: Nice Guys, No Titles 84

The 1950–1957: A Miracle and a Move 100

The 1958–1969: Big-Time Bridesmaids 118

The 1970s: A Long Struggle 140

The 1980s: Earth-Shaking Developments 156

The 1990s: Staying Put, Moving Forward 176

The 2000s: Champs Again, At Long Last 192

Index 220

Heartache and Happiness

Giants fans endure decades of "torture," from McCovey's lineout to the World Series collapse of 2002, before embracing two improbable runs to glory in the 2010s.

Being a fan of the Giants—whether you date yourself to the glory days of New York's Polo Grounds, the frigid summers at San Francisco's Candlestick Park, or the renewed success in AT&T Park—means coming to terms with a storied but tortured history.

My first lesson came quickly. When I moved to the Bay Area in 1989, a newspaper headline proclaimed "Baseball Heaven" as the Giants and Oakland A's won their leagues and prepared to meet in a "Bay Bridge World Series." The joy turned quickly to tragedy as a now-infamous earthquake struck the region moments before the Giants' first World Series home game in 27 years. The A's swept the Series, and the Giants continued their ringless run in San Francisco.

My love for the Giants deepened as Barry Bonds joined manager Dusty Baker and the team showed a knack for winning everything but the big one. In 2002, I received my most painful lesson. With the Giants leading that year's World Series three games to two over the Angels, and leading Game Six 5–0 in the seventh inning, their history of heartbreak caught up with them, and they blew that game and the next one, losing it all again. A colleague posted her young son's lament in our in-house computer system: "They broke our hearts, and we knew they were going to break our hearts, because they always break our hearts."

I knew that the Cubs and Red Sox claimed cursed histories, but I hadn't quite realized the extent to which the Giants traveled under a similar cloud. The more I looked into it, though, the more uncanny it appeared. A light-hitting shortstop—it was the Cardinals' Jose Oquendo, but it might as well have been Bucky Dent—blasted a home run to destroy the 1987 season. A 103-win season in 1993 ended in second place and out of the playoffs, a year before baseball instituted the wildcard. J. T. Snow hit a clutch playoff home run against the Mets, but the game was lost in extra innings; Gold Glove right fielder Jose Cruz Jr. made a critical error to cost another playoff series.

Maybe it was in the genes. Their predecessors, the fabled New York Giants, won five championships but lost many more in the most gut-wrenching ways imaginable. For every "Miracle at Coogan's Bluff," the history includes a "Merkle's Boner" and "Snodgrass's Muff."

Heinie Zimmerman blew a rundown in the 1917 World Series, inspiring calls of game-fixing that pre-dated the Black Sox scandal. A 12th-inning bad hop ended the 1924 World Series.

John McGraw's teams won 10 pennants but only three World Series. Legendary Hall of Famers Bill Terry, Carl Hubbell, and Mel Ott could lead the Giants to only one title. Even after Bobby Thomson hit the famed "Shot Heard 'Round the World" in 1951, the Giants lost the World Series to the dreaded Yankees. New York didn't have long to savor the Giants' victory in the 1954 Fall Classic; three years later, the team left town.

In making baseball a national pastime in the 1950s, the Giants brought their legacy for both triumph and tragedy to the West Coast—and took it to a new level. Despite fielding some of the greatest teams in history, the San Francisco Giants also endured one of the game's longest championship droughts, spanning more than half a century. They came inches away from a title in 1962, losing Game Seven to the Yankees 1–0 after Willie McCovey, with runners on second and third, lined out to Bobby Richardson. Teams loaded with Willie Mays, Juan Marichal, and McCovey never finished first again.

They suffered along with the fans through the years at Candlestick Park, as misbegotten a ballpark as baseball has ever known. Yet against all odds, the team returned to winning ways, built a gem in downtown San Francisco, and kept alive the legacy of good—but not championship—baseball.

Finally, in 2010 and again in 2012, the Giants brought an end to the torture and produced not just one but two improbable titles for San Francisco. Fueled by castoffs and misfits, pitching and defense, the genius of Bruce Bochy and the brilliance of Buster Posey, the Giants managed to take ownership of their penchant for heartache and turn it on its head. They won in 2010 by squeaking out so many tight games that broadcaster Duane Kuiper would cry in anguish, "Giants baseball—it's torture!" Fans and players embraced the call. In 2012, torture reached new heights, as the Giants found themselves with their backs against the wall six times, yet each time they staved off elimination, ultimately sweeping the heavily favored Detroit Tigers in the World Series.

So now as a Giants fan I've seen it all. I've endured the frustration, and I've stood with the throngs one million strong along Market Street, screaming ourselves hoarse at the victory parades. *The Giants Baseball Experience* aims to give you a taste of the highs and lows—the thrills and agony of more than a century of Giants baseball.

I can't wait to see what comes next.

—Dan Fost

The Polo Grounds during the 1905 World Series. *Library of Congress Prints and Photographs Division*

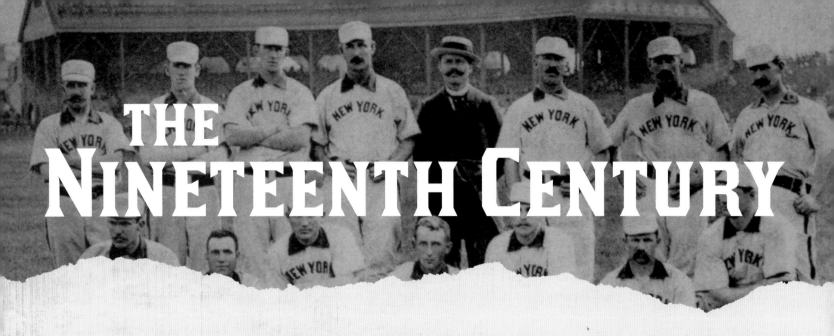

THE NINETEENTH CENTURY

GROWING INTO GIANTS

In the 1800s, the team evolves from the Mutuals and Mets to the Gothams and Giants. Along the way, a tip from a shoeshine boy leads to a new home in Manhattan, at a field called the Polo Grounds.

If you ask old New York Giants fans what year the team left for San Francisco, they will respond in an instant: 1958. They wear that number on a black band across their baseball soul. But if you ask these same fans what year the New York Giants *began*, you likely would be met with a puzzled look. That's to be expected.

The New York Giants were never exactly born. They just sort of evolved.

For all intents and purposes, the Giants began in 1883. But they weren't known as the Giants then. They were the New York Nationals, a.k.a. the Gothams. Actually, we need to begin this complicated tale during the year of America's Centennial celebration, 1876.

That was the year that William Hulbert, a former official with the Chicago White Stockings of the National Association (NA), spearheaded the formation of the National League. Hulbert had been repulsed by the lack of integrity in the NA: fans and even players getting drunk during games; players ignoring the terms of their contracts and signing with the highest bidder; teams that were out of contention deciding to skip late-season road trips; and players, under the influence of gamblers, tanking games. "Fixing" was such a big problem that law enforcement officials sometimes posted signs at ballparks announcing that the outcomes of games should not be trusted.

As president of the new eight-team National League, Hulbert demanded more disciplined behavior. Gambling and alcohol were banned from ballparks, and baseball would not be played on the Sabbath (Sunday). Players were not allowed to jump teams, and teams were required to play every game on their schedules.

That last rule proved to be the demise of the New York Mutuals, an NL team that played on a ragged field in Brooklyn. Near season's end, Mutuals owner and manager Bill

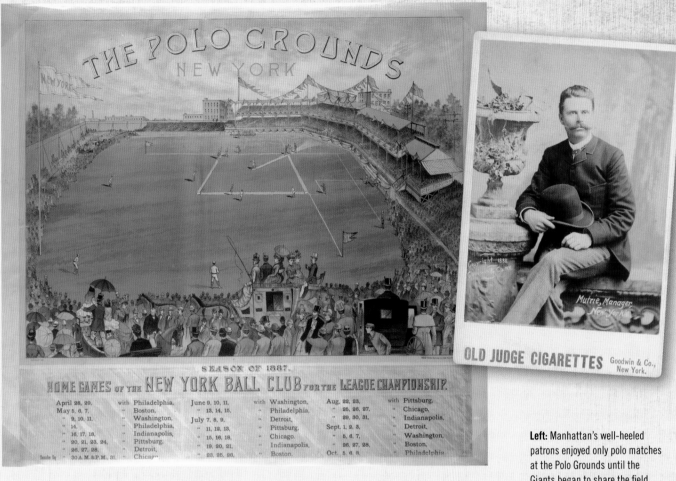

SEASON OF 1887.
HOME GAMES OF THE NEW YORK BALL CLUB FOR THE LEAGUE CHAMPIONSHIP.

April 28, 29.	with Philadelphia.	June 9, 10, 11.	with Washington.	Aug. 22, 23.	with Pittsburg.
May 5, 6, 7.	" Boston.	" 13, 14, 15.	" Philadelphia.	" 25, 26, 27.	" Chicago.
" 9, 10, 11.	" Washington.	July 7, 8, 9.	" Detroit.	" 29, 30, 31.	" Indianapolis.
" 14.	" Philadelphia.	" 11, 12, 13.	" Pittsburg.	Sept. 1, 2, 3.	" Detroit.
" 16, 17, 18.	" Indianapolis.	" 15, 16, 18.	" Chicago.	" 5, 6, 7.	" Washington.
" 20, 21, 23, 24.	" Pittsburg.	" 19, 20, 21.	" Indianapolis.	" 26, 27, 28.	" Boston.
" 26, 27, 28.	" Detroit.	" 23, 25, 26.	" Boston.	Oct. 5, 6, 8.	" Philadelphia
" 30 A.M.&P.M., 31.	" Chicago.				

OLD JUDGE CIGARETTES Goodwin & Co., New York.

Left: Manhattan's well-heeled patrons enjoyed only polo matches at the Polo Grounds until the Giants began to share the field. *Library of Congress Prints and Photographs Division.* **Above:** "Truthful" Jim Mutrie, the first to call New York's National League team the Giants, managed the club to World Series titles in 1888 and 1889. *Library of Congress Prints and Photographs Division*

Cammeyer—pressed for cash—decided not to send his team on a road trip. With the team well below .500, Cammeyer didn't think it was a big deal. To Hulbert, it was. At a league meeting that December, the Mutuals were expelled from the league. For the same reason, so too were the Philadelphia Athletics.

For the president of the fledgling league, it was a bold move to kick out the teams representing the two largest markets in America. The National League needed New York City. Yet, when Hulbert went to his grave in April 1882, the only New York teams were from New York State—the Buffalo Bisons and Troy Trojans.

Talent was wasting away in Troy. Despite dismal attendance figures—for example, 25 fans on the last day of the 1882 season—the Trojans fielded four future Hall of Famers: pitching greats Tim Keefe and Mickey Welch, catching legend Buck Ewing, and first baseman Roger Connor, who would go on to become the major league home run king until Babe Ruth demolished his career record of 138 four-baggers.

In 1882, a new league emerged to challenge the NL. The American Association (AA) was a low-class operation that charged just 25 cents for admission (half the NL rate). Players wore gaudy silk uniforms and games attracted working-class fans, many of whom used the experience as an excuse to get drunk. Nevertheless, the AA was a threat to the National League, and the NL needed to step up its game to remain the superior circuit. Entering 1883, both the AA and NL craved what they did not have: a team in New York City. John B. Day sought to appease both leagues.

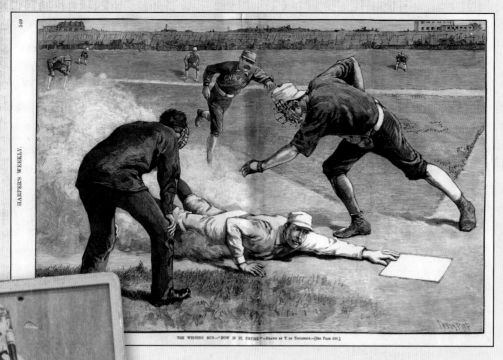

A young, well-to-do tobacco merchant, Day was also a frustrated jock. In the late 1870s, he had organized a team in Orange, New Jersey, and served as the pitcher—until he realized he couldn't get hitters out. In 1880, Day teamed with James Mutrie to form the Metropolitans, an independent pro ball club that played in Brooklyn. Known as the Mets, the team fielded good players but had a hard time drawing spectators.

Day would have preferred to play in Manhattan, which had double the population of Brooklyn (1.2 million compared to 600,000). Unfortunately, as Day explained to a shoeshine boy, he didn't know of a place to play ball in Manhattan.

"I know a place," the boy replied. "The polo grounds at 110th Street and Sixth Avenue."

Day discovered that the field was owned by James Gordon Bennett, Jr., the son of the owner of the New York *Herald* newspaper. They played polo there, of course, but Day leased the grounds and prepped it for baseball. It was a gorgeous venue, with an impressive wooden grandstand and a level, grassy field.

The Mets won 81 games in 1881, including 18 in skirmishes with National League teams. With terrific talent, a great field, and a fan base in New York City (Manhattan, no less), Day's Mets were invited to join the American Association in their inaugural 1882 season. Day and Mutrie decided to decline, preferring to remain independent while trying convince the more prestigious NL to accept them.

After the '82 campaign, Day stunned everyone. He submitted his Mets to the AA while also accepting an invitation to join the NL. The National League club would be managed by a veteran catcher named John Clapp and populated by players from the Troy Trojans, who had disbanded after the '82 season due to poor attendance. Buck Ewing, Roger Connor, and Mickey Welch went to the new National League team, known as both the New York Nationals and New York Gothams. Troy pitching great Tim Keefe suited up with Day's Mets of the American Association.

For the inaugural 1883 season, Day fielded both of his teams at the Polo Grounds. But like a theater owner in the Jim Crow South, he segregated them—not by race, but by class. Day believed that the more "civilized" National League fans, who paid a full 50 cents for admission, would not want to mingle with the drunken, rowdy AA "cranks." So he installed a canvas fence down the middle of the large Polo Grounds. The Nationals played on one side, where the towering grandstand stood, while the Mets got the "back of the bus" treatment by playing on the crummy side, where Day's men poured raw garbage to fill in uneven sections.

Hall of Famer John Montgomery "Monte" Ward, who formed baseball's first players union, stole 111 bases for New York in 1887. *Library of Congress Prints and Photographs Division*

The 1883 New York Gothams is the same franchise as the New York Giants. The latter moniker came about in mid-decade, when Mutrie—who would become New York's manager—began to refer to his dominating ball club as his "giants." As with other clubs of the era, the new nickname stuck when the majority of reporters and fans started using it.

When the Gothams took the field for Opening Day on May 1, 1883—their very first game—no one could have imagined that the franchise would remain intact 130 years later. Reports indicate that a large crowd flocked to the Polo Grounds that day and enjoyed a 7–5 triumph over the Boston Beaneaters. Even former president Ulysses S. Grant was on hand to root for the home team.

The Gothams finished at 46–50 in their inaugural season, as Connor batted .357 and Welch went 25–23. In 1884, the Gothams improved to 62–50 (fourth place) while the Mets won the American Association pennant—but lost money. That prompted Day to take advantage of his dual ownership. For 1885, he transferred Mets manager Jim Mutrie and pitching ace Tim Keefe to the Giants. That gave the NL squad a pair of aces, as Welch had gone 39–21 in 1884 and Keefe had a 37–17 record for the Mets.

Sure enough, that dynamic duo helped propel the Giants to greatness in 1885: an 85–27 record, although a second-place NL finish. (The Chicago Cubs won 87 games.) While Connor bashed a league-high .371 with 15 triples, Keefe went 32–13 with a 1.58 ERA, and Welch had one of the greatest pitching seasons of all time: 44–11 with a 1.66 ERA and 55 complete games. Mightily impressive for a 5-foot-8, 160-pounder.

Through the end of the decade, New York's core group of players, including six future Hall of Famers, remained with the team. Catcher Buck Ewing, a .303 lifetime hitter, was the finest catcher of his era. His throws were so accurate that it was said that he "handed the ball to the second baseman from the batter's box." Shortstop Monte Ward stole a league-high and franchise-record 111 bases in 1887. He would become a successful lawyer and the head of the first successful players union. Orator Jim O'Rourke, a 13-time .300 hitter, led the league in five-dollar words. When he was a player/manager of a Buffalo team in 1881, he denied an infielder's request for a raise. "I'm sorry," he said, "but the exigencies of the occasion and the condition of our exchequer will not permit anything of the sort at this period of our existence."

From 1884 through 1890, the champions of the National League and American Association played each other in what was alternatively called the Championship of the

United States, the World's Championship Series, and the World's Series. In 1888, the Giants played in the Series after topping the eight-team NL with an 84–47 record. Keefe claimed 35 of the team's victories while leading the league in wins, ERA (1.74), and strikeouts (335). A 10-game postseason tilt was scheduled with the AA champion St. Louis Browns, and New York took six of the first eight to take the title. Since 10 games were on the slate, 10 were played, and the Giants lost the last two 14–11 and 18–7 with a lineup filled with substitutes.

In 1889, Connor amassed an NL-best 130 RBI, as the Giants cruised to an 83–43 record and beat out the Boston Beaneaters for their second and last league title of the century. In '89, the AA champion Brooklyn Bridegrooms were appropriately named, as New York won the World's Series six games to three.

In terms of drama, the 1889 series rivaled that of any modern World Series. Brooklyn won three of the first four games, all of which were called on account of darkness by umpire John Gaffney. The Giants felt that something fishy was in the air, especially in Game Three. Trailing Brooklyn 8–7 in the bottom of the ninth, New York loaded the bases as Connor strode to the plate. Gaffney raised his hands to end the game, and then ran to the umpire's dressing room before the appalled crowd could get to him. Nevertheless, New York stormed back to win the next five games to win the Series. After a 4–2 triumph in the Game Nine clincher, Giants fans stormed the Polo Grounds field and, amid a cold rain, linked arms and chanted, "We are the people!"

It seems like a strange celebratory chant, but at the time Americans were angry with the growing chasm between the wealthy capitalists and the poor working-class folks who labored all day for pennies. That spirit infected the National League. Led by Monte Ward, players formed the game's first union, the Brotherhood of Professional Base-Ball Players. Together, they started the Players' League (PL), which lasted one year (1890) and was filled with former NL players. The PL's New York team, managed by Buck Ewing, was even called the Giants, and Keefe, Connor, and O'Rourke were among the stars. When the league disbanded after just one season, this famous trio went back to the NL Giants.

The whole episode took a toll on Giants owner John Day. Attendance was so bad for the 1889 NL Giants that the financial strain affected his tobacco business. Day was eventually forced to sell controlling interest in the team to Edward Talcott, a Wall Street broker. In 1895, shrewd businessman Andrew Freedman purchased a controlling interest in the Giants for $53,000. Freedman would become notorious for his poor treatment of umpires, sportswriters, and players. In 1896, Freedman endured the wrath of fans when pitcher Amos Rusie sat out the entire season in a contract dispute.

Hall of Fame Hurlers

The Giants would feature dominating pitching duos in the 20th and 21st centuries, such as Christy Mathewson/ Joe McGinnity and Matt Cain/Tim Lincecum. But at one point in the 1800s, they had three Hall of Famers on their pitching staff. In 1890 and '91, the Giants' rotation included Tim Keefe, Mickey Welch, and Amos Rusie—all bound for Cooperstown.

A submarine-style pitcher, "Smiling" Tim Keefe won 341 career games, including a 174–82 slate with New York (1885–91). Keefe went 42–20 for the Giants in 1886, and two years later he won 19 in a row. He retired as MLB's career strikeout leader with 2,533.

Mickey Welch was also nicknamed "Smiling," probably because he won 307 of 517 decisions. The crafty right-hander, who wore Giants duds from 1883 to 1892, peaked with a 44–11, 1.66 season in 1885. A year earlier, he won 39 games but logged more than 557 innings.

Nicknamed the "Hoosier Thunderbolt," the Indiana-born, flame-throwing Amos Rusie averaged just shy of 30 wins a year during his eight seasons with the Giants (1890–95; 1897–98). He may have been the most important New York Giant of all time, because he was later traded for Mathewson. Combined, the two hurlers won 619 games, 606 with the Giants.

The 1890s Giants wallowed in mediocrity, with the exception of two seasons. The 1894 team, managed by Monte Ward, went 88–44 to finish second in the 12-team National League. That season was a pitcher's nightmare, as the league's hitters batted .309 (and the Baltimore Orioles rapped .343!). For New York, "Dirty" Jack Doyle led the way with 44 steals and 103 RBI, while Rusie went 36–13 on the hill.

In 1897, shortstop George Davis enjoyed one of the most productive seasons in Giants history. Known for his clean play during a rough-and-tumble era, Davis smashed .353 on the season with 65 steals, 112 runs, and a league-high 135 RBI—all achieved in just 131 games. The Giants placed third in the league at 83–48.

The Giants stumbled in 1898 and '99, as Freedman became overly involved. When a Baltimore Orioles player insulted Freedman with a racial slur during a game, the owner stormed down to the field and demanded that the player be removed from the game. Instead, the umpire forfeited the game to Baltimore.

Freedman made four managerial changes in 1898 and '99, including the hiring of a down-on-his-luck John Day. Freedman got rid of him after the team started 1899 at 29–35 and replaced him with a crony named Fred Hoey, who had never managed before and never would again. The Giants were 31–55 under Hoey and finished at 69–90—their worst record of the 1800s.

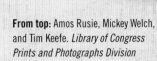

From top: Amos Rusie, Mickey Welch, and Tim Keefe. *Library of Congress Prints and Photographs Division*

1900–1909

BIG SIX AND BIG BRAWLS

The Giants dominate the 1905 World Series, but they set standards for bad behavior in a decade marked by arrests, ejections, and the most famous base-running blunder in history: "Merkle's Boner."

MATHEWSON, N. Y. NAT'L

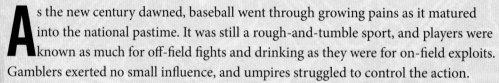

As the new century dawned, baseball went through growing pains as it matured into the national pastime. It was still a rough-and-tumble sport, and players were known as much for off-field fights and drinking as they were for on-field exploits. Gamblers exerted no small influence, and umpires struggled to control the action.

Yet the sport was becoming increasingly professional. The establishment of the American League in 1901 expanded interest and brought a healthy dose of rules.

Andrew Freedman still owned the Giants as they entered the modern era, and he remained as controversial as ever. He churned through five managers from 1900 to 1902, but he did a few things right as well. He traded worn-out Amos Rusie to Cincinnati for young prospect Christy Mathewson, possibly the most lopsided trade of all time, and hired John McGraw to manage the team in July 1902. McGraw brought some of his stars from the old Baltimore Orioles with him, including Hall of Famers "Iron" Joe McGinnity and Roger Bresnahan.

Considering how lousy Freedman's Giants were at the start of the century—finishing eighth, seventh, and eighth in an eight-team league—the injection of McGraw and his stars was just what the team needed. And it didn't hurt when, later in 1902, Freedman sold the team to John T. Brush, who gave "Little Napoleon" McGraw complete authority over baseball matters.

McGraw brought a combative, winning style. "McGraw eats gunpowder every morning and washes it down with warm blood," Giants coach Arlie Latham said. A short, feisty fireplug, "Mugsy" stood in sharp contrast to Mathewson, his biggest star, a tall, college-educated gentleman. But both burned with the desire to win, and in their unlikely partnership, they quickly became kings of the baseball world.

The Giants won the pennant in 1904, but McGraw still seethed at the upstart American League and refused to play in the World Series. After a few rules changes for 1905—a best-of-seven format, umpires from both leagues, and revenue sharing—the Giants agreed to participate. Facing the Philadelphia A's, Mathewson turned in the greatest performance in World Series history, one likely never to be equaled—three shutout victories. Only one runner made it as far as third base.

After those back-to-back 100–win seasons, the Giants kept winning, but they didn't bring home another pennant until 1911. They might have had one in 1908 if it hadn't been for the base-running blunder that's debated to this day: "Merkle's Boner." Rookie Fred Merkle was on first base when Al Bridwell delivered a game-winning hit against the Chicago Cubs in a game with pennant implications. When the run scored, Merkle ran to join the celebration and the Cubs' Johnny Evers tagged second base. The umps ruled Merkle out, the league president backed them up, and the end of the game was replayed at season's end, with the Cubs winning. Merkle's defenders continue to insist that he either touched the base or that Evers didn't have the right ball, but the final score stands. Perhaps it's no coincidence that the Cubs have not won a World Series since that season.

In establishing a consistent winner, McGraw had the perfect formula for winning in the Deadball Era: great pitching and scratching out runs. Mathewson was almost always paired with another Hall of Famer, first McGinnity and later Rube Marquard. The scrappy lineup included characters such as "Turkey" Mike Donlan, who twice quit baseball for vaudeville, and "Bad" Bill Dahlen, a dazzling shortstop. In trading for the pugnacious Dahlen in 1904, McGraw declared, "Now I have the man I've wanted ever since I've had charge of this team."

When it came to the Giants, McGraw usually had his way.

Above: These fans are among the record-setting crowd of 40,000 who witnessed the replayed Cubs-Giants game that decided the 1908 pennant. *Library of Congress Prints and Photographs Division.* **Opposite page:** Christy Mathewson posted a 236–112 record and 1.98 ERA for New York from 1900 to 1909. *Library of Congress Prints and Photographs Division*

Highlights

April 19: The New York Giants open the first season of the new century with a new manager, future Hall of Famer Buck Ewing.

April 26: Giants players George Davis, Mike Grady, and Kid Gleason rescue two women and a child from a burning building, then head to the Polo Grounds for a game.

May 20: After a seventh straight loss, New York is 6–16, nine games out, and doomed for the season.

July 17: Giants pitcher Christy Mathewson hits three batters in his major league debut.

July 4: Giants first baseman Jack Doyle is arrested on the field in Cincinnati after slugging an umpire. The team loses its 12th consecutive game.

July 13: With the club in last place, manager Buck Ewing resigns. Shortstop George Davis replaces him.

September 14: The Giants pull off the NL's first triple play of the century.

NOTES

Outfielder **Kip Selbach** leads the team with a .337 average.

Third baseman **Charlie Hickman** paces the club with nine homers, 17 triples, and 91 RBI.

Bill Carrick leads the Giants in wins and losses (9–22).

NOT NEW YORK'S FINEST

Impromptu Firefighting Is the Giants' Bright Spot

On April 26, 1900, catcher Mike Grady and infielders George Davis and Kid Gleason were on their way to work. The three New York Giants were riding a streetcar headed toward the Polo Grounds when they spotted a burning building on West 144th Street. The trio hopped out of the moving streetcar and rushed to the scene. Davis saved two women and children from the blaze as the ballplayers, according to the *New York World*, "worked like Trojans in carrying down the helpless." More than 200 people were in the building when the fire started, and thanks in part to Grady, Davis, and Gleason, none of those lives were lost. Afterward, with burn blisters on his face and humility in his heart, Davis said, "I didn't do much. I just went up the ladder and helped to carry down women and children."

The heroes continued to the ballpark, where they contributed to a 10–10 tie with the Boston Beaneaters. The three Giants' brief foray into firefighting would stand as the high point in an otherwise abysmal season for New York. Even with one of the best offenses in the National League—Charlie "Piano Legs" Hickman led the team with 91 RBI—the Giants still found a way to disappoint.

Though the New Yorkers may not have always won the game, they were never going to lose a fight, and for team captain "Dirty" Jack Doyle, that fight could be against anybody. On July 4, after being called out on a steal attempt by umpire Bob Emslie, Doyle hopped up and punched Emslie in the face. The umpire retaliated as fans at League Park in Cincinnati rushed the field to join the brawl. Players from both teams eventually broke up the fight, and Doyle left the field in handcuffs. The Giants finished the season in last place with a record of 60–78, 23 games behind first-place Brooklyn.

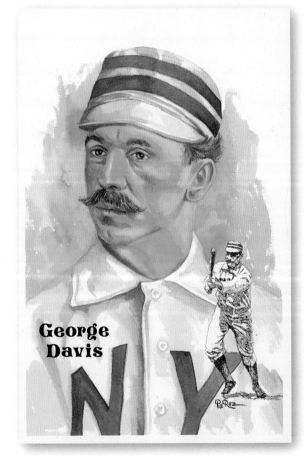

George Davis

Hall of Fame shortstop George Davis, who rapped .332 in his 10 seasons with the Giants, also managed the team in 1900 at the age of 29. *MVP Books Collection*

MATTY CHOOSES GIANTS

Phenom Mathewson Almost Jumps to Philadelphia

In 1901, the best thing to happen to the Giants occurred in March, before the season even started. Christy Mathewson, a 20-year-old pitcher, had gone 0–3 for the New Yorkers in his rookie season in 1900, but Connie Mack saw his enormous potential. Mack ran the Philadelphia Athletics, one of the eight teams that formed the brand-new American League. In January 1901, Mathewson signed a contract with Philly and accepted advance money from Mack, but in March the young pitcher decided to stay with the Giants.

Mack considered taking the case to court, but he eventually decided against it. The A's manager must have been beside himself in the fall of 1905. That year, Mathewson would post a 1.28 ERA, record his 128th career victory—at the age of 25—and shut out Mack's A's three times in the World Series. Argh!

In 1901, the 20-year-old from Bucknell University finished the year with a 20–17 record and a 2.41 ERA. Mathewson was the youngest player on an inexperienced staff, which had an average age of 25. After Mathewson, the Giants' best hurler was Luther "Dummy" Taylor. Taylor was a deaf mute who finished with an 18–27 record while tossing 37 complete games.

Mathewson and Taylor's disappointing winning percentages were due to an inept New York offense. Outfielder George Van Haltren was one of only two Giants to hit above .300, and no player had more than 66 RBI. Third baseman Sammy Strang offered a dose of excitement by stealing 40 bases, third most in the league.

New York followed a respectable 33–29 record in the first half with an abysmal 19–56 mark in the second half. The Giants limped to the finish line by losing 10 of their last 11 games, landing in seventh place in the eight-team league. Although the season was an overall disappointment, the right arm of "Matty" had the Giants' future looking bright.

With 40 stolen bases, third baseman Sammy Strang was among the few bright lights on the woeful 1901 Giants. *MVP Books Collection*

Highlights

February 9: Tom O'Brien, a star Giants outfielder in 1899, dies after drinking seawater for the purpose of curing seasickness.

May 21: Giants owner Andrew Freedman kicks out the umpire for alleged incompetence in a home game versus Pittsburgh. Christy Mathewson's streak of 39 consecutive scoreless innings ends.

June 9: The Giants bang out 31 hits in a 25–13 rout of Cincinnati.

June 10: New York improves to 19-13 and holds first place for the last time.

July 15: Mathewson no-hits St. Louis. He walks four and strikes out four.

October 5: After a 33–29 first half, the Giants close the season with a 19–56 second half.

December 16: Giants owner Andrew Freedman is granted a court injunction preventing newly elected NL President Albert Spalding from assuming the position. Henry Clay Pulliam will be elected president instead.

NOTES

Outfielder **George Van Haltren** spearheads a weak offense with a .335 average.

Third baseman **Sammy Strang** steals 40 bases.

Christy Mathewson, a 20-year-old sensation, goes 20–17 with a 2.41 ERA.

Deaf-mute **Luther "Dummy" Taylor** posts an 18–27 record and a 3.18 ERA.

1902

Highlights

May 7–8: Chicago's two home wins over New York are voided after the Giants discover that the distance between the pitching rubber and home plate is 15 inches short.

June 2: Giants manager Horace Fogel leaves the team due to the death of his father and will not return. Second baseman George Smith will become manager.

July 6: The team loses its 13th consecutive game.

July 8: Former Baltimore Orioles (AL) manager John McGraw officially signs with New York to manage the Giants.

July 16: Joseph France, acting for Giants owner Andrew Freedman, buys controlling interest in the Orioles. He releases several star players, all of whom will sign with the Giants.

August: Cincinnati Reds owner John T. Brush sells that team and buys the Giants from Freedman.

NOTES

John McGraw makes the Giants players learn sign language so they can communicate with pitcher **Dummy Taylor**. The signals become the earliest form of "signs" in baseball.

New York hitters belt just **six home runs** all year.

Christy Mathewson is the staff ace (14–17, 2.12 ERA).

NEW SHERIFF IN TOWN

John McGraw Becomes the Giants' New Manager

On July 8, 1902, the entire fortune of the New York Giants franchise changed with the stroke of a pen. After managing the Baltimore Orioles for three years, John McGraw signed a contract to manage the Giants. Though the short, combative, deeply knowledgeable field general would become one of the most successful managers in baseball history, his first season as New York's skipper was not among his finest. While the talent cupboard for McGraw was bare, the new manager looked for unique ways to make New York competitive in the National League.

To accommodate for the hearing deficiencies of deaf Giants pitcher Luther "Dummy" Taylor, McGraw made the entire team learn sign language in order to communicate with him. This was the earliest evidence of "signs" being used in baseball. Though innovative and creative, the Giants' foray into sign language could not mask the rest of their shortcomings.

New York's offense was anemic, with no player tallying more than 43 RBI and the entire team hitting a combined six home runs. The club's slugging average was a meager .287. With little run support, emerging staff ace Christy Mathewson went 14–17 despite posting a 2.12 ERA. The Giants would finish the 1902 season in last place with a 48–88 record, 53½ games behind the 103–36 Pittsburgh Pirates, who won the pennant by 27½.

As New York sputtered on the field, a more interesting subplot occurred in the Giants' front office. In July, Joseph France, acting for Giants owner Andrew Freedman, bought controlling interest in the Orioles. He then promptly released stars Joe McGinnity, Roger Bresnahan, Jack Cronin, and Dan McGann, all of whom would go on to sign with New York. Later that summer, Cincinnati Reds owner John T. Brush sold his team and bought the Giants from Freedman.

New York's introduction to the 20th century had not been pleasant. However, Giants fans anticipated an end to futility as McGraw prepared for his first full season as manager in 1903.

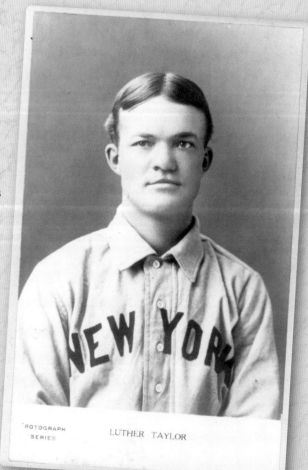

Giants players learned to use sign language to communicate with deaf pitcher Luther "Dummy" Taylor, who won 119 games with New York over nine seasons.
Library of Congress Prints and Photographs Division

ROTOGRAPH SERIES   LUTHER TAYLOR

Two-Headed Monster

McGinnity and Mathewson Are the Class of the NL

After posting what would be their worst record of the 20th century in 1902, the Giants raced to the top of the National League the following spring with a 16–7 start. On the day of their 16th win, New York pitcher Christy Mathewson brought home the victory in front of a record-setting crowd at the Polo Grounds. Mathewson and "Iron" Joe McGinnity gave the Giants one of baseball's most formidable one-two punches of the 20th century.

McGinnity (31–20) and Mathewson (30–13) were the only pitchers in the league with more than 25 wins. McGinnity led the circuit with 434 innings pitched, and Mathewson struck out an NL-best 267 batters.

When Mathewson or McGinnity were pitching, the Giants always had a chance to win. However, manager John McGraw did not have quite enough firepower in his arsenal. After outfielder Sam Mertes (104 RBI), no hitter tallied more than 55 RBI. The New Yorkers hung around first place during the first half of the season. But by the time they left for Chicago on July 1 and lost to the Cubs in their next game on July 4, the Giants dropped from 2½ to 5 games out. They never recovered. The Giants finished with an 84–55 record, 6½ games behind the Pirates.

The one player who could have pushed the Giants past the Pirates never made it to New York City. With his Washington Senators floundering in last place, 35-year-old outfielder Ed Delahanty hopped on a train headed for New York, hoping to suit up for the Giants the following day. While slugging a bottle of whiskey, the .346 lifetime hitter (and reigning AL batting champion) became uncontrollable. The conductor stopped the train near Niagara Falls and asked Delahanty to calm down. He refused. Delahanty was then kicked off the train, and—either intentionally or accidentally—he fell off a bridge and plummeted to his death . . . leaving New York's chances at an NL pennant at the bottom of the Niagara River.

John McGraw: "With my team, I am an absolute czar. My men know it. I order plays and they obey. If they don't, I fine them." *Library of Congress Prints and Photographs Division*

Highlights

May 16: Christy Mathewson prevails over Pittsburgh in front of a Polo Grounds–record 31,500 fans.

June 17: The Giants defeat Philadelphia to improve to 35–15. They will fall from first place for good after this day, as Pittsburgh is just too strong.

June 26: Giants catcher Frank Bowerman starts a fight with Pirates player-manager Fred Clarke in the Giants office before the game.

July 2: Washington Senators star Ed Delahanty, a .346 lifetime hitter, takes a train to New York in an attempt to play for the Giants. He is kicked off the train for rowdy behavior and then falls to his death in the Niagara River.

August 1: Iron Joe McGinnity starts and wins both games of a doubleheader against Boston.

December 12: New York acquires shortstop Bill Dahlen in a trade with Brooklyn.

NOTES

Outfielders **Roger Bresnahan** (.350) and **Sam Mertes** (104 RBI) lead the New York attack on offense.

Joe McGinnity (31–20) and **Christy Mathewson** (30–13) finish first and second in the NL in wins. McGinnity leads the league with 44 complete games, while Mathewson is tops with 267 strikeouts.

Regardless of fan resistance, the Giants were an unstoppable juggernaut. New York finished the season with a 106–47 record, 13 games ahead of the second-place Chicago Cubs, for the first of McGraw's 10 pennants with the franchise.

The Giants were so good that their greatness probably didn't need another test. Still, McGraw and New York owner John T. Brush refused to play the Boston Americans, the AL pennant-winners, in a "World Series." Although McGraw and Brush acted out of hubris, fans and sports journalists saw the two of them as cowards. The two would not budge, and the most victorious Giants team of the 20th century was never officially crowned "world champions."

World Series? We'll Pass

In 1904, a man named Ban Johnson would cause the World Series that year to be, well, banned. Johnson was the president of the American League, a former sportswriter, and an abhorrent critic of the National League. In a ploy to gain a competitive edge over the NL in 1901, Johnson had the AL clubs raise their salary ceiling above the NL's cap of $2,400.

That allowed AL team owners to offer players more money, and the owners began picking players from NL clubs. This shrewd business move enraged Giants manager John McGraw and owner John T. Brush, and in 1904 they sought revenge.

The Giants (106–47) were the best baseball team in America in 1904, but they refused to play in that year's World Series (the first of which was played a year earlier) against the pennant-winner from Johnson's "inferior" American League. McGraw thought that a team from the American League tainted what his team had worked so hard to accomplish, and he declined to play in "a haphazard box-office game with Ban Johnson and Company."

The absence of a World Series in 1904 disappointed fans, but it caused the two leagues to agree on a set of rules in the offseason, laying the groundwork for an annual World Series that has lasted for more than 100 years.

1905

Highlights

April 29: In Philadelphia, Christy Mathewson slugs a teenage fan in the mouth.

May 1: Mathewson wins his 100th career game at age 24.

May 19: At the Polo Grounds before a game, John McGraw berates Pirates owner Barney Dreyfuss, accusing him of controlling the NL umpires. McGraw will be suspended for 15 games, but the suspension will be overturned.

August 2: The Giants win their 13th straight game to improve to 69–25.

October 1: New York downs Cincinnati 5–4 to clinch the NL pennant.

October 9: Mathewson shuts out the Philadelphia A's 3–0 in Game One of the World Series.

October 12: Matty throws his second four-hit shutout of the Series, winning 9–0 in Game Three.

October 13: Joe McGinnity shuts out the A's 1–0 in Game Four.

October 14: Mathewson ends the Series in Game Five with a five-hit, 2–0 shutout.

NOTES

Outfielder **Mike Donlin** rips .356 with an NL-high 124 runs.

Sam Mertes ranks second in the circuit with 108 RBI.

Christy Mathewson leads the league in wins (31–9), ERA (1.28), and strikeouts (206).

THE WORLD'S GREATEST

Mathewson Fires Three Shutouts in World Series

Christy Mathewson had been great, but up until 1905 he wasn't the best. The 24-year-old, back-to-back 30-game winner wasn't even the best pitcher on his team. That distinction belonged to "Iron" Joe McGinnity. Mathewson had been the powerful cross to McGinnity's stinging jab in New York's superb one-two punch of a pitching staff. That changed in 1905. That season, no one could dispute that Mathewson, or the Giants, were the best in the league.

Mathewson started the season strong—just ask the teenage lemonade salesman he punched in the teeth for heckling him during the Giants' 10–3 victory in Philadelphia in April. The brief altercation was the only black eye on a truly beautiful season by Matty. After winning his 100th career game in May, Mathewson would go on to lead the league in wins (31), ERA (1.28), and strikeouts (206), becoming the third Giant to win the pitching triple crown (Tim Keefe won in 1888 and Amos Rusie did so in 1894).

With a spectacular season from Mathewson, a solid effort from McGinnity (21 wins), and the league's best offense for the second year in a row (New York was tops in batting average, runs), the Giants were again the class of the National League.

From atop Coogan's Bluff, Giants fans get a bird's-eye view of Game Two of the 1905 World Series, the only game won by Philadelphia. *Transcendental Graphics/Hulton Archive/Getty Images*

New York was strong all season long, jumping out of the gate at 35–10 and finishing the regular season with a 105–48 record, nine games ahead of second-place Pittsburgh.

Unlike the previous year, the Giants were headed to the World Series, where New York was heavily favored to win the best-of-nine fracas against the AL champion Philadelphia Athletics. The series opened at Philadelphia's Columbia Park with a pitcher's duel between Mathewson and Philly's Eddie Plank. Mathewson threw a complete-game, four-hit shutout. He allowed only one runner to make it past second base in the 3–0 victory.

Game Two took place the next day in New York. Although McGinnity was magnificent, yielding no earned runs, A's hurler Chief Bender flipped the script on New York, shutting out the Giants 3–0. Game Three was the sloppiest of the Series, as New York put up five runs in the top of the fifth while the A's committed four errors in the Giants' 9–0 victory. Mathewson authored his second shutout, allowing four hits and a lone walk. He looked untouchable.

In Game Four, McGinnity outlasted Plank in another pitcher's duel, with the Giants winning 1–0 on a Billy Gilbert single in the fourth. New York was in position to win its first World Series of the 20th century at home in the Polo Grounds.

McGraw once again handed the ball to Mathewson, his third start in six days. Fatigue was not a factor for the 25-year-old as he baffled the A's hitters once again, allowing only five hits and no walks. He even impacted the game from the batter's box, drawing a walk and scoring from third on a George Browne ground out for an insurance run in the 2–0 Series-clinching victory.

Mathewson's three complete-game shutouts in a World Series is a magnificent feat that has never been matched, and it solidified his status as the best pitcher in the majors. Moreover, the Giants' convincing World Series victory—they yielded only three runs in the five games—signaled to the rest of the league that in upcoming years, the road to the World Series would have to go through New York.

With 216 hits, 16 triples, and 124 runs scored, Mike Donlin was far and away the leading hitter on the 1905 "World's Champion" Giants. *Library of Congress Prints and Photographs Division*

Highlights

February 8: On a train leaving New York for an awards ceremony, Giants star Mike Donlin is accused of pulling a gun on a porter and assaulting the conductor. Other Giants players assault passengers.

April 26: John McGraw punches a fan.

May 2: The Giants top Boston 4–3 for their 10th straight win, improving their record to 14–3.

May 5: Still weak from diphtheria, Christy Mathewson pitches just seven innings in his first start of the year.

June 7: The Cubs, who are en route to MLB's best record of the century (116–36), rout the Giants 19–0 in New York.

July 12: The Giants purchase outfielder Cy Seymour, the reigning NL batting champion, from Cincinnati.

August 7: McGraw refuses to admit umpire James Johnstone into the Polo Grounds, which will result in the Giants forfeiting the game to Chicago.

October 5: Henry Mathewson, Christy's younger brother, starts for the Giants against the Braves and sets a modern National League record with 14 walks.

NOTES

Cy Seymour paces the Giants with a .320 average.

Third baseman **Art Devlin** bats .299 and leads the team in steals (54) and RBI (65).

Joe McGinnity (27–12) and **Christy Mathewson** (22–12) anchor the staff.

No Match for Chicago

Giants Unable to Repeat, as Cubs Romp to Pennant

On October 5, 1906, Henry Mathewson, the younger brother of Giants ace Christy Mathewson, took the mound against the Boston Beaneaters. Henry had a lot in common with his superstar brother; they were both right-handed, were Bucknell-educated, and had the long, lanky frame that's well suited for being a productive starting pitcher. Though the table was set for Henry to imitate his brother's greatness, he simply was not the same. That day against Boston, he set a modern NL record by walking 14 batters in a 7–1 loss.

While Christy would go on to an illustrious 17-year career, Henry would play in only one more game and was out of the league by 1907. Similarly, the 1906 Giants looked a lot like the 1905 World Series champions. Their jerseys still read "New York" and they had most of the same players, but they simply could not match the success of the previous year's ball club. The 1906 Giants won an impressive 96 games, but they finished a distant second in the standings.

One of the biggest additions to the 1906 team was outfielder Cy Seymour. After being purchased from Cincinnati in midseason, Seymour led the Giants in batting (.320) and home runs (four). New York also got production from their youngest position player, as 26-year-old third baseman Art Devlin led the team with 54 steals and 65 RBI while batting .299.

The Giants failed to repeat as champions because the Chicago Cubs turned in one of the greatest seasons in baseball history. Chicago recorded the best record of the century (116–36), finished 20 games ahead of New York in the standings, and had one of the best young nucleuses in baseball with the combination of first baseman Frank Chance, second baseman Johnny Evers, and shortstop Joe Tinker—not to mention a team ERA of 1.75.

The Cubs directly asserted their dominance over New York with 15 wins in 22 matchups. In a three-game stretch in June, they routed New York by the scores of 6–0, 11–3, and 19–0. Yet somehow, they couldn't beat the White Sox in the World Series.

Cy Seymour, who won 61 games as a pitcher for the Giants from 1896 to 1900, returned in 1906 as an outfielder and led the team with a .320 average. *Library of Congress Prints and Photographs Division*

SEYMOUR, N. Y. NAT'L

THE MODERN CATCHER

Giants' Bresnahan Helps Construct the "Tools of Ignorance"

In addition to being one of the greatest franchises in baseball history, the Giants were instrumental in shaping "America's Pastime" into the game you see today. We already mentioned the signs introduced by manager John McGraw in 1902 as well as the work by management to establish the current World Series system. In 1907, Giants catcher Roger Bresnahan also helped change the game forever.

On Opening Day in 1907, Bresnahan became the first player to don protective catcher's gear. During spring training, Bresnahan had practiced in shin guards that were modeled after a cricketer's leg pads and decided to use them on the first day of the season. Although fans and the media were critical of Bresnahan's innovation, catchers around the league began to adopt his idea. Bresnahan was also a pioneer in improving player safety. On June 18, the catcher was hit in the head by a pitch and was subsequently hospitalized for 10 days. He returned wearing a helmet similar to what football players of his era wore. He was also the first catcher to add padding to his catcher's mask.

While Bresnahan's actions were revolutionary, his team was not as impressive. After sprinting out to a 24–3 record in 1907—thanks to a 16-game winning streak—the Giants sputtered from June 5 to July 4, when they played only three games at home. During that stretch, the Cubs increased their first-place lead, and they would go on to win their second consecutive NL pennant.

The Giants regressed in 1907, finishing with an 82–71 record after posting more than 95 victories in their three previous seasons. Even though Christy Mathewson led the NL in wins (24–12), the story of the 1907 Giants was about new ideas and safety instead of titles and glory.

Catching trendsetter Roger Bresnahan (center) was no slouch with the bat, fashioning a .293 average in seven seasons with the Giants. *Library of Congress Prints and Photographs Division*

Highlights

April 11: The Giants have to forfeit a game at the Polo Grounds after fans fire snowballs at players and then run around the field. New York catcher Roger Bresnahan wears shin guards, considered a novelty at the time.

May 17: Christy Mathewson prevails 1–0 in 12 innings after stroking a walk-off single. It's New York's 15th straight win.

May 18: The Giants win their 17th consecutive game to improve to 24–3.

May 30: With a loss to the Phillies, New York falls to 27–9 and out of first place for good. The Cubs will run away with the flag.

June 18: Bresnahan is given last rites after being beaned by Reds pitcher Andy Coakley, who also breaks Dan McGann's arm with a pitch in the same inning. Bresnahan will be hospitalized for 10 days.

July 25: Bresnahan appears in a game wearing headgear.

NOTES

Cy Seymour powers the offense with a .294 average and a team-high 75 RBI.

Christy Mathewson leads the NL in wins (24–12) and strikeouts (178) while fashioning a 2.00 ERA.

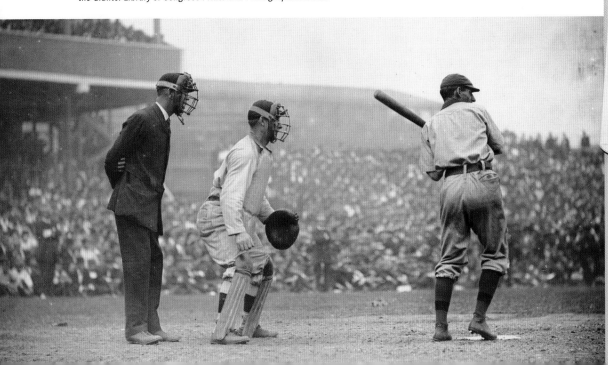

Highlights

July 4: Giants lefty Hooks Wiltse authors a 10-inning no-hitter against Philadelphia.

September 15: New York sweeps the Pirates in a doubleheader in front of an NL record-setting crowd of 35,000 at the Polo Grounds.

September 18: The Giants beat Pittsburgh for their 11th straight win.

September 23: The Giants appear to win a battle-for-first-place game against the Cubs on a walk-off single in the ninth by Al Bridwell. But the runner on first, Fred Merkle, never runs to second. As the crowd overruns the field, the Cubs pick up a ball and make a force at second, negating the run.

September 24: NL President Harry Pulliam declares the previous day's game a tie.

October 7: The season ends with the Giants and Cubs at 98–55 and Pittsburgh at 98–56.

October 8: In a makeup of the September 23 tie, nearly 250,000 fans descend on the Polo Grounds. Two fans die when they fall off an elevated subway platform. The Cubs win 4–2.

NOTES

Mike Donlin (.334, 106 RBI) powers the offense.

Christy Mathewson leads the NL in wins (37–11), ERA (1.43), strikeouts (259), and shutouts (11).

MERKLE'S BONER

First Baseman's "Bonehead" Mistake Costs NY the Pennant

After a disappointing season in 1907, the Giants found themselves in a three-way tie for first place in the National League near the end of September 1908. With Joe McGinnity's old age finally catching up to him, the 37-year-old crawled to an 11–7 record. Giants ace Christy Mathewson needed a new complement to his brilliance. As Mathewson turned in another dominant campaign—he led the NL in wins (37–11) while posting a 1.43 ERA—he was greeted with the best season of Hooks Wiltse's career.

The 28-year-old left-hander racked up 23 wins and orchestrated a no-hitter against Philadelphia on the Fourth of July. Mathewson and Wiltse accounted for more than 60 percent of the Giants' victories, while "Turkey" Mike Donlin powered the offense. Donlin was the catalyst of a New York team that scored the most runs in the league, led the team in nearly all offensive categories (including 106 RBI), and finished second in the NL in batting to Pittsburgh's Honus Wagner.

The Giants were once again the class of the National League and the hottest ticket in New York. They had all the makings of a championship ball club and were looking to return to the World Series. Then, on September 23, all of those hopes came to a screeching halt with one "bonehead" play.

With the Cubs and Giants tied for first place and the Pirates only 1½ games back, Mathewson took the mound at the Polo Grounds against Chicago on the 23rd to try

To witness the replayed game, thousands of fans rushed past a torn-down fence to enter the Polo Grounds. Mounted police and the hoses of firefighters could not deter them. *Library of Congress Prints and Photographs Division*

Top: Even the replayed Cubs-Giants game was marred by a dispute (pictured). Chicago prevailed 4–2 to clinch the pennant. *Library of Congress Prints and Photographs Division.* Bottom: Fred Merkle was the youngest player in the National League (19), and used mostly as a pinch hitter, when he made his unfortunate base-running mistake. *Library of Congress Prints and Photographs Division*

and put New York in the driver's seat in the NL pennant race. A Joe Tinker inside-the-park home run in the fifth and a Donlin RBI single in the sixth made the score 1–1 entering the bottom of the ninth. After Moose McCormick reached first base safely on a fielder's choice, 19-year-old Fred Merkle laced a single down the right field line, advancing McCormick to third. New York's chances of winning the game and sole possession of first place in the NL stood on third base.

Next up was Al Bridwell, who promptly whacked the first pitch from Chicago pitcher Jack Pfiester up the middle. McCormick sprinted home to score the winning run; the victory and first place now belonged to the Giants. At least that's what everyone thought. After Bridwell's single, Giants fans poured out of the stands and onto the field, but the young Merkle—thinking the game had ended as soon as McCormick had scored—retreated to the dugout without ever touching second.

Cubs second baseman Johnny Evers saw what Merkle had done and shouted for center fielder Solly Hofman to retrieve the ball amid the thousands of celebrating Giants fans. Evers finally got the ball and touched second base as umpire Bob Emslie ruled Merkle out. This force-out negated McCormick's game-winning run. Amid the chaos, umpire Hank O'Day called the game because of darkness. It went in the books as a 1–1 tie.

In what remains the most controversial ending in baseball history, nearly everyone had a different account of what happened on the last play. One newspaper claimed that Cubs players physically restrained Merkle from advancing to second. Evers said that he swore he saw McGinnity (who was not playing in the game) pick up the ball and throw it into the stands.

The next day, NL President Harry Pulliam confirmed that the previous day's game was a tie, and he scheduled a makeup game for October 8 at the Polo Grounds. The game was so anticipated that tens of thousands of fans—those who couldn't get a ticket—swarmed the field. Many risked their lives by watching from the roof of the park's grandstand, from elevated train tracks, and even from the tops of subway cars. With a sluggish Mathewson on the mound, the Giants fell behind early and Chicago went on to a 4–2 victory, winning the NL pennant for the third straight year.

While Merkle would go on to a very successful career as New York's everyday first baseman, he will always be remembered for his bonehead play.

Highlights

April 20: The National Commission learns of an effort to bribe the umpires of the Giants-Cubs makeup game in 1908. Dr. Joseph Creamer, a New York physician, will be called out as the alleged briber, and he will be barred from Major League ballparks.

May 24: Christy Mathewson's 24-game winning streak against the Cardinals comes to an end.

May 31: Mathewson defeats Philadelphia with an eighth-inning homer in front of 35,000 fans at the Polo Grounds.

July 5: The Giants win their 14th game in 15 tries to improve to 38–23, but they are well behind the rampaging Pirates.

September 6: Mathewson laces a walk-off 10th-inning triple to defeat Boston.

September 16: New York wins in Chicago 2–1 with President William Taft in attendance.

NOTES

Outfielder **Red Murray** paces the NL in homers (seven) and ranks second in RBI (91) and steals (48).

Second baseman **Larry Doyle** strokes .302 and leads the NL in hits (172).

Christy Mathewson goes 25–6 with eight shutouts and tops the circuit in ERA (1.14).

The Giants lead the league in **attendance** for the third straight year (783,700).

MATTY, MURRAY NOT ENOUGH

Despite 92 Wins, Giants Are No Match for Powerful Pirates

Even after the bizarre events that caused the Giants to fall short of winning the NL pennant in 1908, New York still possessed one of the most loyal and vast fan bases in baseball. Though they weren't the best team in the game in 1909, they were certainly the most popular. For the third straight season, the Giants led the league in attendance.

At the beginning of the year, the New Yorkers gave their capacity crowds a lot to cheer about. By July 9, the team was 40–26 and had just come off a torrid 16–2 stretch. However, their fans' jubilation quickly ended when they glanced at the standings in the New York papers. Even with the Giants 14 games over .500, they were still nine games back in the standings and stuck in third place.

As Chicago and Pittsburgh continued to distance themselves from New York, Christy Mathewson relentlessly tried to close the gap. In a season that saw the 28-year-old post the best winning percentage and ERA of his career (.806 and 1.14), Matty also won games with his bat. A .263 hitter on the year, Mathewson belted an eighth-inning homer to defeat the A's in May and laced a walk-off, 10th-inning triple to thwart Boston in September.

Mathewson's stellar season helped complement a strong New York offense that led the NL in home runs. Outfielder Red Murray ranked among the most versatile offensive weapons in baseball, as he led the league in homers (seven) and finished runner-up in stolen bases (48).

The Giants continued to win at a steady clip throughout the summer but couldn't match the pace of Pittsburgh. Even after winning 92 games, New York finished 18½ games behind the Pirates. Pittsburgh went 110–42 and became World Series champions, as Honus Wagner and Co. defeated Ty Cobb and the Detroit Tigers in seven games.

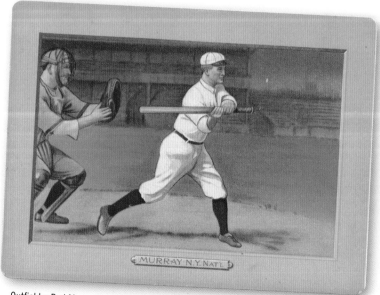

Outfielder Red Murray led the National League with seven homers in 1909.
Library of Congress Prints and Photographs Division

Matty: Master of Them All

As a student-athlete, Christy Mathewson was extraordinarily promising. The class president at Bucknell University, "Matty" played on the football and baseball teams and was named to the Walter Camp All-America football team in 1900.

As a soldier, he was heroic. Opposing his wife's vehement wishes that he stay, Mathewson enlisted in the United States Army for World War I and served as a captain in the newly formed Chemical Service.

As a man, he was genuine. A role model of a ballplayer in a time when the game was infested with players who usually spent their free time gambling and drinking, Mathewson never pitched on Sundays, fulfilling a promise he had made to his mother.

Mathewson was all these things, but he was never better than when he was on the pitcher's mound. The 6-foot-1 right-hander controlled both sides of the plate with pinpoint accuracy. Mathewson truly was "master of them all," as his plaque in Cooperstown reads, but he was one thing above everything else: the greatest pitcher in New York Giants history.

Mathewson won 373 games and lost 188 during his 17-year-career. Only Cy Young and Walter Johnson won more. Nicknamed "Big Six" after a New York fire engine, Mathewson posted a career ERA of 2.13 and amassed 79 shutouts, third most in MLB history. In 1905, Mathewson led the Giants to their first World Series championship of the 20th century by throwing three shutouts in New York's 4–1 series victory over the Philadelphia A's. With superb control and an inventive pitch, famously called the "fadeaway" (now known as a screwball), Matty was unquestionably the best pitcher of the Deadball Era's first decade. He became one of the first five players to be elected in the Hall of Fame's inaugural class in 1936.

Even after Mathewson retired in 1917, his impact on the game remained large. Always respected for his clean-cut conduct off the field, Mathewson played a role in exposing one of baseball's biggest scandals. Hugh Fullerton, one of the journalists to break the story of the 1919 "Black Sox," consulted Mathewson for information about gambling in baseball. With his writing skills and unbiased opinion, Mathewson was the only ballplayer among the group of investigating journalists.

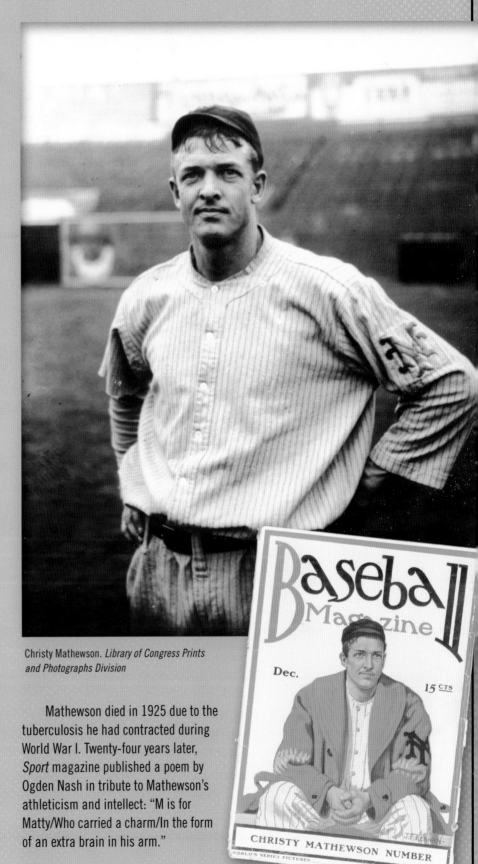

Christy Mathewson. *Library of Congress Prints and Photographs Division*

Mathewson died in 1925 due to the tuberculosis he had contracted during World War I. Twenty-four years later, *Sport* magazine published a poem by Ogden Nash in tribute to Mathewson's athleticism and intellect: "M is for Matty/Who carried a charm/In the form of an extra brain in his arm."

THE 1900–1909 RECORD BOOK

Team Leaders

(*Italics* indicates NL leader)

Batting Average
1900: Kip Selbach, .337
1901: George Van Haltren, .335
1902: George Browne, .319
1903: Roger Bresnahan, .350
1904: Dan McGann, .286
1905: Mike Donlin, .356
1906: Art Devlin, .299
1907: Cy Seymour, .294
1908: Mike Donlin, .334
1909: Larry Doyle, .302

Home Runs
1900: Charlie Hickman, 9
1901: George Davis, 7
1902: Steve Brodie, 3
1903: Sam Mertes, 7
1904: Dan McGann, 6
1905: Bill Dahlen, 7
      Mike Donlin, 7
1906: Cy Seymour, 4
      Sammy Strang, 4
1907: George Browne, 5
1908: Mike Donlin, 6
1909: *Red Murray, 7*

RBI
1900: Charlie Hickman, 91
1901: John Ganzel, 66
1902: Billy Lauder, 43
1903: *Sam Mertes, 104*
1904: *Bill Dahlen, 80*
1905: Sam Mertes, 108
1906: Art Devlin, 65
1907: Cy Seymour, 75
1908: Mike Donlin, 106
1909: Red Murray, 91

Runs
1900: George Van Haltren, 114
1901: Kip Selbach, 89
1902: Heinie Smith, 129
1903: George Browne, 105
1904: *George Browne, 99*
1905: *Mike Donlin, 124*
1906: Art Devlin, 76
1907: *Spike Shannon, 104*
1908: *Fred Tenney, 101*
1909: Larry Doyle, 86

Doubles
1900: George Van Haltren, 30
1901: Kip Selbach, 29
1902: Billy Lauder, 20
1903: *Sam Mertes, 32*
1904: Sam Mertes, 28
1905: Mike Donlin, 31
1906: Art Devlin, 23
1907: Cy Seymour, 25
1908: Mike Donlin, 26
1909: Larry Doyle, 27

Triples
1900: Charlie Hickman, 17
1901: George Davis, 7
1902: Dan McGann, 7
1903: Sam Mertes, 14
1904: Sam Mertes, 11
1905: Sam Mertes, 17
1906: Art Devlin, 8
      Dan McGann, 8
1907: George Browne, 10
1908: Mike Donlin, 13
1909: Red Murray, 12

Sam Mertes topped 100 RBI twice in his three seasons with New York. *MVP Books Collection*

Stolen Bases
1900: *George Van Haltren, 45*
1901: Sammy Strang, 40
1902: Heinie Smith, 32
1903: Sam Mertes, 45
1904: Bill Dahlen, 47
      Sam Mertes, 47
1905: *Art Devlin, 59*
1906: Art Devlin, 54
1907: Art Devlin, 38
1908: Mike Donlin, 30
1909: Red Murray, 48

Wins
1900: Bill Carrick, 19
1901: Christy Mathewson, 20
1902: Christy Mathewson, 14
1903: *Joe McGinnity, 31*
1904: *Joe McGinnity, 35*
1905: *Christy Mathewson, 31*
1906: *Joe McGinnity, 27*
1907: *Christy Mathewson, 24*
1908: *Christy Mathewson, 37*
1909: Christy Mathewson, 25

ERA

1900: Bill Carrick, 3.53
1901: Christy Mathewson, 2.41
1902: Christy Mathewson, 2.12
1903: Christy Mathewson, 2.26
1904: *Joe McGinnity, 1.61*
1905: *Christy Mathewson, 1.28*
1906: Dummy Taylor, 2.20
1907: Christy Mathewson, 2.00
1908: *Christy Mathewson, 1.43*
1909: *Christy Mathewson, 1.14*

Strikeouts

1900: Pink Hawley, 80
1901: Christy Mathewson, 221
1902: Christy Mathewson, 164
1903: *Christy Mathewson, 267*
1904: *Christy Mathewson, 212*
1905: *Christy Mathewson, 206*
1906: Red Ames, 156
1907: *Christy Mathewson, 178*
1908: *Christy Mathewson, 259*
1909: Red Ames, 156

Top: Christy Mathewson, who won 30 games four times in the decade, has a wealth of artifacts on display at Cooperstown. *Baseball Hall of Fame Museum and Library.* **Bottom:** Art Devlin manned the "hot corner" for the Giants from 1904 to 1911. *MVP Books Collection*

GIANTS 1900–1909 All-Decade Team

1B	DAN MCGANN
2B	LARRY DOYLE
SS	GEORGE DAVIS
3B	ART DEVLIN
C	ROGER BRESNAHAN
OF	SAM MERTES
OF	CY SEYMOUR
OF	MIKE DONLIN
SP	CHRISTY MATHEWSON
SP	JOE MCGINNITY

THE 1910s

No Cigars, Only Heartache

The Giants win four pennants—and finish second in four other seasons—but never win a championship. Fred Snodgrass muffs a fly ball, and allegations of throwing a World Series in 1917 foreshadow the Black Sox scandal.

Perhaps it was the arrival of a Kansas farm boy, sent to John McGraw by a fortune teller, that brought back the Giants' pennant-winning ways. Charles "Victory" Faust showed up in the middle of the 1911 season, and when it became clear that he was more amateur than athlete, McGraw tried to lose him in St. Louis. But Faust stuck with the team, became a beloved mascot, and suited up every day, although he never made it into a meaningful game.

Why not try a good-luck charm? Nothing else was working. Even the Polo Grounds had burned down that year, although in what seemed like record time, the wooden ballpark was rebuilt and reopened three months later as a concrete-and-steel structure that stood for the next half century.

The Giants did indeed win the pennant in 1911, and if they had won the World Series, McGraw might have even brought back "Victory" Faust. But this time, Connie Mack's Philadelphia A's had McGraw's number. Even though Fred Merkle—a distinguished player despite his rookie mistake of 1908—staved off elimination with a sacrifice fly in Game Five of the World Series, the A's took Game Six to win it all.

It was the first of three straight pennants for the Giants, none of which led to a world championship. In 1912, McGraw relied on a balanced attack. Rube Marquard complemented 23-game winner Christy Mathewson, winning his first 19 decisions of the season, and Jeff Tesreau won 17 games. Second baseman Larry Doyle hit .330 with 90 RBI and was league MVP, while catcher Chief Meyers ripped .358 and Fred

Snodgrass stole 43 bases. But misfortune awaited again in the World Series, which the Red Sox won in seven games (eight, if you count a tie).

In the deciding contest, the Giants held a 3–2 lead in the 10th inning when the usually sure-fielding Snodgrass dropped an easy fly ball. Even though Snodgrass made a great catch on the next play, the Giants then blew a foul pop. That gave Hall of Famer Tris Speaker one more chance. He delivered an RBI single, and Boston's Larry Gardner won the game with a sacrifice fly. Snodgrass never lived it down. The "$30,000 Muff," as the newspapers called it, headlined his obituary more than 60 years later.

In 1913, the Giants faced the Athletics again, and again the A's had their number. Hall of Famer Eddie Plank proved too much for Mathewson. The Giants nearly made it four straight pennants in 1914, but Boston's "Miracle Braves" reeled off 50 wins down the stretch to turn a 15-game deficit into a 10-game lead and the pennant.

Age caught up to the Giants, and in what would now be called a "rebuilding year," McGraw suffered his only last-place finish in 1915. The struggles continued into 1916, but a series of trades finally paid off, and the Giants won 26 straight games—a record—and nearly overtook the archrival Brooklyn Dodgers.

By 1917, the pennant once again belonged to the Giants—as did the peculiar misery known only to the losers of the World Series. Third baseman Heinie Zimmerman had led the league in RBI that year, but his fielding fell apart in the decisive sixth game against the Chicago White Sox. A throwing error put speedy Eddie Collins on base. After an outfield error put runners at the corners, pitcher Rube Benton induced a comebacker. He threw to Zimmerman, hoping to hang up Collins off third, but as the catcher came up the line for a rundown, Collins sprinted for the plate. Zimmerman gave chase, to no avail. (When blamed for letting the run score, Zimmerman supposedly said, "Who was I supposed to throw the ball to, [umpire Bill] Klem?" The quote was later revealed to be the work of writer Ring Lardner.)

Whispers of gamblers' influence dogged the Giants after that Series. Two years later, after the Black Sox scandal, McGraw suspended Zimmerman and Hal Chase on suspicion of throwing games, ending their careers.

With second-place finishes in 1918 and 1919, McGraw kept rebuilding. In 1919, he acquired a hometown second baseman who would provide a new nucleus for the next dynasty—Frankie Frisch, the "Fordham Flash."

Above: John McGraw's Giants lost twice to the Philadelphia Athletics in the World Series during the decade, and in 1913 they batted a mere .201 in the series. *MVP Books Collection*
Below: The Giants smile on a sunny day just before the start of the 1912 World Series. Eight games later, they would suffer a gut-wrenching loss to Boston in extra innings. *Library of Congress Prints and Photographs Division*

Highlights

June 9: The New Yorkers hold first place for the last time.

June 23: Three Giants players, including Art Devlin, are jailed for attacking a Brooklyn fan.

June 29: The Giants defeat Philadelphia in 10 innings on a walk-off single by Christy Mathewson.

July 10: The Giants nip the first-place Cubs 10–9 to move within a half game of the lead. However, Chicago will pull away over the rest of the season.

August 19: Mathewson wins his 20th game of the season and logs his 17th straight victory over Cincinnati.

August 27: New York takes its frustrations out on the league-dominating Cubs, winning 18–9 in Chicago.

September 30: Giants outfielder Beals Becker cranks a pinch-hit, inside-the-park grand slam in a 17–8 rout of Brooklyn.

NOTES

Outfielder **Fred Snodgrass** cracks a team-best .321.

Red Murray leads the club in RBI (87) and steals (57).

Christy Mathewson paces the league in wins (27–9) and fashions a 1.89 ERA.

Working primarily in relief, **Doc Crandall** goes 17–4 with a 2.56 ERA.

EXTRACURRICULAR ACTIVITIES

Off-the-Field Antics Distract from Team's Success

The 1910 New York Giants were an excellent team, but some of their off-the-field exploits were beyond belief. With a 3–2 lead against Pittsburgh on June 17, the Giants called on reliever Bugs Raymond to bring home the victory. Unfortunately, Raymond could barely stand up straight, let alone throw strikes. Instead of warming up in the bullpen, Raymond had snuck out to enjoy some libations at a nearby saloon. The 28-year-old hit two batters and threw a wild pitch as the Pirates came back to win 6–3.

Less than a week later, three Giants players, including star third baseman Art Devlin, were thrown in jail for assaulting a Brooklyn fan. The season would soon turn sour. Although the Giants were able to hover around first place until early July, their struggles during a three-week road trip that month left them 6½ games back.

Giants fans did enjoy outfielder Fred Snodgrass's breakthrough season. The 22-year-old center fielder finished fourth in the batting race (.321) and second in on-base percentage (.440). Despite the productive hitting and base-stealing of Red Murray (57 swipes), as well as the always reliable Christy Mathewson (27 wins), the Giants couldn't keep up with the blistering pace of Chicago. Though the Giants finished with a 91–63 record as well as a winning mark against every other NL club, New York did not have what it took to overcome the Cubs, ending the season with an 8–14 record against the North Siders and finishing 13 games behind them in the NL standings.

In the offseason, New York got even more depressing news when former first baseman Dan McGann, a member of the 1905 World Series championship team, committed suicide by shooting himself in the heart. As successful as their season was, the 1910 Giants would, sadly, be defined by unfortunate happenings off the field.

Though best known for his "muff" in the 1912 World Series, Fred Snodgrass led the Giants with his .321 average in 1910. *Library of Congress Prints and Photographs Division*

COMING UP SHORT

Giants Win Pennant but Are Thwarted by Philly

On April 14, 1911, fire ripped through the stands of the Polo Grounds, virtually destroying the Giants' home park. New York would play the rest of the season at the Yankees' home field, Hilltop Park in Washington Heights. Their stadium may have been damaged but their spirit wasn't, as the 1911 Giants began one of the great winning eras in franchise history.

Offensively the Giants finished one run shy of the league lead. All the while, their pitchers allowed the fewest. Second baseman Larry Doyle led the New York attack, batting .310 with a league-leading 25 triples. The Giants players were fleet afoot, and manager John McGraw used the stolen base to his advantage. The team stole a league-high 347 bags, with outfielders Josh Devore (61 steals), Fred Snodgrass (51), and Red Murray (48) among the league leaders.

As for pitching, Christy Mathewson racked up another sublime season (26–13 and an NL-best 1.99 ERA), but for the first time in the last few seasons, the Giants had a No. 2 pitcher that could at least attempt to match Mathewson's excellence. Rube Marquard, a 24-year-old lefty from Cleveland, came into his own in 1911. Marquard went 24–7 while overpowering batters with his blazing fastball.

After finishing with a 99–54 record, New York was rewarded with a World Series matchup against Connie Mack's Philadelphia Athletics in the World Series. Although the Giants were able to squeak by the A's in Game One, 2–1, Philadelphia would eventually prevail in six games. Game Three was a heartbreaker for the New Yorkers, as Philly scratched out two runs in the top of the 11th to beat Mathewson 3–2. And though the Giants won Game Five in 10 innings on a walk-off sac fly by Fred Merkle, Philadelphia romped 13–2 in the Game Six finale.

A's first baseman Frank "Home Run" Baker earned his nickname in the Series as he terrorized New York's pitchers, going 9-for-24 and hitting home runs off both Mathewson and Marquard.

Two legendary managers—New York's John McGraw and Philadelphia's Connie Mack—shake hands prior to the opening game of the 1911 Fall Classic. *Library of Congress Prints and Photographs Division*

Highlights

April 14: Hours after an 18-inning game, a fire erupts in the Polo Grounds stands. The Giants will play their games at Hilltop Park until a new, steel-and-concrete Polo Grounds opens for play.

May 13: In a 19–5 win over St. Louis, Fred Merkle tallies six RBI in one inning.

August 21: New York defeats the Cubs to move into first place for good.

September 1: Rube Marquard throws his second straight one-hitter, defeating Philadelphia.

September 12: New York defeats Boston 11–2 as Christy Mathewson (who steals home) faces Cy Young for the only time.

September 21: The Giants win their 12th straight game.

October 25: In Game Five of the World Series against Philadelphia, New York staves off elimination thanks to Merkle's sacrifice fly in the bottom of the 10th.

October 26: The A's crush the Giants 13–2 in Game Six to win the Series.

NOTES

The Giants steal 347 bases, topped by outfielder **Josh Devore's** 61.

Larry Doyle bats .310 with a league-high 25 triples.

Christy Mathewson (26–13) leads the NL in ERA (1.99), and **Rube Marquard** (24–7) is tops in strikeouts (237).

The New, Fireproof Polo Grounds

On Friday, April 14, 1911, a fire began to engulf the horseshoe-shaped grandstand of the Polo Grounds. As the wood was instantly swallowed up by the blaze, only the steel uprights of the stadium remained intact. Due to the gaps between some sections of the stands, most of the outfield seating and the clubhouse could be salvaged. Owner John T. Brush was determined to resurrect a new Polo Grounds from the ashes out of concrete and steel. In the meantime, the Giants needed a new place to play. They rented Hilltop Park from the AL's New York Highlanders (Yankees) while the Polo Grounds was under construction.

The stadium was rebuilt at a healthy pace, and it opened three months later on June 28. It became the ninth concrete- and-steel stadium in the major leagues. The construction workers were able to keep some of the old wooden bleachers, and they left gaps on each side between the newly constructed fireproof areas.

The old bleachers remained until the 1922 season, when they were demolished in favor of a permanent double deck that extended around a majority of the rest of the field. This gave the 54,555-seat stadium its famous shape and a new nickname to go with it: The Giants now played in "The Bathtub."

This unusual nickname was fitting for a ballpark with such unique dimensions. The distances down the left and right field lines were 279 and 257 feet, while a 21-foot overhang in left field consistently turned otherwise catchable

The 1911 fire obliterated the Polo Grounds' wooden grandstand, leaving only steel uprights in place. *Library of Congress Prints and Photographs Division*

fly balls into home runs. Contrasting the extremely short distances down the lines were 450-foot distances in the gaps—and a center field fence that stood 475 feet from home plate. Willie Mays's iconic over-the-shoulder catch in the 1954 World Series was made possible by the cavernous center field. The bullpens were technically in play, located in the left- and right-center field gaps. The outfield sloped slightly downward from the infield, with people in the dugouts able to see only the top half of outfielders.

The Polo Grounds was truly a stadium unlike any other. Like Ebbets Field in Brooklyn and Yankee Stadium in the Bronx, it remains one of the most iconic ballparks in baseball history.

Below: The glorious rebuilt Polo Grounds was constructed of steel and concrete and featured a double-decked, horseshoe-shaped grandstand. The new ballpark seated 34,000. *Library of Congress Prints and Photographs Division* **Right:** The renovated Polo Grounds: The house that McGraw built. *MVP Books Collection*

National League Baseball Park, New York

1912

▶ 103-48   1st ◀

Highlights

April 22: The Giants and Yankees play a fundraiser game at the Polo Grounds for the victims of the Titanic.

June 10: New York's Chief Meyers becomes the first MLB catcher to hit for the cycle.

June 13: The Giants sweep the Cubs to improve to 37–8.

June 20: The Giants steal 11 bases in a 21–12 win over Boston.

July 3: A 16-game winning streak puts the Giants at 54–11 with a 16½-game lead. Rube Marquard improves to 19–0.

September 7: Bugs Raymond, a pitcher with New York the previous year, dies from injuries suffered in a barroom brawl.

September 26: The Giants take a doubleheader from the Braves to clinch the pennant.

October 16: Boston wins the Game Eight finale of the World Series 3–2, due in part to Fred Snodgrass's dropped fly ball in the 10th.

NOTES

Chief Meyers ranks second in the NL in batting (.358).

Red Murray leads the team with 20 triples and 92 RBI.

Rube Marquard (26–11), **Christy Mathewson** (23–12), and **Jeff Tesreau** (NL-best 1.96 ERA) star on the hill.

The $30,000 Muff

Snodgrass Error Costs Giants the World Series

As expected, the Giants were a powerhouse in 1912. The offense was led by second baseman Larry Doyle, who plated 90 runs, and catcher Chief Meyers, who rapped .358. New York continued to terrorize teams on the base paths, swiping 319 bags. On the hill, Rube Marquard blazed through batters en route to a 19–0 start. The Giants finished the year at 103–48, with only the Boston Red Sox standing in their way of another World Series title.

In Game One, Boston's "Smoky" Joe Wood nearly handicapped himself in the Red Sox's 4–3 victory. He said after the game, "I threw so hard, I thought my arm would fly right off my body." The following day at Fenway Park, Game Two ended in controversy. After 11 innings, the umpire decided to call the game due to darkness with the score tied at 6–6. New York would tie the series the next game, as Marquard held Boston to one run on seven hits.

The Red Sox won Games Four and Five, giving them a commanding 3–1 series lead. New York responded by mashing 16 total runs in Games Six and Seven to even the series at 3–3 and force a deciding eighth game.

Boston flamethrower "Smoky" Joe Wood (left) beat New York's Jeff Tesreau (right) in two of their three World Series matchups in 1912. *Library of Congress Prints and Photographs Division*

The Giants lost two of three home games during the 1912 series, including a 3–1 loss in Game Four (seen here).
Library of Congress Prints and Photographs Division

In Game Eight at Fenway, with the Giants leading 2–1 in the 10th, a simple mistake cost them a championship. Boston's Clyde Engel lofted a fly ball toward Giants outfielder Fred Snodgrass. Snodgrass, one of the best fielders in the NL, waited to make the catch that would put his team just two outs away from a World Series victory. Then something unexpected happened: The ball caromed off his glove and fell to the ground as Engle scampered to second.

Boston had momentum and new life. Tris Speaker brought Engle home on a two-out single, and Larry Gardner hit a bases-loaded sacrifice fly to finish the Giants.

Snodgrass's error would go down in history as "the $30,000 muff," a difference in the winning and losing shares. When he died in 1974, the *New York Times* headline on his obituary read: "Fred Snodgrass, 86, Dead; Ball Player Muffed 1912 Fly."

1913

Highlights

February 1: Olympic legend Jim Thorpe signs with the Giants. He will bat .216 in four years with the team.

April 17: The Yankees begin to share the Polo Grounds with the Giants.

June 30: New York beats Philadelphia 11–10 and moves into first place for good.

July 9: The Giants win their 14th straight game.

July 18: Christy Mathewson's 68-inning walkless streak comes to an end.

September 14: The Giants lose 7–0 despite stroking 14 hits.

September 27: A Phillies loss means the Giants clinch the pennant.

October 8: Christy Mathewson tosses a 10-inning, 3–0 shutout over Philadelphia in Game Two of the World Series.

October 11: The A's beat the Giants 3–1 in Game Five to win the World Series.

October: The Giants and Chicago White Sox begin five-month, five-continent exhibition-game tour following the season.

NOTES

Keystone mates **Larry Doyle** (73 RBI, 38 steals) and **Art Fletcher** (71 RBI, 32 steals) help power a balanced Giants offense.

Christy Mathewson (25–11), **Rube Marquard** (23–10), and **Jeff Tesreau** (22–13) get the job done on the hill.

38

CAN'T GET OVER THE HUMP

Giants Lose World Series for Third Straight Year

After winning back-to-back NL titles, the Giants still weren't satisfied with their roster. They still wanted more, something extra that could turn them from pennant-winners to World Series champs. On February 1, 1913, they didn't just get a ballplayer; they got a national hero. That day, Jim Thorpe became a New York Giant.

Fresh off winning gold medals in the pentathlon and decathlon at the 1912 Stockholm Olympics, Thorpe decided to take a crack at professional baseball. Coming to a team that returned all but one of its starters, Thorpe wasn't asked to do much and played in only 19 games. Thorpe's play was underwhelming—he finished the season with a .143 batting average—but the rest of New York's offense was not.

Led by shortstop Art Fletcher and second baseman Larry Doyle (a combined 144 RBI and 70 steals), the Giants found themselves in first place by June 30 and would remain in the top spot the rest of the year.

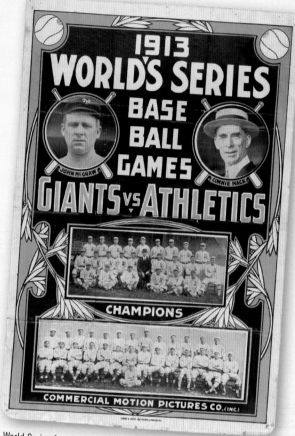

World Series foes Connie Mack (3,731 career victories) and John McGraw (2,763) remain the two winningest managers in Major League history. *MVP Books Collection*

A balanced pitching staff helped sustain New York's early success. In Christy Mathewson (25 wins), Rube Marquard (23), and Jeff Tesreau (22), Giants manager John McGraw always had a pitching stud he could rely on. The Giants finished the season with a 101–51 record, earning their third straight NL pennant.

The 1913 World Series featured the Giants versus the A's in a rematch of the '11 Fall Classic. After a 6–4 Philly triumph in Game One, Mathewson tossed a 10-inning, 3–0 shutout in Game Two. From there, the A's rolled, winning 8–2, 6–5, and 3–1 to take the Series in five games. Giants pitchers could not contain Home Run Baker, Eddie Collins, and Wally Schang, who combined to hit .432 with 17 RBI. Meanwhile, the New York hitters batted just .201.

Frustrated and disappointed once again, the Giants were in dire need of a vacation.

GLOBETROTTERS

Giants and White Sox Take Baseball Abroad

In an idea hatched by Chicago White Sox owner Charles Comiskey and Giants manager John McGraw, their teams spent the 1913–14 offseason on "The Tour to End All Tours." The clubs played baseball for five months on five different continents.

Although he was one of the least accomplished and talented baseball players on the tour, New York's Jim Thorpe proved to be extremely influential in generating popularity for the two teams' games overseas. Thorpe's 1912 Olympic triumphs in Stockholm increased the publicity for the tour and helped bring over 20,000 people to watch the two teams play in London. Traveling also to Japan, China, the Philippines, Australia, Egypt, Italy, France, and Ireland, the two teams were instrumental in spreading baseball across the globe.

After their globetrotting was finished, the Giants still had a pennant to defend. McGraw's squad boasted a balanced attack, as it led the league in runs while no player drove in more than 79. Outfielder George Burns was the catalyst, pacing the league in runs (100) and stolen bases (62). Jeff Tesreau led the Giants pitching staff with a 26–10 record and a 2.37 ERA. Christy Mathewson turned in another solid performance (24–13), although Marquard (12–22) greatly digressed from his excellence in the previous years.

The Giants looked to be on their way to a fourth straight pennant, as they held a 6½-game lead over St. Louis in August. However, they couldn't have expected the storm that was brewing in Boston.

Spending close to half of the year in last place, Boston was 26–40 on the Fourth of July. The "Miracle Braves" responded by going 68–19 in their last 87 games, winning the NL by 10½ and sweeping the defending champion A's in the World Series. The Giants, who finished in second place at 84–70, could at least look forward to a quiet offseason.

Voted the greatest athlete of the first half of the 20th century by the Associated Press, Jim Thorpe batted only .216 in 152 games as a Giants outfielder. *Library of Congress Prints and Photographs Division*

Highlights

February 1: The Giants and White Sox play an exhibition game in the shadows of the Egyptian pyramids.

April 27: Hot dogs are sold at the Polo Grounds for the first time.

July 4: Christy Mathewson shuts out Philadelphia for his 350th career victory.

July 17: Rube Marquard goes the distance in a 21-inning, 3–1 win over Pittsburgh.

August 10: A triumph over St. Louis gives New York a 6½-game lead in the NL.

September 7: The Boston Braves move to Fenway Park to accommodate the 74,000 fans who attend a morning/afternoon Labor Day doubleheader against New York. The teams split, as fans heckle Giants outfielder Fred Snodgrass mercilessly.

September 8: The "Miracle" Braves, en route to a 61–16 second-half record, defeat the Giants to take over first place for good.

NOTES

Giants outfielder **George Burns** raps a team-high .303 and leads the NL in runs (100) and stolen bases (62).

Art Fletcher tallies a team-best 79 RBI.

Jeff Tesreau leads the staff in victories (26–10).

Christy Mathewson goes 24–13 while walking just 23 batters all year.

1915

▶ 69-83   8th ◀

Highlights

April 15: Giants pitcher Rube Marquard no-hits Brooklyn at the Polo Grounds, striking out two and walking two.

April 24: A 2–7 start puts the Giants at six games back.

May 6: Yankees fans at the Polo Grounds witness Babe Ruth's first Major League home run. He's a pitcher for the Boston Red Sox.

August 7: Though just 49–47, the Giants move to within three games of first place.

August 17: New York releases Fred Snodgrass.

August 26: A 3–13 skid drops the Giants out of pennant contention.

August 31: On a day that Chicago's Jimmy Lavender no-hits the Giants, New York sells Marquard to Brooklyn for $7,500.

NOTES

Larry Doyle leads the league in batting (.320), hits (189), and doubles (40).

Third baseman **Hans Lobert**, the "fastest man in baseball," steals 14 bases in 29 attempts for New York.

Jeff Tesreau (19–16, 2.29 ERA) becomes the ace of the staff as **Christy Mathewson** slips to 8–14, ending a skein of 12 straight 20-win seasons for Matty.

FALL FROM GRACE

NY Finishes Last for First Time in 13 Years

In the 1910s, the Giants enjoyed an incredibly successful decade. In their second worst year of the '10s, they were still 14 games over .500. The 1915 campaign, however, was an anomaly. That season, the New Yorkers finished 14 games under .500.

New York stumbled out to a 2–7 start and continued to sputter, due largely to their disappointing pitching staff. Nearing the end of his illustrious Hall of Fame career, Christy Mathewson finally began to show signs of age in 1915. For the first time since 1902, the 34-year-old logged fewer than 20 wins, posting an 8–14 record while recording only 57 strikeouts. Rube Marquard, who had won 26 games just three years prior, continued to struggle, and the Giants let him go before the season was over. The one bright spot of the Giants staff was Jeff Tesreau, who was able to scrape together a 19–16 record and a 2.29 ERA.

To make up for their weak pitching, the Giants ranked among the better hitting teams in the league. "Laughing" Larry Doyle led the charge, winning the batting title (.320) and helping the Giants move to within three games of first place with two months left in the season.

Unfortunately for McGraw's ball club, the Giants began to slide in August. A 2–8 stretch near the end of the month dropped New York to 52–60, 10½ games out of first place. The Giants finished the season at 69–83, 21 games behind the first-place Philadelphia Phillies. It was the first time they finished in last place since 1902.

New York was officially in rebuilding mode. After selling Marquard and releasing Fred Snodgrass, and with Mathewson's career winding down, the Giants were faced with the daunting task of rejuvenating their roster with players that would help them return to their former glory.

Known for his cheery disposition, "Laughing" Larry Doyle stroked .300 five times with the Giants, with a high of .320 in 1915. *Library of Congress Prints and Photographs Division*

By the time Christy Mathewson (right) said goodbye to John McGraw (left), he was washed up. He won just one game with Cincinnati in 1916. Between McGraw and Matty is Buck Herzog, the player Mathewson was traded for. *Library of Congress Prints and Photographs Division*

Highlights

April 29: New York's Fred Merkle wins a car by hitting a ball off an advertisement on the Polo Grounds wall.

May 29: The Giants improve to 19–13 with their 17th win in a row—all on the road.

July 20: New York trades three future Hall of Famers—Christy Mathewson, Edd Roush, and Bill McKechnie— to Cincinnati for Buck Herzog and Red Killefer.

August 20: The Giants deal Fred Merkle to Brooklyn for catcher Lew McCarty.

August 28: Larry Doyle and Herb Hunter are shipped to the Cubs for Heinie Zimmerman and Mickey Doolan.

September 25: The Giants defeat St. Louis for their 21st consecutive victory, setting the NL record.

September 30: Rube Benton one-hits the Braves to secure New York's 26th consecutive victory. Incredibly, the Giants are still in fourth place (85–62).

October 3: After a third straight loss, John McGraw rips his team for not trying hard enough.

NOTES

Outfielder **David Robertson** shares the NL home run title (12).

George Burns paces the NL in runs scored (105).

Jeff Tesreau (18–14) and **Pol Perritt** (18–11) lead the mound corps.

26 IN A ROW!

Giants' Record-Setting Streak Doesn't Lead to Pennant

It was 1–0 in the bottom of the fourth on a dreary September afternoon. The darkness at the Polo Grounds was becoming so thick that you couldn't see the outfielders from the dugout. The Giants were up and they needed to strike out. Aiming to play five full innings before the umpires called the game, Giants manager John McGraw scolded catcher Lew McCarty—after he hit a single to left—for extending the game.

New York would run out of time; the game would be called and the Giants would have to wait another day to make history. The following day, September 30, Giants pitcher Rube Benton threw a one-hitter in New York's 4–0 victory over Boston. The win was New York's 26th in a row, a streak that remains the longest in baseball history. It was all part of a gigantic 31-game homestand. Incredibly, back in May, the Giants won 17 in a row, all of which were on the road.

The Giants had already broken the previous record of 21 straight wins, held by the 1880 Chicago White Stockings, earlier in the week. Nevertheless, even after consecutive win No. 26, New York was still in fourth place. Although the Giants had a fabulous September, it was not enough to make up for their long stretches of sour play earlier in the year.

In rebuilding mode after a last-place 1915 campaign, the Giants traded the face of their franchise, Christy Mathewson, to Cincinnati in July of '16. While Mathewson was nearing retirement and his exodus from New York was inevitable, his presence on the pitching staff was sorely missed. For only the third time in the 20th century, the Giants did not have a pitcher who won more than 20 games, as Jeff Tesreau (18–14) and Pol Perritt (18–11) spearheaded the pedestrian pitching staff.

The Giants would fall flat after their 26th win, losing four of their last five to end the year at 86–66. They remained in fourth place.

▶ 98-56   1st ◀

Highlights

March 30: Detroit's Ty Cobb spikes the leg of Giants second baseman Buck Herzog during an exhibition game. The two fight on the field and, later, at a hotel.

June 8: John McGraw punches the face of umpire Bill Byron, incurring a 16-day suspension by the league.

June 27: The Giants improve to 35–21 and move into first place for good with a win over Philadelphia.

August 10: New York is now 65–31 with its largest lead of the season: 14 games.

August 19: The Giants play their first official game on Sunday, against the Reds, with Europe-bound troops in attendance.

October 10: In Game Three of the World Series against the Chicago White Sox, the Giants win their first game, 2–0, behind Rube Benton's shutout.

October 11: Ferdie Schupp shuts out Chicago 5–0 in Game Four.

October 15: The White Sox win the Series with a 4–2 triumph in Game Six.

NOTES

Dave Robertson (league-high 12 homers), **Heinie Zimmerman** (NL-high 102 RBI), and **George Burns** (NL-best 103 runs) lead the attack.

Ferdie Schupp (21–7, 1.95) shines on the hill.

ANOTHER SERIES HEARTBREAK

Star-less Giants Win the Pennant but Fall to the ChiSox

After getting rid of most of the players who had propelled them to three straight World Series appearances at the beginning of the decade, the Giants were looking for an identity. Larry Doyle, Fred Merkle, and Christy Mathewson were gone, and John McGraw was left with few players he could count on. Although his team

John Brush's Giants led all NL teams with 98 wins and 4 runs per game during the 1917 season, but they came up short once again in October. *MVP Books Collection*

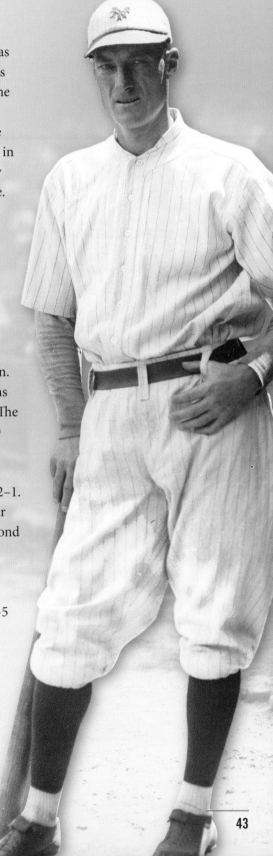

was competitive, McGraw was frustrated during a three-loss series at Cincinnati from June 5 to 8. He let his emotions boil over on June 8 when he punched umpire Bill Byron in the face, incurring a 16-day suspension from the league.

McGraw's act of aggression seemed to ignite the Giants, who won seven of their next eight and were in first place when he returned from the suspension. They would hold the top spot the rest of the season.

New York did not have any true superstars (Heinie Zimmerman and George Burns were the "big names"), but what they lacked in talent they made up for with grit. The Giants led the league in both runs scored and fewest runs allowed and finished 10 games ahead of the second-place Phillies.

In Game One of the World Series, the Giants were no match for the trickery of Chicago White Sox pitcher Eddie Cicotte. The knuckleballer outshined Slim Sallee 2–1. Game Two saw the Giants' newest ace, Ferdie Schupp (21–7, 1.95 ERA in the regular season), get pummeled by the Sox, who knocked Schupp out of the game in the second inning on their way to a 7–2 win.

Back in New York, Giants pitchers Rube Benton and Schupp both recorded shutouts, 2–0 and 5–0, evening the Series. But in the Windy City, Chicago pitcher Red Faber baffled New York on his way to victories in Games Five (in relief of an 8–5 win) and Six (a complete-game 4–2 triumph). In a year in which little was expected of them, the Giants still felt disappointed after suffering their fourth World Series defeat in seven years.

1918

Highlights

May 9: The Giants jump out to an 18–1 start.

June 6: New York falls out of first place for good.

June 20: Giants pitcher Jeff Tesreau says he has taken a job with a steel company.

July: NL and AL officials agree to end the season on Labor Day due to the war raging in Europe. Secretary of War Newton D. Baker rules that baseball players will be subject to the "work-in-essential-industries-or-fight" rule.

July 9: Giants part-timer Jim Thorpe homers in the 10th inning in Chicago to defeat the Cubs.

July 18: Giants star Heinie Zimmerman leaves the team for several days after getting chewed out by manager John McGraw.

August 30: The Giants defeat Brooklyn 1–0 in one of the fastest games ever: 57 minutes.

October 5: Former Giants infielder Eddie Grant is killed during combat in France.

December 31: Giants pitcher Fred Toney is sentenced to four months in jail after taking a woman across state lines for "immoral" purposes.

NOTES

George Burns stands out with 40 steals and 80 runs scored.

Pol Perritt (18–13) is the team's only big winner.

WAR GAMES

Giants Fall Flat in a Season Marred by Global Conflict

In 1917 and 1918, America was at war and baseball players across both leagues responded to their country's call. By the end of World War I, 247 baseball players had enrolled in the Armed Forces, and three of them were killed in action. One of those men was former Giants infielder Eddie Grant.

Harvard educated, Grant became a lawyer after concluding his career with the Giants in 1915. When the United States entered the conflict in 1917, he was among the first to enlist. Grant, who served as a captain with the 77th Infantry Division, was killed by an exploding shell in the Battle of Meuse-Argonne.

As the war raged in Europe, baseball became a distraction from the fighting across the Atlantic. Early in the season, the Giants were an especially fun diversion for New Yorkers, as they rushed to an 18–1 start that included a 27–0 three-game sweep of Philadelphia. Unfortunately, New York's early-season success could not be sustained.

The Giants followed their hot start with a 5–10 stretch, and players began fleeing a roster that already had been hurt by the war. Pitcher Jeff Tesreau left the team in June for a job at a steel company, due to a rule that required baseball players to either work in essential industries or go off to war. Third baseman Heinie Zimmerman fled the team in July for a few days after feuding with manager John McGraw.

The squad that McGraw was left with simply wasn't competitive. New York's offense was middle of the pack, and Pol Perritt (18–13) was the only pitcher to win more than 11 games.

The season ended early on Labor Day due to the war, and New York finished 71–53, 10½ games behind the first-place Cubs. Fortunately, the war would come to an end that November, and MLB teams would return to full strength.

A military band leads the Giants on the field prior to the home opener at the Polo Grounds in 1918, a season abbreviated due to the Great War. *Library of Congress Prints and Photographs Division*

UNDER NEW MANAGEMENT

Stoneham, McQuade, and McGraw Buy the Giants

After the war-shortened season of 1918, there was a general fear among the baseball community that the game would not be able to recapture its fan base. This anxiety prompted the managers of the John Brush estate to sell the Giants. New York manager John McGraw, New York City magistrate Francis X. McQuade, and Charles A. Stoneham purchased the team. Stoneham, a jowly 42-year-old stockbroker who loved racehorses, gambling, and baseball, owned controlling interest of the club.

Stoneham wasn't one to care about his friends' reputations, and he applied that same philosophy to his players. Prior to the season, the Giants acquired first baseman Hal Chase from the Reds. Chase was an incredible fielder, the NL batting champ in 1916, and a player who had repeatedly been accused of throwing games.

Although New York was wrapped in uncertainty with new management and allegedly one of the biggest gamblers in all of baseball playing first base, the Giants were one of the best teams in the NL. On July 30, New York was 55–26 and tied for first place with Cincinnati. Outfielder George Burns had a career year, as he was tops in the NL in runs (86) and stolen bases (40). Outfielder Ross Youngs cracked .311, and pitchers Jesse Barnes and Rube Benton combined for 42 wins.

However, the Giants couldn't keep up their torrid pace, and the Reds ran away with the NL flag, beating out the second-place New Yorkers by nine games. Still, after an offseason that was filled with drastic changes in the front office and in the clubhouse, the Giants' final record of 87–53 served as a pleasant surprise. As the dust settled and all the shuffling began to feel permanent, the Giants were ready to reclaim their spot as the premier team in the National League.

Ross Youngs, a 5-foot-8 outfielder, stroked .322 in his 10-year career, all with the Giants. In 1919, he rapped .311. *Library of Congress Prints and Photographs Division*

Highlights

January 14: John McGraw, Charles A. Stoneham, and Judge Francis X. McQuade buy controlling interest in the Giants from the estate of John T. Brush.

February 19: The Giants acquire alleged gambler, but 1916 NL batting champion, Hal Chase from Cincinnati.

March 7: Christy Mathewson joins the Giants as the pitching coach after serving as a captain in the Army during the war.

May 30: A doubleheader sweep of Brooklyn puts the first-place Giants at 21–7.

July 30: New York holds first place for the final time, as the Reds will begin to run away with the flag.

August 3: After a game in Cincinnati, a police officer goes to punch McGraw but hits Chase, who retaliates by slugging the officer.

September 28: On the last day of the season, the Giants beat Philadelphia 6–1 in just 51 minutes—the shortest game in MLB history.

NOTES

George Burns leads the NL in runs (86), walks (82), and stolen bases (40).

Outfielder **Ross Youngs** tops New York in batting (.311) and the league in doubles (31).

Jesse Barnes paces the NL in victories (25–9).

THE 1910-1919 RECORD BOOK

Team Leaders

(*Italics* indicates NL leader)

Batting Average
1910: Fred Snodgrass, .321
1911: Larry Doyle, .310
1912: Larry Doyle, .330
1913: Art Fletcher, .297
1914: George Burns, .303
1915: *Larry Doyle, .320*
1916: Dave Robertson, .307
1917: Benny Kauff, .308
1918: Ross Youngs, .302
1919: Ross Youngs, .311

Home Runs
1910: Larry Doyle, 8
1911: Larry Doyle, 13
1912: Fred Merkle, 11
1913: Larry Doyle, 5
    Tillie Shafer, 5
1914: Fred Merkle, 7
1915: Larry Doyle, 4
    Fred Merkle, 4

1916: *Dave Robertson, 12*
1917: *Dave Robertson, 12*
1918: George Burns, 4
1919: Benny Kauff, 10

RBI
1910: Red Murray, 87
1911: Fred Merkle, 84
1912: Red Murray, 92
1913: Larry Doyle, 73
1914: Art Fletcher, 79
1915: Art Fletcher, 74
1916: Benny Kauff, 74
1917: *Heinie Zimmerman, 102*
1918: Heinie Zimmerman, 56
1919: Benny Kauff, 67

Runs
1910: Larry Doyle, 97
1911: Larry Doyle, 102
1912: Larry Doyle, 98
1913: George Burns, 81
1914: *George Burns, 100*
1915: Larry Doyle, 86
1916: *George Burns, 105*

1917: *George Burns, 103*
1918: George Burns, 80
1919: *George Burns, 86*

Doubles
1910: Fred Merkle, 35
1911: Red Murray, 27
    Fred Snodgrass, 27
1912: Larry Doyle, 33
1913: George Burns, 37
1914: George Burns, 35
1915: *Larry Doyle, 40*
1916: George Burns, 24
    Larry Doyle, 24
1917: George Burns, 25
1918: George Burns, 22
1919: *Ross Youngs, 31*

Triples
1910: Larry Doyle, 14
    Fred Merkle, 14
1911: *Larry Doyle, 25*
1912: Red Murray, 20
1913: Fred Merkle, 14
    Tillie Shafer, 12

Richard "Rube" Marquard (left) won 20-plus games in each season from 1911 to 1913, while star backstop John "Chief" Meyers (right) batted .301 in 7 seasons with New York. *Library of Congress Prints and Photographs Division*

Jeff Tesreau emerged as an effective sidekick to Christy Mathewson in the 1910s, leading the league in ERA as a rookie in 1912 followed by two 20-win seasons. *Library of Congress Prints and Photographs* Division

1914: George Burns, 10
1915: George Burns, 14
1916: Benny Kauff, 15
1917: George Burns, 13
1918: Heinie Zimmerman, 10
1919: Larry Doyle, 10

Stolen Bases

1910: Red Murray, 57
1911: Josh Devore, 61
1912: Fred Snodgrass, 43
1913: George Burns, 40
1914: *George Burns, 62*
1915: George Burns, 27
1916: Benny Kauff, 40
1917: George Burns, 40
1918: George Burns, 40
1919: *George Burns, 40*

Wins

1910: *Christy Mathewson, 27*
1911: Christy Mathewson, 26
1912: *Rube Marquard, 26*
1913: Christy Mathewson, 25
1914: Jeff Tesreau, 26
1915: Jeff Tesreau, 19
1916: Jeff Tesreau, 18
　　　　Pol Perritt, 18
1917: Ferdie Schupp, 21
1918: Pol Perritt, 18
1919: *Jesse Barnes, 25*

ERA

1910: Christy Mathewson, 1.89
1911: *Christy Mathewson, 1.99*
1912: *Jeff Tesreau, 1.96*
1913: *Christy Mathewson, 2.06*

1914: Jeff Tesreau, 2.37
1915: Jeff Tesreau, 2.29
1916: Pol Perritt, 2.62
1917: Pol Perritt, 1.88
1918: Slim Sallee, 2.25
1919: Fred Toney, 1.84

Strikeouts

1910: Christy Mathewson, 184
1911: *Rube Marquard, 237*
1912: Rube Marquard, 175
1913: Jeff Tesreau, 167
1914: Jeff Tesreau, 189
1915: Jeff Tesreau, 176
1916: Pol Perritt, 115
　　　　Rube Benton, 115
1917: Ferdie Schupp, 147
1918: Pol Perritt, 60
1919: Jesse Barnes, 92

Feisty shortstop Art Fletcher garnered MVP recognition in 1913 and '14. *Library of Congress Prints and Photographs Division*

FLETCHER, N. Y. NAT'L

GIANTS 1910–1919 All-Decade Team

1B	FRED MERKLE
2B	LARRY DOYLE
SS	ART FLETCHER
3B	HEINIE ZIMMERMAN
C	CHIEF MEYERS
OF	GEORGE BURNS
OF	FRED SNODGRASS
OF	RED MURRAY
SP	CHRISTY MATHEWSON
SP	JEFF TESREAU

THE 1920s

A NEW DYNASTY

McGraw finally puts it all together, winning four straight pennants and two World Series. But the Yankees go on to greater glory, beating Mugsy's men in 1923 and dominating the decade.

I f only John McGraw could have known the changes the Roaring '20s would bring. It was a decade of great triumph for the manager, with four straight pennants and two World Series championships, but also a decade in which his beloved "inside game" forever took a back seat to the long ball as ushered in by his crosstown nemesis, Babe Ruth of the Yankees.

Baseball faced some major challenges entering the decade. The 1919 Black Sox scandal, in which the Chicago White Sox had deliberately lost the World Series, shook the game's foundations. In 1920, Cleveland's Ray Chapman died after being struck in the head with a pitch. New MLB commissioner Kenesaw Mountain Landis was given unprecedented powers to restore order and trust.

By 1921, all eyes were on New York. The Yankees had obtained Ruth the year before, and the star had blossomed after giving up pitching and devoting all his energy to batting. He had one of his best years ever in '21, bashing .378 with 59 home runs. The Yankees—playing in the Polo Grounds as tenants of the Giants—made it to the World Series, where they faced their hosts.

After three straight second-place finishes, the Giants had assembled a star-studded cast. Led by Frankie Frisch at second base, the team featured future Hall of Famers Dave "Beauty" Bancroft at shortstop, George "High Pockets" Kelly at first base, and Ross Youngs in the outfield. Despite losing the first two games of the World Series,

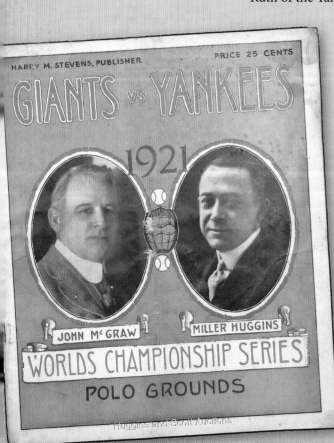

The 1921 World Series pitted 5-foot-7 Giants manager John McGraw against 5-foot-6 Yankees skipper Miller Huggins. It was the first of three straight series matchups between the rivals. *MVP Books Collection*

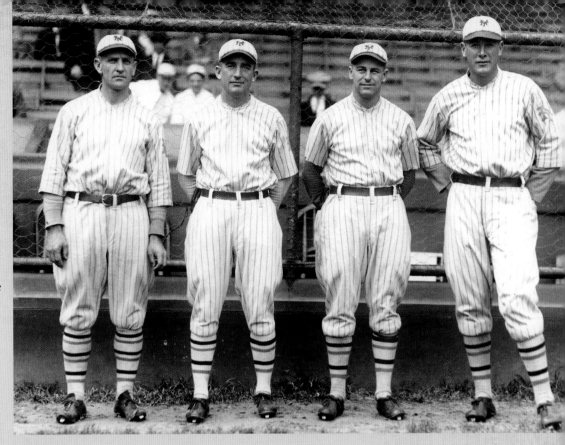

the Giants roared back to win five of the next six—it was the last of a three-year experiment with a best-of-nine format—and become champions for the first time since 1905. They repeated the feat the following year, beating the Yankees again.

By 1923, however, the Yankees had opened their own ballpark across the Harlem River from the Polo Grounds, and the teams met one more time in the Series. In what would prove a poetic twist, the Giants' Casey Stengel hit the first World Series home run in Yankee Stadium—a game-winning, inside-the-park homer in the ninth inning of Game One—but the Yankees won the Series in six. It was their first of many championships.

McGraw still had one pennant left in him in 1924—his eighth in 14 seasons, but also his last. (Only his protégé Stengel would make more trips to the Fall Classic as a manager, 10 to McGraw's 9.) All the Giants' infielders were future Hall of Famers by this time, with Bill Terry at first, Frisch at second, Freddie Lindstrom at third, and Travis Jackson at short. But the Washington Senators eked out a seven-game victory in one of the most closely contested Series of all time. The final game was decided in the 12th inning, with two bad-hop grounders doing the Giants in.

The Giants suffered only one sub-.500 season in the decade. After a spat with Frisch, McGraw traded his star for Rogers Hornsby, a blockbuster swap of Hall of Famers. Teenager Mel Ott joined the team in 1926, and popular star Ross Youngs died of Bright's disease in 1927, breaking McGraw's heart. Valiant runs for the pennant fell short in the late Septembers of 1927 and 1928.

Perhaps it was only a coincidence, another in a long line of baseball's myriad superstitions, but the Giants' decade-opening run of four straight pennants came after the team erected a monument honoring former infielder Eddie Grant, the only major-leaguer to die in World War I. The plaque was mounted on a concrete pillar that stood in center field, in play, from 1921 until 1957. The plaque did not join the team in the move to San Francisco, and it has never been seen since. Some have theorized that the "Curse of Captain Eddie" hung over the team since it forsook Coogan's Bluff for Candlestick Point. After losing the 2002 World Series, the Giants commissioned a replica of the plaque for display in AT&T Park, and ultimately the curse was broken.

1920

▶ **86-68   2nd** ◀

Highlights

February 9: The Joint Rules Committee bans the doctoring of baseballs, but the NL allows current "spitballers," including New York's Phil Douglas, to continue to do so for one more year.

May: Due to a rift between the Giants and the co-tenant Yankees, the Yanks begin plans to build their own ballpark.

May 3: The Giants lose and fall to 3–9. They will never reside in first place this season.

May 11: New York's Ross Youngs laces three triples against Cincinnati.

June 8: New York acquires slick-fielding Phillies shortstop Dave Bancroft for shortstop Art Fletcher, pitcher Bill Hubbell, and $100,000.

June 28: Bancroft goes 6-for-6 in an 18–3 rout of Philadelphia.

September 13: The Giants whitewash St. Louis to move into second place for the first time, a spot they won't relinquish.

September 17: New York's George Burns hits for the cycle

NOTES

George Burns leads the NL in runs (115), first baseman George Kelly is tops in RBI (94), and Ross Youngs is runner-up for the batting title (.351).

Art Nehf (21–12), Fred Toney (21–11), and Jesse Barnes (20–15) provide a strong pitching trio.

UPSTAGED BY THE BABE

The Yankees Become the Main Attraction in New York

With the Roaring '20s set to begin, a ticket to see a game at the Polo Grounds was the hottest pass in New York. Unfortunately for John McGraw's club, most fans weren't coming to see the Giants. The Yankees were significantly outdrawing the Giants in the latter's own ballpark. Everyone in the Big Apple wanted to see the Yankees' newest acquisition from Boston, a 25-year-old, homer-belting behemoth named George Herman "Babe" Ruth.

The previously dormant Yankees were now a sensation, and the Giants were suddenly New York's "other" team. While Ruth was en route to a stunning 54-homer season, the Giants in mid-July were languishing in seventh place at 35–41.

The Giants' woes went beyond their cold bats. Early in the season, third baseman Frankie Frisch underwent an emergency appendectomy that would force him to miss 40 games. Christy Mathewson, who would fill in as manager when McGraw was suspended for five games in May (for relentless umpire heckling), was diagnosed with tuberculosis. And after a loss to the Cubs in August, McGraw showed up at the Polo Grounds the next day with two black eyes, facial bruises, and a fractured skull—the result of a fight at the Lambs Club.

The Giants rebounded from a lackluster first half of the season by going 50–27 in the second half. Led by George "High Pockets" Kelly (11 homers, 94 RBI) and three 20-game winners—Jesse Barnes, Art Nehf, and Fred Toney— New York was only 1½ games back in the standings with less than a month remaining. However, the Giants' first half proved to be too big of a hurdle to overcome, as they finished in second place, seven games behind the Brooklyn Robins.

The 1920 season was a very forgettable year for the New York Giants. With off-the-field issues and the commandeering of their ballpark by their cross-town rivals, the Giants were looking for good news. It would come the following season.

Hailed by John McGraw as his best clutch hitter, George "High Pockets" Kelly averaged 110 RBI for New York from 1920 to '25. In his first full season of 1920, he led the NL with 94 RBI. *Library of Congress Prints and Photographs Division*

50

UNDER NEW MANAGEMENT

"There has only been one manager," said Connie Mack, who won more games than any other manager in MLB history, "and his name is John McGraw."

Though McGraw would become one of the greatest winners in American sports, his upbringing seemed to set him up for failure. After running away from his abusive father in the poor town of Truxton, New York, in 1885, the 12-year-old quickly learned that nothing in life was going to be given to him; he had to take it. It was this philosophy that drove him to the pinnacle of his profession.

The scrappy and diminutive McGraw burst into the big leagues in 1891 with the Baltimore Orioles at the age of 18 and quickly became one of baseball's best hitters. Nicknamed "Mugsy" for his slight, 5-foot-7 frame, McGraw had quick wrists and a sharp eye. He batted over .320 for nine years in a row, eclipsed 100 walks in a season three times, and played superb defense at third base.

McGraw was an extraordinary player; his .466 career on-base percentage is third all-time behind the marks of Ted Williams and Babe Ruth. However, his accomplishments as a player are largely lost to history. John McGraw's more noteworthy career began on July 8, 1902, the day he became the manager of the New York Giants.

After three mediocre seasons as the player/manager of the Orioles, McGraw in New York began one of the most successful managerial tenures in baseball history. In his 33 years as the Orioles' and Giants' skipper, McGraw led his troops to three World Series titles, 10 NL pennants, and a 2,763–1,948 record. A feisty and fiery leader, he was ejected 132 times (second most ever), yet he seemed to get more out of players with limited abilities than any other manager. While never consistently blessed with the best talent, McGraw recorded only two losing seasons during his time in New York, not counting his first and last campaign, when he managed only a fraction of each season.

Like his nickname suggested, "Little Napoleon" was a masterful strategist and committed to controlling every aspect of the game from the dugout. McGraw became the first major league manager to call pitches from the bench, and he was the first to utilize relief specialists.

Giving up baseball was not easy for McGraw, as illness and infirmity kept him away from his team for much of the time near the end of his managerial career. Baseball was his life, and without one he didn't seem to need the other. McGraw died in 1934 at the age of 60, two years after he retired from the game. He was inducted into the Baseball Hall of Fame three years later.

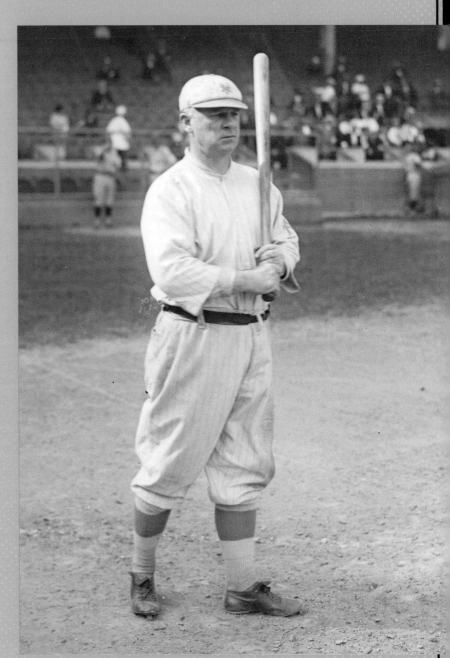

Though second to Connie Mack in all-time managerial wins, McGraw's .586 winning percentage is 100 points higher than Mack's. *Library of Congress Prints and Photographs Division*

1921

▶ **94-59   1st** ◀

Highlights

May 30: The Giants unveil a memorial to former player Eddie Grant, who was killed in combat during the war.

June 1: Dave Bancroft hits for the cycle, but he faints in the dugout after his inside-the-park homer.

July 1: The Giants acquire outfielder Casey Stengel in a trade with Philadelphia.

September 9: A 6–2 win over Brooklyn launches the Giants into first place for good.

September 17: New York tops Pittsburgh 6–1 for its 10th straight victory.

October 7: Down two games to none in the best-of-nine World Series, the Giants crack 20 hits in a 13–5 win over the Yankees.

October 10: Phil Douglas earns a 2–1 victory in Game Seven to put the Giants up four games to three.

October 11: The Giants score in the first inning, and Art Nehf shuts out the Yankees 1–0 to win Game Eight to clinch the World Series.

NOTES

George Kelly plates 122 runs and leads the NL in homers (23).

Third baseman **Frankie Frisch** rips .341 with 211 hits and a league-high 49 steals.

Art Nehf leads the mound corps with a 20–10 record.

KINGS OF NEW YORK!

Giants Knock Off Rival Yankees in World Series

After a year in which the Yankees were suddenly the toast of New York, the Giants were ready to take back their city. While the Yankees had the sheer power and explosiveness of Babe Ruth, the Giants had a budding nucleus of young players who were hungry to bring home a title for the original owners of the Polo Grounds.

Frankie Frisch, a 22-year-old third baseman out of Fordham University, led the Giants in batting (.341) and the league in stolen bases (49). Outfielder Ross Youngs, age 24, drove in 102 runs. And catcher Earl Smith, 24, finished second on the team with 10 home runs while hitting .336. But the key to the Giants reclaiming the "City That Never Sleeps" lay in a man with exceptionally large trousers.

George "High Pockets" Kelly was a 6-foot-4, 190-pound first baseman out of San Francisco—and the Giants' answer to the "Sultan of Swat." While Kelly certainly couldn't match the output or sheer distance of Ruth's moon shots, he was the best power hitter in the NL. Kelly paced the league with 23 home runs, finished second in RBI with 122, and was the main catalyst for an offense that led the league in runs.

Even though McGraw didn't have the workhorse ace that his past teams had been blessed with, New York still had one of the most productive staffs in the league. Southpaw Art Nehf led the team in victories with 20, and none of the starters had a losing record.

For most of the year, the Giants were looking up at the Pirates from second place in the NL. As it became clear that the Yankees were going to take home the AL flag, the Giants rattled off 10 straight victories to upend Pittsburgh and capture the pennant.

The stage was set for an all-New York World Series, and Giants manager John McGraw

Frankie Frisch, the "Fordham Flash," ripped .321 in exactly 1,000 games for the Giants. He batted .341 in 1921. *Library of Congress Prints and Photographs Division*

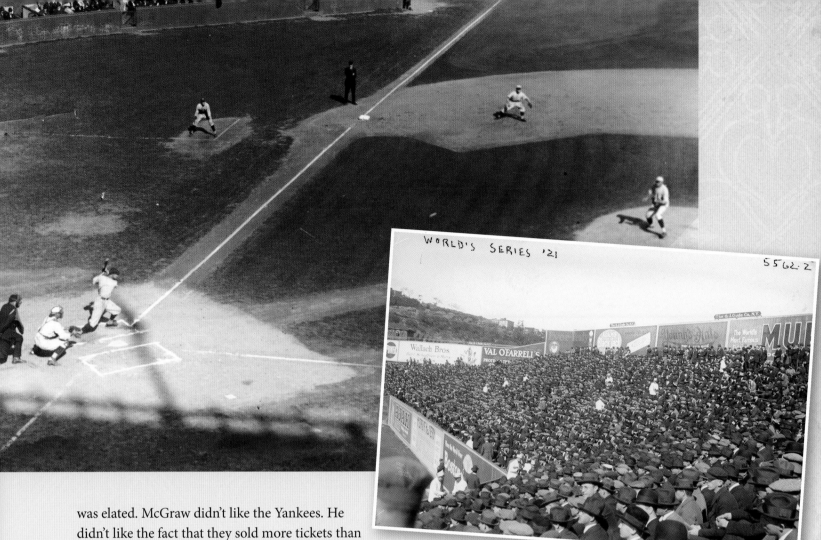

was elated. McGraw didn't like the Yankees. He didn't like the fact that they sold more tickets than his Giants, and he didn't like Babe Ruth. McGraw vowed to reestablish the Giants' supremacy on the New York baseball scene.

The 1921 World Series was a best-of-nine affair and the first Fall Classic to take place entirely in one ballpark. The Yankees took a commanding 2–0 Series lead after winning Games One and Two by identical 3–0 scores. While Giants fans were concerned, McGraw was calm and confident that his team's offense would show up. "I am anything but discouraged," he said after Game Two.

McGraw was right, as the Giants exploded for 20 hits in a 13–5 Game Three victory. The good fortune continued for the Giants in Game Four as "Shufflin'" Phil Douglas outpitched the Yankees' Carl Mays while Ruth played through an elbow injury. The Babe was able to score a key run (after beating out a bunt!) in the Yankees' 3–1 Game Five victory, but he batted only once more during the rest of the Series.

The absence of Ruth was a major blow to the Yankees offense. After the Giants won Game Six 8–5, McGraw's pitchers held their rivals to one run and 12 hits over the final two games. The Giants won Game Seven 2–1 and then, after scoring in the first inning, took the Game Eight clincher 1–0 behind the arm of Art Nehf, who went all the way for a four-hit shutout.

After winning his second World Series title, and first in 16 years, McGraw praised the grit of a team that was more than just New York's finest. "I have the greatest baseball club in the world," he said, "and unquestionably the gamest."

Top: The Yankees battle the Giants at the Polo Grounds—the home of both teams—in the 1921 World Series. The Giants won the best-of-nine affair in eight games. *Baseball Hall of Fame Museum and Library;* **Inset:** The Polo Grounds bleachers were packed with bowler- and derby-wearing men for the World Series matchup between the Yanks and the Giants. *Library of Congress Prints and Photographs Division*

1922

▸ **93-61   1st** ◂

Highlights

July 10: The Giants bang out 28 hits in a 19–2 route of Pittsburgh.

July 30: New York's Phil Douglas (11–4, NL-best 2.63 ERA in 1922) pitches his last game in the majors. He will be banned from MLB for requesting inducement money from the Cardinals to join them.

September 25: The Giants edge St. Louis 5–4 in 10 innings to clinch the pennant.

October 4: The Giants rally for three in the bottom of the eighth to defeat the Yankees in Game One of the World Series.

October 6: Jack Scott shuts out the Yankees in Game Three after Game Two ended in a 3–3 tie.

October 8: A two-out, two-run single in the eighth by George Kelly puts the Giants ahead 4–3 in Game Five, and they win 5–3 to sweep the Series.

NOTES

The Giants bat .305 as a team, with Casey Stengel (.368) and catcher Frank Snyder (.343) leading the team in average.

Irish Meusel (.331-16-132) and George Kelly (.328-17-107) are the big guns.

Art Nehf (19–13) leads the staff in wins.

SHUFFLIN' TO GLORY

Douglas Is Banned, but Giants Repeat as World Champs

With the Giants in position to defend their World Series championship for the first time since 1906, one would think that every member of the team would have been committed to bringing home another title. Not quite.

In 1922, "Shufflin'" Phil Douglas was the Giants' most reliable pitcher and posted the staff's lowest earned-run average. After a great first half of the season that saw him win 11 games, Douglas's downward spiral began. First he was fined $100 and five days' pay by manager John McGraw for passing out dead drunk on the Upper West Side after a game. Soon after that, Douglas lumbered into the press box and threatened to kill a local sportswriter. But the last straw came in the form of a letter that Douglas sent to his friend, St. Louis outfielder Leslie Mann. In the letter, Douglas professed his hatred for McGraw and his disinterest in competing for the Giants. Mann, an honest guy, turned the letter over to league officials, who banned Douglas from baseball for life.

Though Douglas' downfall was tragic, his expulsion from the Giants had little effect on the team, which went 34–22 in August and September. The staff ended up boasting the lowest ERA (3.45) in the league. Art Nehf paced the Giants with 19 wins, and youngster Bill "Rosy" Ryan won 17. Outfielder Irish Meusel, brother of Yankees slugger Bob Meusel, led the offense with 132 RBI. But he wasn't the only big bopper; seven regulars batted above .320. The Giants cruised to their second straight pennant, finishing with a 93–61 record and seven games ahead of second-place Cincinnati.

With the Yankees taking care of business in the AL, the World Series was a rematch of the previous year. Although Babe Ruth was in the midst of one of the worst seasons of his storied career, the Giants refused to be beaten by the Bambino and were committed to pitching around the portly power hitter. McGraw was convinced that if his pitchers threw Ruth curveballs in the dirt, he wouldn't hurt them.

McGraw's strategy worked, as his pitchers stifled Ruth and the entire Yankees offense in Game One, 3–2, which the Giants won with three in the eighth. Game Two ended in confusion when umpires Ernie Hildebrand and Bill Klem decided to call the game due to darkness with the score tied at 3–3. The 10-inning tie would be the closest the Yankees would get to a win in the Series.

The fan who paid $3.30 (about 46 bucks in today's money) for a ticket to Game One of the 1922 World Series saw the Giants rally for three runs in the eighth for a 3–2 win. *MVP Books Collection*

Jack Scott threw a four-hit shutout in Game Three, Hugh McQuillan outdueled Carl Mays 4–3 in Game Four, and George "High Pockets" Kelly hit a game-winning, two-run single in the eighth inning of Game Five—a 5–3 Giants victory—to seal the repeat.

The Giants players, each of whom were $4,500 richer due to their World Series share, celebrated with a party at the Waldorf hotel—a celebration that lasted till dawn. According to reporter Westbrook Pegler, celebrants left the hotel looking "bruised and disheveled, like bums out of a barrel house." It was a heck of a drunken bash—and Shufflin' Phil Douglas wasn't even there.

The front page of the October 9, 1922, edition of the *Daily News* celebrates the Giants' clinching victory over the Yankees in the World Series. Below, the caption under John McGraw's photo credits his "masterly strategy" in leading the club to its third championship. *New York Daily News Archive/Getty Images*

Giants Kick Yankees Out of Polo Grounds

Before relocating to the Bronx, the New York Yankees shared their cavernous 55,000-seat home on West 155th Street and Eighth Avenue in Manhattan with the New York Giants. Giants manager John McGraw hated having to share the Polo Grounds with the Yankees, and he was especially angry that the home run exploits of Babe Ruth were drawing more fans to see Ruth's Yankees than his Giants.

En route to defeating the Yankees in back-to-back World Series, the Giants decided to one-up the Yanks one last time. The Giants told Yankees owners Jacob Ruppert and Cap Huston that 1922 would be the last year they could lease the Polo Grounds, with McGraw saying they should move their team "to some out-of-the-way place, like Queens." Although it wasn't in Queens, the Yankees did have a new ballpark by 1923. Yankee Stadium was built on the other side of the Harlem River in the Bronx.

By playing in two different leagues, the Giants and Yankees rarely met, but when they did, their games had major implications. After relocating to Yankee Stadium, the Yanks and Giants faced each other four times in the World Series, with the Yankees winning all four meetings.

The Polo Grounds (left) lay in Manhattan, across the Harlem River from Yankee Stadium (right) in the Bronx. *Joe Caneva/AP Images*

1923

Highlights

April 19: The Giants open the season at 4–0. They will reside in first place every day of the season.

May 20: The Giants draw an NL-record 42,000 fans at the newly expanded Polo Grounds.

June 1: The New Yorkers score in all nine innings of a 22–8 win at Philadelphia.

September 17: George Kelly homers in the third, fourth, and fifth innings against the Cubs. He also singles and doubles.

October 10: The Giants upend the Yankees in Game One of the World Series 5–4 on a Casey Stengel inside-the-park homer in the top of the ninth.

October 12: A Stengel homer and Art Nehf's shutout result in a 1–0 Giants victory in Game Three.

October 15: The Yankees down the Giants 6–4 in Game Six to clinch the Series.

NOTES

Frankie Frisch cracks .348 and leads the NL in hits (223) and total bases (311).

Irish Meusel leads the league in RBI (125), while **Ross Youngs** tops the circuit in runs (121).

Jack Scott (16–7) and **Rosy Ryan** (16–5) lead the team in wins.

JUST SHY OF A THREE-PEAT

Giants Go Wire to Wire Before Falling to Yankees

By 1923, the Giants were on top of the world. They were back-to-back World Series champs, finally had the Polo Grounds to themselves, and were once again the class of the National League. By May 27, the Giants were 28–8, causing *Sporting News* editor Joe Vila to proclaim New York "the most powerful ball team ever put together." In fact, the 1923 Giants became the first MLB club in the 20th century to reside in first place for the entire season.

Four Giants starters hit over .300. Second baseman Frankie Frisch paced the team with a .348 average while leading the circuit in hits. Irish Meusel slugged 14 triples and 19 homers while driving in 125 runs. And fellow outfielder Ross Youngs ripped .336 with 121 runs scored.

New York finished at 95–58, beating out second-place Cincinnati by 4½ games. Though the Yankees had moved across the river, the Giants still couldn't get away from their familiar foe, as they met the Yankees in the World Series for the third straight year.

Before he would become one of the Bronx Bombers' most beloved managers, Giants outfielder Casey Stengel proved to be a huge thorn in the Yankees' side during the 1923 World Series. In Game One, Stengel's inside-the-park home run off "Bullet" Joe Bush broke a 4–4 tie in the ninth and gave the Giants an early edge in the Series.

Still, the Giants weren't able to avoid the heroics of the Babe, as Ruth belted home runs in the fourth and fifth innings of Game Two to help give the Yankees a 4–2 victory. In Game Three, Stengel's homer provided the lone run in Art Nehf's 1–0 shutout. Unfortunately for the Giants, that would be the end of Stengel's heroics. The Yankees took the next three games (8–4, 8–1, 6–4) to finally beat the Giants in the World Series and win the first of their many world championships in Yankee Stadium.

Right: The Polo Grounds' capacity increased dramatically due to an extension of the upper deck. All but center field would be enclosed. *Library of Congress Prints and Photographs Division*
Opposite page: The Giants' Casey Stengel slides home with an inside-the-park home run in Game One of the 1923 World Series. The two-out blast in the top of the ninth gave the Giants a 5–4 victory. *Bruce Bennett/ Getty Images*

▶ 93-60   1st ◀

Highlights

June 14: George Kelly tallies three homers and eight RBI in an 8–6 triumph over Cincinnati.

July 29: Pitcher Art Nehf belts two home runs in a 5–2 win over St. Louis.

September 10: Frankie Frisch's six hits help the Giants rout Boston 22–1.

September 27: New York beats Philadelphia 5–1 to clinch its fourth straight NL flag.

October 1: Giants outfielder Jimmy O'Connell is banned from MLB after it's discovered that he asked the Phillies shortstop to "go easy" on the Giants on September 27.

October 4: The Giants score twice in the 12th and defeat Washington 4–3 in Game One of the World Series.

October 5: A walk-off Roger Peckinpaugh double in the ninth gives the Senators a 4–3 win in Game Two.

October 10: Washington captures the Game Seven finale 4–3 on a bad-hop single in the eighth and an Earl McNeely walk-off double in the 12th.

NOTES

Frankie Frisch leads the league in runs (121), and **George Kelly** is the RBI king (136).

Ross Youngs strokes .356.

Virgil Barnes and **Jack Bentley** lead the staff with 16 wins each.

A ROCKY FINISH

Ball Hits Pebble, Costs Giants the World Series

Near the end of May 1923, Giants manager John McGraw stepped off a high curb in Chicago, fell in the street, and badly injured the same knee he had damaged during his playing days in 1902. While McGraw would limp the rest of the year, his Giants would soar—until another bad break ruined their season.

New York spent most of the 1924 campaign in first place. The team batted an even .300 and led the National League in nearly every major category. Standouts included Frankie Frisch (.328, 121 runs), George Kelly (.324-21-136), Ross Youngs (.356, 112 runs), and Irish Meusel (.310, 102 RBI).

The Giants withstood a late-season charge by Brooklyn to claim their fourth straight pennant. However, over in the other league, a force was emerging in Washington. The Senators, led by legendary fireballer Walter Johnson, had just given the nation's capital its first baseball championship of any kind. President Calvin Coolidge would attend three of the World Series games at Griffith Stadium in Washington.

New York dampened Washington's momentum in Game One by scoring twice in the 12th inning to win 4–3. The Senators responded the next day, as shortstop Roger Peckingpaugh's ninth-inning double gave his team its first World Series victory. The two clubs split the next four games, setting the stage for an epic Game Seven in Washington.

Unfortunately for Giants fans, another freak happening deprived the team of a championship. Sparking memories of Merkle's Boner and Snodgrass's Muff, a seemingly harmless grounder toward third baseman Freddie Lindstrom in the bottom of the eighth hit a pebble and bounced over his head. Two runners scored on the play, which knotted the game at 3–3. After Walter Johnson pitched four innings of shutout relief, Earl McNeely laced a walk-off double in the 12th to give the Senators their first (and only) World Series championship.

This photo was snapped right before Game Seven of the 1924 World Series, which would turn into a 12-inning epic that was decided by a small stone. *Library of Congress Prints and Photographs Division*

A SICKENING SEASON

McGraw's Health Issues Correlate With Subpar Play

In 1925, New York manager John McGraw was 52 years old, in his 24th year at the helm of the Giants, and the wear and tear of a life given to baseball was beginning to show. McGraw's health became such an issue that his players had become accustomed to seeing the fat little man at the end of the bench sneezing and coughing into his handkerchief. However, McGraw refused to let his ailments prevent him from managing. When asked by reporters if it was time to retire, he said, "I will manage the Giants as long as I live. The game is my life. That's all there is to it!"

"Little Napoleon" swore that his deteriorating health had no impact on his players, but their play on the field indicated otherwise. As McGraw's health began to slip, so did the Giants in the standings. After climbing to first place with a 42–26 record by July 1, New York began to fall behind Pittsburgh as McGraw began to stay home during road trips. He ended up missing more than 30 games during the 1925 campaign, as his close friend Hughie Jennings—the longtime former Tigers manager—filled in for him when he was ill.

Even with their leader's medical situation uncertain, the Giants were just three games behind Pittsburgh when the Pirates came to town for a five-game series at the Polo Grounds in late August. The Pirates won four of those contests on their way to winning the pennant by 8½. After the series, a furious McGraw told his players in the clubhouse, "I won't manage this team next year."

McGraw would manage the team the following season, but it was becoming clear that his days at the helm of the Giants were numbered. New York's second-place finish marked the first time in four years that the team hadn't ended the season in the World Series. New York's time at the pinnacle of the baseball world was coming to an end.

From 1922 to 1925, Giants outfielder Irish Meusel averaged .316 and 118 RBI per season. In 1925, he led the team in homers (21), RBI (111), and slugging (.548). *Library of Congress Prints and Photographs Division*

1925

▶ 86-66   2nd ◀

Highlights

May 18: An eight-game winning streak puts the Giants at 21–6.

June 10: The Giants beat the Cubs to improve to 33–15 and extend their NL lead to 6½ games, but a six-game losing streak will immediately follow.

June 12: Against Pittsburgh, New York pulls off a 6–2–5–9–4–3 triple play.

July 1: Young outfielder Hack Wilson clubs two homers in one inning in a 16–7 rout of the Phillies.

August 8: The Giants send future Hall of Famer Wilson to Toledo, and he'll never return to New York. Also this day, the New Yorkers lose their sixth straight to fall five games back (after leading the NL a week earlier).

September 2: New York pummels the Phillies 24–9 on 30 hits.

NOTES

Illness forces manager **John McGraw** to miss more than 30 Giants games throughout the season. Coach **Hughie Jennings** fills in.

Frankie Frisch paces the Giants with a .331 average and 89 runs.

Irish Meusel clubs .328 with 21 homers and 111 RBI.

Virgil Barnes (15–11) leads Giants pitchers in wins.

Highlights

January: Giants pitcher Hugh McQuillan breaks bones in his pitching hand when he punches a cab driver.

April 13: The Giants attract 45,000 in an Opening Day loss to Brooklyn.

April 23: New York improves to 7–1 with a 6–3 win over Brooklyn.

May 11: The Giants drop from first to fourth after a 2–9 skein. They will not rise above fourth place over the rest of the season.

August 20: John McGraw chews out star second baseman Frankie Frisch, who responds by leaving the team. He won't play again until September 7.

September 3: The New Yorkers score 12 runs in the fifth inning of a 17–3 trouncing of the Braves.

December 20: The Giants trade Frisch and Jimmy Ring to the Cardinals for Rogers Hornsby, winner of six straight NL batting titles through 1925, including three .400 seasons.

NOTES

Five Giants regulars hit above .300, led by shortstop **Travis Jackson** at .327.

Mel Ott, age 17 at season's end, bats .383 in 60 at-bats.

Freddie Fitzsimmons's 14 wins are enough to lead the staff.

FRUSTRATIONS BOIL OVER

McGraw and Frisch Go At It During Sub-.500 Season

In 1926, Giants owner Charles Stoneham rewarded manager John McGraw with a three-year contract extension. Yet McGraw would need to earn every cent of his new $50,000 salary, as 1926 was shaping up to be one of his toughest coaching jobs yet. With a group of underachieving veterans and inexperienced youngsters, McGraw quickly became frustrated with his ball club. "The trouble with the team," he said, "is due to the indifference of certain players and the downright insubordination of others."

All of McGraw's anger came to a head on August 20 when the manager verbally filleted star second baseman Frankie Frisch in front of the whole team for missing a sign. Back at the hotel in St. Louis, Frisch ordered a bellhop to buy him a train ticket to New York. The next morning, Frisch paid his own tab at the hotel and boarded the train. "I was finished with the Giants," he said. "I wouldn't take it anymore."

Frisch would later rejoin the club, but it made little difference to a team that did seem to feel indifferent about winning and losing. Even as five Giants regulars hit above .300, New York was pretty much out of the pennant race in late May and never rose above fourth place for most of the season. The Giants' offense produced a mediocre 663 runs, while Fred Fitzsimmons's pedestrian 14 victories led the pitching staff.

New York limped into the offseason with a 74–77 record, as their fifth-place finish marked the worst showing for a McGraw-led team since 1915. A glimmer of hope came in the form of Melvin Ott. The 17-year-old from Louisiana racked up a .383 average in his 60 late-season at-bats. With the Giants struggling, the future of the New York franchise seemed to be on the teenager's shoulders.

Like the famous Civil War general, Travis Jackson was nicknamed "Stonewall," but his moniker was due to his tremendous range at shortstop, sealing his side of the infield like a stone wall. He chipped in with the bat, too, with a team-high .327 average in 1926.
MVP Books Collection

"THE RAJAH" COMES TO NY

Hornsby Cracks .361 as Giants Make a Pennant Run

In what was considered the marquee trade in baseball up to that point, John McGraw finally got his man. In exchange for the troublesome Frankie Frisch and mediocre starting pitcher Jimmy Ring, the Giants acquired second baseman Rogers Hornsby from the St. Louis Cardinals.

McGraw had admired Hornsby for some time, and with good reason. From 1920 through '25, "The Rajah" had won six consecutive batting titles with the Cardinals, hitting .370, .397, .401, .384, .424, and .403. After learning of the trade, Hornsby returned the manager's praise. "I'm mighty glad to be with John McGraw," he said. As expected, Hornsby shined on offense. He bashed .361-26-125 and led the NL in runs (133) and walks (86).

Complementing Hornsby was first baseman Bill Terry, who ripped .326 while driving in 121 runs. The Giants had one of the league's most powerful offenses—they led the NL in homers with 109—but a disappointing start to the season proved to be their downfall. The Giants followed a 42–38 first half with a 50–24 record in the second half. Hornsby actually managed the Giants for much of the later months, as McGraw suffered from upper respiratory ailments.

After a win against the Cubs on September 9 that put them just a half game out of first place, the New Yorkers began to slip. The Giants slowly fell to third place, finishing just two games behind first-place Pittsburgh. The Pirates were promptly swept in the World Series by the legendary '27 Yankees.

The hard-bitten McGraw found reasons to smile in 1927. He learned that the new athletic field at St. Bonaventure College would bear his name, and on July 19 the Giants staged a Silver Jubilee for McGraw at the Polo Grounds, commemorating his quarter century as team manager. That day, the Lambs Club, a social club that had kicked out McGraw in 1920, publicly honored the Giants skipper.

Rogers Hornsby, said Frankie Frisch, for whom he was traded, "is the only guy I know who could hit .350 in the dark." The "Rajah" hit .358 for his career, second-best in MLB history, and rapped .361 in his lone season playing for John McGraw's Giants. *MVP Books Collection*

Highlights

February 9: The Giants trade George Kelly to the Reds for outfielder Edd Roush, a two-time NL bat champ.

April 8: Newly acquired Giant Rogers Hornsby agrees to sell his stock in the St. Louis Cardinals for $100,000.

May 17: New York improves to 19–9, but the team will lose its next six.

July 19: The Giants hold John McGraw Day at the Polo Grounds, in tribute to his 25 years as team manager.

September 4: New York wins its 10th straight game to go from eight games out to two back.

September 5: The Giants draw 58,000 fans for a Labor Day doubleheader.

September 9: A win over the Cubs puts the Giants within a half game of first place. However, they will drop back and out of the race.

October 22: Longtime Giants star Ross Youngs dies of Bright's disease at age 30.

NOTES

Rogers Hornsby leads the NL in runs (133), ranks second in batting (.361), and finishes third in homers (26) and RBI (125).

First baseman **Bill Terry** bats .326 with 121 RBI.

Burleigh Grimes is the staff's big winner (19–8).

Highlights

January 10: Troubled by Rogers Hornsby's abrasive style and involvement in gambling, the Giants trade him to the Braves for catcher Shanty Hogan and outfielder Jimmy Welsh.

February 11: New York trades pitcher Burleigh Grimes to Pittsburgh for pitcher Vic Aldridge.

April 11: Jewish player Andy Cohen replaces Hornsby at second base on Opening Day. After he collects three hits, hundreds of Jewish fans storm the field and carry him off on their shoulders.

July 12: New York acquires lefty pitcher Carl Hubbell from Beaumont of the Texas League.

September 25: A 16–2 run puts the Giants within a game of first place, but that's as close as they'll get to the Cardinals.

September 27: The Giants fall to the Cubs 3–2 after a controversial call at the plate.

NOTES

Freddie Lindstrom bats .358 with 107 RBI while leading the NL with 231 hits.

Teenage outfielder **Mel Ott** raps .322 and paces the team with 18 homers.

Bill Terry cracks .326 with 101 RBI.

Larry Benton leads the NL in wins (25–9), while **Freddie Fitzsimmons** finishes 20–9.

A YOUTH INFUSION

Giants Contend Thanks to Ott, Lindstrom, Fitzsimmons

The Rogers Hornsby era in New York quickly came to a close in January 1928. Troubled by Hornsby's abrasive personality and gambling ties, Giants owner Charles Stoneham traded him to the Boston Braves. Stoneham said after the trade, "It occurred to me that to prevent any possible conflict in authority, it would be best to send Hornsby elsewhere." The deal came as a surprise to John McGraw, who, upon hearing the news, said, "The trade has been made, and that's all there is to it."

Replacing a player of Hornsby's caliber would be tough, but the play of outfielder Mel Ott, third baseman Freddie Lindstrom, and pitcher Freddie Fitzsimmons helped soften the loss. Ott and Lindstrom were just 19 and 22, respectively, but the two youngsters carried much of the offensive load for New York. Lindstrom led the club with 107 RBI and mashed 14 home runs, while Ott socked a team-high 18 dingers in his first full major league season. Fitzsimmons, a 26-year-old from Indiana, won 20 games for the first time in his career and formed a dynamic tandem with 25-game winner Larry Benton.

With four games left in the season and the Giants down just one game to the Cardinals in the pennant race, New York went to Chicago for a four-game tilt at Wrigley Field. In the first meeting, with the Giants trailing 3–2, New York infielder Andy Reese collided with Cubs catcher Gabby Hartnett en route to home plate. As Reese was still tangled with Hartnett, Chicago's Clyde Beck ran over and tagged him out. McGraw leapt from the dugout, screaming for interference, as it seemed that Hartnett had deliberately held Reese down.

McGraw's protests fell on deaf ears, and New York lost the game and the series. Failing to take care of business in Chicago allowed the Cardinals to walk away with the pennant, as New York finished two games behind at 93–61.

Freddie Lindstrom ranks second in Giants history with 231 hits in a season, a feat he achieved in both 1928 and 1930.
MVP Books Collection

Mel Ott Emerges

New York Outfielder Belts 42 Homers in Breakthrough Year

The right field foul pole in the Polo Grounds stood just 257 feet away from home plate. No one took advantage of this quite like Mel Ott, a 5-foot-9 left-handed hitter. The 20-year-old had his breakthrough season in 1929. In addition to leading the Giants in RBI (151) and runs (138), he also finished second in the majors in home runs (42) by becoming a master at pulling pitches to the right field corner of the Polo Grounds.

While Ott was an expert at exploiting the Polo Grounds' comically short right field wall, his talent transcended the ballpark's unique quirk. The Louisiana-born outfielder hit more home runs on the road in 1929 (22) than at the Polo Grounds (although that wasn't true for his career), and he was a dynamo on defense, recording a league-high 26 outfield assists. "He is a standout with me," John McGraw said. "Ott is the best-looking young hitter in my time with the Giants."

As Ott announced himself as a superstar, the rest of the Giants tried to keep up with his torrid pace. First baseman Bill Terry batted .372 and drove in 117 runs, Edd Roush cracked .324, and Travis Jackson's 21 home runs set a major league season record for a shortstop. Every Giants regular stroked .290 or better, while Carl Hubbell recorded 18 wins.

Though the Giants were statistically impressive, the season was an overall disappointment. Most of New York's futility lay in their inability to win close games. The Giants were 15–28 in games decided by one run or less—remarkable considering that they were 84–67 overall.

As the Giants continued to drop nail-biters, they saw the Cubs sprint to the top of the National League. McGraw's club finished in third place, 13½ games behind Chicago, and watched another team claim the pennant for the fifth straight year. The Giants were stocked with talent, but they would have to suck it up during the late innings if they were to contend in 1930.

While Mel Ott would belt 323 of his 511 career homers at the Polo Grounds, he swatted most of his 1929 big flys on the road. His 151 RBI that year are the most in Giants history. *MVP Books Collection*

Highlights

May 8: Carl Hubbell twirls an 11–0 no-hitter against Pittsburgh.

May 22: The Giants lose to fall to 9–16. They are buried in sixth place, eight games back.

June 15: The Giants score eight runs in the 14th inning to defeat Pittsburgh 20–15. The teams combine for 52 hits.

June 18: Bill Terry amasses nine hits and six RBI in a doubleheader against the Dodgers.

September 24: Mel Ott ties the NL season record with his 42nd home run.

October 5: On closing day for the Phillies, against the Giants, Philadelphia's Chuck Klein homers to finish with 43 round-trippers. Philly's Lefty O'Doul, whom the Giants traded a year earlier, ends his season with a .398 average and an NL-record 254 hits.

December 24: Giants officials file a $200,000 damage suit against former team treasurer Francis McQuade, claiming that he had sought to "destroy" the team.

NOTES

Mel Ott breaks out with a .328-42-151 season.

Bill Terry bashes .372 with 117 RBI.

Every Giants regular hits .290 or better, and the **team average** is .295.

Carl Hubbell leads the staff in wins (18–11).

THE 1920-1929 RECORD BOOK

Team Leaders

(*Italics* indicates NL leader)

Batting Average
1920: Ross Youngs, .351
1921: Frankie Frisch, .341
1922: Ross Youngs, .331
1923: Frankie Frisch, .348
1924: Ross Youngs, .356
1925: Frankie Frisch, .331
1926: Travis Jackson, .327
1927: Rogers Hornsby, .361
1928: Freddie Lindstrom, .358
1929: Bill Terry, .372

Home Runs
1920: George Kelly, 11
1921: *George Kelly, 23*
1922: George Kelly, 17
1923: Irish Meusel, 19
1924: George Kelly, 21
1925: Irish Meusel, 21
1926: George Kelly, 13
1927: Rogers Hornsby, 26
1928: Mel Ott, 18
1929: Mel Ott, 42

RBI
1920: *George Kelly, 94*
1921: George Kelly, 122
1922: Irish Meusel, 132
1923: *Irish Meusel, 125*
1924: *George Kelly, 136*
1925: Irish Meusel, 111
1926: George Kelly, 80
1927: Rogers Hornsby, 125
1928: Freddie Lindstrom, 107
1929: Mel Ott, 151

Runs
1920: *George Burns, 115*
1921: Dave Bancroft, 121
     Frankie Frisch, 121
1922: Dave Bancroft, 117
1923: *Ross Youngs, 121*
1924: *Frankie Frisch, 121*
1925: Frankie Frisch, 89
1926: Freddie Lindstrom, 90
1927: *Rogers Hornsby, 133*
1928: Bill Terry, 100
1929: Mel Ott, 151

Doubles
1920: George Burns, 35
1921: George Kelly, 42
1922: Dave Bancroft, 41
1923: Dave Bancroft, 33
     Ross Youngs, 33
1924: George Kelly, 37
1925: Irish Meusel, 35
1926: Freddie Frisch, 29
1927: Freddie Lindstrom, 36
1928: Freddie Lindstrom, 39
1929: Bill Terry, 39

Triples
1920: Ross Youngs, 14
1921: Freddie Frisch, 17
1922: Irish Meusel, 17
1923: Irish Meusel, 14
1924: Freddie Frisch, 15
1925: Freddie Lindstrom, 12
1926: Irish Meusel, 10
1927: Bill Terry, 13
1928: Bill Terry, 11
1929: Travis Jackson, 12

Stolen Bases
1920: Frankie Frisch, 34
1921: *Frankie Frisch, 49*
1922: Frankie Frisch, 31
1923: Frankie Frisch, 29
1924: Frankie Frisch, 22
1925: Frankie Frisch, 21
1926: Frankie Frisch, 23
1927: Edd Roush, 18
1928: Freddie Lindstrom, 15
1929: 4 tied with 10

A great table-setter, George Burns led the NL in walks and runs several times each with the Giants. *Library of Congress Prints and Photographs Division*

Wins

1920: Art Nehf, 21
Fred Toney, 21
1921: Art Nehf, 20
1922: Art Nehf, 19
1923: Rosy Ryan, 16
Jack Scott, 16
1924: Virgil Barnes, 16
Jack Bentley, 16
1925: Virgil Barnes, 15
1926: Freddie Fitzsimmons, 14
1927: Burleigh Grimes, 19
1928: *Larry Benton, 25*
1929: Carl Hubbell, 18

ERA

1920: Jesse Barnes, 2.64
1921: Jesse Barnes, 3.10
1922: *Phil Douglas, 2.63*
1923: Hugh McQuillan, 3.41
1924: Hugh McQuillan, 2.69
1925: Jack Scott, 3.15
1926: Virgil Barnes, 2.87
1927: Burleigh Grimes, 3.54
1928: Larry Benton, 2.73
1929: *Bill Walker, 3.09*

Strikeouts

1920: Fred Toney, 81
1921: Art Nehf, 67
1922: Rosy Ryan, 75
1923: Jack Bentley, 80
1924: Art Nehf, 72
1925: Jack Scott, 87
1926: Jack Scott, 82
1927: Burleigh Grimes, 102
1928: Larry Benton, 90
1929: Carl Hubbell, 106

NL Awards

NL MVP Voting

1924: Frankie Frisch, 3rd
Ross Youngs, 5th
George Kelly, 6th
1925: Kelly, 3rd
Frisch, 9th
1926: Freddie Lindstrom, 9th
1927: Rogers Hornsby, 3rd
Travis Jackson, 5th
1928: Lindstrom, 2nd
Larry Benton, 4th
Shanty Hogan, 8th
Jackson, 9th
1929: Bill Terry, 3rd

GIANTS 1920–1929 All-Decade Team

1B	GEORGE KELLY
2B	FRANKIE FRISCH
SS	TRAVIS JACKSON
3B	FREDDIE LINDSTROM
C	FRANK SNYDER
OF	ROSS YOUNGS
OF	IRISH MEUSEL
OF	MEL OTT
SP	ART NEHF
SP	JESSE BARNES

Above: Known for his twisting windup, "Fat" Freddie Fitzsimmons won 170 games with the Giants. *MVP Books Collection.*
Left: Reporters who covered the 1921 World Series received this press pin. *MVP Books Collection.*

THE 1930s

PASSING THE TORCH

John McGraw retires, turning the team over to his biggest star, Bill Terry, who leads the Giants to three pennants in the '30s and a revenge victory over Washington for another world championship.

B y 1930, John McGraw was at last running out of steam. As his health began to fail, he was unable to get the Giants back to the World Series. But he did leave the team in great shape for another run at glory.

In 1930, the Giants' biggest star, Bill Terry, hit .401—the last National Leaguer to top that hallowed mark. McGraw and "Memphis" Bill had feuded over the years, usually over Terry's annual holdouts for more money. After Terry "slumped" in 1931 to .349, McGraw actually cut his salary, from $23,000 to $18,000, and the two went weeks into the 1932 season before speaking.

McGraw broke the ice, and in the most surprising fashion. Neither he nor the team was well; McGraw suffered from sinus trouble (a lingering result of being struck in the nose by an errant throw from Luther "Dummy" Taylor in 1904) and ptomaine poisoning, and his kidneys began to fail. All the while, the Giants languished in eighth place, and the players were ready to mutiny. McGraw's old-fashioned characteristics began to grate at his young stars; ace pitcher Carl Hubbell resented McGraw calling every pitch from the bench, and others chafed as McGraw hired coaches to act as spies (making sure, for instance, that outsized catcher John "Shanty" Hogan didn't eat too much).

It was time. McGraw called Terry into his office, and he offered him the managerial reins. Terry was speechless, but he took the job.

He inherited a team ready to make a move in 1933. "King" Carl Hubbell and "Prince" Hal Schumacher, though not pitching royalty yet, would be a formidable duo, with Freddie Fitzsimmons rounding out the

Not only did Joe Cronin and Bill Terry manage Washington and New York, respectively, to the World Series in 1933, but these player/managers each finished in the top five in MVP voting. *MVP Books Collection*

rotation. Terry and Mel Ott provided two tough outs in the middle of the lineup. Terry told sportswriters before the season that the Giants would finish at least in third place, and when they laughed at his prediction, he retorted, "If any of you think I'm kidding, put your money where your mouth is."

At age 30, Hubbell finally showed his Hall of Fame form, pitching an 18-inning shutout against the Giants' most formidable rival for the pennant, the Cardinals. He was 23–12 overall with a 1.66 ERA. Schumacher won 19 games, and the Giants won the pennant. They exacted a measure of revenge for 1924, beating Washington in the World Series. McGraw threw a party for the team at the New Yorker Hotel, but it was his last victory celebration. He died in the spring of 1934.

Terry managed for the rest of the decade, winning two more pennants. But in 1936 and 1937, he ran into a Yankees team so good that it seemed unfair, and his playing days ended after the 1936 Series. Although the Yankees felt the loss of Babe Ruth, they quickly restocked, with Bill Dickey and Joe DiMaggio joining Lou Gehrig to create another dynasty. While all New York—and all of baseball—anticipated seeing Hubbell facing Gehrig in the Fall Classic, Hubbell won only one game in each Series, and the Giants proved no match for the pinstriped powerhouse. "That club has everything," Terry said. "They're the toughest club I've ever faced." Those wins were the first of four straight championships for the Yankees.

While the Yankees kept rolling, the Giants ran out of steam. Baseball kept evolving, with radio broadcasts and night games coming to the game, but the Giants faded into fifth place as the decade closed.

At the top of his game in 1936 (26 regular-season wins), Carl Hubbell defeated the Yankees in Game One of that year's World Series, though the Yankees prevailed in six. *Transcendental Graphics/Hulton Archive/Getty Images*

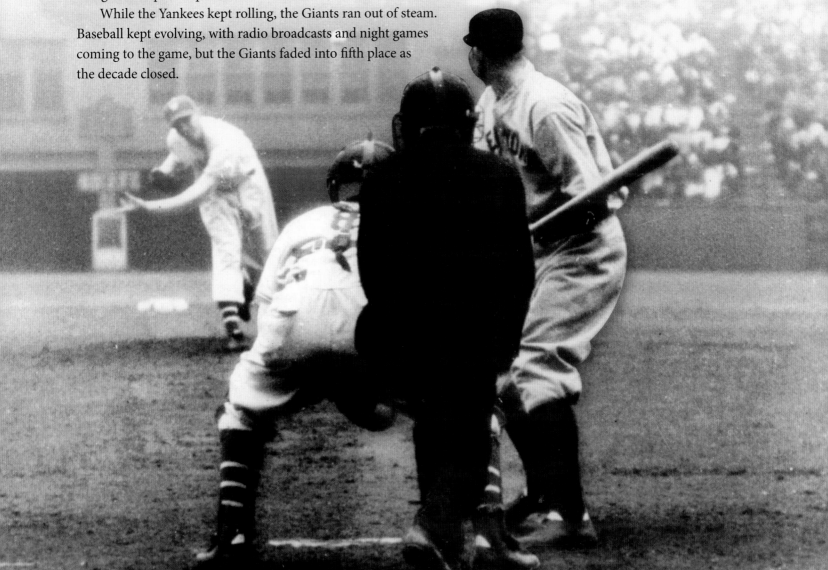

Highlights

June 1: The Giants erupt for 12 runs in the third inning en route to a 16–3 whipping of the Braves.

June 11: A ninth straight win puts the Giants at 26–22. They will spend the remainder of the season between 2 and 7½ games out of first place.

July 10: New York routs the Phillies 19–8 at the tiny Baker Bowl.

Late July: John McGraw repeats his claims that the new lively ball is hurting baseball.

July 31: Fred Lindstrom collects his 1,000th MLB hit. He is only 24.

August 31: Mel Ott belts three straight homers in a game against Boston.

September 3: With 19 hits in his last seven games, Bill Terry is batting .414.

NOTES

The Giants bat .319, which sets and will remain a **20th-century MLB record**.

Bill Terry becomes the last NL player of the century to bat .400 (.401). He also drives in 129 runs and leads the NL with 254 hits.

Other big hitters include **Fred Lindstrom** (.379-22-106), **Mel Ott** (.349-25-119), **Travis Jackson** (.339), and **Shanty Hogan** (.339).

Freddie Fitzsimmons is tops on the staff with a 19–7 record.

POWER SURGE

Giants Finish Second in Record-Setting Offensive Year

In 1930, for the first time, the Polo Grounds had a voice. On Opening Day, the 35,000 customers who filed into the Manhattan stadium were greeted with an electrically amplified loudspeaker system. The Polo Grounds and Philadelphia's Shibe Park were the only two stadiums to have such a system.

Giants fans heard mostly good things to begin the year as their team won its first seven games of the season. In Bill Walker (17–15), Carl Hubbell (17–12), and Freddie Fitzsimmons (19–7), McGraw had three first-class pitchers in a record-setting year for scoring throughout the majors. While everyone agreed that the game was being played with a ball that was much livelier than ever, John McGraw was disgusted with the new style of offense. "Nowadays, the game has become a case of burlesque slugging," McGraw complained. He yearned for the days of "tight pitching, sensational fielding, base stealing, and scientific methods."

While the game was certainly different than it had been in previous years, attendance spiked thanks to the power explosion. Bill Terry's .401 batting average for the Giants and Hack Wilson's 56 home runs and MLB-record 191 RBI for the Cubs were just some of the feats that prompted people to spend more of their money on baseball tickets than ever before.

Although they led the league with a .319 team batting average, the Giants were simply no match for the Cardinals. With a lineup comprised entirely of .300-plus hitters, St. Louis scored more than 1,000 runs and finished five games ahead of New York in the pennant race. The Giants ended the season in third place with an 87–67 record.

Even though McGraw didn't like the direction the game was headed, he believed he could make the Giants successful in a game that was rapidly beginning to favor the strong rather than the tactful. Despite his chronically poor health, "Little Napoleon" would return in 1931 for his 30th season as Giants skipper.

Run production was so high in 1930 that Freddie Fitzsimmons led the NL in winning percentage (.731; 19–7) despite posting a 4.25 ERA. *MVP Books Collection*

The Giants' .400 Hitter

Strength was never the issue for Bill Terry. Emotionally, he was hardened by his parents' separation while he was just a teenager. Physically, his chiseled figure was a product of working at the rail yards in Atlanta, where he heaved heavy flour sacks onto trucks.

Completely independent by the time he was 15, Terry played on various baseball teams in the South before settling down in the early 1920s. With a wife, a baby, and a sales job with Standard Oil, he was content playing semipro ball on the weekends. In 1922, John McGraw saw Terry play and invited him to join the Giants. Terry initially indicated that he wasn't interested, but money talked, and he signed with the New York organization for $800 a month.

That year, the 23-year-old slugger played for the Toledo Mud Hens, New York's minor league affiliate. His defense and plate discipline were suspect, but his power was never in question. "On June 29, Terry hit a ball that cleared the scoreboard for the first time in a regulation game," author Peter Williams noted.

After solidifying himself as one of the best hitters in the NL from 1927 to '29—batting .326, .326, and .372, with more than 100 RBI each season—Terry had the best year of his career in 1930. "Memphis Bill" led the National League with a .401 average, becoming the first player to hit over .400 since Rogers Hornsby in 1925 and the only NL player to do it since. Moreover, Terry's 254 hits tied—and remain—the National League record. Over the next five years, he batted .349, .350, .322, .354, and .341.

Right: Hitting .398 on September 19, 1930, Terry rapped .456 over the remaining seven games to finish at .401. *Baseball Hall of Fame Museum and Library.* **Above:** Terry's Goudey baseball card from 1934, a season in which he batted .354. *MVP Books Collection*

As his career was winding down, Terry was assigned the seemingly impossible task of taking over managerial duties from the legendary McGraw. Terry shined as the Giants' new manager, winning three pennants and one World Series during his 10-year tenure (1932–41).

Always adamant about his desire to keep his baseball career separate from his personal life, Terry garnered resentment from the media for refusing to give out his home phone number to reporters. As strong a businessman as he was a hitter, Terry turned down an offer to manage the Brooklyn Dodgers in 1953 because it would have meant giving up the grandiose income from his cotton trading and car dealership enterprises.

Over his 14-year Hall of Fame career, Terry scored more than 100 runs seven times, had six seasons with at least 200 hits, and batted .320 or higher in nine consecutive seasons. Not only does his .341 average rank 15th all-time, but Ted Williams is the only player since Terry to record a higher career batting mark.

February 21: The Giants play the AL's Chicago White Sox in a night game.

May 26: Bill Walker and then Carl Hubbell shut out the Braves in a doubleheader.

July 2: The Giants win to rise to 40–27, 1½ games back, but following a subsequent four-game losing streak, they will be outside of striking distance for good.

July 11: New York enjoys a 23–5 laugher at Philly's Baker Bowl. Freddy Leach leads the way with a homer, two doubles, and two singles.

July 12: At age 22, Mel Ott belts his 100th career home run, becoming the youngest MLB player to do so. The record will last the century.

July 18: Manager John McGraw's tirade over an umpire's call will earn him a three-game suspension.

September 18: Ott is done for the season after getting beaned.

September 24: The Polo Grounds hosts fundraising games for the Depression's unemployed. The Giants, Yankees, and Brooklyn participate.

NOTES

Bill Terry leads the NL in runs (121) and triples (20) and ranks in the top three in batting (.349), doubles (43), and RBI (112).

Mel Ott is second in the league in home runs (29) and RBI (115).

Freddie Fitzsimmons is the staff's top winner (18–11).

ANOTHER LACKLUSTER YEAR

Giants Fall Short of Pennant for Seventh Straight Season

By 1931, John McGraw didn't recognize his own team. On one occasion, he complained that "the men don't get out and fight for games like they used to— that's what is wrong with baseball."

The game was certainly changing. In the 1930–31 offseason, the horsehide covering the baseball was made slightly thicker to make the ball deader and easier to grip. Also, the sacrifice fly rule was (temporarily) abolished, making a run-scoring fly ball a regular at-bat that counted against a hitter's average. With the Giants, McGraw had bigger concerns. His team's competitive spirit was slipping, and the skipper viewed his team as being "just another ball club."

Even though McGraw believed that his team was starting to underachieve, the Giants were still one of the NL's most talented clubs in 1931. The combination of the aging Bill Terry and the upstart Mel Ott propelled New York to a 41–31 first-half record. Terry paced the Giants with a .349 average and tied for the league lead in runs scored (121).

Ott continued to reign as one of the best outfielders in baseball by crushing a team-high 29 home runs and driving in 115 runs. On the mound, Freddie Fitzsimmons and Bill Walker took the lead. Fitzsimmons led the Giants with 18 wins, while Walker went 16–9 with a 2.26 ERA. A pleasant surprise came at the end of the year with the play of left-handed rookie Jim Mooney (7–1 2.01 ERA), whom McGraw called "one of the greatest southpaws ever seen in the league."

For the fifth straight year, the Giants were stuck in baseball purgatory—not good enough to win a pennant but not terrible enough to begin to rebuild. New York led the league in homers (101) and batting average (.289) but couldn't match the excellence of St. Louis, as the Giants finished the year at 87–65, 13 games behind the first-place Cardinals.

Outfielder Freddy Leach, who batted .309, was one of seven Giants regulars to hit at least .300 in 1931.
MVP Books Collection

END OF AN ERA

Terry Takes Over as Manager for Retiring McGraw

The regime change was surprisingly smooth. On June 2, John McGraw called first baseman Bill Terry into his office. It was the first time they had spoken since February, and McGraw cut straight to the point. "Do you want to manage the Giants?" he asked.

Terry was initially stunned, but he quickly composed himself and said yes. Terry was flattered, but he still had his reservations. If he was going to be the boss, he wanted no interference from McGraw. He wanted complete control of the reins, and McGraw gave it to him. "I am giving full and complete charge and control of the team to Terry," McGraw said. "I am turning over a good team, and I believe he will capably handle it."

The Giants welcomed Terry by sweeping a doubleheader from Philadelphia in his June 4 debut. Unfortunately for the Giants, the sweep was not a sign of things to come. New York would go 55–59 under Terry and finish in sixth place, 18 games behind the NL champion Cubs.

One of Terry's most reliable hitters was himself; he cracked a team-high .350 and clubbed 28 home runs. Ott continued to be the Giants' best player, driving in 123 runs and belting 38 homers. Outside of Ott and Terry, the Giants didn't get much offensive production, as only one other player, outfielder Jo-Jo Moore, hit above .300. Carl Hubbell gave Terry some consistency on the mound, posting an 18–11 record with a 2.50 ERA. No one else won more than 11 games.

Although New York finished the season with its worst record since 1915, McGraw and owner Charles Stoneham felt confident in their new manager. With the former skipper's endorsement, Stoneham gave Terry a two-year contact at the end of the season. It was now up to "Memphis Bill" to show New York's fans that there was life after John McGraw.

Mel Ott was in the midst of eight straight 100-RBI seasons in 1932. His 1,860 career ribbies rank 12th in MLB history. *MVP Books Collection*

Highlights

January 11: Giants star Bill Terry, who batted .373, .401, and .349 the previous three seasons, is appalled when the team asks him to take a $9,000 pay cut from his $22,500 salary.

April 12: In an omen of things to come, the Giants get blown out in the opener at the Polo Grounds, losing 13–5 to Philadelphia.

April 23: Terry clouts his sixth home run in four games.

May 28: A loss to Brooklyn drops the Giants to 14–20 and in the unfamiliar position of last place.

June 3: After managing the team for 30 years, John McGraw resigns. He led the Giants to a 2,583–1,790 record, 10 pennants, and three world titles. Terry takes over as manager.

August 12: In a 1–0 loss to Brooklyn, the Giants tie an MLB record by turning six double plays.

NOTES

Mel Ott leads the NL in homers (38) and walks (100) and drives in 123 runs.

Bill Terry strokes .350 with 28 home runs and 117 RBI.

Carl Hubbell ranks among the NL's top four in wins (18–11), ERA (2.50), and strikeouts (137).

1933

Highlights

June 10: The Giants win their seventh straight game to improve to 29–17. They will not relinquish their hold on first place.

July 2: Hubbell goes all the way in an 18-inning, 1–0 shutout of the Cardinals.

July 6: The first MLB All-Star Game includes Giants Carl Hubbell, Lefty O'Doul, Hal Schumacher, and Bill Terry.

August 1: Hubbell sets an NL record with 46⅓ consecutive scoreless innings.

September 19: The Giants clinch the pennant thanks to a Pirates loss.

October 3: New York beats Washington 4–2 in Game One of the World Series, as Mel Out goes 4-for-4 with a homer.

October 4: Six in the sixth gives the Giants a 6–1 win in Game Two.

October 6: New York rides the arm of Hubbell in a 2–1, 11-inning win in Game Four.

October 7: The Giants clinch the title in Game Five, 4–3, on an Ott homer in the top of the 10th.

NOTES

Mel Ott (.283-23-103) is the Giants' big stick.

Carl Hubbell takes NL MVP honors after leading the league in wins (23–12) and ERA (1.66).

McGraw Who?

Skipper Terry Leads Giants to World Title

Washington second baseman Buddy Myer erases New York's Travis Jackson on a double-play ball in Game Three of the 1933 World Series, won by the Senators 4–0. *Transcendental Graphics/Hulton Archive/Getty Images*

For the first time since 1902, the New York Giants began a season without John McGraw. As early as Opening Day, it became clear that Bill Terry's Giants were going to be much different than the bunch commanded by "Little Napoleon." Terry's club was much more laid-back than McGraw's teams. Among the differences were Terry's refusal to conduct morning practices, employment of a relaxed curfew policy, and his preference for a simpler, pinstripe-less uniform.

Terry's new attitude seemed to work, as the Giants were in a four-way catfight with Pittsburgh, Chicago, and St. Louis early in the year. Superb starting pitching from Carl Hubbell helped New York take a commanding six-game lead by early July. The acquisition of standout defensive catcher Gus Mancuso from the Cardinals helped Hubbell win 23 games and post a microscopic 1.66 ERA.

In June, the *Chicago Tribune* announced that the paper would sponsor an exhibition game between selected stars of the two major leagues—baseball's first All-Star Game.

McGraw was chosen to manage the National League team, which fell to the American Leaguers 4–2.

After the All-Star Game, the Giants continued to put pressure on the rest of the NL. A notable, if merely anecdotal, moment occurred on August 27 at the Polo Grounds. After a disputed call at first base, Terry went ballistic, yelling at the umpire and kicking his cap and glove. Giants fans, who had viewed Terry as a cool, emotionally removed player, loved watching his fiery side come out. John Kieran of the *New York Times* noted that "fans stood up and roared approval of Memphis Bill's explosion. They never knew that he cared."

Though the Giants again led the league in round-trippers (82) thanks to the home run haven that was the Polo Grounds, New York's climb to the top of the league was actually on account of its pitching. The Giants led the league in ERA at 2.71, and all the team's starting pitchers had winning records.

Perhaps because he was distracted by his managerial duties, Terry's production on the field slipped drastically in 1933. The 34-year-old player/manager had fewer than 100 RBI for the first time in seven years (58), and he cracked only six home runs. Thankfully for the Giants, Mel Ott was able to pick up the offensive slack. Ott led the team in home runs (23), RBI (103), and runs scored (98).

Through outstanding pitching and an offense that was just good enough to squeak out close games—New York was 28–18 in one-run contests—the Giants were able to reach the World Series in Terry's first full season as manager. After winning the pennant by five games, the Giants battled the Washington Senators, the team that had spoiled their last trip to the Fall Classic.

Hubbell continued his stellar play in the Series. The "Meal Ticket" gave up five hits and two unearned runs as Ott provided four hits in New York's 4–2 Game One victory. "Prince" Hal Schumacher dominated the Senators in Game Two, winning 6–1 as the New Yorkers quickly found themselves up 2–0 in the Series. After the Giants bats fell flat in Game Three, a 4–0 shutout by Washington's Earl Whitehill, Hubbell went the distance in New York's 2–1, extra-innings victory in Game Four. Hubbell pitched 20 innings in the Series and give up no earned runs.

The fans were greeted with extra baseball again in Game Five, as Giants reliever Dolf Luque and Washington pitcher Jack Russell battled in the late innings before an Ott home run in the top of the 10th sealed the Series for New York.

Through all the uncertainty that had surrounded Terry taking over for McGraw, one thing was now clear: The New York Giants were champions of the world for the first time in 11 years.

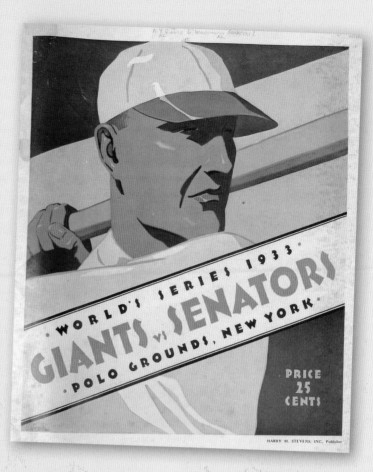

Attaining revenge for 1924, the Giants broke the Senators' hearts in the 1933 World Series with extra-inning wins in the last two games, both at Griffith Stadium. *MVP Books Collection*

King Carl

Detroit Tigers manager Ty Cobb didn't know what he was talking about. As a young left-hander in the Tigers system in 1926–27, Carl Hubbell had a pitch in his repertoire that baffled hitters by breaking the other way. It was a lethal pitch, but Cobb forbade him from throwing it. Cobb was concerned about the longevity of a hurler who threw a pitch that required such a violent snapping of the arm. The lefty bounced around the Tigers farm system and considered quitting baseball before being sold to Beaumont of the Texas League.

In Texas, Hubbell regained command of the pitch, and Giants manager John McGraw took notice. Hubbell and his screwball were headed to the Polo Grounds, where he would pitch for 16 seasons. Cobb's trash would be McGraw's treasure,

Control was the name of Hubbell's game throughout his 16-year career. *MVP Books Collection*

as Hubbell would go on to become one of the best pitchers in franchise history.

Hubbell cracked New York's rotation in 1928 and became the Giants' ace for close to a decade. His breakthrough season came in 1933. That year, Hubbell led the NL in wins (23), ERA (1.66), and shutouts (10), earning him league MVP honors as the Giants cruised to a World Series championship. In the Series, Hubbell threw 20 innings without giving up a single earned run.

After a season that seemed impossible to follow, Hubbell confirmed his dominance in the following year's All-Star Game at the Polo Grounds. As the starter for the National League, "King Carl" and his screwball struck out five future Hall of Famers in succession: Babe Ruth, Lou Gehrig, Jimmie Foxx, Al Simmons, and Joe Cronin. In 1936–37, Hubbell set the major league record for consecutive wins by a pitcher with 24.

With his easy delivery, pinpoint accuracy, and a pitch that seemed to break effortlessly away from right-handed batters, Hubbell at times seemed more of an artist than a pitcher. Over his 16 years with the Giants, the "Meal Ticket" was selected to nine All-Star Games, collected two MVP Awards, and amassed a career record of 253–154. He became the first NL player to have his number, 11, retired by his team, and he was elected to the Baseball Hall of Fame in 1947.

Despite nearly quitting the game after his trademark pitch wasn't accepted, Hubbell proved to be a model of perseverance and consistency. "A fellow doesn't last long on what he has done," Hubbell said. "He has to keep on delivering."

Carl Hubbell's 253 career wins rank him 12th all-time among lefties, and his 24 consecutive victories in 1936–37 remain an MLB record. *MVP Books Collection*

A LEGEND PASSES

John McGraw Dies at 60, and Giants Finish Second

Highlights

January 25: Manager Bill Terry's comment "Is Brooklyn still in the league?" will come back to haunt the Giants.

February 25: John McGraw dies at age 60.

June 2: The Giants win to move into first place, a position they will hold for nearly four months.

August 4: Mel Ott belts two homers and scores six runs, and New York scores 11 times in the ninth, in a 21–4 pounding of the Phillies.

September 16: In front of a Polo Grounds–record crowd of 62,573, the Giants are swept in a doubleheader by second-place St. Louis, as brothers Dizzy and Paul Dean earn the wins. New York's lead is cut to 3½ games.

September 30: Entering the season finale up one game on the Giants, the Cardinals win on Dizzy Dean's 30th victory, and New York loses to Brooklyn for the second straight day.

NOTES

Mel Ott leads the NL in home runs (35) and RBI (135).

Bill Terry rips .354, while shortstop **Travis Jackson** drives in 101 runs.

Carl Hubbell goes 21–12 and wins his second straight ERA crown (2.30).

Before a single pitch was thrown in 1934, tragedy struck the New York Giants. After a long battle in the hospital that included blood transfusions and multiple oxygen tanks, former manager John McGraw died on February 25. McGraw's death was not a surprise—his failing health had been public knowledge for some time—but his passing still was painful to a populace that had known him for more than 30 years. The *New York Times* honored McGraw on page one the day after his passing. The headline read: "John J. McGraw Is Dead At 60. Called Baseball's Greatest Figure." Few could argue differently.

The Giants grieved, but there was still a season to play. New York manager Bill Terry, who was feeling confident following his team's World Series victory in 1933, was asked about Brooklyn's chances in '34. Terry responded, "Brooklyn? I haven't heard anything from them lately. Are they still in the league?"

The Giants backed up their manager's tough talk early in the year, claiming first place on June 2, a position they held until the season's final weekend. Outfielder Mel Ott tore up NL pitching, belting a team-high 35 home runs and amassing 135 RBI. Terry himself hit .354 with 109 runs scored, and shortstop Travis Jackson knocked in 101. Carl Hubbell continued as the Giants' ace, going 21–12 en route to his second straight ERA crown (2.30).

The lead that New York built early in the year began to dwindle as the season reached its final weekend. The Giants needed to win their final two games to bring home a pennant. Standing in their way was, of course, the Dodgers. Brooklyn proved to Terry and the rest of the Giants that they were very much still in the league, winning the final two games of the season in the Polo Grounds, 5–1 and 8–5. The Giants, who lost their last five games, finished at 93–60, two games behind the pennant-winning Cardinals.

A .298 hitter in 12 seasons with the Giants, outfielder Joe "Jo-Jo" Moore rarely fanned—just 247 strikeouts compared to 1,615 hits in his career. He posted a career-best .331 average in 1934 while striking out just 23 times in more than 600 plate appearances. *MVP Books Collection*

Highlights

April 23: The Giants draw 47,000 fans on Opening Day, largely because Babe Ruth is playing for the opposing Boston Braves.

May 30: During a Memorial Day doubleheader sweep of Brooklyn, the Giants set an NL record with a crowd of 63,943.

June 23: Freddie Fitzsimmons notches his fourth shutout of the year. He'll finish at 4–8.

July 4: A doubleheader sweep at Brooklyn increases the Giants' first-place lead to nine games. They are 47–19.

July 23: The New Yorkers lose their sixth straight game and briefly drop to second place.

August 24: Giants outfielder Hank Leiber clouts two homers in the second inning against the Cubs.

August 25–28: The Giants lose four straight and fall out of first place for good. The Cubs, with 21 straight late-season victories, will take the flag.

December 14: The Giants sign AL umpire Firpo Marberry as a pitcher.

NOTES

Mel Ott (.322-31-114) and **Hank Leiber** (.331-22-107) lead the way on offense.

Hank Leiber (203), **Bill Terry** (203), and **Jo-Jo Moore** (201) each tally more than 200 hits.

Carl Hubbell ranks second in the NL in wins (23–12), while **Hal Schumacher** goes 19–9.

STREAKING IN CHICAGO

Giants Lose Pennant as Cubs Win 21 Straight

In April 1935, "Rowdy Richard" Bartell was introduced at the Polo Grounds. In the offseason, the Giants had sent George Watkins, Johnny Vergez, Blondy Ryan, minor-leaguer John "Pretzel" Pezzullo, and $75,000 in cash to the Phillies for the 27-year-old shortstop. Bartell was a grinder, the type of player whom John McGraw would have loved and a great start in manager Bill Terry's attempt at rebuilding the Giants' roster.

Bartell was en route to 14 home runs and 141 hits as the Giants found themselves in first place for most of 1935. In his first full major league season, outfielder Hank Leiber clubbed 22 homers and cracked .331, while the always-reliable tandem of Mel Ott (31 homers and 114 RBI) and Bill Terry (.341) served as the backbone for a powerful New York offense. On the mound, Carl Hubbell finished second in the NL in wins (23–12), while 24-year-old Hal Schumacher went 19–9.

Schumacher almost didn't see the end of the year after a frightening moment in late July. On a sweltering day in St. Louis, the right-hander collapsed on the mound. Team doctors rushed onto the field and, in the words of Blondy Ryan, "brought him back from the dead."

After finding themselves in first place in the NL with a 74–43 record, the Giants, like everyone else in the league, were forced to succumb to Chicago. Beginning on September 4, the Cubs won 10 straight games to tie St. Louis for first place. But they were just getting started. A sweep of the Giants at Wrigley Field in mid-September, by the combined score of 34–10, gave Chicago 16 consecutive victories, and they wound up winning 21 in a row.

Though the Giants posted a respectable 91–62 record, they still finished in third place, 8½ games behind Chicago. Yet the Cubs, in typical team fashion, eventually blew it, losing the World Series to Detroit in six games.

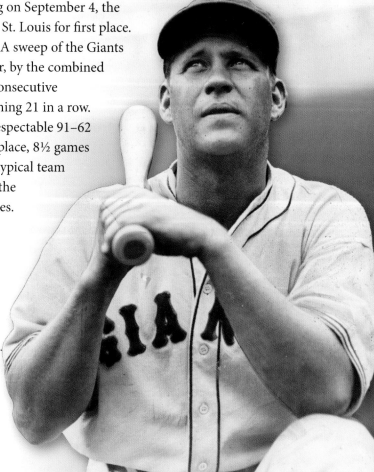

Hank Leiber was a full-time starter in only one of his seven seasons with the Giants (1935), but he took advantage of it, finishing 11th in NL MVP voting. *Baseball Hall of Fame Museum and Library*

President Franklin Roosevelt, posing with managers Bill Terry (left) and Joe McCarthy (right), threw out the ceremonial first pitch in Game Two of the 1936 World Series, won by the Yankees 18–4. *New York Daily News/Getty Images*

BOMBED IN THE BRONX

Giants Win NL Flag but Fall to Yankees in World Series

For the second time in three years, an unfortunate death served as a prelude to the season for the New York Giants. After John McGraw's passing in 1934, the death of club owner Charles Stoneham on January 6 left the Giants with no surviving members of the trio that had purchased the team in 1919. Stoneham's son, Horace, would be the team's principal owner over the next 40 years.

On the field, Carl Hubbell enjoyed his finest season, leading the league with 26 wins, an .813 winning percentage, and a 2.31 ERA. Hubbell's 16-game winning streak helped him earn MVP honors for the second time in four years. At the plate, outfielder Mel Ott continued to shine, leading the league in homers (33) and slugging (.588).

As good as the Giants were—they would finish 92–62 and win the pennant by five games—the nation's attention was focused on the team from the other side of the Harlem River. The Yankees were putting together one of the most impressive seasons in baseball history. Led by Lou Gehrig and Joe DiMaggio, the Bronx Bombers scored 1,065 runs and batted an even .300 as a team. The Yankees won the pennant with a 102–51 record, setting up the first "Subway Series" since 1923.

Hubbell stifled the Yankees in Game One, claiming a 6–1 victory on a rainy day at the Polo Grounds. Any momentum the Giants may have had quickly disappeared, as the Yankees exploded for 18 runs in a Game Two rout. The Bombers took the next two games, 2–1 and 5–2, and looked poised to clinch the title before a Bill Terry run-scoring fly out in the top of the 10th kept the Series alive in Game Five. However, the Yankees proved to be too much, racking up seven runs in the ninth inning to win Game Six 13–5. "That club," Terry said after the game, "has everything."

Highlights

January 6: Giants President Charles Stoneham dies. His son will assume the position.

July 17: Carl Hubbell shuts out Pittsburgh, sparking a personal 16-game winning streak through the end of the season.

August 11–28: The Giants win 15 straight games to rise from third place to first, three games ahead.

September 13: The Polo Grounds attracts an NL-record 64,417 for the Cardinals-Giants doubleheader.

September 24: New York clinches the pennant with a 10th-inning win over Boston.

September 30: Hubbell cruises to a 6–1 victory in Game One of the World Series against the Yankees.

October 5: A Bill Terry sacrifice fly in the top of the 10th helps the Giants beat the Yanks 5–4 in Game Five.

October 6: The Yankees romp to a 13–5 win in Game Six to win the Series.

NOTES

Mel Ott bats .328-33-135, leading the league in homers and slugging (.588).

Carl Hubbell cops the NL MVP Award after leading the circuit in wins (26–6) and ERA (2.31).

Christy Mathewson is included among the initial inductees into the National Baseball Hall of Fame.

Highlights

February: The Giants open spring training in Havana, Cuba.

May 31: Brooklyn ends Carl Hubbell's MLB-record 24-game winning streak in front of 61,756 fans at the Polo Grounds.

June 4: Giants first baseman Gus Suhr's NL-record 822 consecutive games comes to an end when he leaves to attend his mother's funeral.

August 13–30: A 13–3 stretch lands the New Yorkers in first place.

September 30: The Giants clinch the pennant with a 2–1 victory over the Phillies.

October 9: After being outscored by the explosive Yankees 21–3 in the first three games of the World Series, the Giants cop Game Four 7–3 behind Hubbell.

October 10: The Yankees take Game Five 4–2 to win the Series.

NOTES

Mel Ott wins his fourth homer crown (31) and leads the team in RBI.

Outfielders **Jimmy Ripple** (.317) and **Jo-Jo Moore** (.310) pace the club in batting.

Carl Hubbell tops the NL in wins (22–8) and strikeouts (159).

John McGraw is inducted into the Baseball Hall of Fame.

A FAMILIAR FOE

Yankees Beat Giants in World Series—Again

Even after bringing home a pennant, Bill Terry had fallen out of favor with the press by 1937. He was "too aloof," wrote one writer. "The most unpopular manager to ever win a pennant," opined another. Regardless of public opinion, Terry's prowess as a manager was undisputed. He had brought home two pennants since taking over for John McGraw, and he was about to bring home a third.

Outfielder Jimmy Ripple ripped a team-high .317 in 1937. Here he takes batting practice before a World Series game while manager Bill Terry looks on with reporters. *Transcendental Graphics/Hulton Archive/Getty Images*

New York spent most of the year nipping at the heels of the Cubs. As Chicago made its late-season slide, the Giants capitalized and claimed first place on September 1. New York rode out a 22–9 September to win the pennant by three games.

An aging Carl Hubbell managed to lead the league in victories with 22, and Cliff "Mountain Music" Melton brought home 20 wins of his own. The offense was led by Mel Ott, who was tops in the league in home runs (31) and paced the Giants in RBI (95). New York's climb to a pennant was rewarded with the opportunity to get clobbered by the Yankees in the World Series.

The Bronx Bombers had won the AL by 13 games and were overwhelming favorites in the Series. Hubbell seemed unfazed, as he shut the Yankees down for five innings in Game One. But even the "Meal Ticket" wasn't immune to the Yankees juggernaut, as they exploded for seven runs in the sixth to take the opener 8–1. The Yanks won the next two games by a combined score of 13–2.

Hubbell was able to rebound from his Game One implosion in Game Four, as the Giants scored six runs in the second inning en route to a 7–3 victory. However, the Yankees were not going to lose two straight Series-clinching games. They took care of business the next day, taking Game Five and the Series, 4–2.

Though the Giants put up a good fight, the result of the Fall Classic was expected. "The turning point of the series," quipped sportswriter Joe Williams, "was when the Yankees suited up for the first game."

Master Melvin

In the small town of Gretna, Louisiana, there wasn't much to do except play baseball—and Melvin Thomas Ott was better at it than everyone else. In addition to playing for his high school team two days a week, Ott served as the catcher for a semipro club. While his peers were studying arithmetic, Ott was hitting game-winning home runs.

After Ott wreaked havoc on a lumber company's semipro team in Patterson, Louisiana, the owner of the company, Harry Williams, relayed a message to Giants manager John McGraw that the 16-year-old was worth a look. Months later, Williams bought Ott a train ticket to New York. The teenager from Gretna was headed to the Big Apple. During his tryout, Ott put on a show, smashing balls all over the field, including blasts that hit high against the advertising signs on the right field wall. After the spectacle, McGraw remarked, "He's got the most natural swing I've seen in years. This lad is going to be one of the greatest left-handed hitters the National League has seen."

McGraw's prediction was spot-on, as Ott would go on to terrorize NL pitching throughout his 22-year career. As a 17-year-old in 1926, Melvin amazed Giants fans by batting .383 in 60 at-bats. And though he managed just one walk and zero homers that season, he would deliver both in abundance in later years.

The 5-foot-9 outfielder enjoyed his breakthrough season in 1929, when he set what would remain career highs in doubles (37), home runs (42), RBI (151), runs scored (138), and slugging (.635). His homer and RBI numbers are the most ever for a major league player age 20 or younger.

Known for his high leg kick before each swing, Ott went on to lead the NL in home runs six times. "Master Melvin" took advantage of the short fence in right at the Polo Grounds, clubbing 63 percent of his career four-baggers at home. He finished his career as the NL home run leader with 511, a record that stood until Willie Mays broke it in 1966. In addition, Ott walked more than 100 times in a season on 10 occasions. He batted .304 for his career and played in 11 consecutive All-Star Games.

Ott took over managerial duties for the Giants in 1942 and continued to manage until 1948. He and Stan Musial are the only players to spend 22 seasons with a National League team. When it was all said and done, the kid from Gretna became one of New York's greatest icons.

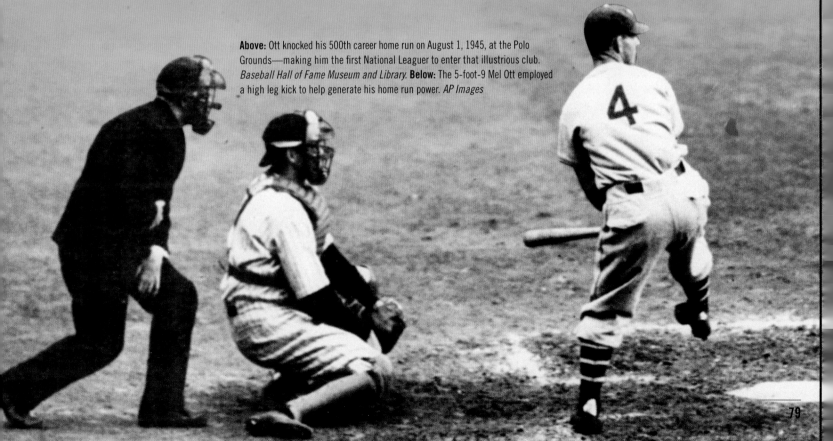

Above: Ott knocked his 500th career home run on August 1, 1945, at the Polo Grounds—making him the first National Leaguer to enter that illustrious club. *Baseball Hall of Fame Museum and Library.* **Below:** The 5-foot-9 Mel Ott employed a high leg kick to help generate his home run power. *AP Images*

Highlights

May 2: New York wins its 11th straight game to improve to 12–1.

May 11: A 5–3 win over St. Louis puts the Giants at 18–3, with a 5½-game lead.

June 24: The Giants purchase outfielder Bob Seeds from the Yankees. In his first 59 games in the International League this year, Seeds amassed 28 homers and 95 RBI.

June 26: Carl Hubbell outclasses the Cubs 5–1 for his 200th career victory.

July 12: The Giants-Dodgers rivalry erupts into tragedy during a game at Ebbets Field, when Dodgers fan Robert Joyce kills Giants supporter Frank Krug.

July 14: A 1–0 loss to Cincinnati drops the Giants out of first place for the first time since June 8.

December 6: The Giants trade Dick Bartell, Hank Lieber, and Gus Mancuso to the Cubs for Billy Jurges, Frank Demaree, and Ken O'Dea.

NOTES

Mel Ott raps .311-36-116, leading the NL in homers, runs (116), and OBP (.442).

Harry Gumbert (15–13) leads a balanced rotation in wins.

Carl Hubbell and outfielders **Hank Leiber**, **Jo-Jo Moore**, and **Ott** are NL All-Stars.

ONE-MAN SHOW

Ott Shines for New York, but Rest of Team Falters

New York started out hot to begin the 1938 season, winning 11 in a row to improve to 12–1. However, the Giants' inability to find a lights-out pitcher would cost them, as they began to fade after their smokin' start and would not regain first place in the NL after July 17.

Carl Hubbell started just 22 games in 1938, and his 13 wins were his lowest total since his rookie season a decade earlier. "King Carl" admitted that his signature screwball pitch had taken a toll on his arm. He began to feel the effects in 1934, and by '38 the pain was excruciating. Somehow, he would muster exactly 11 wins a year from 1939 to '42.

Harry Gumbert led the Giants in victories (15–13) in 1938, but he had the second highest ERA (4.01) among New York's starting pitchers. No Giants moundsman seemed to be anything more than average—except for 255-pound reliever Walter "Jumbo" Brown, who logged a 1.80 ERA over 90 innings. The unexceptional pitching was not good news for an offense that was essentially a one-man show.

Outside of Mel Ott, New York lacked a big stick. Although Ott's standards were nearly impossible to match—he led the NL in homers (36), runs (116), and OBP (.442)—the Giants had no one to complement the slugger. Ott's closest thing to a sidekick was outfielder Jo-Jo Moore, who was second to Ott in hits (153) and batted .302.

The Giants followed a 45–25 first half with a subpar 38–42 second half. The key stretch of the season came during a 15-game western road trip in July, when New York fell from a half game up to four games back.

The Cubs took advantage of New York's slide to take the pennant, finishing two games ahead of the Pirates and five in front of the Giants. In the World Series, the crosstown Yankees again proved why Chicago was the "Second City," as they broomed the Cubs in four games.

Jo-Jo Moore (shown here on a 1940 Playball card) was named to his fifth straight All-Star team in 1938 thanks to a fourth season with an average above .300. *MVP Books Collection*

"JO-JO" MOORE

Bottom Billing

Giants Are Just the Third Best Team in New York

I n 1939, America's attention turned to Europe, as Nazi Germany invaded Poland and plotted future conquests. Americans were anxious and uncertain about what was going to happen next. MLB attendance dropped significantly that year, including at the Polo Grounds, where the Giants dropped from second in the NL in fan support in 1938 to fourth in '39. After back-to-back World Series appearance in 1936 and '37, the team seemed to be trending downward.

While the New York Yankees were the marquee team in the AL and the Brooklyn Dodgers were beginning a 19-year run of success (18 winning seasons), the Giants' reign of dominance seemed to have run its course. In 1939, there was little to cheer about in Manhattan.

The Giants actually started the season respectably. By the All-Star break, they were 40–33, 5½ games out. Harry "Gunboat" Gumbert, a crafty right-hander, led the Giants with 18 wins, but he was the sole bright spot on a lackluster New York staff. No other pitcher won more than 13 games. Unlike the previous season, the so-so performance of the Giants' hurlers couldn't be covered up by Mel Ott's bat. In a down year, Ott belted 27 homers and drove in only 80 runs. Ott was not even the team's leader in RBI, as first baseman Zeke Bonura was tops with 85.

As the Giants sputtered to a 37–41 second-half record, Cincinnati soared to the top of the NL. New York finished the season with a 77–74 mark and in fifth place, their worst season since 1932. Meanwhile, Brooklyn went 84–69 to finish in third place, and the Yankees took home another World Series, sweeping the Reds in the Fall Classic.

The Giants' fears were becoming reality, as they were slowly becoming the worst team in New York City. But across Manhattan and around the world, far greater problems loomed ahead.

A national javelin-throwing champion at age 16, first baseman Zeke Bonura could launch a baseball a ways, too. He averaged .311-20-101 in five AL seasons before starring with the Giants in 1939. *Baseball Hall of Fame Museum and Library*

► 77-74 5th ◄

Highlights

June 6: New York hitters bash seven home runs, including two by Jo-Jo Moore, in a 17–3 rout of the Reds.

June 17: The Giants defeat St. Louis for their ninth straight victory, but they're still just 29–25 and seven games out of first place.

July 2: In front of more than 50,000 fans at the Polo Grounds, Dodgers player-manager Leo Durocher spikes first baseman Zeke Bonura, triggering a wrestling match between the two.

July 15: Giants shortstop Billy Jurges and umpire George Magerkurth spit at each other, resulting in 10-game suspensions for each.

July 28: New York's 5–4 loss at Chicago's Wrigley Field caps a 1–12 tailspin.

August 13: The Giants crank seven home runs, including two by Frank Demaree, in an 11–2 trouncing of the Phillies.

NOTES

Mel Ott (.308-27-80) finishes a homer shy of a sixth NL home run crown.

First baseman **Zeke Bonura** (.321) and catcher **Harry Danning** (.313) pace the Giants in batting.

Harry Gumbert is the club's winningest pitcher (18–11).

THE 1930-1939 RECORD BOOK

Team Leaders

(*Italics* indicates NL leader)

Batting Average

1930: *Bill Terry, .401*
1931: Bill Terry, .349
1932: Bill Terry, .350
1933: Bill Terry, .322
1934: Bill Terry, .354
1935: Bill Terry, .341
1936: Mel Ott, .328
1937: Jimmy Ripple, .317
1938: Mel Ott, .311
1939: Zeke Bonura, .321

Home Runs

1930: Mel Ott, 25
1931: Mel Ott, 29
1932: *Mel Ott, 38*
1933: Mel Ott, 23
1934: *Mel Ott, 35*
1935: Mel Ott, 31
1936: *Mel Ott, 33*
1937: *Mel Ott, 31*
1938: *Mel Ott, 36*
1939: Mel Ott, 27

RBI

1930: Bill Terry, 129
1931: Mel Ott, 115
1932: Mel Ott, 123
1933: Mel Ott, 103
1934: *Mel Ott, 135*
1935: Mel Ott, 114
1936: Mel Ott, 135
1937: Mel Ott, 95
1938: Mel Ott, 116
1939: Zeke Bonura, 85

Runs

1930: Bill Terry, 139
1931: *Bill Terry, 121*

1932: Bill Terry, 124
1933: Mel Ott, 98
1934: Mel Ott, 119
1935: Mel Ott, 113
1936: Mel Ott, 120
1937: Mel Ott, 99
1938: *Mel Ott, 116*
1939: Mel Ott, 85

Stolen Bases

1930: Freddie Lindstrom, 15
1931: Chick Fullis, 13
    Travis Jackson, 13
1932: Freddie Lindstrom, 6
    Mel Ott, 6
1933: Kiddo Davis, 10
1934: Joe Moore, 5
1935: Mel Ott, 7
    Bill Terry, 7
1936: Burgess Whitehead, 14
1937: 3 tied at 7
1938: George Myatt, 10
1939: Jo-Jo Moore, 5

Wins

1930: Freddie Fitzsimmons, 19
1931: Freddie Fitzsimmons, 18
1932: Carl Hubbell, 18
1933: *Carl Hubbell, 23*
1934: Hal Schumacher, 23
1935: Carl Hubbell, 23
1936: *Carl Hubbell, 26*
1937: *Carl Hubbell, 22*
1938: Harry Gumbert, 15
1939: Harry Gumbert, 18

ERA

1930: Carl Hubbell, 3.87
1931: *Bill Walker, 2.26*
1932: Carl Hubbell, 2.50
1933: *Carl Hubbell, 1.66*
1934: *Carl Hubbell, 2.30*
1935: Hal Schumacher, 2.89
1936: *Carl Hubbell, 2.31*
1937: Cliff Melton, 2.61
1938: Carl Hubbell, 3.07
1939: Carl Hubbell, 2.75

Right: Dick Bartell, pictured on this 1985 Renata Galasso reprint, earned the nickname "Rowdy Richard" for his fiery play. *MVP Books Collection.* **Below:** This press pin from the 1933 World Series represents the last Giants championship for another 21 years. *MVP Books Collection*

Strikeouts

1930: Carl Hubbell, 117
1931: Carl Hubbell, 155
1932: Carl Hubbell, 137
1933: Carl Hubbell, 156
1934: Carl Hubbell, 118
1935: Carl Hubbell, 150
1936: Carl Hubbell, 123
1937: *Carl Hubbell, 159*
1938: Carl Hubbell, 104
1939: Cliff Melton, 95

NL Awards

NL MVP Voting

1930: no award
1931: Bill Terry, 3rd
　　　Travis Jackson, 7th
1932: Terry, 6th
　　　Mel Ott, 10th
1933: *Carl Hubbell, 1st*
　　　Terry, 4th
　　　Gus Mancuso, 6th
　　　Blondy Ryan, 9th
1934: Jo-Jo Moore, 3rd
　　　Jackson, 4th
　　　Ott, 5th
　　　Terry, 7th
　　　Hubbell, 9th
　　　Hal Schumacher, 9th
1935: Hubbell, 6th
　　　Terry, 6th
1936: *Hubbell, 1st*
　　　Ott, 6th
　　　Mancuso, 8th
1937: Hubbell, 3rd
　　　Dick Bartell, 6th
　　　Ott, 7th
1938: Ott, 4th
1939: Harry Danning, 9th

NL All-Stars

(*Italics* indicates starter)

1933: Carl Hubbell, P
　　　Lefty O'Doul, OF
　　　Hal Schumacher, P
　　　Bill Terry, 1B
1934: Hubbell, P
　　　Travis Jackson, SS
　　　Jo-Jo Moore, OF
　　　Mel Ott, OF
　　　Terry, 1B
1935: Hubbell, P
　　　Gus Mancuso, C
　　　Moore, OF
　　　Ott, OF
　　　Hal Schumacher, P
　　　Terry, 1B

1936: Hubbell, P
　　　Moore, OF
　　　Ott, OF
1937: *Dick Bartell, SS*
　　　Hubbell, P
　　　Mancuso, C
　　　Moore, OF
　　　Ott, OF
　　　Burgess Whitehead, 2B
1938: Hubbell, P
　　　Hank Leiber, OF
　　　Moore, OF
　　　Ott, OF
1939: Harry Danning, C
　　　Bill Jurges, SS
　　　Ott, OF

Hal Schumacher, shown on this 1933 Goudey card, won 117 games for New York in the '30s. *MVP Books Collection*

GIANTS 1930–1939 All-Decade Team

1B	BILL TERRY
2B	HUGHIE CRITZ
SS	TRAVIS JACKSON
3B	JOHNNY VERGEZ
C	GUS MANCUSO
OF	MEL OTT
OF	JO-JO MOORE
OF	HANK LEIBER
SP	CARL HUBBELL
SP	HAL SCHUMACHER

THE 1940S

NICE GUYS, NO TITLES

Mel Ott takes the reins from Bill Terry, and the Giants slug their way to a lot of wins but no pennants. At the end of the decade, the club is remade in the image of its new manager, scrappy Leo Durocher.

As the 1940s dawned, the Giants were not able to maintain their winning ways. In the words of author Noel Hynd, Giants owner Horace Stoneham "shelled out $125,000 to equip the Polo Grounds for night baseball. But the ball that was played there would have been better left in the darkness."

In the first two years of the decade, manager Bill Terry couldn't get his team within 25 games of first place. Making matters worse, the archrival Brooklyn Dodgers—long a perennial laggard—were in ascendance, finishing second in 1940 and first in 1941. Giants legend Carl Hubbell, his arm permanently disfigured from throwing the screwball, never won more than 11 games in a season after 1939. An era had ended.

Power-hitting Johnny "Big Cat" Mize (far left) joined the Giants in 1942, teaming with Dick Bartell, Joe Orengo, Mel Ott, and Bill Werber (left to right). *Transcendental Graphics/Hulton Archive/Getty Images*

The 1940s was a long, frustrating decade for the Giants, who never finished higher than third place. *MVP Books Collection*

Stoneham eased Terry out of the manager's spot and appointed another Hall of Fame Giant player in his place: Mel Ott. Diminutive "Master Melvin," with his high leg kick, was on his way to clubbing a National League–record 511 home runs, a mark that would stand until another Giant, Willie Mays, passed it on his way to 660. (Although Mays was eventually passed by Hank Aaron for the NL record, Aaron gave way to another Giant, Barry Bonds, in 2007.)

Ott sought to remake the team in his own slugging image. Named manager only days before Pearl Harbor was bombed in 1941, he completed a trade only days after that infamous event, sending three players and $50,000 to St. Louis for the "Big Cat," Johnny Mize. "I know what kind of baseball New Yorkers want, and I promise to give it to them," Ott said.

The Giants turned in a winning season in 1942, as Ott clubbed 30 homers and Mize 26, but they finished a distant third behind the Cardinals and Dodgers. The next year, Mize was off to World War II along with many other big-leaguers, not to return until after the war ended in 1945. The Giants lost 98 games in 1943 and 87 in 1944. A winning record in 1945 was followed by a return to the cellar in 1946.

It was in that season that Leo Durocher, then a longtime Giants enemy as the manager of the Dodgers, used Ott and his team as the foils for one of the most famous baseball quotes of all time. In praising his own star, Eddie Stanky, Durocher acknowledged that maybe "The Brat" didn't have the sweetest personality. "Take a look at that No. 4 out there," Durocher told sportswriters, pointing to Ott. "A nicer guy never drew breath than that man there." He ticked off the names of other Giants. "Take a look at them. All nice guys. They'll finish last." The writers truncated the quote to "Nice guys finish last," and a legend was born.

In 1947, the Giants shattered the MLB home run record of 182, walloping 221 dingers and earning the nickname "Window Breakers." Paced by Mize with 51, every member of the starting lineup save shortstop Buddy Kerr hit in double figures. In his first full season, young Bobby Thomson belted 29 homers. But with a team ERA of 4.44, the Giants finished in fourth place.

With the Giants languishing just shy of .500 in 1948, Horace Stoneham made an inconceivable move. He replaced Ott with Durocher, the hated Dodgers manager. Durocher set about remaking the Giants in his own image, unloading Ott's lumbering sluggers such as Walker Cooper and Willard Marshall and bringing in infielders Stanky and Alvin Dark.

The turnaround took some time. The Giants stayed stuck in fifth place in 1948 and 1949, but better times were in store.

Highlights

May 26: Playing their first night game at the Polo Grounds, the Giants beat Boston 8–1 in front of 20,260 fans.

May 30: Carl Hubbell limits Brooklyn to a single and no walks in a 7–0 whitewash.

June 15: The Giants rout the Pirates 12–1 for their eighth straight victory, putting them at 30–15, two games back. New York's Harry Danning achieves a rare feat for a catcher, hitting a single, double, triple, and inside-the-park home run.

August 7: In a loss to the Dodgers, 53,997 fans turn out at the Polo Grounds for Mel Ott Night.

September 4: A seven-game losing streak has dropped New York below .500.

September 19: The Giants lose their 11th straight game, as they get swept by four straight teams in the Polo Grounds.

NOTES

Harry Danning (.300-13-91) and first baseman Babe Young (.286-17-101) emerge as New York's top hitting stars.

At 13–13, Hal Schumacher has the most wins and the only non-losing record in the rotation.

Giants All-Stars include Danning, Carl Hubbell, Bill Jurges, Jo-Jo Moore, and Mel Ott.

A New Babe in Town

Giants' "Babe" Stars, but New Yorkers Finish in Sixth

Two decades earlier, the Yankees became the premier team in New York behind the historic slugging of a robust left-hander named Babe Ruth. Now with the Giants slipping into irrelevance in the Big Apple, they called on their own Babe to help resurrect the franchise. Norman Robert "Babe" Young was a New York thoroughbred, born in Astoria and Fordham educated, who took over first base for the Giants during his first full season in 1940.

The 24-year-old was a shot in the arm for a Giants team that was lacking in excitement. Young led New York with 101 RBI and belted 17 home runs. This was the bat that the Giants had needed to supplement Mel Ott's heavy lumber. Sadly, after carrying New York's offense for years, Ott was beginning to slow down, at least by his sky-high standards. He still led the Giants with 19 home runs, but it was his lowest total in 12 seasons.

Besides Ott, three other position players made the All-Star team. They included catcher Harry "The Horse" Danning (.300, 91 RBI), outfielder Jo-Jo Moore (.276), and shortstop Billy Jurges, who wound up playing just 63 games.

Once again, the story of the Giants' failures revolved around a mediocre pitching staff. First, no Giants starting pitcher had a winning record; Hal Schumacher came the closest with a mark of 13–13. Harry Gumbert digressed from his breakthrough season in 1939, going 12–14 with an exceptional 3.76 ERA. Carl Hubbell, whose arm had the strength of overcooked linguini at 37 years old, hobbled to an 11–12 record.

A 32–52 finish in the second half solidified the Giants' fall from grace. While Cincinnati crossed the finish line at 100–53, New York finished in sixth place, 27½ games behind. New York opened the 1940s with one of the worst seasons in franchise history. Yet much to the Giants' chagrin, things were about to get worse.

Harry "The Horse" Danning, who caught Carl Hubbell's screwballs for many years, represented the Giants at the All-Star Game from 1938 to '41. He drove in a career-high 91 runs in 1940. *Baseball Hall of Fame Museum and Library*

A Troubling Year

Giants Finish Fifth as War Rhetoric Escalates

On May 27, 1941, baseball took a backseat to a national crisis. In a game between the Giants and Boston Braves at the Polo Grounds, umpire Jocko Conlon stopped play as fans sat and listened to President Roosevelt address the nation. For 45 minutes, they heard Roosevelt proclaim America's intention to stand up to further Nazi efforts to interfere with American shipping to Europe.

Three weeks later, another Giants game was stopped and the radio was played on the PA system. This time, it was so that fans could learn about a different type of fighting. With New York playing in Pittsburgh, Pirates management played boxer Joe Louis's thrashing of Billy Conn over the loudspeakers. Due to the delay, the game was halted by the midnight curfew with the score 1–1. Giants manager Bill Terry was furious. "Next time they might as well hold up the game to listen to Bob Hope," he fumed. Terry's anger was justified, but even he couldn't have enjoyed watching his team play.

Winning didn't come easy for the Giants in 1941, and they were 11 games out of first place by the middle of June.

Babe Young followed his breakthrough season by leading the Giants in RBI (104) and finishing second in home runs (25). Ott was once again New York's best home run hitter (27), but his average dipped to .286. Few players besides Ott and Young contributed much, and third baseman Dick Bartell was the only regular to hit over .300.

Things weren't a whole lot better on the mound. Hal Schumacher led the Giants with 12 wins, and no starter had an ERA under 3.00. The team fell apart in July, winning only eight games the entire month. Terry, whose frustration was now focused completely on his floundering team and not the radio, hinted to reporters that he would retire at the end of the season. The Giants finished in fifth place, 25½ games behind the first-place Brooklyn Dodgers.

First baseman Babe Young topped 100 RBI in both 1940 and '41. A year later, he was forced to the outfield due to the arrival of Johnny Mize. *Sporting News and Rogers Photo Archive/Getty Images*

Highlights

July 6: The Giants enter the All-Star break at 40–37 and in fourth place, 14 games out of first.

August 3: For a twilight game in which revenue goes to aid the war effort, the Giants and Dodgers attract 57,303 fans at the Polo Grounds. This game (and the next day's game) end prematurely because of a government-mandated 9:14 curfew on lights.

August 30: Mel Ott cracks his 2,500th hit.

August 31: A 19–11 record in August doesn't help the Giants, as the Cardinals and Dodgers are on pace for 106 and 104 wins, respectively.

September 25: Giants outfielder Hank Leiber pitches a complete game against Philadelphia but loses 9–1.

September 26: Kids are admitted free to the Polo Grounds for bringing scrap metal to aid the war effort, but the Giants have to forfeit the game after the kids storm the field.

NOTES

New manager **Mel Ott** wins his sixth homer crown (30) and leads the league in runs (118).

Newcomer **Johnny Mize** smashes .305-26-110 and leads the NL in slugging (.521).

Bill Lohrman tops the staff in wins (13–4) and ERA (2.56).

MEL THE MANAGER

Ott Becomes the Third Giants Skipper Since 1902

Bill Terry retired from managing the Giants following the 1941 season. This did not come as a surprise, as Terry had made it public that his interest in managing was dwindling. The question now was who would replace him. The Giants had employed only two managers since 1902, and the team was coming off two miserable years. They needed strength. They needed stability. They needed Mel Ott.

Ott was shocked that the job was offered to him, and he initially was reluctant to accept the position. "Go on, son, take it," Terry told Ott, who was only 32 years old. "I want you to take it." Ott took it on December 2, 1941, just five days before Pearl Harbor was bombed.

Although the world was at war, Ott still faced the tough task of putting together a team capable of winning a pennant. His first big move was acquiring Johnny Mize via a trade with St. Louis. The acquisition of the sweet-swinging first baseman was a success, as he led the Giants in RBI (110) and batting (.305). Ott helped himself by leading the club in homers (30) and runs scored (118). If only Mize and Ott could pitch.

Once again, New York's pitching staff was the source of its misery. Bill Lohrman's 13 wins led all Giants hurlers. Somehow, the 39-year-old Carl Hubbell was still able to throw strikes, as "King Carl" chipped in 11 wins in what would be his last full season. Consistency was New York's biggest issue. Over the course of the year, 13 different pitchers started for the Giants.

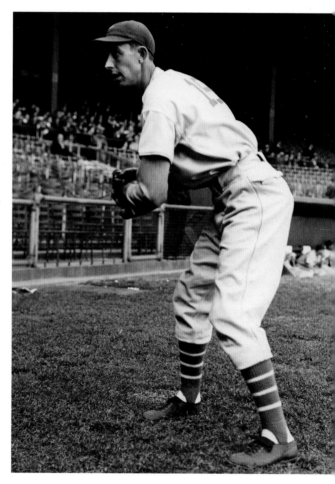

Out of rugged Brevard, North Carolina, 6-foot-5 Cliff "Mountain Music" Melton averaged a dozen wins a year for the Giants from 1937 to '43. He was named to the All-Star team in 1942 but did not appear in the game. *Baseball Hall of Fame Museum and Library*

New York's hopes at being a major player in the pennant race faded before summer. Although they finished with their best record in four years, 85–67, the Giants simply were not in the same class as Brooklyn and St. Louis. The Cardinals won the pennant by two games over the Dodgers and 20 over the Giants.

ROCK BOTTOM

Giants Finish Last for the First Time Since 1900

The 1943 season was a brutal one for the Giants. Before the campaign began, Bill Terry resigned from his position as the team's farm director. Terry had played a pivotal role in the Giants' previous successes, and his departure after two decades was felt throughout the organization. Next, the Giants roster was decimated by the military draft. Johnny Mize, Harry Danning, Hal Schumacher, and Dave Koslo were no longer Giants. They were soldiers. This left New York with no first baseman, no catcher, and huge holes in its already ailing pitching staff. Although every team in baseball felt the effects of the war, few were hit as hard as the Giants.

Ott quickly tried to find replacements for his departed players, but what he found was disappointing. Joe Orengo, Mize's stand-in at first, cracked only six home runs and batted just .218, the second worst average among the Giants' everyday players. The worst mark (.198) belonged to catcher Gus Mancuso, who had starred for the team in the 1930s but by now was washed up. In July, the Giants acquired star first baseman Dolph Camilli from the Dodgers, but the 1941 NL MVP chose to retire instead of reporting to the Polo Grounds.

The group of pitchers that Ott put together wasn't much better. Only one hurler on the entire Giants roster had a winning record, reliever Ace Adams (11–7). Cliff Melton's nine wins were the most of any Giants starting pitcher, and 40-year-old Carl Hubbell managed four wins before calling it a career. It came as no surprise that New York had the worst team ERA in the NL (4.08).

The Giants spent the last three months in the basement and ended the season on an eight-game winless streak. They finished at 55–98, 49½ games behind the first-place Cardinals. It was the first time they had finished in last place since the beginning of the century. "It was just a season," Ott said, "when everything went wrong."

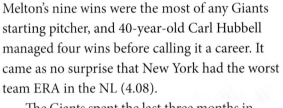

Though "Ace" connotes a standout starting pitcher, Adams was a relief specialist who led the NL in games pitched each year from 1942 to '44. His given name was Ace Townsend Adams.
MVP Books Collection

Highlights

April 27: In a trade with the Braves, the Giants acquire catcher and reigning NL batting champion Ernie Lombardi.

May 1: The Giants are shut out for the first of 13 times this year, as cheaper, harder baseballs are used due to war restrictions.

June 5: Carl Hubbell defeats Pittsburgh 5–1 for his 250th career victory.

June 30: The Giants end the month at 25–39 and in last place. They will remain in the basement for the rest of the season.

July 31: New York trades three players to Brooklyn for Johnny Allen and first baseman Dolph Camilli, the NL MVP in 1941. Camilli decides to retire instead.

August 7: The Giants strand 18 runners, two in every inning, in a 9–6 loss to the Phillies.

NOTES

Second baseman **Mickey Witek** leads New York in batting (.314) and is second in the league in hits (195).

Mel Ott finishes second in the NL homer race with just 18. He hits all of them at home.

Reliever **Ace Adams** leads the staff in wins (11–7) and ERA (2.82).

Highlights

April 30: The Giants walk 17 times during a 26–8 rout of Brooklyn before 58,068 at the Polo Grounds. First baseman Phil Weintraub logs two doubles, a triple, a homer, and 11 RBI.

May 12: In a deal with the Pirates, the Giants acquire 6-foot-9 pitcher Johnny Gee, who is too tall to be drafted for military service.

June 2: A seven-game winning streak puts New York at 20–20.

June 3: The Giants-Pirates game at the Polo Grounds is interrupted by a PA announcement: The invasion of Europe has begun. The report turns out to be false.

June 26: In front of 50,000 at the Polo Grounds, the Yankees, Dodgers, and Giants play an exhibition game to raise money for the war effort.

August 20–29: The streaky Giants win seven of eight immediately after losing 13 in a row.

NOTES

Joe Medwick leads New York in batting (.337) and RBI (85).

Phil Weintraub cracks .316, while **Mel Ott** paces the team with 26 home runs.

Bill Voiselle emerges as the staff ace, going 21–16 with a 3.02 ERA.

RAVAGED BY WAR

With a Decimated Roster, the Giants Finish Fifth

During a June 3 game between the Giants and Pirates, the PA system in the Polo Grounds was flipped on and play was stopped. The 9,000 fans perked up their ears as the public address announcer proclaimed what many had feared: "The invasion of Europe has begun." Although the announcement was premature—the invasion of Normandy would not begin until three days later on June 6—America was entering one of the tensest times in the country's history.

Along with every other ball club, New York had to make due with a roster that had been picked apart by the military draft. While the Giants' outfield of Mel Ott, Johnny Rucker, and Joe Medwick remained the same in 1944, the entire infield featured a new cast of regulars. One of the newcomers was backup outfielder Danny Gardella, who became one the most colorful characters on the Giants. Sneaking into high school proms and dressing up as Hitler was a typical "Dauntless Dan" activity. Gardella's hijinx provided humor to an otherwise forgettable season.

Medwick led New York's offense in batting (.337) and RBI (85) while Ott continued to reign as the Giants' home run king, as he belted 26. One of New York's oldest players, 36-year-old first baseman Phil Weintraub, proved to be one of their best hitters, as he knocked in 77 runs and stroked .316.

The once-leaderless Giants pitching staff finally boasted a true ace, as rookie Bill Voiselle went 21–16 and posted a 3.02 ERA. Voiselle was the only Giants pitcher to have an ERA under 4.00, and he was the only starter with a winning record. Voiselle was named the NL Pitcher of the Year by *The Sporting News*.

The Giants' inconsistencies—for example, they lost 13 in a row before winning seven of eight—would ultimately be their downfall. New York finished in fifth place with a 67–87 record, 38 games behind St. Louis.

Joe "Ducky" Medwick, a Triple Crown winner with the Cardinals in 1937, recaptured some old glory with the Giants in 1944, his last All-Star season. *Baseball Hall of Fame Museum and Library*

The Polo Grounds Experience

It was home to eight different teams, and it possessed some of the most head-scratching dimensions of any ballpark in major league history. Unusual and quirky, the Polo Grounds—like Ebbets Field and Yankee Stadium—became an icon in New York City, hosting some of the most memorable events in the history of sports.

If the Polo Grounds could talk, what stories it could tell. . . . It probably would start at the very beginning, when it was constructed in 1876 for the sport of . . . you guessed it, polo. It would tell tales of battles on the gridiron; Yale University football teams played there, and the Buffalo All-Americans of the American Professional Football Association brought the pigskin to "The Bathtub" in 1920. It would recall bouts between some of boxing's greatest warriors. Jack Dempsey, Joe Louis, and Floyd Patterson all had fights inside the Polo Grounds. But if the Polo Grounds could really speak, it would go on for hours about its most famous tenant, the New York Giants.

From 1883 to 1957, the Giants called the Polo Grounds home. No team in the majors was as connected to its ballpark as the Giants were with their home in Manhattan. With the left and right field fences both standing less than 280 feet from home plate, the Giants had one of the most unique home-field advantages in all of baseball—provided that they stocked their lineup with pull-hitting long-ballers. Remarkably successful, the Giants won 16 pennants and seven World Series championships during their time on West 155th Street and Eighth Avenue.

As the years ticked by, problems with the Polo Grounds began to arise. The stadium was not properly maintained and ticket sales began to decline, even as the Giants continued to be one of the marquee teams in baseball. With the New York Giants football team migrating to Yankee Stadium in 1956 and the baseball Giants leaving for San Francisco in 1957, the Polo Grounds stood vacant and without a purpose.

The New York Titans of the American Football League began play there in 1960, and the newly formed Mets of the National League called the ballpark home in 1962, but their stays were merely temporary as both teams were waiting for their permanent homes to be built. Though the Polo Grounds was finally demolished in 1964, it will always be regarded as one of the premier sports cathedrals of the early 20th century.

Behind the massive center field of the Polo Grounds were two "cigar box" bleacher sections that straddled the "batter's eye," which gave hitters a dark background amid a sea of white shirts. *MVP Books Collection*

Highlights

May 20: With their 13th win in 14 games, the first-place Giants improve to 21–5.

May 24: Hours after playing a suicide prank on his hotel roommate, New York's Danny Gardella belts a pinch home run for a 7–6 win at Cincinnati.

May 30: Mel Ott surpasses Honus Wagner's career total of 4,888 total bases (since adjusted) to set the NL record.

June 1: Manager Ott fines pitcher Bill Voiselle $500 for throwing a fat pitch to a Cardinals batter.

June 17: After getting swept by Philadelphia in a doubleheader, the New Yorkers fall out of first place for good.

July 5: New York's Whitey Lockman, 18, homers in his first Major League at-bat.

August 1: Ott becomes the third major leaguer to reach 500 home runs, as he goes deep against Boston at the Polo Grounds.

September 26: The Giants reach the million mark in attendance for the first time.

NOTES

Mel Ott leads the team in batting (.308), homers (21), and RBI (79).

After returning from military duty, **Van Mungo** (14–7, 3.20 ERA) is the team's most productive pitcher.

JESTER OF NEW YORK

Outfielder's Pranks Highlight Mediocre Year

The acquisition of outfielder Danny Gardella provided joy to most of the Giants players and misery to others. Nap Reyes was one of the others. Reyes served as Gardella's roommate on the road and was often the target of Dauntless Dan's relentless pranks.

After setting up Reyes for days with talks of depression and suicide ("life is too much for me"), Gardella pulled off his masterpiece in St. Louis. One morning, Reyes woke to the sound of Gardella screaming "Here I go! Goodbye!" Reyes ran to the open window and looked down to see a smiling Gardella hanging onto the windowsill with his arms, high above the sidewalk. While Reyes was angry, the rest of the Giants tolerated such ludicrous behavior because of Gardella's performance on the diamond. Just hours after feigning his death, Gardella came off the bench to hit a game-winning home run against Cincinnati.

Giants pitcher Van Mungo went 14–7 in his last-hurrah season in 1945 despite departing in the second inning of this August game. He glowers at umpire Ziggy Sears before he leaves. *AP Images*

While Gardella provided comic relief, news from across the Atlantic caused even more jubilation. By May, the war in Europe was over. Unfortunately for the Giants, their hopes of winning a pennant would end as well. New York fell out of first place for good on June 17, as Chicago stormed to the top of the league. The Giants' biggest issue was their inability to get their base runners in scoring position. They ended up leading the NL in home runs while finishing third worst in the league in runs scored.

Taking time away from hanging out of windows, Gardella belted 18 homers and drove in 71 runs, while catcher Ernie Lombardi tallied 19 round-trippers of his own. Mel Ott continued to defy old age as he led the Giants in homers (21), RBI (79), and batting (.308) at 36. On the mound, Van Mungo, months removed from military duty, became the Giants' most reliable pitcher with a 14–7 record. New York finished at 78–74, 19 games back of the NL-champion Cubs.

NICE GUYS FINISH LAST

Giants Are "Too Nice," Finish in the Basement

"Look over there," Dodgers manager Leo Durocher proclaimed. "Do you know a nicer guy than Mel Ott? Or any of the other Giants? Why, they are the nicest guys in the world, and where are they? In last place!"

Durocher's tirade came after Dodgers radio broadcaster Red Barber questioned him about splitting a doubleheader against the Giants. The Dodgers manager was upset that the Giants had hit five home runs that he believed would have been line drives and fly outs in any ballpark other than the Polo Grounds. Barber asked him why he couldn't admit that the hits were real home runs and why he couldn't just "be a nice guy for a change?" Durocher's response, "nice guys finish last," would be repeated millions of times by those in such fields as sports, business, and politics.

At the beginning of the season, the Giants' fortunes looked to be turning, as they signed a bundle of young prospects to go with their strong crop of returning veterans. Then, a crisis arose. With most athletes suffering from some sort of financial hardship due to the impact of the war, some ballplayers were looking for any way to make more money. Jorge Pasquel and his brother Bernardo provided that option. The Pasquels created the Mexican League, a baseball circuit that offered big-league players exceptionally large contracts. Jorge's offers were enticing enough to lure Danny Gardella and two other players away from the Giants. Months later, Sal Maglie, Roy Zimmerman, and George Hausmann also walked away from New York. The Giants roster that had looked so stout before was now without several of its key players.

To make things even worse, Mel Ott injured his knee in the beginning of the season and finished the year with a .074 average. It was Master Melvin's last year playing in a Giants uniform. Other than Johnny Mize (.337), no New York hitter batted above .300. The Giants finished at 61–93 and, to Durocher's satisfaction, in last place.

Walker Cooper made the All-Star team eight times in his career, including 1946. He enjoyed a career year as a "Window Breaker" in '47, when he caught for his brother Mort. *Baseball Hall of Fame Museum and Library*

Highlights

January 5: The Giants acquire catcher Walker Cooper from the Cardinals for $175,000.

February: Danny Gardella is the first of several Giants to jump to the "outlaw" Mexican League.

April 16: Against Philadelphia, Mel Ott clouts his 511th and last home run.

April 28: The Giants attract 54,181 fans for a Sunday doubleheader against the Dodgers, as attendance is up sharply across the majors.

June 9: Manager Ott is tossed from both games of a doubleheader versus Pittsburgh.

July 5: Dodgers manager Leo Durocher makes his famous "nice guys finish last" remark in reference to "nice guy" Mel Ott, manager of the last-place Giants.

September 7–26: A 2–16 stretch secures a last-place finish for the Giants.

September 29: New York's Buddy Kerr breaks the NL record by playing in his 52nd consecutive game at shortstop without an error.

NOTES

Johnny Mize leads the Giants in batting (.337) and RBI (70) while finishing one off the NL homer lead (22).

Outfielder **Sid Gordon** is second on the team in hitting at .293.

Lefty **Dave Koslo** (14–19) is the only double-digit winner on the staff.

Highlights

April 18: Facing Brooklyn, New York's Dave Koslo gives up Jackie Robinson's first career home run.

May 25: Buddy Kerr's NL record for consecutive games at shortstop ends at 68.

June 9: The Giants erupt for 12 runs in the eighth and ninth innings to defeat Pittsburgh 13–10.

June 13: New York acquires pitcher Mort Cooper, brother of Giants catcher Walker Cooper.

June 18: At 29–21, the Giants hold first place for the last time.

July 3: The Giants jump out to a 19–0 lead in the fourth inning against the rival Dodgers at Ebbets Field.

July 5: With two homers from Johnny Mize, the New Yorkers have now belted 37 long balls over the last 16 games.

NOTES

Johnny Mize shares the NL homer crown with 51, which will stand as the all-time New York Giants record. He leads the league in RBI (138) and runs (137).

Catcher **Walker Cooper** (.305-35-122) and outfielder **Willard Marshall** (.291-36-107) also swing heavy lumber, as the Giants set the MLB record for homers with 221.

Rookie **Larry Jansen** goes 21–5.

THE "WINDOW BREAKERS"

Giants Set MLB Homer Mark but Finish Fourth

It was a big deal when Johnny Mize reached 50 homers in 1947. Only three American Leaguers (Babe Ruth, Jimmie Foxx, Hank Greenberg) and one NLer (Hack Wilson) had ever done it before. *W. Eugene Smith/Time & Life Pictures/Getty Images*

By 1947, the Giants had gone nine seasons without bringing a pennant back to Manhattan. This level of play was not acceptable for a franchise as historic as the Giants. Changes needed to be made. Manager Mel Ott, John McGraw's native son, made alterations to the Giants roster that may have turned Mac over in his grave. Diverting from the McGraw teams that relied on bunting, stealing, and timely hitting, Ott constructed a club that lived for the home run and the marathon inning.

The "Window Breakers" shattered all types of records for home runs in 1947. The Giants crushed 37 homers in a 16-game stretch and broke the old team record of 144 by the beginning of August. By the end of the season, New York had hit a startling 221 long balls to set a major league record.

A new generation of sluggers fueled New York's power surge. The quartet of catcher Walker Cooper (35), first baseman Johnny Mize (51), and outfielders Willard Marshall (36) and Bobby Thomson (29) combined for more home runs than six other teams in the NL. Shortstop Buddy Kerr was the only starter to hit fewer than 10 four-baggers.

While the Giants had no problem hitting the long ball, their pitchers had no problem giving it up. Ranked next to last in runs and homers allowed, New York operated under a "bend but don't break" philosophy. Other than Larry Jansen (21–5) and Dave Koslo (15–10), Giants pitchers couldn't get it done. New York's lack of quality pitching caused the team to drop out of first place for good on June 19.

Still, the Giants finished the season in the top half of the league at 81–73. No one could argue that New York's offense was bordering on unstoppable. With a plethora of power hitters playing in a hitter-friendly ballpark, the sky was the limit. It was the feeling around the league that if the Giants could acquire or groom a couple more quality pitchers, they would claim the pennant.

The Giants–Dodgers Rivalry

The New York Giants and Brooklyn Dodgers were perhaps too closely intertwined. After all, they were the only teams in Major League Baseball history to play in the same city in the same league at the same time. Their rivalry was so intense that it pushed fans to the edge. As sportswriter Bruce Lowitt put it, perhaps half-jokingly, "people got knifed over who was a better pitcher, Carl Erskine or Sal Maglie."

Although the two teams shared a city, their fans couldn't have been more different. Particularly in the early years, Giants supporters were viewed as wealthy elitists of bourgeois Manhattan. On the other hand, Dodgers fans were more blue-collar with more newly arrived immigrants. The rivalry was fierce in the early decades of the 1900s, and the tempers of Dodgers owner Charles Ebbets and Giants manager John McGraw only made it worse.

Ebbets and McGraw seemed to disagree on everything, from how National League profits should be split to how to run a ball club, and they used their teams to carry out their feud. On more than one occasion, fists flew between Giants and Dodgers players. This passion was carried out through the fans as well. In 1940, umpire George Magerkurth was severely beaten during a game by an enraged Dodgers fan after Magerkurth made a pro-Giants call.

In 1934, Giants manager Bill Terry fueled the rivalry when he responded to a question by saying, "Brooklyn? I haven't heard anything from them lately. Are they still in the league?" In 1946, Dodgers manager Leo Durocher made his famous "nice guys finish last" quote in discussing Giants manager Mel Ott.

Even though the Dodgers and Giants rivalry was marred by physical altercations, they also played some darned good baseball. During their 68-year series in New York, the Giants had a slight edge on the Dodgers, winning 722 and losing 671. The Giants won 16 pennants during their stay in New York, taking home seven World Series titles (including two in the 1800s). The Dodgers were less successful, as they won 11 NL championships and one World Series.

The Giants and Dodgers parted from New York after the 1957 season, as neither team could fill their dilapidated stadiums. But during the first half of the 1950s, the Giants and Dodgers were the top teams in the National League. The two squads finished 1-2 in the standings three times from 1951 to 1954, and the Giants (1954) and Dodgers (1955) both won a World Series. Around this time, New Yorkers argued about who had the best center fielder—the Giants with Willie Mays, the Dodgers with Duke Snider, or the Yankees with Mickey Mantle.

The Dodgers-Giants feud continued after their migration to California, as the LA Dodgers and San Francisco Giants were the two premier teams in the league during the 1960s. The rivalry would continue to rage well into the 21st century.

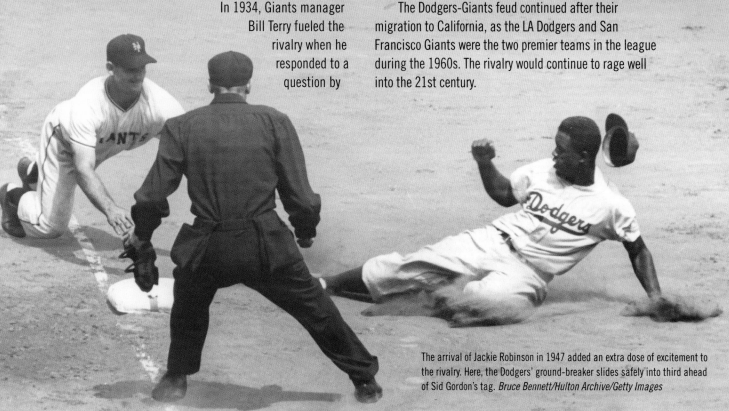

The arrival of Jackie Robinson in 1947 added an extra dose of excitement to the rivalry. Here, the Dodgers' ground-breaker slides safely into third ahead of Sid Gordon's tag. *Bruce Bennett/Hulton Archive/Getty Images*

Highlights

June 7: New York erupts for four runs in the last two innings to defeat Pittsburgh 9–5 and take over first place.

June 13–18: The Giants lose five straight games to fall out of first place for good.

June 20: Johnny Mize, Willard Marshall, and Sid Gordon smash back-to-back-to-back home runs in the eighth to lift New York to a 6–4 win over St. Louis.

July 4: Both teams score four runs in the ninth as Brooklyn edges New York 13–12 at Ebbets Field.

July 13: Gordon, Mize, Walker Cooper, and Bobby Thomson represent the Giants at the All-Star Game.

July 16: In a provocative managerial change, the Giants replace Mel Ott with outspoken Dodgers skipper Leo "The Lip" Durocher.

August 2: The Cardinals crush the Giants 21–2.

NOTES

Johnny Mize, who ties for the NL lead in homers with 40, also leads the Giants with 125 RBI.

Third baseman **Sid Gordon** is New York's second biggest stick (.299-30-107).

Larry Jansen (18–12, 3.61) and starter/reliever **Sheldon Jones** (16–8, 3.35) are the pitching standouts.

Bully Turned Manager

Leo Durocher Leaves Dodgers for Giants

Two years earlier, Dodgers manager Leo Durocher made the infamous remark that the Giants were too nice and that "nice guys finish last." On July 16, 1948, it became Durocher's responsibility to keep the Giants from finishing the season on the NL floor.

After a 37–38 start, manager Mel Ott resigned during a private meeting with Giants owner Horace Stoneham. Stoneham instantly set his sights on Durocher and signed the most hated Dodger in all of Manhattan to be the Giants' manager later that evening. "The Lip" understood that getting the fans to like him would be tough, but he just didn't care. "Like me or not," he said. "I'm going to give Giant fans a ball club so exciting that they'd come out in spite of me and in spite of themselves."

Durocher's "us against the world" attitude seemed to energize the troops, as the Giants went 13–5 after his induction as manager. Leading The Lip's club were the power-hitting tandem of first baseman Johnny Mize and third baseman Sid Gordon. Mize tied for the NL crown with 40 and led the Giants with 125 RBI. Gordon pounded out 30 home runs, plated 107, and led New York in batting with a .299 average.

Still, the Giants pitching staff continued to falter. New York hurlers yielded the most home runs in the NL and posted a team ERA just a shade under 4.00. Larry Jansen emerged from the mediocre pack to post an 18–12 record. Sheldon Jones, who finished with a 16–8 record and posted a fine 3.35 ERA, complemented Jansen. They were two of three pitchers who had double-digit win totals.

New York ended the year two games above .500 at 78–76, as the fifth-place finish marked 10 years since the Giants won a pennant. However, with Durocher now at the helm, anything was possible.

A Brooklyn native with a sunny disposition, third baseman Sid Gordon played the bulk of his career with the Giants. He posted triple digits in runs and RBI in 1948 and finished fourth in NL MVP voting. *Baseball Hall of Fame Museum and Library*

BREAKING THE BARRIER

Irvin, Thompson Become Giants' First Black Players

After the 1948 season concluded, Giants owner Horace Stoneham met with manager Leo Durocher to discuss what changes needed to be made to New York's roster for 1949. Durocher's answer was simple. "Back up a truck," he said. "In other words, get a whole new team."

The changes were drastic. The team fired two of Ott's old coaches, sold Johnny Mize (whose power production dipped) in midseason, and after the season traded regulars Buddy Kerr, Willard Marshall, and Sid Gordon to the Boston Braves. While many of Durocher's moves were unpopular, nothing was more controversial than the two players he called up from Jersey City in early July.

By summoning outfielder Monte Irvin and second baseman Hank Thompson to New York, Durocher brought in the first two African American players in Giants history. The move was met with much resistance. Baseball's color barrier had just recently been broken (Jackie Robinson with Brooklyn in 1947), and Thompson's claims to fame were serving as a machine gunner during the Battle of the Bulge and playing for the AL's lowly St. Louis Browns. Still, no one could argue with Thompson's production, as he became New York's everyday second baseman and hit .280. Irvin, a World War II veteran and a football star in college, batted .224 in 36 games—but great things lay ahead for him.

The newly formed Giants were no longer the "Window Breakers," but they did have a rising young star who could hit the long ball. Bobby Thomson, a 25-year-old outfielder from Staten Island, led the Giants in batting (.309), home runs (27), and RBI (109). The news wasn't as hopeful on the mound. Sheldon Jones (15–12) was the only Giants starter to post a winning record. Dave Koslo managed to lead the league in ERA while going 11–14.

New York once again finished in the lower half of the NL, ending the year in fifth place with a 73–81 record.

Monte Irvin toiled for 11 years in the Negro Leagues before breaking the Giants' color barrier on July 8, 1949, nine days before African American Hank Thompson joined the team. *MVP Books Collection*

1949

▸ 73-81   5th ◂

Highlights

April 28: A fan at Ebbets Field charges Giants manager Leo Durocher with assault. MLB will suspend but then absolve Durocher.

May 5: Johnny Mize's walk-off homer against Pittsburgh is his 300th career big fly.

June 6–10: With a five-game losing streak, New York tumbles out of first place for good.

June 13: The Giants trade Walker Cooper to the Reds for fellow catcher Ray Mueller.

July 3: Giants pitcher Monte Kennedy belts a grand slam and shuts out Brooklyn 16–0.

July 8: Outfielder Monte Irvin and second baseman Hank Thompson are the first African Americans to play for the Giants.

July 19: New York scores in every inning of a 13–3 home win over Cincinnati.

August 21: When Philly fans whip bottles at the umpires, the Giants win by forfeit.

August 22: The Giants sell Johnny Mize to the Yankees for $40,000.

NOTES

Bobby Thomson spearheads the Giants in batting (.309), home runs (27), and RBI (109).

Dave Koslo leads the NL in ERA (2.50) but posts just an 11–14 record.

Larry Jansen (15–16) and **Sheldon Jones** (15–12) lead the team in wins.

Team Leaders

(*Italics* indicates NL leader)

Batting Average

1940: Frank Demaree, .302
1941: Dick Bartell, .303
1942: Johnny Mize, .305
1943: Mickey Witek, .314
1944: Joe Medwick, .337
1945: Mel Ott, .308
1946: Johnny Mize, .337
1947: Walker Cooper, .305
1948: Sid Gordon, .299
1949: Bobby Thomson, .309

Home Runs

1940: Mel Ott, 19
1941: Mel Ott, 27
1942: *Mel Ott, 30*
1943: Mel Ott, 18
1944: Mel Ott, 26
1945: Mel Ott, 21
1946: Johnny Mize, 22
1947: *Johnny Mize, 51*

1948: *Johnny Mize, 40*
1949: Bobby Thomson, 27

RBI

1940: Babe Young, 101
1941: Babe Young, 104
1942: *Johnny Mize, 110*
1943: Sid Gordon, 63
1944: Joe Medwick, 85
1945: Mel Ott, 79
1946: Johnny Mize, 70
1947: *Johnny Mize, 138*
1948: Johnny Mize, 125
1949: Bobby Thomson, 109

Runs

1940: Mel Ott, 89
1941: Johnny Rucker, 95
1942: *Mel Ott, 118*
1943: Mickey Witek, 68
1944: Mel Ott, 91
1945: George Hausmann, 98
1946: Johnny Mize, 70
1947: *Johnny Mize, 137*

1948: Whitey Lockman, 117
1949: Bobby Thomson, 99

Stolen Bases

1940: Burgess Whitehead, 9
1941: Johnny Rucker, 8
1942: Billy Werber, 9
1943: Mel Ott, 7
1944: Buddy Kerr, 14
1945: George Hausmann, 7
1946: Buddy Blattner, 12
1947: Billy Rigney, 7
1948: Buddy Kerr, 9
1949: Whitey Lockman, 12

Wins

1940: Hal Schumacher, 13
1941: Hal Schumacher, 12
1942: Bill Lohrman, 13
1943: Ace Adams, 11
1944: Bill Voiselle, 21
1945: Van Mungo, 14
  Bill Voiselle, 14
1946: Dave Koslo, 14
1947: Larry Jansen, 21
1948: Larry Jansen, 18
1949: Larry Jansen, 15
  Sheldon Jones, 15

ERA

1940: Hal Schumacher, 3.25
1941: Cliff Melton, 3.01
1942: Bill Lohrman, 2.56
1943: Cliff Melton, 3.19
1944: Bill Voiselle, 3.02
1945: Van Mungo, 3.20
1946: Monte Kennedy, 3.42
1947: Larry Jansen, 3.16
1948: Sheldon Jones, 3.35
1949: *Dave Kolso, 2.50*

Shown here on his 1952 Topps card, Larry Jansen went an impressive 21–5 as a 26-year-old rookie in 1947. He finished second to Jackie Robinson in Rookie of the Year voting.
MVP Books Collection

Strikeouts

1940: Hal Schumacher, 123
1941: Cliff Melton, 100
1942: Carl Hubbell, 61
    Cliff Melton, 61
1943: Ken Chase, 86
1944: *Bill Voiselle, 161*
1945: Bill Voiselle, 115
1946: Dave Koslo, 121
1947: Larry Jansen, 104
1948: Larry Jansen, 126
1949: Larry Jansen, 113

NL Awards

NL MVP Voting

1940: Harry Danning, 7th
1942: Mel Ott, 3rd
    Johnny Mize, 5th
1944: Bill Voiselle, 5th
1947: Mize, 3rd
    Larry Jansen, 7th
1948: Sid Gordon, 4th

NL All-Stars

(*Italics* indicates starter)

1940: Harry Danning, C
    Carl Hubbell, P
    Bill Jurges, SS
    Joe Moore, OF
    Mel Ott, OF
1941: Danning, C
    Hubbell, P
    Ott, OF
1942: Hubbell, P
    Willard Marshall, OF
    Cliff Melton, P
    Johnny Mize, 1B
    Ott, OF

1943: Ernie Lombardi, C
    Ott, OF
1944: Joe Medwick, OF
    Ott, OF
1945: No All-Star Game played
1946: *Walker Cooper, C*
    Mize, 1B
1947: Cooper, C
    Marshall, OF
    Mize, 1B
1948: *Cooper, C*
    Sid Gordon, 3B
    Mize, 1B
    Bobby Thomson, OF
1949: Gordon, 3B
    Marshall, OF
    Mize, 1B
    Thomson, OF

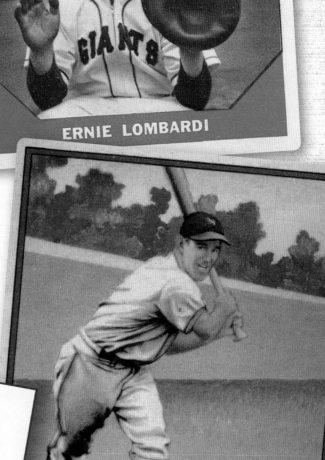

ERNIE LOMBARDI

GIANTS 1940–1949 All-Decade Team	
1B	JOHNNY MIZE
2B	MICKEY WITEK
SS	BUDDY KERR
3B	SID GORDON
C	WALKER COOPER
OF	MEL OTT
OF	WILLARD MARSHALL
OF	BOBBY THOMSON
SP	LARRY JANSEN
SP	HAL SCHUMACHER

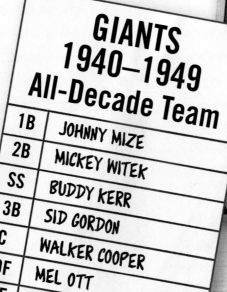

"BILL" JURGES

From top: Catcher Ernie Lombardi, posing on this Fleer card, batted .300 10 times, including twice with the Giants. Shortstop Billy Jurges, who was nearly murdered by a former girlfriend in 1932, made the NL All-Star team with the Giants in 1940. *MVP Books Collection*

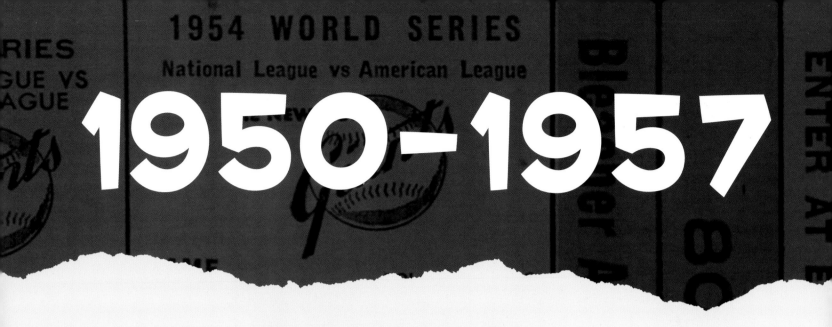

1950–1957

A MIRACLE AND A MOVE

Giants fans enjoy the highest of highs with the "Miracle at Coogan's Bluff" and a stunning World Series sweep of Cleveland. But the move to San Francisco in 1958 sends New Yorkers into despair.

The Giants' sweep of the Indians ranks among the top World Series shockers in history, as Cleveland had set an American League record with 111 victories—one more than the fabled 1927 Yankees.
MVP Books Collection

The 1950s hold a reputation for placidity, an era of postwar peace and prosperity memorialized in bland suburban sitcoms such as *Leave It to Beaver*. But you'd have a hard time telling that to Giants fans. On the New York side, their emotions were whipsawed from the greatest single moment in Giants history—Bobby Thomson's 1951 "Shot Heard 'Round the World"—and a World Series title in 1954 to the worst thing that could happen to a fan: the loss of the team to another city.

Above all, the 1950s brought the arrival and blossoming of the greatest star the Giants, and maybe any team, had ever known: Willie Mays. The "Say Hey Kid" burst on the scene in 1951, winning Rookie of the Year honors and contributing to the Giants' first pennant since 1937. (Mays was on deck when Thomson slugged his homer.) Even though he lost two productive years to military service in the Korean War, Mays still amazed, winning the MVP Award in 1954 and then making the greatest catch in World Series history to help the Giants to their fifth title. His first manager, Leo Durocher, described him as "Joe Louis, Jascha Heifetz, Sammy Davis, and Nashua, rolled into one." In other words, a boxer, violinist, entertainer, and racehorse.

Durocher, the tempestuous "Leo the Lip," was only the fourth Giants manager since 1902—and, like his predecessors, a future Hall of Famer. A former Dodger, Durocher helped author the greatest Dodgers-killing moment of all time, leading the Giants from a 13½-game deficit in 1951 to tie Brooklyn at season's end. Later accounts told how the team used a sophisticated system involving a telescope and

After clinching the 1954 World Series with a Game Four win at Cleveland, the Giants were greeted by this elated crowd at LaGuardia Field. *New York Daily News Archive/Getty Images*

buzzers to steal opponents' signs and fuel the comeback, but nothing could tarnish the unforgettable moment when Thomson launched Ralph Branca's pitch into the left field stands at the Polo Grounds, with announcer Russ Hodges exulting in near-hysteria, "The Giants win the pennant! The Giants win the pennant!"

That the Giants lost the World Series to the Yankees hardly mattered. "We had done the one thing we wanted to do, and that was beat the Dodgers," Giants star Monte Irvin said. By 1954, the Giants were back in the Series. Again they assumed the role of heavy underdogs, this time to a Cleveland Indians juggernaut that had won 111 games. With heroics from Mays and pinch hitter Dusty Rhodes, the Giants swept the Tribe in four straight.

It was the beginning of the end. Durocher resigned after the 1955 season, seeing in his third-place Giants the dark times ahead. Bill Rigney succeeded him, but victories were few and fans grew sparse. When Stoneham decided to join Dodgers owner Walter O'Malley in the audacious move to California after the 1957 season, he was asked what he would tell the New York kids who loved the team. "I feel sorry for the kids," he said. "But I haven't seen many of their fathers recently."

Moments after the Giants' final game at the Polo Grounds, fans swarmed the field while players ran for the safety of the clubhouse. New Yorkers ripped up such souvenirs as sod, home plate, and the plaque commemorating Eddie Grant. As dusk descended, the remaining fans chanted, "We want Willie! We want Willie!" But their favorite son did not come out of the clubhouse. His days in the Polo Grounds were over. He was going to San Francisco.

Highlights

May 11: Several teams, including the Giants, travel in airplanes due to a railroad strike.

May 28: A seventh straight loss puts New York at 10–20.

June 24: New York catcher Wes Westrum clouts three homers and a triple in a 12–2 drubbing of Cincinnati.

June 27: Pitcher Larry Jansen's scoreless-innings streak ends at 30.

July 4: At a Giants-Dodgers game at the Polo Grounds, 56-year-old fan Bernard Doyle is killed by a bullet fired from outside the ballpark.

August 12: This Phillies-Giants game is marred by second baseman Eddie Stanky's ouster for distracting a Phillies batter, Hank Thompson being knocked unconscious in a collision, and a bench-clearing brawl.

August 16: Thompson laces two inside-the-park home runs at the Polo Grounds.

September 9: Giants pitcher Sal Maglie tosses his fourth consecutive shutout.

NOTES

Eddie Stanky leads the NL in walks (144), is second in runs (115), and bats .300.

Bobby Thomson paces New York in home runs (25), and **Hank Thompson** is tops in RBI (91).

Larry Jansen goes 19–13 and ranks third in the circuit in ERA (3.01) and strikeouts (161).

A POWER FINISH

Stanky, Dark, and the Thom(p)sons Help NY Close Strong

After a pair of disappointing seasons, Giants manager Leo Durocher was angry. Durocher detested losing, but as the 20th century turned 50, his team looked to be turning a corner. He was especially confident in the play of his new double-play combination: second baseman Eddie Stanky and shortstop Alvin Dark, each acquired from the Boston Braves.

Stanky was a holdover from Durocher's days with the Dodgers, and Dark possessed one of the best gloves in the NL. But it was their tenacity that pleased Durocher the most. "We have two guys who can do things with the bat and can run the bases," Durocher said. "They come to kill you."

In addition to having two killers on their roster, the Giants also welcomed the return of Sal Maglie. Maglie, who had been restricted from playing in the majors due to his time in the Mexican League, bounced between the bullpen and starting rotation and proved to be New York's strongest arm. Maglie's 18–4 record and 2.71 ERA were complemented by an outstanding season by midseason acquisition Jim Hearn. A gift from the St. Louis Cardinals, Hearn went 11–3 for New York and registered a league-leading 2.49 ERA (1.94 with NY).

Giants ace Sal "The Barber" Maglie earned his nickname because he often gave hitters "close shaves." He ranked second among NL hurlers with 10 hit batters in 1950. *MVP Books Collection*

On offense, Bobby Thomson led the Giants with 25 home runs and Hank Thompson drove in 91 runs. Although he was expected to kill, Stanky mostly walked. The 5-foot-8 second baseman led the NL in bases on balls (a staggering 144) and was second in runs (115) while hitting .300.

The Giants gelled late in the year, going 41–21 from August 1 to the end of the season. Even after New York's torrid finish, the hole they had dug was too deep. A 52–28 second half after a 34–40 first half was not enough to push the Giants higher than third place. New York's 86–68 record put the Giants five games behind the Phillies. For the 13th straight year, the season ended without a pennant in the Polo Grounds.

"It Will Take a Miracle . . ."

Giants Win the Pennant on Shot Heard 'Round the World

There are certain seasons in baseball that live on long after the final out is recorded. Men with gloves and bats become heroes, and conversations recounting it are laced with hyperbole that last entire afternoons. As the years pass, the legend grows. Nineteen fifty-one was one of those seasons.

However extraordinary the 1951 season would turn out to be, it certainly didn't look that way for the Giants at the beginning of the year. New York lost 12 of its first 14 games, including a stretch that saw them drop 10 in a row. Nearly every aspect of the Giants ball club was floundering. They couldn't hit, they couldn't pitch, and their defense was prone to errors. As the Dodgers flew out of the gate, the Giants continued to slide. Arthur Daley, one of the most respected writers at the *New York Times*, wrote, "It will take a miracle for the Giants to win the championship now."

The Giants didn't get a miracle, but they did get the next best thing: a lanky, fleet-footed outfielder from Alabama. Willie Mays, who had been crushing pitching in the American Association for Minneapolis, was called up in late May. Unfortunately, the "Say Hey Kid" didn't make the instant impact that Giants manager Leo Durocher was hoping for. Mays went hitless in his first 12 at-bats, and the confidence that had allowed him to hit .477 back in Minnesota was gone.

Giants manager Leo Durocher is restrained as Bobby Thomson skips home with his pennant-winning homer, concluding what *ESPN Sports Century* ranked as the No. 2 sporting event of all time (behind the 1958 NFL Championship Game). *Transcendental Graphics/Hulton Archive/Getty Images*

1951

▶ 98–59   1st ◀

Highlights

August 11: New York trails rival Brooklyn by 13 games.

August 12–27: The Giants win 16 straight but are still five games out.

September 30: Against Boston, New York closes the season with its seventh straight win (12th in 13 games) to tie Brooklyn for first place.

October 1: A two-run homer by Bobby Thomson keys a 3–1 Giants win over Brooklyn in the first of a three-game playoff at Ebbets Field.

October 3: After losing the second playoff game 10–0 at home, New York wins the third contest 5–4 on a three-run walk-off homer by Thomson.

October 6: With a 6–2 victory in Game Three, the Giants take a two-games-to-one lead over the Yankees in the World Series.

October 10: The Yankees clinch the Series at home in Game Six, 4–3, after Sal Yvars lines out to right with a man in scoring position to end the game.

NOTES

Monte Irvin tallies a league-high 121 RBI, and rookie **Willie Mays** cracks 20 homers.

Shortstop **Alvin Dark** tops the NL with 41 doubles.

The Giants' **Sal Maglie** (23–6) and **Larry Jansen** (23–11) tie for the NL lead in wins.

Durocher refused to give up on Mays and continued to offer the 20-year-old encouragement. "You are my center fielder from now until the end of the season," Durocher told him. "Now go out there and just play ball." His manager's vote of unwavering confidence seemed to be all that Mays needed, and he regained the stroke he had in the minors. As Mays's bat heated up, so did the Giants.

A 16-game winning streak in the middle of August electrified Manhattan and moved the Giants from 13 games out to just 5 behind. Perhaps feeling the Giants breathing down their necks, the first-place Dodgers began to slide. Brooklyn players could feel the "Creeping Terror" inching closer and closer as the year began to wind down.

Riding the arms of Sal Maglie (23–6, 2.93 ERA) and Larry Jansen (23–11, 3.04), along with the hot bat of outfielder Monte Irvin (24 home runs and 121 RBI), the Giants found themselves tied with the Dodgers at the end of September. A three-game playoff between the two New York clubs would decide the pennant.

The Giants won the first game of the much-ballyhooed series 3–1 at Ebbets Field on the strength of a Bobby Thomson two-run homer. The Dodgers responded with a 10–0 blowout at the Polo Grounds in the second game, setting the stage for the finale in the Giants' home park.

On the morning of Game Three, the skies were dark and threatening. It was a day that seemed unfit for baseball as Durocher entrusted his ace, Maglie, to bring the pennant home for New York. Maglie was holding his own against counterpart Don

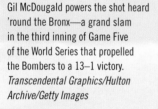

Gil McDougald powers the shot heard 'round the Bronx—a grand slam in the third inning of Game Five of the World Series that propelled the Bombers to a 13–1 victory. *Transcendental Graphics/Hulton Archive/Getty Images*

Newcombe until the eighth inning. Brooklyn put up three runs in the top of the inning to go ahead 4–1, held the Giants scoreless in the bottom half, and was now three outs away from going to the World Series. However, New York had spent all season fighting and was in no mood to quit.

With the Giants needing three runs to tie and four to win, Alvin Dark kicked off a rally with a base hit. Don Mueller followed with a single of his own, advancing Dark to third. Representing the tying run, Whitey Lockman stepped into the box and cracked a double down the left field line. Dark scored (making the score 4–2) and Mueller advanced to third, breaking his ankle during his slide. With Bobby Thomson set to hit next, Newcombe was pulled for Ralph Branca, No. 13.

Branca's first pitch painted the inside corner. His next offering was a high fastball that was designed to set up Thomson for a curveball low and away. Thomson didn't oblige with Branca's plan.

It is known as the "Shot Heard Round the World," but as soon as Thomson's fly ball curled into the left field bleachers, nothing could be heard other than the sound of 34,320 Giants fans screaming with excitement. People flooded from the grandstand onto the diamond as Thomson hopped in jubilation around the bases.

It was the perfect ending to a season that had seen more than its fair share of tense moments. When the cheering subsided and the last celebratory champagne bubble fizzed flat, the Giants had to regroup. Now they had a World Series to win.

Still riding high from their dramatic victory, the Giants were able to jump on the Yankees early for a 5–1 win in Game One. The Yankees bounced back the next day to even the Series at 1–1. After winning Game Three 6–2, it looked like the Giants actually had a shot at beating the seemingly unstoppable Yanks. The Bronx Bombers were not going to let that happen. The Yankees put the Giants away over the next three games— winning 6–2, 13–1, and 4–3—to claim their third straight World Series title.

Although they came up short of their ultimate goal, the Giants could always claim ownership of the most legendary pennant victory in the history of baseball.

Voice of the Giants

Russ Hodges's career as the Giants' radio broadcaster spanned 22 magnificent years. But he is most remembered for a certain 90 seconds on October 3, 1951.

"Here's a long drive. . . . It's gonna be, I believe. . . . The Giants win the pennant! The Giants win the pennant! The Giants win the pennant! The Giants win the pennant! Bobby Thomson hits into the lower deck of the left field stands. The Giants win the pennant, and they're goin' crazy! They're goin' crazy! Hee-oh!"

It is the most famous call in baseball history—the beautiful sound of Hodges shrieking with excitement as Thomson rounded the bases.

Hodges began his broadcasting career in 1934 and became the voice of the Giants in 1949. When the team moved west to San Francisco in 1958, he followed. In addition to his work with the Giants, Hodges lent his voice to one of the most famous bouts in boxing history, calling Muhammad Ali and Sonny Liston's first fight in 1964. Hodges also joined partner Lon Simmons in broadcasting San Francisco 49ers games over the airwaves.

Hodges died from a heart attack in 1971 at age 60. He was posthumously awarded numerous broadcasting awards, and the Giants made sure that his legacy was maintained. In 2000, they named their broadcast booth the Hodges-Simmons Broadcast Center.

Russ Hodges. *MVP Books Collection*

Highlights

April 2: Giants star Monte Irvin breaks his ankle. He will miss most of the season.

April 23: In his first of 1,070 games (a since-broken record for an MLB pitcher), New York's Hoyt Wilhelm homers in his first at-bat. He'll never homer again.

May 28: With a 6–2 drubbing of Brooklyn, the Giants stretch their lead to 2½ games.

May 29: Willie Mays, batting .236, is inducted into the Army.

June 6: A 2–8 skid drops the New Yorkers to four games back, and they will spend the rest of the season in Brooklyn's rearview mirror.

June 15: After trailing New York 11–0 through three innings, the Cardinals score 14 in the last four frames to win 14–12.

June 16: Bobby Thomson is at it again, belting a walk-off grand slam to defeat St. Louis 8–7.

NOTES

Bobby Thomson spearheads the New York offense with 24 homers, 108 RBI, and an NL-best 14 triples.

Sal Maglie (18–8, 2.92) is second in the NL in wins, and rookie knuckleball reliever **Hoyt Wilhelm** goes 15–3 and leads the league in ERA (2.43).

TOUGH ACT TO FOLLOW

Giants Can't Replicate Previous Year's Miracle

The Giants' miraculous run to the pennant in 1951 was certainly a hard act to replicate. After one of the most exciting seasons in the history of the game, what could possibly serve as an encore? New York started its quest to defend its NL pennant by trading away walk machine Eddie Stanky and acquiring two rookies that would be key to their future success. Pitcher Hoyt Wilhelm, who led the National League in ERA in 1953, would befuddle hitters with his knuckleball, and Dusty Rhodes would serve the Giants as one of the finest pinch hitters the game had ever seen.

Brooklyn took control of first place in early June 1953, but the Giants stayed in the Dodgers' rear view. Still riding high from his pennant-winning home run, Bobby Thomson paced a powerful Giants offense with 24 homers and 108 RBI. Shortstop Alvin Dark rapped .301, and first baseman Whitey Lockman batted .290. No Giants starter hit fewer than 10 long balls, as the team finished second in the league with 722 runs.

On the mound, New York relied on veteran starters Jim Hearn, Sal Maglie, and Larry Jansen. Though all were in their 30s, their old age didn't show. Maglie led the team with 18 wins while Hearn and Jansen combined for 25. Wilhelm proved to be dynamite out of the bullpen, grabbing 15 wins without starting a single game.

Hoyt Wilhelm went 15–3 with the Giants as a 30-year-old rookie in 1952. No one could have dreamed that he would become the first major-leaguer to pitch in 1,000 career games. *MVP Books Collection*

While the Giants stayed close to the first-place Dodgers, New York wasn't as fortunate as it had been the previous season. Monte Irvin broke his ankle and played in just 46 games, and Willie Mays was called to serve his country in May. The absence of two of their best hitters prevented the Giants from making a late-season push like the year before. New York finished at 92–62, 4½ games behind the Dodgers.

"THE GIANTS IS DEAD"

NY Finishes With First Losing Record in Four Years

Two years removed from an epic season that had fans on the edge of their seats into October, 1953 was rather boring. New York was so lifeless that Brooklyn Dodgers manager Chuck Dressen proclaimed, "The Giants is dead!" Giants manager Leo Durocher took offense to Dressen's grammatically poor barb and took it upon himself to show the Dodgers that his team still had some life.

In early September, with the Giants nearly 30 games back of first, New York traveled to Ebbets Field to try and spoil Brooklyn's inevitable run to the pennant. A brawl started between the two teams after Giants pitcher Ruben Gomez plunked Brooklyn's Carl Furillo on the wrist. A fight started but was quickly broken up. As both teams returned to their dugouts, Durocher hollered at Furillo. The Brooklyn outfielder was Durocher's least favorite Dodger, and the Giants manager wanted a piece of him.

Furillo accepted Durocher's invitation for combat, and one of the largest brawls in Giants-Dodgers history ensued. The benches emptied, punches flew, and jerseys were ripped. Durocher emerged from the scuffle unscathed, but Furillo suffered a finger injury that forced him to miss the rest of the regular season. That day, Durocher proved one thing: The Giants may have had a lousy record and dull arms, but they certainly weren't dead.

They also had a quartet of hitters as good as any other in the NL. Shortstop Alvin Dark, third baseman Hank Thompson, and outfielders Bobby Thomson and Monte Irvin each swatted more than 20 home runs. Thomson led New York with 106 RBI, and Don Mueller was tops in average at .333.

Things were less exciting on the mound. When he wasn't instigating bench-clearing brawls, Gomez was the Giants' best pitcher (13–11, 3.40 ERA). Unfortunately, he was the only rotation regular with a winning record. Brooklyn took the pennant as the Giants finished at 70–84, their first sub-.500 season in four years.

Hank Thompson debuted with the AL's St. Louis Browns on July 17, 1947, 12 days after Larry Doby broke the league's color barrier. Thompson batted .302 for the Giants in 1953.
MVP Books Collection

Hank THOMPSON
outfielder NEW YORK GIANTS

Highlights

April 30: Sal Maglie tosses a 1–0 shutout against the Milwaukee Braves, as Bobby Thomson accounts for the only run with a ninth-inning homer off the left field foul pole at the Polo Grounds.

May 13: A 10–14 start puts the Giants back of the pack—for good.

June 5: The Giants beat the Cubs thanks in part to Puerto Rican pitcher Ruben Gomez and Cuban catcher Ray Noble.

July 5: New York kicks off an eight-game winning streaking with a 20–6 trouncing of Brooklyn, as Hank Thompson swats a grand slam and a three-run homer.

August 26: Outfielder Dusty Rhodes cracks three straight home runs in a 13–4 win over St. Louis.

September 6: Brooklyn's Carl Furillo, the NL's leading hitter, gets hit on the wrist by a pitch. When Furillo attacks Giants manager Leo Durocher for ordering the brushback, a Giants player steps on and breaks Furillo's finger.

NOTES

Five hitters swing heavy lumber: **Alvin Dark** (.300-23-88, 126 runs), **Hank Thompson** (.302-24-74), **Bobby Thomson** (.288-26-106), **Monte Irvin** (.329-21-97), and **Don Mueller** (.333).

Ruben Gomez (13–11) is the best of a mediocre rotation.

1954

▶ **97-57**   **1st** ◀

Highlights

April 13: Back with the Giants after serving in the Army, Willie Mays powers a home run on Opening Day to help beat Brooklyn 4–3.

May 25: The New Yorkers win a 21–4 laugher over Pittsburgh.

June 15: A walk-off homer by Hank Thompson versus Cincinnati puts the Giants in first place for good.

July 6–8: A three-game sweep of second-place Brooklyn puts the Giants up by 6½.

September 20: New York clinches the pennant with a 7–1 win over the Dodgers.

September 29: The Giants defeat favored Cleveland 5–2 in Game One of the World Series thanks to Willie Mays' famous catch in the eighth inning and Dusty Rhodes' three-run homer in the bottom of the 10th.

October 2: After 3–1 and 6–2 victories, New York sweeps the Indians with a 7–4 win at Cleveland in Game Four.

NOTES

Willie Mays is named NL MVP after leading the circuit in batting (.345) and triples (13) and belting 41 home runs.

Don Mueller raps 212 hits, more than any other NLer.

Lefty **Johnny Antonelli** goes 21–7 and leads the NL in ERA (2.30) and shutouts (six).

Willie Mays catches Vic Wertz's blast in the deep recesses of the Polo Grounds in Game One of the World Series. Larry Doby might have tagged at second and scored if Mays hadn't made an epic throw to the infield.
New York Daily News Archive/Getty Images

"SAY HEY!"

Mays's Legendary Catch Helps Giants Win World Series

Sometimes, the past must be purged to make way for the future. Before the 1954 season began, the Giants received pitcher Johnny Antonelli from the Milwaukee Braves in exchange for outfielder Bobby Thomson. Thomson, of "Shot Heard 'Round the World" fame, had been New York's best hitter over the previous few seasons and was one of the most popular Giants in team history. While some fans grumbled at the loss of Thomson, Antonelli shined. The 24-year-old lefty posted 21 wins and led the league with a 2.30 ERA. While the addition of Antonelli was a significant boost to the Giants roster in 1954, it was a mere afterthought compared to New York's other new toy.

After missing most of 1952 and all of '53 due to military service, the "Say Hey Kid" returned to Manhattan. From Opening Day, Willie Mays looked at home patrolling the cavernous center field at the Polo Grounds. En route to winning his first NL MVP Award, Mays led the league in batting at .345 while amassing 41 home runs and 110 RBI. He was the focal point of a devastating New York attack. Hank Thompson crushed

26 home runs and Alvin Dark chipped in 20, as the Giants tied Brooklyn for the league lead in homers with 186.

The Giants were just as impressive on the mound. With a newly acquired ace in Antonelli, New York led the league in ERA. Ruben Gomez registered 17 wins while 37-year-old Sal Maglie defied old age to contribute 14 Ws. Another newly minted Giant helped New York out of the bullpen. Marv Grissom, a waiver-wire pickup from the Red Sox, logged 19 saves. First-class play from every corner of their roster allowed the Giants to jump out to a 57–27 record by the All-Star break, 5½ games ahead of second-place Brooklyn.

Even with one of the best teams he ever had in New York, manager Leo Durocher was still prone to making head-scratching decisions in the name of winning. Late in the year, the Giants had the bases loaded with two outs as they trailed Brooklyn 5–4. New York's last hope for victory was Wes Westrum, a defensive-oriented catcher who was in the middle of a terrible slump. Knowing that if he pulled Westrum he would have no one left to catch for the remainder of the game, Durocher called on Dusty Rhodes to pinch-hit. Rhodes promptly crushed a pitch to deep center to win the game. "I'd rather be in the 10th inning without a catcher than in the clubhouse with a loss," Durocher said afterward.

The Giants finished at 97–57, five games ahead of second-place Brooklyn, and earned a date with the Cleveland Indians. Loaded with such star pitchers as Bob Lemon, Early Wynn, and Bob Feller, the Tribe had won an AL-record 111 games in 1954. Some pundits were predicting a sweep. They were right, except they got the winner wrong.

It takes a pretty spectacular event for a play to be known simply as "The Catch." This "Catch" was not just amazing, it affected the entire World Series. With Game One tied at 2–2 in the eighth, Cleveland's Vic Wertz crushed a ball to deep, deep center field with none out and runners at first and second. Mays, who knew the Polo Grounds' cavernous center field better than anyone, instantly sprinted back at the crack of the bat. Mays caught the ball over his left shoulder on a dead sprint and quickly spun and whipped the ball toward the infield. Larry Doby tagged at second and went to third, but the great throw prevented him from scoring on the play. Sportswriter Arnold Hanno described Mays's toss as "the throw of a giant, the throw of a howitzer made human."

The historic play kept the game tied, and Rhodes's three-run homer in the bottom of the 10th allowed New York to claim Game One 5–2. The Giants rode the momentum the rest of the Series. Antonelli went the distance in Game Two, scattering eight hits in a 3–1 victory.

The Series went back to Cleveland, but the story was the same. Gomez earned the Game Three win, 6–2, with Hoyt Wilhelm notching the save. The Giants closed out the Series 7–4 the next day to complete the sweep. New Yorkers, who welcomed home their world champions with a ticker-tape parade, saved their loudest cheers for their biggest hero: Willie Mays.

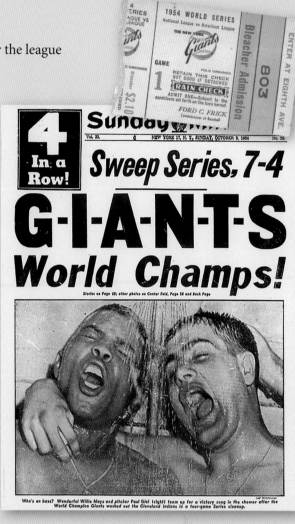

4 In a Row! Sweep Series, 7-4 **G-I-A-N-T-S World Champs!**

Stories on Page 58; other photos on Center Fold, Page 58 and Back Page

Who's on boss? Wonderful Willie Mays and pitcher Paul Giel (right) team up for a victory song in the shower after the World Champion Giants washed out the Cleveland Indians in a four-game Series cleanup.

Top: Incredibly, the Giants charged just $2.10 for this bleacher ticket to the 1954 World Series. That's just $18 in today's money. *MVP Books Collection.* **Bottom:** Paul Giel, who pitched only 4⅓ innings for the Giants in 1954 (none in the World Series), nevertheless took a celebratory shower with Willie Mays after the series triumph. *MVP Books Collection*

The Amazing Willie Mays

Willie Mays was in the mood to take in a movie. The 20-year-old from rural Alabama deserved a break after ravaging Triple-A pitching. Mays was hitting .477 in 35 games for the Minneapolis Millers when he took a seat in a Sioux City movie theater. What appeared on the screen next was better than any John Wayne or Gary Cooper film. Before the movie began to roll, a message popped up on the screen: "WILLIE MAYS CALL YOUR HOTEL." The movie would have to wait. Willie Howard Mays was being called up to the big leagues.

Deemed the "Say Hey Kid" by sportswriter Jimmy Cannon due to Mays's penchant for not knowing the names of his teammates and instead saying "Say hey," Mays had a hard time greeting NL pitching. In fact, Willie's start in the major leagues was infamously abysmal. The center fielder began his career by going 0-for-12 in 1951. However, Mays's first career hit was a home run off Hall of Fame hurler Warren Spahn. Spahn would later joke, "I'll never forgive myself. We might have gotten rid of Willie forever if I'd only struck him out."

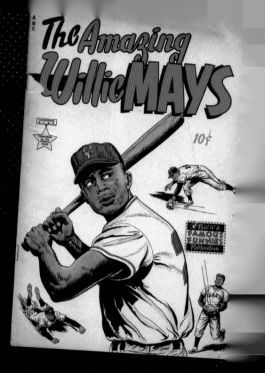

After that first hit, there was no stopping this five-tool wunderkind. That first season, Mays cracked .274 while amassing 20 home runs and 68 RBI in 121 games. While a legendary career was ahead of him, Mays was almost at the focal point of baseball history in his rookie season. When Bobby Thomson hit the "Shot Heard 'Round the World" to give the Giants the pennant in 1951, Willie was waiting in the on-deck circle.

Mays would miss most of the 1952 season and all of the 1953 campaign due to his military service during the Korean War, but he made up for lost time when he returned to Manhattan. In 1954, straight out of the Army, Mays won the NL MVP Award. In addition to swatting 41 home runs and driving in 110 runs that year, Mays led the NL in batting average (.345), slugging (.667), and triples (13). He would prove to be a key cog in the Giants' run to the 1954 World Series crown.

In the 18 years that followed Mays' first MVP season, the Giants center fielder established himself as the premier superstar in the National League. From 1954 to 1972, he played in 23 All-Star Games, won 12 Gold Glove Awards (tied for the most ever by an outfielder), and won a second MVP Award (1965). His ability to relate well to fans, such as playing stickball with kids on the New York streets, only added to his immense popularity.

While his home run totals piled up—he would hit his 600th career home run in 1970—Mays was also lethal on the base paths. From 1956 to 1959, he led the league in steals each year. In 1957, Mays became the second player in Major League history to join the 20–20–20–20 club (26 doubles, a league-leading 20 triples, 36 home runs, and 38 steals).

Above: There was nothing comic about Mays's amazing play on the baseball diamond. *MVP Books Collection.* **Left:** Leo Durocher: "If somebody came up and hit .450, stole 100 bases, and performed a miracle in the field every day, I'd still look you in the eye and say Willie was better." *MVP Books Collection*

Defensively, Mays was without peer in center field. While the "basket catch" was his trademark, he also dazzled with his amazing range and rocket arm. He gunned down 188 runners in his career, and he remains the only outfielder in Major League history with more than 7,000 catches.

With his beaming smile, infectious enthusiasm, and electrifying play, Mays immediately won over San Francisco fans after the team moved west in 1958. While his stolen base totals diminished, his power improved, as he averaged more than 40 homers a year from 1959 to '66, with a high of 52 in 1965.

With his career winding down, Mays returned to where it all began. At 41 years old, he was traded to the New York Mets in 1972. Willie appeared in only 135 games for the Mets during his stay in Queens, but he still found ways to set records. In 1973, he became the oldest position player to appear in a World Series game.

Mays retired in 1973, but his impact on the game remained, as he became one of baseball's greatest ambassadors. He was elected into the Hall of Fame on his first year of eligibility with 95 percent of the vote. His No. 24 was not only retired by the Giants, but AT&T Park sits at 24 Willie Mays Plaza.

Mays's iconic status became apparent to President Barack Obama. "Two years ago, I invited Willie to ride with me on Air Force One on the way to the All-Star Game in St. Louis," Obama recalled when the Giants visited the White House in 2011. "It was an extraordinary trip. Very rarely when I'm on Air Force One am I the second most important guy on there. Everybody was just passing me by. 'Can I get you something, Mr. Mays?'"

Mays was not only the most popular guy on that plane, but some historians consider him the greatest all-around player who ever lived—especially those who had the privilege of watching him play.

Running like the wind, Mays often lost his cap on the field, whether he was scoring one of his 2,062 runs or making one of his still-standing MLB-record 7,095 outfield catches. *MVP Books Collection*

Highlights

April 13: In a bad omen, the Giants are nearly no-hit on Opening Day. They crack their first hit with one out in the ninth off Philadelphia's Robin Roberts.

April 24: At Ebbets Field, the Giants score six runs in the top of the 10th and hold on to beat Brooklyn 11–10.

May 10: Though 12–11, the Giants are 9½ games behind the 22–2 Dodgers, who will breeze to the pennant.

July 31: Cleveland selects Giants pitcher Sal Maglie off waivers.

September 13: Hurler Johnny Antonelli allows just six hits from the mound in a 9–1 victory over the Milwaukee Braves while cracking two singles, a double, and a home run at the plate.

September 20: Against Pittsburgh, Willie Mays homers for the sixth consecutive game to reach 50 for the year.

September 24: Manager Leo Durocher resigns. Bill Rigney will replace him.

September 25: In their last game of the season, a 3–1 loss to Philadelphia, the Giants hit into double plays in the seventh and eighth innings and a triple play in ninth.

NOTES

Willie Mays leads the league in triples (13) and homers (51, which ties the team record) while batting .319 with 127 RBI.

Don Mueller cracks .306 with 83 RBI.

Johnny Antonelli and **Jim Hearn**, both of whom go 14–16, are the staff's top winners.

NO MORE LIP

Durocher Retires after Giants Place Third

It was quickly made clear that 1955 would be very different than the world championship season of a year earlier. On Opening Day against the Phillies, the Giants were nearly victims of the season's first no-hitter. They narrowly avoided the blanking by mustering a hit with one out in the top of the ninth.

It was that kind of season for the Giants. By May 10, they were 9½ games behind first-place Brooklyn. While there wasn't a ton to cheer about in the Polo Grounds, one guy whom every Giants fan could count on was Willie Mays. At 24 years old, the "Say Hey Kid" was showing the entire league what the beginning of a Hall of Fame career looked like. Already one of the best players in baseball, Mays went on an offensive tear that was outright Ruthian. Willie finished the year with 51 home runs, good enough for the league lead and a share of the club record with Johnny Mize. He also led the league in triples and hit a team-high .319 with 127 RBI. Don Mueller's 83 RBI served as a nice complement to Mays's production, although no other Giant drove in more than 63 runs.

At spring training in 1955, Giants manager Leo Durocher poses with his two favorite people—his wife (actress Laraine Day) and Willie Mays. It would be Leo the Lip's last season with New York. *Hy Peskin/ Sports Illustrated/Getty Images*

Though the Giants had the second-best ERA in the league, you wouldn't have known it by their pitchers' win-loss records. Johnny Antonelli, the previous year's pitching hero, finished with a 14–16 record despite a 3.33 ERA. Jim Hearn, a 34-year-old right-hander, was also 14–16. No one else won more than 10 games.

On the last day of the season, with New York's third-place finish secured, manager Leo Durocher announced that he would not return to manage the Giants. His replacement, longtime Giants infielder Bill Rigney, was certainly a capable hire, but he wasn't the caliber of Durocher, a Hall of Fame–bound manager. With a new skipper and a roster that had huge question marks, New York's future was quite uncertain.

ROUGH FOR RIGNEY

Giants Finish Sixth in Manager's First Season

Bill Rigney was in a tough spot. Not only did he have the arduous task of replacing one of baseball's greatest managers, he didn't have nearly enough tools to put together a winning ball club. Outfielder Monte Irvin was lost to the Cubs in the Rule 5 draft. Ageless wonder Sal Maglie was waived. And the Giants' one blockbuster move, a trade for the aging but still productive Jackie Robinson in December 1956, was squelched before the ink on the trade papers was dry. Robinson decided to retire from baseball rather than report to the Giants. Rigney didn't have a lot, but he still had Willie Mays.

Mays's talent would have made him a star on any team in the league, but the ragtag bunch that New York put on the field in 1956 made the "Say Hey Kid" look superhuman. Mays led the Giants in virtually every offensive category while stealing a league-high 40 bases. To say that New York's offense was stagnant would be a gross understatement. While Mays scored 101 runs, first baseman Bill White had the second most with 63. New York finished with a league-worst 540 runs scored. If they weren't going to score, at least the Giants had players who could field. Second baseman Red Schoendienst set a league record for his position with a .9934 fielding percentage.

Johnny Antonelli bounced back from a lackluster 1955 campaign to finish second in the NL in wins (20–13). However, his 20 wins were as many as the next three best New York pitchers' win totals combined.

It was a rough first year for Rigney, as New York finished at 67–87 and in sixth place. Ominously, the Giants finished last in the league in attendance at just 629,179, including five games below 2,000 during the season's final homestand. With a crummy team, a dilapidated ballpark, and loss of fan support, Giants owner Horace Stoneham pondered what to do next.

Johnny Antonelli was a true ace for the Giants, averaging 17 wins from 1954 to '59 and making the NL All-Star team five times. In 1956, he won as many games (20) as the next three winningest Giants pitchers combined. *MVP Books Collection*

1956

▶ 67-87   6th ◀

Highlights

May 2: The Giants use 25 players in a 6–5, 17-inning win over the Cubs.

July 8: New York wallops seven home runs in an 11–1 cakewalk over Pittsburgh, including two each by Willie Mays, Daryl Spencer, and Wes Westrum.

July 17: Milwaukee's Joe Adcock is so enraged after getting hit on the wrist by a Ruben Gomez pitch that he goes to the clubhouse and grabs an ice pick before being restrained.

July 31: After a dismal 8–20 July, the Giants are 34–58 and in last place.

December 13: New York trades pitcher Dick Littlefield and $30,000 to Brooklyn for Jackie Robinson, but the 37-year-old trailblazer decides to retire.

NOTES

The Giants' 540 runs are by far the fewest in the league.

Willie Mays clouts 36 home runs and pilfers a league-high 40 bases.

Rookie first baseman **Bill White** socks 22 home runs.

Midseason acquisition **Red Schoendienst** sets a league record with a .9934 fielding average for a second baseman.

Johnny Antonelli ranks second in the NL in wins (20–13) and third in ERA (2.86).

113

Highlights

May 1–5: The Giants' five-game losing streak drops them to sixth place, a spot they'll occupy for almost the entire rest of the season.

May 28: The National League approves the proposed relocation of the Giants and Dodgers to the West Coast.

August 19: Based on poor attendance at the aging Polo Grounds, the Giants board of directors votes 8–1 to move to California in 1958. The city of San Francisco promises a new stadium.

September 27: The owner of Seals Stadium in San Francisco agrees to rent the ballpark to the Giants until Candlestick Park is ready.

September 29: In their final game as a New York team, the Giants fall 9–1 to Pittsburgh in front of 11,606 at the Polo Grounds.

November 29: New York Mayor Robert Wagner forms a committee to find replacement teams for the Giants and Dodgers.

NOTES

Willie Mays bats .333-35-97 and leads the league in triples (20), steals (38), and slugging (.626).

Forty-year-old outfielder **Hank Sauer** blasts 26 home runs.

Ruben Gomez tops the staff in victories (15–13).

The Giants finish last in the NL in **attendance**, averaging 8,493 per game.

END OF AN ERA

Giants Play Their Last Season in New York

When 1957 began, few people thought it would be the Giants' last season in New York. Sure, there had been rumblings, but no one actually believed that a New York institution such as the Giants would really move 3,000 miles away. However, as the season dragged on, a migration to the West Coast seemed more and more likely.

There was still a season to play, and it wasn't pretty. The Giants couldn't crack the .500 barrier, and they were 10 games out of first by early June. Willie Mays continued to shine in the field, at the plate, and on the bases (35 home runs, 38 steals, and a .333 average), and 40-year-old Hank Sauer mashed 26 homers. However, New York had little production outside of those two sluggers, as Mays was the only Giants regular to hit above .260.

Pitcher Johnny Antonelli continued to be a mystery, as he followed his 20-win campaign in 1956 with a stinker. He finished at 12–18, while Ruben Gomez (15–13) proved to be the only Giants starter capable of a winning record.

However, not all of the Giants' struggles could be blamed on the players, as the team's uncertain future was being decided by executives. On May 28, the NL approved the proposed relocation of the Giants to the West Coast. With the wheels already in motion for a move to California, New York's floundering attendance didn't help the

Fans serenaded the Giants after their last-ever game at the Polo Grounds: "We hate to see you go/We hate to see you go/We hope to hell you never come back/We hate to see you go." *AP Images*

A Bad Breakup

When the New York Giants announced that they intended to uproot the franchise and move to California in 1957, there was outrage. Many sportswriters and onlookers seemed surprised with the fans' reaction. If people were so distraught to see the Giants go, why had they not come to the ballpark in recent years? As fans stormed the field following the Giants' last game at the Polo Grounds, Giants PR man Garry Schumacher remarked, "If all the people who will claim in the future that they were here today had actually turned out, we wouldn't have to be moving in the first place."

By 1957, the Giants had fallen from the pinnacle of New York baseball. The Dodgers had energized their fan base with the beloved and highly successful "Boys of Summer," and the Yankees had won five straight world titles through 1953. The Giants were a second-division ball club. Although some Giants fans felt betrayed, the team's exodus to California was extremely influential in expanding baseball's popularity. By moving cross-country with the Dodgers, the Giants were able to spread the game of baseball to the western half of the United States.

Giants fans would have preferred a better ballpark and a better team in New York.

Movers load the Giants' equipment and memorabilia out of the Polo Grounds on November 7, 1957. *New York Daily News Archive/Getty Images*

Giants' case for staying in Manhattan. New York again finished with the lowest mark in the NL, as only 653,923 passed through the gates at the Polo Grounds.

Then, on August 19, it all became official. Citing poor attendance and the potential financial windfall that came with relocating to California, the Giants' board of directors voted almost unanimously to uproot the franchise for a move to San Francisco. With their fate sealed, the Giants' game against Pittsburgh on September 29 would be the last the Giants would play as the home team at the Polo Grounds. On a dreary New York afternoon, the Pirates stomped the Giants 9–1. A Dusty Rhodes sacrifice fly in the first inning proved to be the last run scored by the New York Giants.

When the game was finished, many of the 11,606 fans rushed the field. Some wanted souvenirs; others wanted blood. While seats were ripped out and bases were unearthed, the more rowdy members of the crowd were calling for Giants owner Horace Stoneham's head. "We want Stoneham, with a rope around his neck!" read one sign. Mrs. John McGraw, the widow of the famed New York manager, was among the last to leave the stadium that her husband had made famous. "This would have broken John's heart," she said.

The move was unpopular. The Giants had been a fixture in New York since 1883, and now they were gone. A new chapter in the franchise's history was set to begin in the City by the Bay.

The final Giants team from New York, shown on the 1957 Topps card. *MVP Books Collection*

THE 1950-1959 RECORD BOOK

Team Leaders

(*Italics* indicates NL leader)

Batting Average
1950: Eddie Stanky, .300
1951: Monte Irvin, .312
1952: Alvin Dark, .301
1953: Don Mueller, .333
1954: *Willie Mays, .345*
1955: Willie Mays, .319
1956: Willie Mays, .296
1957: Willie Mays, .333
1958: Willie Mays, .347
1959: Orlando Cepeda, .317

Home Runs
1950: Bobby Thomson, 25
1951: Bobby Thomson, 32
1952: Bobby Thomson, 24
1953: Bobby Thomson, 26
1954: Willie Mays, 41
1955: *Willie Mays, 51*
1956: Willie Mays, 36
1957: Willie Mays, 35
1958: Willie Mays, 29
1959: Willie Mays, 34

RBI
1950: Hank Thompson, 91
1951: *Monte Irvin, 121*
1952: Bobby Thomson, 108
1953: Bobby Thomson, 106
1954: Willie Mays, 110
1955: Willie Mays, 127
1956: Willie Mays, 84
1957: Willie Mays, 97
1958: Orlando Cepeda, 96
   Willie Mays, 96
1959: Orlando Cepeda, 105

Runs
1950: Eddie Stanky, 115
1951: Alvin Dark, 114
1952: Whitey Lockman, 99
1953: Alvin Dark, 126
1954: Willie Mays, 119
1955: Willie Mays, 123
1956: Willie Mays, 101
1957: Willie Mays, 112
1958: *Willie Mays, 121*
1959: Willie Mays, 125

Wins
1950: Larry Jansen, 19
1951: *Sal Maglie, 23*
   Larry Jansen, 23
1952: Sal Maglie, 18
1953: Ruben Gomez, 13
1954: Johnny Antonelli, 21
1955: Johnny Antonelli, 14
   Jim Hearn, 14
1956: Johnny Antonelli, 20
1957: Ruben Gomez, 15
1958: Johnny Antonelli, 16
1959: *Sam Jones, 21*

ERA
1950: *Sal Maglie, 2.71*
1951: Sal Maglie, 2.93
1952: *Hoyt Wilhelm, 2.43*
1953: Ruben Gomez, 3.40
1954: *Johnny Antonelli, 2.30*
1955: Johnny Antonelli, 3.33
1956: Johnny Antonelli, 2.86
1957: Curt Barclay, 3.44
1958: *Stu Miller, 2.47*
1959: *Sam Jones, 2.83*

Strikeouts
1950: Larry Jansen, 161
1951: Sal Maglie, 146
1952: Sal Maglie, 112
1953: Ruben Gomez, 113
1954: Johnny Antonelli, 152
1955: Johnny Antonelli, 143
1956: Johnny Antonelli, 145
1957: Johnny Antonelli, 114
1958: Johnny Antonelli, 143
1959: Sam Jones, 209

Monte Irvin
Slugging star of the New York Giants

DRINK
Coca-Cola
IN BOTTLES

Left: Monte Irvin was a Giants' slugging star and Coca-Cola pitchman in the early 1950s. *MVP Books Collection.* **Below:** It's the most cherished ticket in New York Giants history— the pass to the third playoff game in 1951. *MVP Books Collection*

NEW YORK GIANTS BASEBALL CLUB POLO GROUNDS
PLAY-OFF GAME
GAME NO.   LOWER BOX SEAT $3.00
            Est. Price $2.50-Tax Paid .50
PO-1   Right reserved to revoke license granted by
            this ticket by refunding purchase price
                        Horace C. Stoneham President

5E 5 BOX

NOT REDEEMABLE FOR CASH
See Other Side For Conditions
Play-off Game   GAME NO.
In the event of a postponement this coupon will admit same holder to the game in place thereof if detailed from RAIN CHECK. Not good herein. Not detached from RAIN CHECK.
PO-1

GAME NO.
N.Y. GIANTS Baseball Club POLO GROUNDS
Play-off Game   GAME NO.
PO-1
PLAY-OFF GAME

RAIN CHECK
SEC. 5E 5
BOX SEAT
LOWER BOX SEAT $3.00
BOX SEAT

Saves

1950: 3 tied with 3
1951: George Spencer, 6
1952: Hoyt Wilhelm, 11
1953: Hoyt Wilhelm, 15
1954: Marv Grissom, 19
1955: Marv Grissom, 8
1956: Hoyt Wilhelm, 8
1957: Marv Grissom, 14
1958: Marv Grissom, 10
1959: Stu Miller, 8

NL Awards

NL MVP Voting

1950: Eddie Stanky, 3rd
Sal Maglie, 10th
1951: Monte Irvin, 3rd
Maglie, 4th
Bobby Thomson, 8th
1952: Hoyt Wilhelm, 4th
1954: *Willie Mays, 1st*
Johnny Antonelli, 3rd
Alvin Dark, 5th
1955: Mays, 4th
1957: Mays, 4th
1958: Mays, 2nd
Cepeda, 9th
1959: Sam Jones, 5th
Mays, 6th

NL Rookies of the Year

1951: Willie Mays
1958: Orlando Cepeda
1959: Willie McCovey

Gold Glove Award Winners

1958: Willie Mays, OF
1959: Willie Mays, OF
Jackie Brandt, OF

NL All-Stars

(*Italics* indicates starter)
1950: Larry Jansen, P
Eddie Stanky, 2B
1951: *Alvin Dark, SS*
Jansen, P
Sal Maglie, P
1952: Dark, SS
Monte Irvin, OF
Whitey Lockman, 1B
Maglie, P
Bobby Thomson, 3B
Wes Westrum, C
1953: Hoyt Wilhelm, P
David Williams, 2B

1954: Johnny Antonelli, P
Dark, SS
Marv Grissom, P
Willie Mays, OF
Don Mueller, OF
1955: Mays, OF
Mueller, OF
1956: Antonelli, P
Mays, OF
1957: Antonelli, P
Mays, OF
1958: Antonelli, P
Mays, OF
Bob Schmidt, C
1959: Antonelli, P
Orlando Cepeda, 1B
Sam Jones, P
Mays, OF

GIANTS 1950–1959 All-Decade Team	
1B	ORLANDO CEPEDA
2B	EDDIE STANKY
SS	ALVIN DARK
3B	HANK THOMPSON
C	WES WESTRUM
OF	WILLIE MAYS
OF	DON MUELLER
OF	MONTE IRVIN
SP	JOHNNY ANTONELLI
SP	SAL MAGLIE
RP	HOYT WILHELM

Alvin Dark's wizardry at shortstop is hinted at on this 1956 Topps card. The "Swamp Fox" led NL shortstops in double plays three times. *MVP Books Collection*

1958–1969

BIG-TIME BRIDESMAIDS

With a new home on the West Coast, the Giants restock. Unfortunately, their winningest decade produces only one pennant along with five straight second-place finishes.

New York cried when the "Jints" left town, but San Francisco threw a parade. The Giants took up residence in Seals Stadium, the minor-league park where native son Joe DiMaggio first made a name for himself, until a permanent home could be built. The honeymoon was brief; San Franciscans wanted a team of their own, and they were slow to warm up to New York stars. "This is the damnedest town," wrote Hearst Newspapers' Frank Conniff while covering a visit to San Francisco by Soviet Premier Nikita Khrushchev. "They cheer Khrushchev and boo Willie Mays."

The City by the Bay soon had its own stars, players such as Orlando Cepeda and Willie McCovey, who came to the majors in 1958 and 1959 and won Rookie of the Year

awards. They were joined by pitchers Juan Marichal and Gaylord Perry, giving the Giants a roster with five Hall of Famers in their prime. The fans ultimately warmed to Mays, of course—what baseball lover wouldn't?—and exulted as the Giants became winners once again.

The ride wasn't smooth. In 1959, in a three-team pennant race, former Giant Herman Franks arrived in San Francisco and hatched a plan to steal opponents' signs. Pitcher Al Worthington, recently "born again" after attending a Billy Graham rally, threatened to quit the team, and the plot fizzled. The Giants finished in third. "You couldn't believe the morale on our team," shortstop Darryl Spencer said. "The bottom fell out."

The Giants did win a pennant in fabulous fashion in 1962. With their rivalry with the Dodgers now transplanted to the West Coast, the Giants caught Los Angeles on the final day of the season, forcing another three-game playoff. As in 1951, it came down to Game Three on October 3—11 years to the day after Bobby Thomson's blast—and the Dodgers again blew a ninth-inning lead. Once again, the Giants faced the Yankees in the World Series, and they nearly beat them this time. It all came down to McCovey in the ninth inning of Game Seven, with Matty Alou at third, Mays at second, and the Giants down 1–0. McCovey scorched a line drive, but right to second baseman Bobby Richardson. "I still say Richardson was playing me out of position," McCovey said 45 years later. "Normally they had a shift toward first, but he was playing me more toward second. Ninety-eight times out of a hundred, I hit a ball like that and I run for mayor and win."

The Giants fell to third place the next year and fourth in 1964 (although only three games behind the pennant-winning Cardinals) before embarking on the most frustrating run yet. For the next five seasons, the Giants finished in second place, twice coming within two games of the pennant. In those days before divisional play, they never once tasted the postseason. "We were never able to get that one guy we needed down the stretch like teams do now to get over the hump," McCovey said. "Somehow Horace [Stoneham] wouldn't do that. He thought we had enough to win."

If Stoneham did make a move, it usually backfired. Matty Alou in 1965 was sent to Pittsburgh, where he won a batting title. Unable to play both McCovey and Cepeda every day—neither first baseman had much aptitude for the outfield—the Giants sent the "Baby Bull" to St. Louis for Ray Sadecki in 1966. While Sadecki proved ineffective, Cepeda won the MVP Award, leading the Cardinals to the World Series.

Marichal won more games in the 1960s than any other pitcher, but he took home no Cy Young Awards while Sandy Koufax and Don Drysdale led Los Angeles to three pennants and two championships. Mays was his usual stellar self, peaking with the 1965 MVP Award, while Mike McCormick earned Cy Young honors in 1967. As the decade closed, the Giants' aging stars tried to muster one more run. And it looked like they might do it: McCovey turned in a great season in 1968 and improved on that with the 1969 MVP Award, and Perry blossomed into a star, with four straight years of double-digit victories and sub-3.00 ERAs. But their finishes in 1968 and '69 were like the three previous: second place.

Opposite page: San Franciscans say hello to Willie Mays and the rest of the Giants during a welcoming parade on April 14, 1958, the day before Opening Day. *Richard Meek/Sports Illustrated/Getty Images*
Above: The two Willies, shown together on this 1967 Topps card, combined to hit 812 doubles, 184 triples, and 1,115 homers as Giants and made the team contenders throughout the 1960s. *MVP Books Collection*

1958

▶ **80-74   3rd** ◀

Highlights

April 15: On Opening Day, Ruben Gomez of the San Francisco Giants shuts out the Los Angeles Dodgers 8–0 in front of an over-capacity crowd of 23,448 at Seals Stadium.

April 18: In their home opener, the Dodgers top the Giants 6–5 at the Los Angeles Coliseum in front of an NL-record 78,682 fans.

May 5: The Giants rally for nine runs in the bottom of the ninth but fall short of Pittsburgh, losing 11–10.

May 13: Willie Mays goes 5-for-5 with two homers and two triples in a 16–9 win over LA.

July 20: The Giants win their sixth straight to improve to 50–39 and a tie for first place.

August 10: After a brutal 21-game road trip, San Francisco is in third place, seven games out.

NOTES

Willie Mays is the NL MVP runner-up after batting .347-29-96 and pacing the league in runs (121) and steals (31).

Rookie of the Year **Orlando Cepeda** bashes .312-25-96 and leads the circuit in doubles (38).

Johnny Antonelli goes 16–13 to lead the staff in wins.

The Giants are fourth in the NL in **attendance** at 1,272,625.

BASEBALL BY THE BAY

The San Francisco Giants Settle In at Seals Stadium

In 1958, after 75 years in New York, the Giants helped lead the charge in baseball's expansion to the West Coast. Due to floundering attendance and the promise of an economic windfall by relocating to California, Giants owner Horace Stoneham moved the team 3,000 miles away from the Polo Grounds to their new home in San Francisco.

Joining the Giants in Major League Baseball's first expedition west of the Mississippi River were their former New York rivals, the Brooklyn Dodgers. The freshly named Los Angeles Dodgers were the first team to take on the Giants in their new temporary home, Seals Stadium. After the announcement that the Giants were coming to San Francisco, the Pacific Coast League powerhouse San Francisco Seals packed their bags for Vancouver. As the Giants waited for their own ballpark to be built at Candlestick Point, they called the 23,500-seat stadium on Bryant Street home.

On April 15, 1958, San Francisco hosted the rival Dodgers on Opening Day. Even Willie Mays, after so many years in New York, embraced the excitement that was in the air. "It's like the World Series," he told reporters. The Giants dominated their new Golden State rivals, knocking out pitcher Don Drysdale in the fourth inning and cruising to an 8–0 victory. In the fifth, first baseman Orlando Cepeda, a 20-year-old rookie from Puerto Rico, blasted a home run off Dodgers reliever Don Bessent. "Baby Bull" would drive in 96 runs on the season en route to the NL Rookie of the Year Award.

In addition to the surprising rise of Cepeda, San Francisco was graced with another superb season from center fielder Willie Mays. In addition to his fifth

A capacity crowd of 23,448 packed Seals Stadium to see the Giants whitewash the Dodgers on Opening Day on April 15, 1958.
Jon Brenneis/Time & Life Images/Getty Images

"Baby Bull"

Growing up in Puerto Rico, Orlando Cepeda didn't have much. His family bounced from slum to slum, usually living in houses without telephone service or a refrigerator. Cepeda had few possessions, but what he did have was as valuable as any dial tone or icebox in the underdeveloped town of Ponce: the ability to absolutely crush a baseball.

As a 20-year-old in 1958, Cepeda put on a yearlong power display. The Giants first baseman smashed .312 with 25 home runs, 96 RBI, and a league-high 38 doubles, earning unanimous NL Rookie of the Year honors. The Giants' new San Francisco fan base adored their "Baby Bull," naming him the "Most Valuable Giant" in a poll conducted by the *San Francisco Examiner*. The team rewarded its emerging superstar with a $9,500 contract, which he used to help buy his mother a house in California, where the telephone and refrigerator worked just fine.

In his seven full seasons with San Francisco, Cepeda drove in at least 96 runs every year while batting over .300 six times and earning six NL All-Star berths. In 1961, he erupted for 46 homers and 142 RBI—both league highs—and finished runner-up for the league MVP Award. In May 1966, after an injury-plagued season, he was traded to St. Louis for pitcher Ray Sadecki.

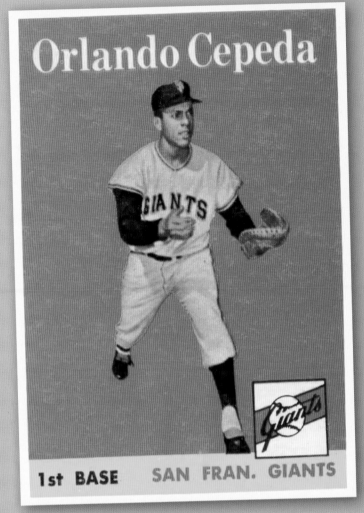

Orlando Cepeda was the NL Rookie of the Year in 1958 and an All-Star in each of his next six seasons with the Giants. *MVP Books Collection*

consecutive All-Star appearance, Mays earned his second straight Gold Glove Award while leading the Giants with a .347 average, 29 home runs, and 31 stolen bases. Even though Mays was brilliant in 1958, Cepeda overshadowed him. Many San Francisco fans considered Mays as being New York's star, while the "Baby Bull" was viewed as a ballplayer that they could claim as their own.

Regardless of their fans' preferences, the Giants had an established superstar in Mays and an emerging one in Cepeda and found themselves on top of the National League standings near the end of July. Unfortunately, the Giants' California honeymoon would not last. Because they were "stuck" on the West Coast in the early days of air travel, the Giants played extremely long homestands followed by arduous road trips that would last nearly three weeks. One of them lasted from July 23 through August 10, during which they fell to seven games out of first place.

San Francisco finished the season with a respectable 80–74 record, good enough for third in the National League. With two of the best hitters in baseball, an excited fan base, and the promise of a brand-new stadium on the horizon, the future looked bright by the Bay.

Highlights

June 12: Giants pitcher Mike McCormick tosses a rain-shortened, five-inning no-hitter over Philadelphia.

June 30: SF's Sam Jones throws a one-hit shutout over LA. An eighth-inning bobbled grounder to shortstop was ruled a hit.

August 13: The Giants lose 20–9 at Chicago in a game that takes three hours and 50 minutes.

September 17: After a 13–6 rout of Milwaukee, San Francisco has a two-game lead over LA in the NL with eight games to go.

September 19–20: The Dodgers sweep three games in San Francisco to move ahead by one game.

September 22–23: The Cubs beat the Giants twice on walk-off homers.

September 27: After losing a doubleheader at St. Louis on the season's last day, the Giants finish three games behind LA.

NOTES

Orlando Cepeda (.317-27-105) and Willie Mays (.313-34-104, NL-best 27 steals) are the heart of the lineup.

First baseman **Willie McCovey** bashes .354-13-38 in 52 games to win the NL Rookie of the Year Award.

Spring training acquisition **Sam Jones** leads the NL in wins (21–15) and ERA (2.83). **Johnny Antonelli** isn't far behind at 19–10, 3.10.

COVETING MCCOVEY

Slugging First Baseman Wins Rookie of the Year Award

The Giants' second season in San Francisco saw the team in a battle for first all season long. From Opening Day until the last weekend of September, the Giants, Dodgers, and Milwaukee Braves were in a three-way tug-of-war for the top spot in the NL. San Francisco gained an edge on its rivals on July 30, when a powerful left-handed first baseman from Alabama donned a Giants jersey for the first time.

Willie McCovey had been destroying pitching in Triple-A Phoenix to the tune of 29 home runs, 92 RBI, and a .372 average. It didn't take the 6-foot-4 slugger long to adjust to the major leagues. In fact, it didn't take a single game. In his debut against the Phillies, McCovey went 4–4 in a 7–2 Giants victory. Two of his four hits were triples— and this after playing all 18 innings of a doubleheader the previous day for Phoenix.

McCovey was unanimously named NL Rookie of the Year after playing in only 52 games. Regardless of sample size, McCovey's .354 average, 13 home runs, and 38 RBI were mightily impressive.

San Francisco's other first baseman (and outfielder), Orlando Cepeda, wasn't bad either. Cepeda (.317, 27 homers, and 105 RBI) and Willie Mays (.313, 34 homers, 104 RBI) were the heart of a very strong Giants lineup. San Francisco's 167 home runs were second in the NL. Trading for 33-year-old "Toothpick" Sam Jones during spring training proved to be the team's smartest move, as Jones wound up as the Giants' ace, leading the NL in wins (21–15) and ERA.

Riding high, the Giants were two games up on Los Angeles with only eight games left to play. Then suddenly, San Francisco collapsed. The Giants dropped seven of their last eight, including a sweep by the Dodgers and back-to-back losses to Chicago. In first place just 10 days earlier, San Francisco finished at 83–71, four games behind their new West Coast rival.

Willie McCovey won his 1959 NL Rookie of the Year Award unanimously despite playing less than one third of a season. *MVP Books Collection*

Loading Up

Add Juan Marichal to the List of Giants Stars

At the start of the 1960 campaign, the Giants were blessed with two of the best young players in all of baseball. In Orlando Cepeda and Willie McCovey, the Giants had the two most recent NL Rookie of the Year winners—not to mention perennial superstar Willie Mays. As the 1960s began, San Francisco welcomed two more franchise-altering pieces. One was their new stadium, Candlestick Park, and the other was a high-kicking 22-year-old veteran of the Dominican Air Force.

Like Cepeda and McCovey, Juan Marichal dominated in the minor leagues before being called up to the big show. His first opponent, on July 19, 1960, was Philadelphia, and he did not disappoint. In one of the most memorable major league debuts in baseball history, Marichal threw a one-hit shutout in a 2–0 San Francisco victory. The "Dominican Dandy" struck out 12 Phillies and did not allow a runner to reach base until the seventh inning. Marichal's encore was a four-hit performance against the Pirates just four days later.

Marichal made just 11 starts, but his 6–2 record and 2.66 ERA served notice that he would be a staff ace for years to come. Another youngster, 21-year-old Mike McCormick, went 15–12, while Sam Jones led the Giants in wins with 18. At the plate, Mays continued to be the story. The center fielder rapped .319 with 29 home runs, 103 RBI, and a league-leading 190 hits. McCovey regressed from his breakout year, hitting just .238 with 13 home runs, but Cepeda excelled. The left fielder was second on the team in home runs (24), RBI (96), and average (.297).

After replacing manager Bill Rigney with Tom Sheehan in June, the Giants began to falter. San Francisco went 12–19 in August and lost 25 one-run games. They finished at 79–75 and in fifth place, but no one doubted that good times lay ahead.

"Toothpick" Sam Jones won 39 games in 1959–1960, third most in the National League behind Warren Spahn and Lew Burdette. Here he looks for the sign during his complete-game, shutout win over the Philadelphia Phillies on May 24, 1960. *John G. Zimmerman/Sports Illustrated/Getty Images*

Highlights

April 12: In front of 42,269 fans, the Giants defeat St. Louis 3–1 on Opening Day in their first game at Candlestick Park.

May 11: Sam Jones and Jack Sanford throw consecutive two-hit, 1–0 shutouts against Philadelphia.

May 13–15: Shutouts over LA by Mike McCormick and Johnny Antonelli put the Giants at 19–8.

May 26: Jack Sanford's 9–0 whitewash of Philly gets first-place San Francisco to 24–12.

June 18: The 33–25 Giants replace manager Bill Rigney with 66-year-old Tom Sheehan.

July 16: A 1–7 stretch drops the Giants to 40–40. They will stay in fifth place every day for the remainder of the season.

July 19: Juan Marichal fires a one-hit shutout over the Phillies in his MLB debut.

September 15: Willie Mays legs out three triples against Philadelphia.

October 31: The Giants acquire Alvin Dark to be their manager.

NOTES

Willie Mays raps .319-29-103 and leads the league in hits (190).

Sam Jones finishes at 18–14, while **Mike McCormick** goes 15–12 with a 2.70 ERA.

The Giants finish second in the NL in attendance at 1,795,356.

Giants Blow in to Candlestick

The creation of Candlestick Park was anything but easy. As a key factor in the Giants migrating west, San Francisco Mayor George Christopher promised Giants owner Horace Stoneham a shiny, new 40,000-seat stadium. It would cost the San Francisco taxpayers $5 million (a third of the cost of the stadium), but Christopher was going to get his team. After the city bought more than 40 acres of the land needed for the project from construction tycoon Charles Harney, groundbreaking began in August 1958. The Giants opened play in Candlestick Park on April 12, 1960.

Candlestick was considered the first modern baseball stadium, as it was the first to be built entirely of reinforced concrete. One thing that technology couldn't fix was the savage force of Mother Nature. Due to the ballpark's close proximity to the San Francisco Bay, frigid winds whipped off the water and caused the mild Northern California temperature to drop 15 to 20 degrees in the evenings. Catching fly balls in the outfield became notoriously difficult at Candlestick, and the grass sometimes became so wet that the water soaked through the players' shoes. The gusts of wind were so strong that during the 1961 All-Star Game, Giants pitcher Stu Miller was blown off balance by a particularly strong blast. He was charged with a balk.

The inaugural game at Candlestick Park welcomed a sellout crowd of 42,269 to watch Sam Jones pitch a three-hitter in a 3–1 Giants victory over the Cardinals. Vice President Richard Nixon threw out the first pitch, and former Giant Leon "Daddy Wags" Wagner christened the new ballpark by hitting Candlestick's first home run.

The Giants were Candlestick's lone occupants until 1971, when the San Francisco 49ers moved to "The Stick" and the stadium's capacity was expanded to around 60,000. Football was the most successful sport played inside Candlestick; the Giants didn't win a World Series during their time there, while the 49ers became the most successful football team of the 1980s, winning four Super Bowls in the decade. In addition to being a crucial part of sports history, Candlestick hosted the Beatles' final full concert there on August 29, 1966. As hard as it is to fathom, the Fab Four could fill only 25,000 of the 42,000 seats, with tickets ranging from $4.50 to $6.50.

The Giants played at "The Stick" for 40 years before moving to Pacific Bell Park in 2000. The 49ers lasted all the way to 2013, as they prepared to move to new Levi's Stadium in Santa Clara, California, the following summer.

Candlestick Park featured natural grass in the 1960s, AstroTurf from 1970 to '78, and grass again beginning in 1979. *Hy Peskin/Sports Illustrated/Getty Images*

WESTWARD BOUND

Giants Go on Japanese Tour Prior to Season

After putting an end to a rather disappointing 1960 season, the Giants quickly regrouped and traveled across the Pacific to spread the message of baseball in Japan. The team had a quick two-day stop in Hawaii for two games against the Hawaiian All-Stars before beginning their 16-game exhibition series in The Land of the Rising Sun. The Giants went 11–4–1 during their month-long stay, and Willie Mays was given a farewell gift for his spectacular play. A group of Japanese tour commissioners awarded the "Say Hey Kid" with a Japanese automobile.

Back in the States, Mays stayed hot. On April 30, he became the ninth player in major league history to belt four home runs in a game. His eight RBI helped the Giants coast to a 14-4 win at Milwaukee. Mays could have had a chance for a fifth, but third baseman Jim Davenport made the final out in the top of the ninth inning with Willie in the on-deck circle.

Mays put on another long ball display later in the season, hitting three home runs against Philadelphia on June 29. However, even with these historic power surges, Mays wasn't even the best hitter on the Giants in 1961. Orlando Cepeda, splitting time between first base and the outfield, had the best year of his career. Cepeda led the league in home runs (46) and RBI (142) while hitting .311, good enough to finish second in NL MVP voting. Mays was a pretty good second banana, amassing 40 home runs, 123 RBI, and a .308 average. Unfortunately for the Giants, no other hitter in the lineup stood out. Only Davenport (65) had more than 52 RBI, and no player besides Mays and Cepeda hit more than 18 dingers.

Stu Miller led all SF pitchers with 14 wins, even though he didn't start a single game. The Giants finished at 85–69, eight games behind the first-place Reds.

Stu Miller's super-slow curveball was more effective at windy Candlestick, where he went 12–1 with a 2.35 ERA in 1961—all in relief. *Baseball Hall of Fame Museum and Library*

Highlights

April 30: Willie Mays becomes the ninth MLB player to swat four home runs in a game. He drives in eight runs, and the Giants belt eight homers overall, in a 14–4 win at Milwaukee.

May 28: A sweep of the Cubs puts San Francisco at 25–13, with a 2½ game lead in the NL.

June 3: The Giants tumble out of first place for good after a 1–6 stretch.

July 4: Orlando Cepeda goes 5-for-5 with eight RBI in a 19–3 romp at Chicago. In the second game of the doubleheader, Mays belts his 300th home run.

July 11: Strong winds mar the MLB All-Star Game at Candlestick Park. The NL wins 5–4 in 10 innings.

August 23: In the ninth inning of a 14–0 drubbing of Cincinnati, the Giants clout five home runs and score 12 runs.

NOTES

Orlando Cepeda is the NL MVP runner-up after leading the league with 46 homers and 142 RBI.

Willie Mays smashes .308-40-123 with a league-best 129 runs scored.

Full-time reliever **Stu Miller** (14–5) leads the staff in wins and posts a 2.66 ERA.

1962

▶ **103-62   1st** ◀

Highlights

May 4: A 10-game winning streak puts San Francisco at 19–5.

September 11: Jack Sanford shuts out Pittsburgh for his 16th straight victory.

September 30: The Giants win and the Dodgers lose, meaning both teams finish at 101–61.

October 1–3: The Giants take two out of three in their playoff against LA. Billy Pierce fires a shutout in the first game, and San Francisco scores four in the top of the ninth of the finale to win 6–4.

October 5: After New York wins the opener, Jack Sanford shuts out the Yankees 2–0 in Game Two of the World Series.

October 15: The Giants take Game Six 5–2 to tie the Series.

October 16: Trailing the Yankees 1–0 in the bottom of the ninth of Game Seven, Willie McCovey lines out to second baseman Bobby Richardson with runners on second and third.

NOTES

Willie Mays (.304-49-141) wins the NL homer crown, while **Orlando Cepeda** bats .306-35-114.

The formidable rotation includes **Jack Sanford** (24–7), **Billy O'Dell** (19–14), **Juan Marichal** (18–6), and **Billy Pierce** (16–6).

OH, SO CLOSE . . .

Season Comes Down to the Last Swing of Game Seven

In 1962, 162 games weren't enough. The Giants, who were four games back of the first-place Dodgers with seven games remaining, scratched and clawed their way to a tie with LA on the last day of the season, when a Willie Mays homer in the bottom of the eighth helped San Francisco beat Houston 2–1.

Led by the masterful pitching of Jack Sanford (24–7) and the power-hitting duo of Orlando Cepeda and Mays, San Francisco racked up 101 wins in the regular season, the most by a Giants team since 1913. Nevertheless, their 101–61 record was no better than the Dodgers'.

Game One of a special three-game playoff series saw the Giants dominate Los Angeles behind a three-hit shutout by Billy Pierce at Candlestick Park. The 8–0 victory was Pierce's 12th straight win at home. The next day, the two teams traveled down the coast for Game Two in Los Angeles. The Dodgers prevailed 8–7 in the ninth on a sacrifice fly by Ron Fairly that scored speedster Maury Willis. At four hours and 18 minutes, it was the longest nine-inning game in National League history.

After 164 grueling games, the NL pennant would be decided in game 165. The Giants' late-season climb that made the playoffs necessary seemed to be for naught, as

The Giants mob pitcher Billy Pierce after the pennant-clinching victory over the Dodgers in their third playoff game. *AP Images*

KSFO presents

"THE GIANTS WIN THE PENNANT"

HI-LITES OF THE 1962 BASEBALL SEASON

Fantasy GB-1962
HIGH FIDELITY

From Left to Right:

Back Row: JIM DAVENPORT, WILLIE MAYS, BOB BOLIN, HARVEY KUENN, MANUAL MOTA and BOB NIEMAH.
Third Row: DON LARSEN, ED BAILEY, TOM HALLER, JUAN MARICHAL, FELIPE ALOU, WILLIE McCOVEY, MIKE McCORMICK.
Second Row: EDDIE LOGAN, JIM DUFFALO, WHITEY LOCKMAN, LARRY JANSEN, AL DARK, WES WESTRUM, JACK SANFORD, ORLANDO CEPEDA, DOC BOWMAN.
Front Row: STU MILLER, BILL PIERCE, ERNIE BOWMAN, CHUCK HILLER, ERNIE RODDICK, MATTY ALOU, JOSE PAGAN, BILLY O'DELL, JOE PIGNATANO.

RUSS HODGES

LON SIMMONS

The radio voices of the Giants, Russ Hodges and Lon Simmons, narrate the team's remarkable pennant-winning season on this record. *MVP Books Collection*

San Francisco fell behind 4–2 in the top of the ninth inning. However, a Mays RBI single, a Cepeda sacrifice fly, and a Jim Davenport bases-loaded walk spurred a Giants rally that pushed them in front 6–4. Billy Pierce, finishing what he started in Game One, held off the Dodgers in the ninth.

The Giants were going to the World Series with what many fans considered to be the best team in franchise history. San Francisco fielded a ball club with five future Hall of Famers: Mays, Cepeda, outfielder Willie McCovey, and pitchers Juan Marichal and Gaylord Perry. Mays and Cepeda combined for 84 home runs, and four pitchers on the Giants' staff teamed for 77 wins. However, their World Series opponent was no slouch, either. The New York Yankees finished the season with a 96–66 record, thanks largely to AL MVP Mickey Mantle.

The teams split the first two games of the Series at Candlestick Park. The Yankees won Game One behind the bats of Roger Maris and Clete Boyer. Sanford took the mound in Game Two and stifled New York's powerful offense, allowing only three hits in a complete-game, 2–0 shutout. After a sloppy 3–2 loss in New York in Game Three, in which they made three errors, the Giants were able to regroup and even the Series. With the bases loaded and the game tied at 2–2 in the seventh, Giants second baseman Chuck Hiller belted a grand slam, the first by a National League player in World Series history. The blow secured a 7–3 San Francisco victory.

After the Yankees won Game Five 5–3, San Francisco staved off elimination with a 5–2 triumph in Game Six. Game Seven took place on October 16, one day after the White House learned that the Soviets had placed ballistic weapons on Cuban soil. A different kind of tension developed during a Jack Sanford-Ralph Terry pitching duel at The Stick. Through eight innings, New York led 1–0, with the only run scoring on a double-play grounder in the fifth.

In the bottom of the ninth, the Giants had a chance to win it. A Matty Alou bunt single and a Mays double put runners at second and third with two outs. Terry chose to pitch to McCovey, who scorched a ball that appeared to be going over second baseman Bobby Richardson's head . . . before it smacked the webbing of his glove. McCovey would later say it was the hardest ball he had ever struck.

In a *Peanuts* cartoon after the Series, Charlie Brown wailed, "Why couldn't McCovey have hit the ball just three feet higher?"

Right: Program to the 1962 World Series, which pitted old-time rivals now on opposite coasts. *MVP Books Collection.* **Left:** This Topps cards commemorates the grand slam that Chuck Hiller (center) cracked in Game Four of the 1962 World Series. It was the first slam ever by a National Leaguer in a World Series. *MVP Books Collection*

SAN FRANCISCO

GIANTS

1962 WORLD SERIES

NEW YORK

YANKEES

WORLD SERIES GAME #4

HILLER BLASTS GRAND SLAMMER

The "Dominican Dandy"

Hailing from the small farming village of Laguna Verde in the Dominican Republic, Juan Marichal burst onto the major league scene in 1960. Although he was a polished 22-year-old pitcher when he made his big-league debut, the hardships he had experienced in Laguna Verde would contribute to his focus and determination. He would become one of baseball's greatest pitchers, posting a sterling record of 243–142 with a 2.89 ERA.

Marichal's childhood home was often without electricity, and Juan worked alongside his other family members on their farm in an effort to make ends meet. His parents urged him to get an education, seeing it as an opportunity to escape the arduous life that he had grown up living. But for Juan, it was always baseball. "My mother used to say that you could not make money playing baseball," Marichal said, "but I was going to show her that I could." In 1956, he left high school after being recruited to play for the United Fruit Company team. A year later, he signed with the Giants.

With a windup that saw his leg go almost completely vertical, Marichal stood out the minute he put on his uniform. One of the first native Dominicans to play in the majors, Marichal dominated the Philadelphia Phillies in his big-league debut, taking a no-hitter into the eighth inning. The "Dominican Dandy" ended up with a one-hit, 12-strikeout shutout.

Just like his iconic leg kick, the expectations for Marichal were sky-high. Besides his searing fastball, he packed a late-breaking slider and a screwball that ate up left-handers. "This guy is a natural," Giants great Carl Hubbell said. "He's got ideas about what he wants to do and does it. He amazes me."

Although he did not receive any votes for the Cy Young Award until 1970, Marichal was one of the most dominant pitchers of the '60s. In addition to winning more games in the decade than any other major league pitcher with 191 (27 more than anyone else), Juan had four consecutive 20-win seasons and six 20-victory campaigns in the decade. Marichal led the league in wins twice—25 in 1963 and 26 in 1968—and had the lowest ERA of his career in 1969 with a league-leading 2.10 figure.

Marichal was at his best when he was playing against the game's greats. In his 10 All-Star Game appearances, he posted a record of 2–0 with a 0.50 ERA. He was named the MVP of the 1965 game—a rarity for a pitcher.

Always the pitching backbone for the strong Giants teams of the 1960s, Marichal retired in 1975 after brief stints with the Red Sox and Dodgers. The Giants retired his No. 27 jersey in 1975, and in 1983 he became the first Latino pitcher inducted into the Baseball Hall of Fame. A statue of Marichal was unveiled outside AT&T Park in 2005, immortalizing the unique windup of one of baseball's greats.

Left: The first great Dominican pitcher in the Major Leagues, Marichal served as his country's Minister of Sports beginning in 1996. *MVP Books Collection.* **Opposite page:** Marichal derived his power from his distinctive high leg kick. *Focus on Sport/Getty Images*

1963

▶ 88-74   3rd ◀

Highlights

May 11: Dodgers ace Sandy Koufax no-hits the first-place Giants in Los Angeles.

May 24: Juan Marichal defeats Sandy Koufax and the Dodgers 7–1 to extend SF's NL lead to two games.

June 15: Marichal throws the first Giants no-hitter since 1929, blanking the Houston Colt .45's 1–0 at Candlestick. He becomes the first Latin American pitcher to author a no-hitter.

June 24: A 4–3 win over St. Louis allows San Francisco to enjoy first place for the last time.

July 2: Willie Mays homers in the bottom of the 16th to defeat Milwaukee 1–0. Remarkably, pitchers Marichal and Warren Spahn go the distance.

September 22: In a blowout win over the Mets, three Alou brothers share the Giants outfield: Matty, Felipe, and Jesus.

NOTES

Juan Marichal ties for the NL lead in wins (25–8) and ranks fourth in ERA (2.41) and strikeouts (248).

Willie McCovey shares the NL home run title (44) and knocks in 102 runs.

Willie Mays (.314-38-103) and **Orlando Cepeda** (.316-34-97) help power the league's second-best attack.

ONE FOR THE AGES

Marichal and Spahn Face Off in Epic Pitcher's Duel

It began as just another game in early July. But it turned into a duel, and it finished as a classic.

On July 2, Giants pitcher Juan Marichal took the mound against Milwaukee's Warren Spahn. Marichal had pitched a no-hitter against Houston just four starts earlier and was on his way to logging 18 complete games. Spahn, age 42, would win 23 games that season and 363 for his career. The two legends battled all through the brisk San Francisco night. Willie Mays finally sent the crowd home with a walk-off home run off Spahn in the bottom of the 16th. The complete-game win pushed Marichal's win streak to nine, and he was on his way to a league-leading 25 triumphs. Unsurprisingly, he also led the league in innings pitched, with 321⅓.

Marichal had the NL's second best offense to thank. In addition to being named the All-Star Game's MVP, Willie Mays smacked .314 with 38 home runs and 103 RBI. Orlando Cepeda was comparably productive, batting .316 with 34 homers and 97 driven in. The third big weapon in SF's powerful arsenal was Willie McCovey. "Big Mac" earned himself a share of the NL home run title with 44 as he drove in 102 runs.

In addition to Marichal and their three-headed offensive monster, Jack Sanford was second on the Giants in wins with 16, and Felipe Alou compiled 82 RBI. If only the Giants could have gotten as much production out of the other two Alous. Benchwarmers for most of the year, Matty and Jesus Alou started in the outfield alongside their brother during a blowout win against the Mets on September 22.

Although they finished with a non-losing record in every month except June (14–15), the Giants couldn't break into the pennant race. San Francisco finished the season at 88–74, 11 games behind the Dodgers, who would sweep the Yankees in the World Series.

Dominican-born brothers Jesus, Matty, and Felipe Alou (left to right) made history on September 22, 1963, becoming the first brotherly trio to man the outfield at the same time. *Baseball Hall of Fame Museum and Library*

COMING TO AMERICA

Giants Sign MLB's First Japanese Players

Prior to the 1961 season, the Giants took a trip to Japan to play against some of that country's best players and help plant the seed of baseball among the Japanese people. In 1961, the Giants' good faith was returned. With the signings of pitcher Masanori Murakami, infielder Tatsuhico Tanaka, and catcher Hiroshi Takahashi, San Francisco became the first MLB team to explore the Japanese market.

Highlights

February 23: The Giants become the first MLB team to explore Japanese talent, as they sign pitcher Masanori Murakami, infielder Tatsuhico Tanaka, and catcher Hiroshi Takahashi.

April 14: San Francisco opens the season with five home runs in an 8–4 win over Milwaukee at Candlestick.

May 31: In the second game of a doubleheader, the Giants defeat the Mets in New York 8–6 in a 23-inning marathon that lasts 7 hours and 23 minutes.

July 10: Jesus Alou goes 6-for-6 in a 10–3 win over the Cubs.

July 21: After hovering around first place all year, the Giants fall out of the top spot for good after a 2–1 loss to the Cubs.

September 1: SF's Murakami becomes the first Japanese-born player to play in the majors.

October 4: The Giants fire manager Alvin Dark and replace him with Herman Franks.

From 1958 to '64 with the Giants, Orlando Cepeda averaged .309-32-107 per season. He fell just shy of those numbers in '64, his last full season with the team. *Focus on Sport/Getty Images*

Murakami posted a 1.80 ERA in his nine games with the Giants in 1964, although he would play just one more season in the major leagues. Tanaka and Takahashi never played a game in the majors. Although professional baseball would become huge in Japan, it would be decades before Japanese stars would make a big impact in the U.S. Hideo Nomo, Ichiro Suzuki, and Hideki Matsui would lead the charge.

When they were not improving relations with the Japanese, the Giants were usually winning. Many of San Francisco's victories in 1964 were somehow tied to Willie Mays. In helping the Giants to a 90–72 record, Mays led the league with 47 home runs and paced San Francisco in nearly every offensive category. Cepeda was able to pass Mays in batting average, as "Baby Bull" belted .304 while tallying 31 home runs and 97 RBI. Willie McCovey had an uncharacteristically somber year, as he hit only .220 and drove in just 54 runs.

Marichal was nearly as good as the year before, winning 21 games while leading all Giants starters with a 2.48 ERA. However, other than Gaylord Perry (12–11, 2.75), Marichal didn't get much help. He and Perry were the only pitchers who threw more than 100 innings and posted a winning record. The Giants hovered around first place until the dog days of July. After relinquishing their hold on first on July 21, the team began to slide.

Besides their World Series season of 1962, the Giants' 90 wins were the most for the franchise in a decade. It wasn't enough in '64, as they finished in fourth place, three games behind the first-place Cardinals and two behind the second-place Phillies and Reds.

NOTES

Willie Mays leads the NL in home runs (47) and slugging (.607) while driving in 111 runs.

Orlando Cepeda continues his heavy production (.304-31-97).

Juan Marichal (21–8, 2.48) is the king of the hill for San Francisco.

Highlights

July 17: Juan Marichal blanks the Houston Astros for his fourth shutout in his last five starts.

July 19: The Giants sign 44-year-old pitcher Warren Spahn, winner (so far) of 360 games.

August 22: Marichal hits Dodgers catcher John Roseboro with a bat, which will incur him an eight-day suspension.

August 29: Willie Mays sets an NL record for homers in a month (17).

September 4–16: A torrid 14-game winning streak launches the Giants from third place to first, with a 4½-game lead.

September 13: In the Houston Astrodome, Mays clouts his 500th career home run off Don Nottebart in a 5–1 Giants victory.

September 17–October 3: While San Francisco follows its winning streak with an 8–8 record to close the season, the Dodgers finish 15–1 to steal the pennant.

NOTES

Willie Mays earns the NL MVP Award after bashing .317 with a league-high (and Giants-record) 52 home runs.

Willie McCovey belts 39 homers, while third baseman **Jim Ray Hart** raps .299-23-96.

Juan Marichal goes 22–13 with a 2.13 ERA and a league-best 10 shutouts.

TWO GAMES SHY

Rookie Linzy, MVP Mays Just Aren't Enough

A few years earlier, it had seemed as if the Giants were snapping up all the good young talent that baseball had to offer. After boasting back-to-back NL Rookie of the Year winners in 1958 (Orlando Cepeda) and 1959 (Willie McCovey), the Giants struck gold again in 1960 with Juan Marichal. In 1965, the Giants appeared to have another young phenom in reliever Frank Linzy. The right-hander out of Oklahoma State appeared in 57 games, recorded nine wins and 21 saves, and posted a microscopic 1.43 ERA. The 24-year-old fireman (as the closer was called in those days) was named the *Sporting News* NL Rookie of the Year.

While Linzy was a welcome surprise, the real story in 1965 was the play of Willie Mays. Mays had been outstanding throughout his years in San Francisco, but this year was something special. On the way to his second NL MVP Award, Mays stroked .317, drove in 112 runs, and clobbered a Giants-record 52 home runs. Mays finished the season with a flurry, blasting 17 homers in August (breaking the National League record for bombs in a month) to keep San Francisco in the thick of the pennant race. It was a season full of milestones for Mays, as he belted his 500th career home run on September 13.

On the back of Mays's torrid hitting, the Giants rattled off a 14-game winning streak in the first half of September to catapult themselves from third place to a 4½-game lead. The pitching of Juan Marichal (22–13 and a league-best 10 shutouts) and the slugging of Willie McCovey (39 home runs) had the Giants poised to claim their second pennant in four years. While San Francisco limped to the finish by winning eight of their last 16 games, the Dodgers went 15–1 (including 13 in a row) to take the pennant by two games. San Francisco finished the season at 95–67.

After belting just two home runs in July 1965, Willie Mays clouted a record-smashing 17 in August and 11 in September/October to finish with 52 for the season. *MVP Books Collection*

Rivaling in California

They say to keep your friends close and your enemies closer. No two entities embody that statement more than the Los Angeles Dodgers and San Francisco Giants. After sharing the same city and playing in the same league for 68 years in New York, the two teams headed west together in 1958. For a while, they were the only MLB teams west of the Rocky Mountains. They often began and ended the season with series against each other, and in one year they battled each other in a special three-game playoff.

In 1962, the Giants and Dodgers both finished with 101 wins and were forced to undergo a three-game series to determine who would go to the World Series. After splitting the first two games, the Giants took the floor out from under the Dodgers in Game Three by scoring four runs in the top of the ninth to take the pennant. It remains the only time that LA and San Francisco have faced each other in a postseason series.

Unfortunately, in a rivalry so intense, tempers can flair and things can turn ugly. In one of the most vicious on-field acts of violence, Juan Marichal took his bat and clocked Dodgers catcher John Roseboro on the head in 1965. He did so after Roseboro had nicked his ear while throwing the ball back to the pitcher. The act was completely out of character for the low-key, gentlemanly Marichal, and he would immediately regret it. However, Roseboro sued Marichal, and sportswriters would not vote the "Dominican Dandy" into the Hall of Fame until 1983, two years after he was eligible.

In 1981, Dodgers outfielder Reggie Smith jumped into the stands and attacked Giants fan Michael Dooley after Dooley had whipped a plastic souvenir batting helmet at him. Smith told

reporters afterward: "He said to me . . . 'If I break your neck, you guys may lose the pennant race., . . . He whizzed the thing at me and I went after him."

Most unfortunate of all, Giants fan Bryan Stow was nearly beaten to death by Dodgers fans in 2011. The former paramedic suffered brain damage that would prevent him, years later, from bathing and dressing by himself.

These acts of aggression mar one of the best rivalries in all of sports. Through 2013, the Giants trailed the all-time series 479–503 since the teams moved to California in 1958.

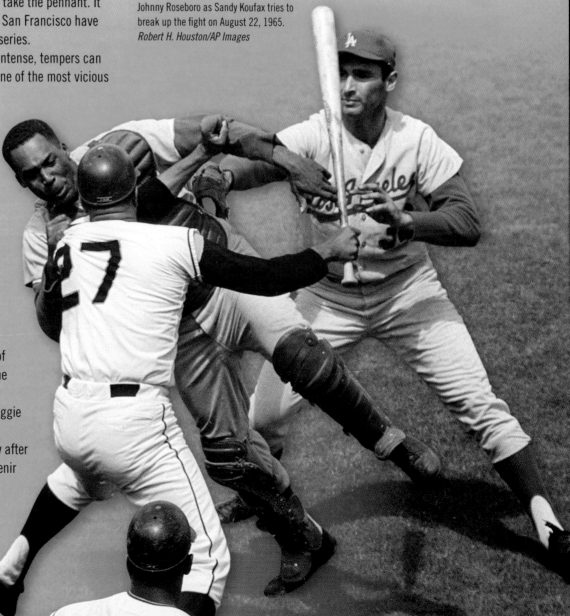

Juan Marichal assaults Dodgers catcher Johnny Roseboro as Sandy Koufax tries to break up the fight on August 22, 1965.
Robert H. Houston/AP Images

1966

Highlights

May 4: Against LA, Willie Mays blasts his 512th home run to break Mel Ott's Giants and NL record.

May 7: San Francisco sets a modern NL record by scoring 13 runs in an inning (the third) in a 15–2 win at St. Louis.

May 8: The Giants trade hometown hero Orlando Cepeda to St. Louis for pitcher Ray Sadecki.

May 13: The Giants' 5–4 win against the Mets—on Jim Davenport's homer in the 17th inning—is their 12th straight win and puts them at 22–7.

May 26: Juan Marichal improves to 9–0 after tossing a 14-inning, 1–0 shutout over Philadelphia.

August 17: Against St. Louis, Willie Mays hammers his 535th home run to move past Jimmie Foxx and into second place on MLB's all-time list.

September 2: A 6–5, 12-inning loss at St. Louis drops San Francisco out of first place for good.

NOTES

Willie Mays (37), **Willie McCovey** (36), and **Jim Ray Hart** (33) are among the NL's top six in home runs.

Juan Marichal (25–6, 2.23 ERA) and **Gaylord Perry** (21–8, 2.99) are a dominant one-two punch.

COMING UP SHORT

Despite Three Big-Time Sluggers, the Giants Finish Second

After winning 90 games in 1964 and 95 a year later, San Francisco was poised for a pennant run in 1966. The Giants were good enough to win the whole thing, but once again they would be frustrated by their old nemesis. Darn those Dodgers.

The Giants were loaded with stars all around the diamond. Willie Mays again spearheaded the attack, leading the team with 37 home runs and 103 RBI. Third baseman Jim Ray Hart and first baseman Willie McCovey were nearly as productive. McCovey belted 36 home runs and drove in 96 runs while leading the Giants with a .295 average. Hart had a career year with 33 homers and 93 RBI.

Together Mays, McCovey, and Hart were among the NL's top six in home runs, although Mays was still the star of the show. On August 17, he became the second greatest home run hitter in baseball history after belting his 535th long ball, surpassing Jimmie Foxx.

San Francisco was just as strong on the mound. In Juan Marichal (25–6, 2.23 ERA) and Gaylord Perry (21–8, 2.99 ERA), the Giants had a one-two punch as good as any in the NL. Frank Linzy digressed from the year before (7–11), but he still put up a strong 2.96 ERA to go with 16 saves, and Lindy McDaniel gave the Giants 10 wins out of the bullpen.

However, the biggest story for the Giants was not what they had but what they lacked. Outside of their three big hitters, San Francisco's offense was dormant. Catcher Tom Haller was the only other player to have more than 40 RBI, as the Giants offense hovered around the league average in runs scored. San Francisco fell out of first place for good on September 2 and finished in second place for the second straight year with a 93–68 record. The Dodgers won 95 games . . . but at least they lost the World Series.

Gaylord Perry, who won 21 games in 1966 and 314 in his career, had a full arsenal of pitches, including his notorious greaseball. *MVP Books Collection*

FULL OF ACES

Giants Boast the Best Pitching Staff in the NL

The Giants have a long history of great pitchers. There was Christy Mathewson in the early 20th century, who sat batters down with his easy delivery and razor-sharp accuracy. Carl Hubbell and his screwball followed. Sal Maglie was next, defying old age in the 1950s, and then Juan Marichal emerged as a dominant force. But despite the preponderance of aces, the Giants rarely had a complete staff that could truly complement all of their record-setting offensive clubs. Yet in 1967, the Giants' strength shifted away from the batter's box as San Francisco had, undisputedly, the best pitching staff in baseball.

Led by NL Cy Young Award winner Mike McCormick, the Giants topped the NL in ERA (2.92), complete games (64), and fewest hits allowed (1,283). McCormick became the first Giant to capture the Cy Young, after winning a league-high 22 games and posting a 2.85 ERA. San Francisco's four-man starting rotation was the envy of pitching coaches everywhere. In addition to McCormick, Gaylord Perry, Ray Sadecki, and Marichal all won at least 12 games and posted ERAs under 3.00. Fireman Frank Linzy was lights-out, as he locked up 17 saves to go with his 1.51 ERA.

Unfortunately, in the year in which San Francisco had great pitching, the offense was lackluster. Jim Ray Hart, not Willie Mays, led the Giants' attack, popping 29 home runs and knocking in 99 runs. Willie McCovey belted 31 round-trippers. The 36-year-old Mays had a down year, hitting only 22 long balls and driving in just 70 runners. No Giant hit above .292, and San Francisco's team average was below the league average at .245.

Still, the Giants were good enough on the mound to stay within sight of first-place St. Louis until mid-July. Although the Cardinals would run away with the pennant, winning the NL by 10½ games over San Francisco, the Giants' 91–71 performance was their fourth straight 90-win season.

Third baseman Jim Ray Hart, who averaged 28 homers a year from 1964 to '68, tallied career-highs with 99 RBI and 98 runs in 1967. *Focus on Sport/Getty Images*

Highlights

June 13: Willie Mays socks a 10th-inning grand slam at Houston for a 6–2 Giants win. It's his 19th extra-inning home run.

July 11: Juan Marichal is the NL's starting pitcher in the All-Star Game.

September 1: Gaylord Perry (16 innings) and Frank Linzy (five frames) pitch a 21-inning, 1–0 shutout at Cincinnati. Dick Groat walks with the bases loaded.

September 1–8: A seven-game winning streak launches San Francisco into second place for good; St. Louis will run away with the pennant.

September 7: The Giants use 25 players in a 15-inning, 3–2 win over the Astros.

September 22: Tom Haller smacks a walk-off homer in the ninth to defeat Pittsburgh 1–0.

September 27: Jim Davenport sets an NL record with his 64th straight errorless game at third base.

NOTES

Jim Ray Hart (.289-29-99) and **Willie McCovey** (.276-31-91) swing the heaviest lumber.

Mike McCormick wins the NL Cy Young Award after leading the league in wins (22–10) and posting a 2.85 ERA.

Giants starters **Gaylord Perry, Juan Marichal**, and **Ray Sadecki** have ERAs that are better than McCormick's.

Highlights

February 13: In a rare trade with the rival Dodgers, the Giants swap Tom Haller and Frank Kasheta for Ron Hunt and Nate Oliver.

May 22–June 1: The Giants enjoy an 11-day stretch in first place.

June 1–July 26: During this stretch, the Giants go 23–28 and drop from first place to 16 games back of the rampaging Cardinals.

June 8: The Mets-Giants game at Candlestick is postponed due to the assassination of U.S. Senator Robert F. Kennedy.

June 25: Giants rookie Bobby Bonds belts a grand slam in his first major league game.

July 20: San Francisco tops Houston 1–0 after Willie Mays scores from first on a single.

August 19: San Francisco wins 1–0 on a Ron Hunt single in a 17-inning marathon at New York.

September 17: Gaylord Perry no-hits the pennant-bound Cardinals 1–0 at Candlestick Park, walking two and fanning nine. Ron Hunt's first-inning homer is the only run of the game.

October 11: The Giants replace manager Herman Franks with Clyde King.

NOTES

Willie McCovey leads the NL in homers (36), RBI (105), and slugging (.545).

Willie Mays and **Jim Ray Hart** pop 23 homers apiece.

Juan Marichal (26–9, 2.43) leads the NL in wins, with four more than league MVP **Bob Gibson** (22–9, 1.12).

ROAD WARRIOR

Pitcher Juan Marichal Dominates in Enemy Parks

The name was Bonds. Bobby Bonds. He may not have been as dapper as the martini-guzzling super spy with whom he almost shares a name, but Giants outfielder Bobby Bonds certainly knew how to make an entrance. In his major league debut, Bonds cracked a grand slam off Dodgers pitcher John Purdin in a 9–0 San Francisco victory. It was the first grand slam by a player in his first major league game since 1898. The 22-year-old rookie would play in 81 games for San Francisco in 1968, belt eight more home runs, and steal 16 bases. He would eventually produce many more of each with the Giants—as would his famous son.

Juan Marichal is congratulated by catcher Jack Hiatt after defeating the New York Mets in mid-June. It wasn't his strongest outing (5 runs and 16 hits allowed), but it was good enough to earn him one of his league-best 26 wins and 30 complete games that year. *Herb Scharfman/Sports Illustrated/Getty Images*

While Bonds was announcing himself as a player to keep an eye on, Juan Marichal was staking his claim as the best pitcher in baseball. The "Dominican Dandy" had a season in which every statistic was more impressive than the last. Marichal led the league in wins (26) and posted a 2.43 ERA. He started a total of 38 games, completed a league-leading 30 of them, and won a mind-blowing 18 games on the road. Twenty-three of his starts happened to be in enemy parks, and he went 18-4 with a 2.27 ERA.

Marichal's offensive counterpart was Willie McCovey. "Big Mac" took the reins from an aging Willie Mays to lead the league in home runs (36), RBI (105), and slugging (.545). While he was getting up there in years, the 37-year-old Mays still put up 23 home runs, 79 RBI, and 12 stolen bases. Jim Ray Hart continued to provide plenty of pop, tallying 23 home runs and 78 RBI in the "Year of the Pitcher."

The Giants were red-hot in August, going 21–10, but they couldn't match the pace of the St. Louis Cardinals and NL MVP Bob Gibson (1.12 ERA). The Giants would finish the season at 88–74, in second place in the 10-team league for the fourth straight year.

ALWAYS A BRIDESMAID

Giants Finish Second for Fifth Straight Season

In 1969, change was sweeping baseball. With the addition of four expansion teams—the San Diego Padres and Montreal Expos in the NL and the Kansas City Royals and Seattle Pilots in the AL—each of the two leagues were split into East and West divisions. This meant that each pennant would be decided by a five-game series between the winners of the two divisions. As the league adjusted to the new format, the Giants were dealing with one of the hardest changes of all: replacing the "Say Hey Kid."

It wasn't like Mays was being shoved out the door—he still played in 117 games and hit 13 home runs—but the Giants were quickly coming to grips with the fact that the 38-year-old center fielder was nearing the end of his career. Thankfully, the play of Willie McCovey and Bobby Bonds lightened the blow of No. 24's looming departure.

Taking advantage of the lowered pitcher's mound in 1969, McCovey led the league in home runs (45), RBI (126), OBP (.453), and slugging (.656), earning the NL MVP Award. His two-homer performance in the All-Star Game also earned him MVP kudos in the Midsummer Classic. Bonds, meanwhile, looked like the reincarnation of Mays. Bobby became the fourth player in baseball history to record at least 30 steals (45) and at least 30 homers (32) in the same season.

Juan Marichal was unaffected by the lowered mound, as he posted a 21–10 record while topping the NL in ERA (2.10) and shutouts (eight). Gaylord Perry provided a strong complement to the Dominican, as he went 19–14 and registered a 2.49 ERA. Still, the Giants couldn't break the second-place curse.

Even in the newly formed West Division, which included just six teams, they were unable to come up on top. The Giants had a winning record every year in the '60s, but they finished 1969 at 90–72, three games back of first-place Atlanta.

With Willie Mays by his side, Willie McCovey hoists the NL MVP Award that he earned for his 1969 performance. *Bruce Bennett/Hulton Archive/Getty Images*

Highlights

April 7: The season begins with the NL and AL teams separated into a total of four divisions. The Giants share the NL West Division with the Dodgers, Reds, Astros, Atlanta Braves, and the new San Diego Padres. The winners of each division will compete in League Championship Series.

April 25: SF catcher Jack Hiatt socks a 13th-inning grand slam and drives in seven runs in a 12–8 win over Houston.

May 4: The Giants ground into seven double plays in a 3–1, nine-inning loss to Houston.

August 21–29: A nine-game winning streak catapults San Francisco into first place.

September 12: Juan Marichal throws a one-hit, 1–0 shutout against Cincinnati.

September 30: The Braves win their 10th straight game to clinch the NL West.

NOTES

Willie McCovey cops the NL MVP Award after batting .320 with league highs in homers (45) and RBI (126).

Bobby Bonds becomes the fifth Major League player with 30 steals (45) and 30 homers (32).

Juan Marichal goes 21–10 with NL bests in ERA (2.10) and shutouts (eight).

THE 1960-1969 RECORD BOOK

Team Leaders

(*Italics* indicates NL leader)

Batting Average
1960: Willie Mays, .319
1961: Orlando Cepeda, .311
1962: Felipe Alou, .316
1963: Orlando Cepeda, .316
1964: Orlando Cepeda, .304
1965: Willie Mays, .317
1966: Willie McCovey, .295
1967: Jesus Alou, .292
1968: Willie McCovey, .293
1969: Willie McCovey, .320

Home Runs
1960: Willie Mays, 29
1961: *Orlando Cepeda, 46*
1962: *Willie Mays, 49*
1963: *Willie McCovey, 44*
1964: *Willie Mays, 47*
1965: *Willie Mays, 52*
1966: Willie Mays, 37
1967: Willie McCovey, 31
1968: *Willie McCovey, 36*
1969: *Willie McCovey, 45*

RBI
1960: Willie Mays, 103
1961: *Orlando Cepeda, 142*
1962: Willie Mays, 141
1963: Willie Mays, 103
1964: Willie Mays, 111
1965: Willie Mays, 112
1966: Willie Mays, 103
1967: Jim Ray Hart, 99
1968: *Willie McCovey, 105*
1969: *Willie McCovey, 126*

Runs
1960: Willie Mays, 107
1961: *Willie Mays, 129*

1962: Willie Mays, 130
1963: Willie Mays, 115
1964: Willie Mays, 121
1965: Willie Mays, 118
1966: Willie Mays, 99
1967: Jim Ray Hart, 98
1968: Willie Mays, 84
1969: *Bobby Bonds, 120*

Wins
1960: Sam Jones, 18
1961: Stu Miller, 14
1962: Jack Sanford, 24
1963: *Juan Marichal, 25*
1964: Juan Marichal, 21
1965: Juan Marichal, 22
1966: Juan Marichal, 25
1967: *Mike McCormick, 22*
1968: *Juan Marichal, 26*
1969: Juan Marichal, 21

ERA
1960: *Mike McCormick, 2.70*
1961: Mike McCormick, 3.20
1962: Juan Marichal, 3.36

1963: Juan Marichal, 2.41
1964: Juan Marichal, 2.48
1965: Juan Marichal, 2.13
1966: Juan Marichal, 2.23
1967: Gaylord Perry, 2.61
1968: Bobby Bolin, 1.99
1969: *Juan Marichal, 2.10*

Strikeouts
1960: Sam Jones, 190
1961: Mike McCormick, 163
1962: Billy O'Dell, 195
1963: Juan Marichal, 248
1964: Juan Marichal, 206
1965: Juan Marichal, 240
1966: Juan Marichal, 222
1967: Gaylord Perry, 230
1968: Juan Marichal, 218
1969: Gaylord Perry, 233

Saves
1960: Johnny Antonelli, 11
1961: *Stu Miller, 17*
1962: Stu Miller, 19
1963: Billy Pierce, 8

Left: Jim Davenport, profiled on this 1962 Topps card, was an All-Star and Gold Glove winner at third base that year. *MVP Books Collection.* Right: Juan Marichal was an All-Star every year from 1962 to 1969, and he won more than 20 games in a season six times during that stretch. *MVP Books Collection*

1964: Bob Shaw, 11
1965: Frank Linzy, 21
1966: Frank Linzy, 16
1967: Frank Linzy, 17
1968: Frank Linzy, 12
1969: Frank Linzy, 11

NL Awards

NL MVP Voting
1960: Willie Mays, 3rd
1961: Orlando Cepeda, 2nd
    Mays, 6th
1962: Mays, 2nd
    Jack Sanford, 7th
1963: Mays, 5th
1964: Mays, 6th
1965: *Mays, 1st*
    Juan Marichal, 9th
    Willie McCovey, 10th
1966: Mays, 3rd
    Marichal, 6th
1967: Mike McCormick, 6th
1968: McCovey, 3rd
    Marichal, 5th
1969: *McCovey, 1st*

NL Cy Young Award Winners
1967: Mike McCormick

NL Gold Glove Award Winners
1960: Willie Mays, OF
1961: Willie Mays, OF
1962: Jim Davenport, 3B
    Willie Mays, OF
1963: Willie Mays, OF
1964: Willie Mays, OF
1965: Willie Mays, OF
1966: Willie Mays, OF
1967: Willie Mays, OF
1968: Willie Mays, OF

NL All-Stars
(*Italics* indicates starter)
1960: Orlando Cepeda, OF
    Willie Mays, OF
    Mike McCormick, P
1961: Ed Bailey, C
    Cepeda, OF
    Mays, OF
    McCormick, P
    Stu Miller, P
1962: Felipe Alou, OF
    Cepeda, 1B
    Jim Davenport, 3B
    Juan Marichal, P
    Mays, OF
1963: *Ed Bailey, C*
    Cepeda, 1B
    Marichal, P
    Mays, OF
    Willie McCovey, OF

1964: *Cepeda, 1B*
    Marichal, P
    Mays, OF
1965: *Marichal, P*
    Mays, OF
1966: Tom Haller, C
    Jim Ray Hart, 3B
    Marichal, P
    Mays, OF
    McCovey, 1B
    Gaylord Perry, P
1967: Haller, C
    Marichal, P
    Mays, OF
1968: Marichal, P
    Mays, OF
    McCovey, 1B
1969: Marichal, P
    Mays, OF
    McCovey, 1B

GIANTS 1960–1969 All-Decade Team	
1B	WILLIE MCCOVEY
2B	RON HUNT
SS	JOSE PAGAN
3B	JIM RAY HART
C	TOM HALLER
OF	WILLIE MAYS
OF	ORLANDO CEPEDA
OF	FELIPE ALOU
SP	JUAN MARICHAL
SP	GAYLORD PERRY
RP	FRANK LINZY

A collage of Willie Mays artifacts. *Baseball Hall of Fame Museum and Library*

THE 1970s

A LONG STRUGGLE

One last blast of glory for Willie Mays and Willie McCovey gives way to a winter of discontent—or to be more literal, many sad, cold, windy evenings at Candlestick Park.

As Willie Mays approached his 40th birthday, time was running out on the Giants. Even though Bobby Bonds showed some potential as another five-tool star, the orange and black needed to make their push soon. Their successors in New York, the Mets, had pulled off a miracle in 1969, the year that divisional play was introduced. Perhaps the Giants could do the same on the West Coast?

A slow start in 1970 led to the firing of manager Clyde King after only 42 games. He was replaced by Charlie Fox, under whom the team went 67–53, but the recovery only carried them to third place. The following year, however, became known as the "Year of the Fox."

In 1971, the Giants led the West by as many as 10 games, and they held a seemingly comfortable eight-game cushion on September 5. However, they lost seven straight games and 11 out of 12 to let the Dodgers back into the race. Only by winning three of their last four (two wins for Juan Marichal, one for Gaylord Perry) did they win the West by one game. They went on to lose to the Pirates in the National League Championship Series, three games to one.

That was the beginning of the end. Perry was dealt to Cleveland for Sam McDowell; Perry went on to win a Cy Young Award and another 180 games over his Hall of Fame career. Mays was traded to the Mets in 1972, to finish his career in New York, and 1973 saw Marichal shipped to the Red Sox and McCovey to the Padres.

After trading away their stars (whose best years were far behind them), as well as young sluggers such as George Foster and Dave Kingman, whose biggest home run totals were yet to come, the Giants fell into a fog-bound funk. Cold, windy nights and losing teams kept fans away from Candlestick Park. The decade was marked by good-

Above: Willie Mays cracks his 3,000th hit on July 18, 1970, at home against Montreal. He finished his career with 3,283. *AP Images*. Right: In the middle of the decade, it looked like the Giants were headed to Toronto—until Bob Lurie saved the day. *MVP Books Collection*

field, no-hit shortstop Johnnie LeMaster getting razzed so much that he once showed up wearing a uniform with "Boo" emblazoned on the back.

The decade had its bright spots. Bobby Bonds did flash 30/30 form, swatting 39 homers and stealing 43 bases in 1973. (He, too, would be traded before the decade was out, to the Yankees for Bobby Murcer.) Gary Matthews won Rookie of the Year honors in 1973, giving the Giants—with Matthews, Bonds, and Garry Maddox—the fastest outfield in baseball. John "The Count" Montefusco won the league's top rookie honors in 1975, and he authored a no-hitter in 1976. Old New York Giants Wes Westrum and Bill Rigney took turns as manager, but neither brought many victories.

Things got so bad that Horace Stoneham was ready to sell the team he had inherited from his father, after more than 50 years of family ownership. A Canadian brewery was ready to move the Giants to Toronto in 1976, but in stepped loyal San Franciscan Bob Lurie, who saved the team.

Before the decade was out, the Giants showed signs of life. Joe Altobelli won the NL Manager of the Year Award after he guided the team to 89 wins and a third-place finish in 1978, and Lurie began assembling a front office and farm system designed to bring more lasting results. As they shivered under their blankets, fans dreamed of better days ahead.

1970

▸ **86-76** **3rd** ◂

Highlights

April 26: Willie McCovey and Dick Dietz swat grand slams in an 11–1 rout of the Montreal Expos.

May 23: After San Francisco blows an 8–0 lead and loses 17–16 in 15 innings to San Diego, Giants manager Clyde King is fired. He'll be replaced by Charlie Fox, the team's Triple-A manager.

July 8: Jim Ray Hart clouts a three-run homer and three-run triple in the fifth inning, and hits for the cycle, in a 13–0 pasting of the Braves.

July 12: After lingering around .500 since Opening Day, the Giants enter the All-Star break at 41–44.

July 18: Willie Mays rips his 3,000th hit off Montreal's Mike Wegener.

August 28: Juan Marichal beats the Pirates 5–1 for his 200th career victory.

September 19: Against San Diego, Gaylord Perry tosses his fourth straight shutout.

NOTES

Willie McCovey rips .289-39-126 with league highs in slugging (.612) and walks (137).

Catcher **Dick Dietz** hits .300-22-107, and **Willie Mays** belts 28 homers.

Bobby Bonds tallies 134 runs, 200 hits, 26 homers, and 48 steals.

Gaylord Perry leads the NL in wins (23-13) and shutouts (five).

NEW DECADE, SAME RESULT

Pennant Drought Continues for Frustrated Giants

As the Giants entered the 1970s, the team was at a crossroads. The Giants had recorded five straight second-place finishes and were looking for anything to help them avoid a sixth. On May 23, San Francisco management felt that current manager Clyde King was not the man who could get that done. After blowing an 8–0 lead to San Diego, King was fired and replaced by Charlie Fox, the team's Triple-A manager.

Fox, whose MLB career encompassed three games with the 1942 New York Giants, wasn't exactly the spark plug that the Giants were hoping for, going 30–30 in his first 60 games. Easing Fox's transition was Willie McCovey. "Big Mac" led the league in slugging (.612) and walks (137) while hitting .289 with 39 home runs and 126 RBI. Bobby Bonds had an outstanding all-around season, scoring 134 runs, amassing 200 hits, belting 26 home runs, and swiping 48 bases. Catcher Dick Dietz batted .300 and drove in 107 runs, while Willie Mays bounced back with 28 home runs.

Juan Marichal recorded his 200th victory on August 28 with a 5–1 defeat of the Pirates. Nevertheless, it was a down year for Marichal, who went 12–10 and recorded a 4.12 ERA, the highest of his career. Thankfully for the Giants, Gaylord Perry was able to pick Marichal up. The famous greaseballer led the league in wins (23–13) and shutouts (five), including four straight late in the season, and finished second in Cy Young Award balloting. However, Perry's magic didn't rub off on the rest of the team.

San Francisco entered the All-Star break at 41–44 and hovered around .500 for the rest of the year. The Giants avoided finishing in second for the sixth straight season, but it certainly wasn't the ending they had hoped for. San Francisco ended the year at 86–76 . . . in third place.

Though he averaged just .261-8-38 for his career, Dick Dietz enjoyed a hugely productive All-Star season in 1970. Here he crosses the plate after delivering a ninth-inning homer during the midsummer classic in Cincinnati to help rally the NL to victory. *AP Images*

"Big Mac" Attack

Alabama has been kind to the Giants. In 1951, 20-year-old Westfield native Willie Mays joined the New York Giants. Eight years later, a 6-foot-4, left-handed slugger from Mobile named Willie McCovey began his first of 19 seasons with San Francisco. You cannot talk about the team's success in the 1960s and '70s without mentioning "Big Mac."

McCovey started his career with a bang. As a rookie in 1959, he socked 13 home runs, drove in 38 runs, and batted .354, winning the NL Rookie of the Year Award despite playing just 52 games. Three years later, McCovey helped lead the Giants to the World Series against the New York Yankees. With the Giants trailing 1–0 in the bottom of the ninth of Game Seven with two outs and runners on second and third, Willie smashed a line drive at second baseman Bobby Richardson, ending the Series with a Yankees victory. It would be the closest McCovey ever got to winning a championship.

"Stretch" was one of the most intimidating hitters in the game. Pitcher Bob Gibson described him as "the scariest hitter in baseball," and Reds manager Sparky Anderson (who admittedly was prone to exaggeration) said, "If you pitch to him, he'll ruin baseball. He'd hit 80 home runs. There's no comparison between McCovey and anybody else in the league."

McCovey led the NL in home runs three times and was consistently a threat to launch the ball into the bleachers with his huge uppercut swing. His finest season came in 1969. That year, McCovey dominated NL pitching, leading the league in home runs (45), RBI (126), OBP (.453), and slugging (.656) en route to the NL MVP Award. From 1968 to 1970, McCovey was tops in the league in slugging and OPS. As with Barry Bonds a generation later, NL pitchers often preferred to walk McCovey rather than pitch to him. In 1970, he led the league in walks with 137.

Even though his body was ravaged by injuries—he topped 130 games in only eight of his 22 seasons—Willie's career numbers put him among the greatest hitters in baseball history. His 521 home runs place him 18th on the all-time list, which includes several players tainted by steroid scandals. In 1986, McCovey was elected to the Baseball Hall of Fame. In his honor, the inlet of San Francisco Bay beyond the right field fence of AT&T Park is nicknamed "McCovey Cove."

"When he belts a home run," Sparky Anderson said about McCovey, "he does it with such authority it seems like an act of God." McCovey's shrine stands outside of San Francisco's AT&T Park. *Shutterstock.com.*

McCovey ranks among the franchise's top five leaders in hits, doubles, home runs, RBI, walks, and games played, among other categories. *MVP Books Collection*

1971

▶ 90-72   1st ◀

Highlights

April 6–10: Willie Mays homers in the first four games of the season.

April 11–19: A nine-game winning streak puts San Francisco at 12–2 and in first place for good.

May 30: Mays scores his 1,950th run to break Stan Musial's NL record.

May 31: The Giants oust New York 2–1 in 11 innings to improve to 37–14. They lead the NL West by 10½ games.

September 30: On the last day of the season, the Giants win the division by one game over LA after Juan Marichal beats San Diego 5–1.

October 2: In Game One of the NL Championship Series, two-run homers in the fifth inning by Willie McCovey and Tito Fuentes key a 5–4 Giants win over Pittsburgh.

October 6: After 9–4 and 2–1 victories, the Pirates eliminate San Francisco in Game Four with a 9–5 triumph.

NOTES

Bobby Bonds drives the offense with 33 homers, 26 steals, 110 runs, and 102 RBI.

Juan Marichal (18–11) and **Gaylord Perry** (16–12) anchor the rotation.

HOT START, COOL FINISH

Giants Win First Division Title but Fall in NLCS

It didn't take long for San Francisco to claim its first NL West Division championship. Two years after the league expanded to two divisions, the Giants started out on fire in 1971 and rolled to a first-place finish.

Willie Mays set the tone for the Giants' season by hitting a home run in each of the team's first four games. After Mays's torrid streak subsided, San Francisco reeled off a nine-game winning streak that put them at 12–2. The Giants were never under .500 the entire season, and they remained in first place from April 12 on.

San Francisco's strong run to the division championship was fueled by a healthy blend of youth and veterans. Even with a knee injury that forced him to miss 57 games, Willie McCovey swatted 18 homers and knocked in 70 runs. McCovey's injuries forced Willie Mays to assume a part-time role as San Francisco's first baseman. Splitting time between first and his usual post in center field, Mays clubbed 18 home runs while drawing 112 walks.

Shortstop Chris Speier, who led all National League players with 33 errors in 1971, drops a pop-up during the opening game of the NLCS against Pittsburgh. *George Long/Sports Illustrated/Getty Images*

Dick Deitz continued to be a strong offensive presence from behind the plate, tallying 19 home runs and 72 RBI, both good enough for second on the team. Bobby Bonds erupted for 33 home runs, 102 runs, and 26 stolen bases. His outstanding play didn't stop in the batter's box, as he received his first career Gold Glove Award to go with his first All-Star selection and a fourth-place finish in the MVP voting.

Rookie Chris Speier led NL shortstops in errors but finished second in assists. He formed a slick double-play combination with Tito Fuentes. Manager Charlie Fox told Speier to take charge in the infield because, Speier recalled, "he said Willie McCovey didn't say too much and Tito Fuentes talked too much and you couldn't understand him." Fuentes would one day say that pitchers shouldn't be throwing at him because "I'm the father of five or six kids."

The pitching staff was led by Gaylord Perry's 2.76 ERA and Juan Marichal's 18 wins and four shutouts. Even with a roster that had no .300 hitters or 20-game winners, the Giants finished with a 90–72 record. Despite being in first since April, San Francisco felt the Dodgers' presence in late September. In the last game of the season, Marichal defeated the Padres in San Diego 5–1 to give his team the championship by one game.

Meeting the Giants in the NL Championship Series were the Pittsburgh Pirates, a team they had defeated nine times in 12 games during the regular season. In Game One in San Francisco, McCovey and Fuentes belted home runs and Gaylord Perry went the distance in a 5–4 Giants victory.

Pittsburgh won a 9–4 slugfest in Game Two and defeated Marichal 2–1 in Game Three at Three Rivers Stadium. The Pirates closed out the Series 9–5 in Game Four by breaking a 5–5 tie with four runs in the bottom of the sixth inning. Alas, the Giants' opening-game victory would be the only postseason win for the team between the years 1962 and 1987.

The 30/30 Man

As a high school athlete in California, Bobby Bonds scored six touchdowns in a football game and won the state championship in the long jump. Bonds parlayed that extraordinary athleticism into an All-Star career in the major leagues, including seven remarkable years with the Giants.

In his second year in the majors, in 1969, Bonds compiled 32 home runs and 45 stolen bases, becoming the fourth member of MLB's 30/30 club. By 1978, four years after he left the Giants, Bobby had compiled five 30/30 seasons, a feat that only his son, Barry, would ever match.

A three-time Gold Glove Award winner due to his tremendous range and powerful arm, Bonds batted .273 with San Francisco. Strikeouts were his only bugaboo. He led the National League in whiffs three times, and his 189 punchouts in 1970 set an MLB record that would last the century.

In 1973, Bonds came one home run shy of becoming the founding member of the 40/40. He would finish just short again in 1977, when his 37 home runs failed to meet his 41 stolen bases. Only four players have accomplished the 40–40 feat, including Bobby's famous son.

Bobby Bonds averaged 30 homers, 41 steals, 118 runs, and 86 RBI from 1969 to 1974. *MVP Books Collection*

1972

▶ **69-86   5th** ◀

Highlights

April 16: Young Giants slugger Dave Kingman hits for the cycle and drives in six runs against Houston.

April 18: Willie McCovey breaks his right arm in a collision against the Padres.

May 11: Batting .184, 41-year-old Willie Mays is traded to the Mets for minor league pitcher Charlie Williams and cash. Mays batted .304-646-1,859 and made 18 All-Star teams with the Giants.

May 16: With SF and Cincinnati tied 3–3, Giants pitcher Ron Bryant gives up the winning run during an intentional walk when Pete Rose hits the 3-0 pitch.

May 18: The Giants lose their seventh straight game to fall to 9–23. They are in last place, 11 games out.

August 29: After retiring the last 21 batters in his previous outing, Giants pitcher Jim Barr extends the streak to an MLB-record 41 in a 3–0 win over St. Louis.

NOTES

Dave Kingman leads SF in homers (29) and RBI (83) but bats just .225.

Bobby Bonds steals 44 bases and ranks second in the NL in runs (118).

The Giants finish last in the league in **attendance**, averaging 8,412 fans per game.

146

SAYING GOODBYE

After 21 Years, Giants Part With Willie Mays

In early January 1972, the San Francisco Giants and Lotte Orions of Japan announced the first international player trade in Major League Baseball history. In exchange for giving Frank Johnson an unconditional release so he could play for the Orions, Lotte released right-handed pitcher Toru Hamaura so that he could ink a contract with the Giants. The trade ended up having little impact, as neither player saw much time on the field. However, another Giants transaction would make headlines all across America.

The Giants decided that it was finally time to part with the "Say Hey Kid." With his age climbing and his numbers declining, The Giants ended their 21-year relationship with Willie Mays and traded him to the New York Mets. Mays had always wanted to return to New York, and the Mets were happy to oblige, sending pitcher Charlie Williams and cash in return for the aging superstar.

Dave Kingman, who was almost the antithesis of Mays, led San Francisco in home runs (29) and RBI (83). "King Kong" could hit the ball a mile, but his surly disposition, subpar glove work (first base and outfield), low batting averages, lack of foot speed, and penchant for strikeouts were a drain on the team. Yet this Giants club had little else to hang its hat on. Bobby Bonds cracked 26 homers and stole 44 bases, but an injury-wracked Willie McCovey played just 81 games and batted .213.

Dave Kingman's output in 1972—.225 average with 29 homers and 140 strikeouts in 135 games—would be typical of his 16-year career. *Baseball Hall of Fame Museum and Library*

Ron Bryant proved to be San Francisco's best pitcher, winning 14 games and posting a 2.90 ERA. Only Bryant and "Sudden" Sam McDowell—the former Indians ace who battled problems with the bottle—and would record double-digit wins for San Francisco.

It was a rough year for the Giants. They lost their franchise player to trade, their best hitter to injury, and a whole heap of games. San Francisco finished the year at 69–86, 26½ games behind an emerging juggernaut: the Cincinnati Reds.

JUST SHY OF IMMORTALITY

Bobby Bonds Nearly Achieves Historic Feat

I n 1973, Bobby Bonds fell one round-tripper short of becoming the first 40-40 player in Major League history. A slender and strong right fielder in the mold of his friend and mentor, Willie Mays, Bonds wreaked havoc on NL opponents in '73, finishing among the league's top five in home runs (39) and stolen bases (43). He also led the Giants in doubles (34), runs (131), and slugging (.530), and he earned MVP honors in the All-Star Game by blasting a home run and legging out a hustle double.

In addition to Bonds, the Giants fielded two other exciting young outfielders: Garry Maddox, 23, and Gary Matthews, 22. Maddox, a tremendous glove man with great range in center field, led the team with a .319 average while amassing 30 doubles and 76 RBI. Matthews cracked .300 and laced 10 triples. His performance earned him *Sporting News* NL Rookie of the Year honors.

On the mound, Ron Bryant led the way. After emerging the previous seasons, Bryant went 24–12 to lead the league in victories, and he finished third in Cy Young balloting behind Tom Seaver and relief ace Mike Marshall. The left-hander was the ace of a mediocre pitching staff that finished ninth in the NL in ERA at 3.79. San Francisco finished the year at 88–74, in third place.

Management made some moves at the beginning of the offseason that would send the Giants in a new direction in the forthcoming years. In a move that enraged many Giants fans, Willie McCovey was sent down the coast to San Diego for a solid starting pitcher named Mike Caldwell. Although McCovey had belted 29 home runs in 1973, he was 35 years old and had dealt with numerous injuries in recent years.

Later that winter, Juan Marichal was sold to the Red Sox. Though only 11–15 in 1973, Marichal had served as a mentor to the young and ailing San Francisco staff. As the 1974 season approached, there was a cloud of uncertainty surrounding the future of the Giants franchise.

Bobby Bonds (center) is greeted by Johnny Bench and Joe Morgan after Bonds' two-run homer gave the NL a 5–1 lead in the fifth inning of the All-Star Game. Bonds earned the game's MVP award. *AP Images*

▸ 88-74   3rd ◂

Highlights

April 12: In a 9–3 win over Houston, Willie McCovey blasts two home runs in the eight-run fourth inning.

April 18–June 16: San Francisco is in first place almost every day while accumulating a record of 40–26.

May 1: Trailing Pittsburgh 7–1 with two outs and a man on first in the bottom of the ninth, the Giants score seven runs to win 8–7. Chris Arnold's pinch grand slam and Bobby Bonds's three-run, game-ending double are the big blows.

June 16–26: A 2–8 stretch drops the Giants to 6½ games back, and they won't come close to catching the Reds.

October 25: San Francisco trades Willie McCovey and a minor leaguer to the Padres for pitcher Mike Caldwell.

December 7: Juan Marichal is sold to the Red Sox.

NOTES

Bobby Bonds amasses 39 homers, 43 steals, 96 RBI, and a league-best 131 runs.

Outfielder **Garry Maddox** leads the team in hitting at .319, while **Willie McCovey** skies 29 home runs.

Giants outfielder **Gary Matthews** (.300 average) wins the NL Rookie of the Year Award.

Lefty **Ron Bryant** leads the NL in wins (24–12).

Highlights

March 15: Giants ace Ron Bryant is injured in a swimming pool. He will go 3–15 in 1974, his last full season.

June: After a 27–25 start, the Giants go 7–20 in June. By month's end, they are 19½ games back.

June 19: Against St. Louis, San Francisco's Ed Goodson belts one over the fence but passes a teammate between first and second. He thus settles for a single.

June 21–23: Rubber-armed Dodgers reliever Mike Marshall logs wins against the Giants in three consecutive games.

September 3: In his first MLB game, Giants pitcher John Montefusco pitches nine innings of relief (yielding just one run) and belts a home run in a 9–5 victory over the Dodgers.

October 22: San Francisco trades Bobby Bonds to the Yankees for outfielder Bobby Murcer.

NOTES

Bobby Bonds leads the team in homers (21) and steals (41).

Catcher **Dave Rader** tops the clubs in batting (.291), while **Gary Matthews** is high in RBI (82).

Mike Caldwell leads the Giants in wins (14–5).

Attendance plummets to just 519,987, lowest in the league.

TAKING A DIP

Giants Ace Ron Bryant Hurts Himself in Pool Accident

Spring training is an important time for all major-leaguers. Many use it as a time to improve on their weaknesses. Most view it as a training period to adjust to the rigors of playing every day during the regular season. Others just want to stay healthy. That was where Ron Bryant fell short.

On a trip to Palm Springs in mid-March, Bryant took a midnight swim at the Giants' motel and tore a huge gash in his side as he whizzed down the pool's slide. The injury kept him out until the end of April, but he was never the same even after he returned. Bryant, who had led the NL in wins the previous year with 24, scraped together a 3–15 record in 1974. When asked about the injury, the 26-year-old apologized and said, "It was probably a dumb thing to do. I probably shouldn't have been in the pool."

The absence of an ace left a huge hole in the Giants' pitching staff. San Francisco ranked in the bottom four of the NL in ERA and strikeouts. Mike Caldwell emerged as the makeshift go-to guy, going 14–5 with a 2.95 ERA. Things weren't much better offensively, as no player hit above .300. Only two teams in the NL scored fewer runs than San Francisco's 634. Bobby Bonds popped 21 homers and drove in 71 runs, and Gary Matthews led the team with 82 RBI. In midseason, manager Charlie Fox was replaced by Wes Westrum, but the former Mets manager could do no better.

As the team's play began to decline, the fans showed their frustration at the box office. By the beginning of September, the Giants were 60–74 and 24½ games out of first place. Attendance at Candlestick Park was just 519,987, the lowest in the NL. In San Francisco's last two games of the season, a short series against San Diego, just 2,541 fans—in both games combined—spun through turnstiles. The Giants finished at 72–90 and in fifth place in the six-team NL West.

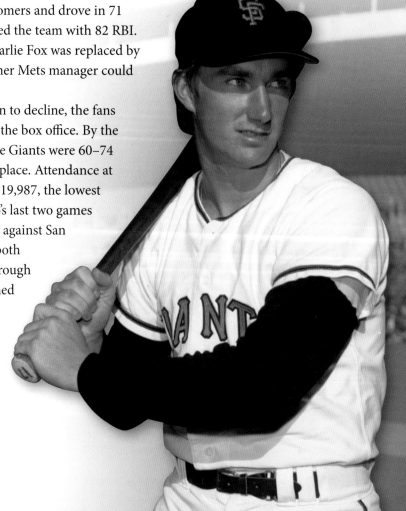

Though error-prone early in his career, shortstop Chris Speier became one of the slickest-fielding shortstops of the 1970s. *Baseball Hall of Fame Museum and Library*

A Fresh Start

Giants Make Multiple Offseason Moves

After an abysmal season that saw the Giants' attendance plummet to the worst in the league, management hit the reset button. Shortly after the 1974 season was over, San Francisco's most talented player, outfielder Bobby Bonds, was traded to the Yankees for outfielder Bobby Murcer. In February, heavy-hitting first baseman Dave Kingman was sold to the Mets for $150,000.

San Francisco thus traded or sold two of its biggest hitters from an already weak offensive ball club. As powerful as Kingman and Bonds's bats were, their exodus was actually a blessing. Although they put up good power numbers, the two sluggers were notorious free-swingers. Bonds had thrice led the league in strikeouts, and Kingman would top the circuit in that dubious distinction three times himself.

San Francisco's new and more conservative offense was effective in 1975, as the Giants finished in the top half of the league in batting average. However, it wasn't enough to vault them into the pennant race. Murcer, a former darling of Yankees fans, hit .298 and led the Giants with 91 RBI, while outfielder Von Joshua—acquired on waivers from the Dodgers—led the team in batting at .318. Second baseman Derrel Thomas paced the Giants with 99 runs scored.

John "The Count" Montefusco went 15–9 with a 2.88 ERA to earn NL Rookie of the Year honors. The brash right-hander guaranteed he would beat the Dodgers on July 4, 1975, and proceeded to deliver a 1–0 shutout victory. Pete Falcone (12–11) was the only other regular Giants starter to record a winning record.

Despite winning eight more games than in the previous season, the Giants still finished last in the NL in attendance (522,919) in the windy, often-chilly Candlestick Park. After parting with Bonds and Kingman, San Francisco had no marquee stars that could draw the attention of fans and sell tickets. That fall, former Giants player Bill Rigney came out of retirement to replace the fired Wes Westrum as manager. Rigney had managed the Giants before—*way* back in 1956 and 1957, during their final days in New York.

John Montefusco won 15 games as a rookie in 1975 and improved to 16 victories in 1976, but he left the game in 1986 with just 90 career wins to his credit.
Baseball Hall of Fame Museum and Library

Highlights

February 28: The Giants sell slugger Dave Kingman to the Mets for $150,000.

May 4: At Candlestick, Houston's Bob Watson scores what is calculated at the time as MLB's one millionth run.

May 25: The Giants win their seventh straight game to improve to 22–19, four games back. They will hover around .500 the entire season, spending most of the year in third place.

August 24: Giants pitcher Ed Halicki no-hits the Mets, although controversy arises over a possible infield hit that was ruled an error on the second baseman.

September 2: In his first Major League at-bat, Giants shortstop Johnnie LeMaster laces an inside-the-park home run.

November 20: The Giants fire manager Wes Westrum. Bill Rigney will come out of retirement to replace him.

NOTES

Bobby Murcer raps .298 and leads the Giants with 91 RBI.

Outfielder **Von Joshua** tops the team in batting at .318, while second baseman **Derrel Thomas** is tops with 99 runs.

John Montefusco (15–9, 2.88) wins the NL Rookie of the Year Award.

Despite an improved record, the Giants are last again in the NL in **attendance** (522,919).

1976

> **74-88   4th**

Highlights

January: Giants owner Horace Stoneham agrees to sell the team to a Toronto group for $13 million. The plan is for the Toronto Giants to begin play in 1976. With fans outraged, San Francisco Mayor George Moscone will work to prevent the deal.

March 4: Real estate magnate Bob Lurie leads a group that buys the Giants for $8 million. The team will remain in San Francisco.

May 23: A 4–19 skid puts San Francisco at 12–27, in last place, 13½ games out.

June 13: The Giants trade Willie Montanez and three others to Atlanta for slugger Darrell Evans and Marty Perez.

July 16: Bobby Murcer belts a walk-off homer in the ninth inning in a 1–0 win over Philadelphia.

September 2–18: The Giants get hot late, winning 14 out of 18 games.

September 29: John Montefusco no-hits the Braves, and walks just one batter, in a 9–0 victory. It's his league-best sixth shutout of the year.

NOTES

Bobby Murcer (.259-23-90) and Gary Matthews (.279-20-84) swing the mightiest bats.

John Montefusco (16–14, 2.84) and Jim Barr (15–12, 2.89) are the heart of the rotation.

THE TORONTO GIANTS?

Stoneham Nearly Sells the Team to Canadian Group

In 1976, San Francisco's biggest battle of the year occurred before the season even started. Ever since play began at the cold and windy Candlestick Park, attendance was an issue. Facing financial hardship, Giants owner Horace Stoneham agreed to sell the team for $13.25 million to a Toronto collective that consisted of Labatt Breweries of Canada, Vulcan Assets, and the Canadian Imperial Bank of Commerce.

The team was set to play the 1976 season at Exhibition Stadium as the Toronto Giants—before a group led by Bob Lurie intervened. Lurie was a Bay Area real estate mogul with a rich San Francisco heritage and a position on the Giants' Board of Directors. With the help of Arizona cattleman Bud Herseth, the two were able to put together a deal with Stoneham and purchase the team for $8 million.

The Giants' residence in San Francisco was now secure, but there were loads of questions up and down their roster. Gary Matthews (.279-20-84) and Bobby Murcer (.259-23-90) led a dormant Giants offense that sent no hitters to the All-Star Game for the first time in team history. Larry Herndon was a nice addition in the outfield, hitting .288 to become the fifth consecutive Giant to earn NL Rookie of the Year honors by *The Sporting News*.

On the mound, reigning *official* league Rookie of the Year John Montefusco continued to stake his claim as the San Francisco ace. The lone Giant at the All-Star Game, Montefusco won 16 games while posting a 2.84 ERA. The 26-year-old's finest moment came in his final start of the season. Montefusco threw a no-hitter against the Braves at Fulton County Stadium to record his league-best sixth shutout of the year.

Hailed as "the next Mickey Mantle," Oklahoma native Bobby Murcer earned four All-Star berths with the Yankees and another with the Giants in 1975. He plated 181 runs in two seasons with San Francisco. *Diamond Images/Getty Images*

Unfortunately, few Giants could match Montefusco's brilliance, as their 74–88 record gave San Francisco its fourth losing season in five years. After the season concluded, the Giants underwent another managerial change, as three-time International League Manager of the Year Joe Altobelli replaced Bill Rigney.

WILLIE'S BACK

But McCovey's Big Bat Can't Get Giants Over the Hump

After a three-year sabbatical down the California coast in San Diego and across the Bay in Oakland, Willie McCovey was back in San Francisco. Joe Altobelli's tenure as manager would begin with one of the best hitters in franchise history returning to his post at first base. McCovey was one of a handful of recognizable faces as Altobelli's team had only two returning starters in the Opening Day lineup. One of the new starters, Gary Thomasson, quickly made his presence felt, hitting a home run on the first pitch of the season opener.

The longtime bench player parlayed his Opening Day shot into a productive season. The 25-year-old hit 17 home runs, drove in 71 runs, and stole a team-high 16 bases. McCovey picked up right where he had left off, instantly becoming the Giants' best hitter by mashing 28 home runs and knocking in 86 runs, both tops on the team. The 39-year-old was named NL Comeback Player of the Year. As impressive as Thomasson and McCovey's performances were, the rest of the offense was underwhelming. Bill Madlock, acquired in a trade with the Chicago Cubs, was the only regular starter to hit above .280.

San Francisco's pitching staff was maligned by the decline of John Montefusco. "The Count," who had been the Giants' ace the previous two seasons, put up a 7–12 record and a 3.49 ERA as he struggled with arm problems. After leading the NL in shutouts the previous season, Montefusco's physical woes would prevent him from throwing another shutout for the rest of his career. Ed Halicki (16–12, 3.32 ERA) led San Francisco in strikeouts (168) and complete games (seven).

The Giants plodded along for much of the year, never rising above .500, and had their only winning month in August (15–14). They finished the season where they had spent most of the second half, in fourth place.

Gary Lavelle, whose 20 saves in 1977 were a career high, pitched in 647 games with the Giants—a still-standing franchise record. *Baseball Hall of Fame Museum and Library*

Highlights

January 6: Willie McCovey, age 39, signs with the Giants after three years with San Diego and Oakland.

February 11: The Giants trade Bobby Murcer, pitcher Steve Ontiveros, and a minor-leaguer to the Cubs for third baseman Bill Madlock (the NL batting champ in 1975 and 1976) and second baseman Rod Sperring.

April 7: San Francisco opens the season with a new manager, former minor league skipper Joe Altobelli. Giants leadoff hitter Gary Thomasson homers against Los Angeles on the first pitch of the game.

May 3: After losing their fifth game in a row, the Giants are 8–13, 10 games out. They will remain at least 10 out over the remainder of the season.

June 27: In a 10-run sixth inning of a 14–9 win over the Reds, McCovey belts two home runs, including a grand slam.

NOTES

Willie McCovey leads the team in home runs (28) and RBI (86).

Bill Madlock is the club's batting leader at .302.

Ed Halicki (16–12, 3.32) is the staff ace, while lefty **Gary Lavelle** saves 20 games.

151

1978

89-73   3rd

Highlights

March 15: The Giants trade seven players and cash to Oakland for 28-year-old pitcher Vida Blue, a three-time 20-game winner.

May 19: The Giants' 10–7 win at LA is their eighth consecutive victory. They improve to 23–12 and have a two-game lead in the NL West.

June 16: San Francisco wins its seventh straight and is now 39–21.

June 30: Willie McCovey slugs his 500th home run, victimizing Jamie Easterly of the Braves.

July 9: The Giants enter the All-Star break at 52–34, with a two-game lead in the division.

July 26: Against St. Louis, new hitting sensation Jack Clark sees his hitting streak stopped at 26 games.

August 16: The Giants fall out of first place for good after a 1–0 loss to Montreal.

NOTES

Outfielder **Jack Clark** emerges with a .306-25-98 season, while **Bill Madlock** raps a team-best .309.

Vida Blue is the new ace, going 18–10 with a 2.79 ERA.

The Giants draw 1,740,477 fans, more than one million more than the preceding year.

FEELING BLUE?

Not Giants Fans, as Vida Makes Team a Contender

After a stretch that saw San Francisco put up five losing seasons in six years, the Giants front office attempted to change the team's losing culture with two trades prior to the 1978 season. In one transaction, the team dealt Derrel Thomas, the first overall pick in the 1969 MLB draft, to the Padres for Mike Ivie, the first overall pick in 1970. In their second big move of the offseason, the Giants sent seven players and cash to Oakland for pitcher Vida Blue. Blue was a former All-Star and AL MVP, but he was coming off the worst season of his career. Many wondered if the Giants had given up too many players for a pitcher that seemed past his prime.

Blue answered his critics by leading all Giants pitchers with 18 wins in 1978. He was named to the All-Star team and finished third in Cy Young voting. Complementing Blue on a Giants pitching staff that finished third in the league in ERA were Bob Knepper and John Montefusco. Knepper was a workhorse, throwing 16 complete games on his way to a 17–11, 2.63 season, and Montefusco regained his previous form and went 11–9.

Outstanding pitching propelled the Giants to first place in mid-May, and they would hold the top spot for most of the next three months. A 1–10 stretch in the first half of September led to their demise.

Forgotten in the magical season by Blue was the steady play of Ivie, who stroked .308. The 22-year-old Jack "The Ripper" Clark led the Giants offense with 25 home runs and 98 RBI. Willie McCovey, defying all doubters by playing 108 games at 40 years old, clubbed 12 home runs in 1978, including his 500th on June 30.

Although they didn't win the division—they would finish at 89–73 and in third place—the Giants had a lot to be happy about in 1978. The four-year streak of losing was over, and fans were excited about the team again. The Giants brought in 1,740,477 fans, more than 1 million more than the previous season.

When Vida Blue started the All-Star Game in 1978, he became the first pitcher to do so in both leagues. *Baseball Hall of Fame Museum and Library*

A STEP BACKWARD

North Steals 58, but Giants Finish South of .500

With players soaring past the 500-, 600-, and 700-homer levels during the steroid era, Willie McCovey is often forgotten as one of the game's all-time great power hitters. But in the previous generation, he was held in high esteem—and rightly so. In June, McCovey became the all-time home run leader in the NL among lefties. The milestone was a highlight in an otherwise disappointing season for San Francisco.

One of the Giants' newest additions, Mike Ivie, paced the offense, leading the team in home runs (27) and RBI (89). Right fielder Jack Clark followed up on his breakout season of 1978 by leading the team in doubles (25) and hits (144) while knocking 26 home runs and driving in 86. Speedy center fielder Bill North led San Francisco in runs (87) and ranked second in the NL with 58 stolen bases. Overall, though, Giants hitters batted just .246 and led the league in strikeouts.

Things weren't much better on the mound. The previous year's success story, Vida Blue, struggled mightily all year and finished with a 14–14 record and a 5.01 ERA. The true bad news for Joe Altobelli's team was that even with his .500 record, Blue was the Giants' winningest pitcher. Other than John Curtis (10–9), no San Francisco pitcher posted double digits in wins. The Giants staff finished third from last in the league in ERA at 4.16.

San Francisco's struggles on the mound and in the batter's box mirrored its overall record. The Giants finished the year with a 71–91 mark and in fourth place in the NL West. With the season winding down, Altobelli was fired and replaced with coach Dave Bristol. In a decade in which they posted six losing records and no pennants, the Giants were happy to see the 1970s come to a close.

A five-tool talent with a prickly personality, Jack "The Ripper" Clark earned his second straight All-Star nod in 1979. *Baseball Hall of Fame Museum and Library*

Highlights

January 23: Willie Mays is voted into the Hall of Fame, but 23 of 432 writers inexplicably vote no.

April 4: Major League umpires picket the opening game of the season: San Francisco at Cincinnati. The Giants score eight runs in the second and win 11–5.

May 25: The Giants beat Atlanta 6–4 to improve to 25–20 and into a first-place tie. A subsequent seven-game losing streak will drop them back in the pack for good.

June 9: Against the Cubs, Willie McCovey clouts his 512th career home run to become the all-time NL leader among lefties, passing Mel Ott.

June 28: The Giants trade Bill Madlock to the Pirates in a multiplayer deal.

September 6: The Giants fire manager Joe Altobelli and replace him with coach Dave Bristol.

NOTES

First baseman/outfielder **Mike Ivie** raps .286-27-89, while **Jack Clark** is right behind at .273-26-86.

Outfielder **Bill North** leads SF in runs (87) and ranks second in the league in steals (58).

Vida Blue struggles at 14–14, 5.01, but he's the only Giants pitcher with more than 10 wins.

THE 1970–1979 RECORD BOOK

Team Leaders

(*Italics* indicates NL leader)

Batting Average

1970: Bobby Bonds, .302
1971: Bobby Bonds, .288
1972: Chris Speier, .269
1973: Garry Maddox, .319
1974: Gary Matthews, .287
1975: Von Joshua, .318
1976: Larry Herndon, .288
1977: Bill Madlock, .302
1978: Bill Madlock, .309
1979: Jack Clark, .273

Home Runs

1970: Willie McCovey, 39
1971: Bobby Bonds, 33
1972: Dave Kingman, 29
1973: Bobby Bonds, 39
1974: Bobby Bonds, 21
1975: Gary Matthews, 12
1976: Bobby Murcer, 23
1977: Willie McCovey, 28
1978: Jack Clark, 25
1979: Mike Ivie, 27

RBI

1970: Willie McCovey, 126
1971: Bobby Bonds, 102
1972: Dave Kingman, 83
1973: Bobby Bonds, 96
1974: Gary Matthews, 82
1975: Bobby Murcer, 91
1976: Bobby Murcer, 90
1977: Willie McCovey, 86
1978: Jack Clark, 98
1979: Mike Ivie, 89

Runs

1970: Bobby Bonds, 134
1971: Bobby Bonds, 110
1972: Bobby Bonds, 118
1973: *Bobby Bonds, 131*
1974: Bobby Bonds, 97
1975: Derrel Thomas, 99
1976: Gary Matthews, 79
1977: Derrel Thomas, 75
1978: Jack Clark, 90
1979: Bill North, 87

Stolen Bases

1970: Bobby Bonds, 48
1971: Bobby Bonds, 26
1972: Bobby Bonds, 44
1973: Bobby Bonds, 43
1974: Bobby Bonds, 41
1975: Derrel Thomas, 28
1976: 3 tied at 12
1977: Gary Thomasson, 16
1978: Bill Madlock, 16
1979: Bill North, 58

Wins

1970: Gaylord Perry, 23
1971: Juan Marichal, 18
1972: Ron Bryant, 14
1973: *Ron Bryant, 24*
1974: Mike Caldwell, 14
1975: John Montefusco, 15
1976: John Montefusco, 16
1977: Ed Halicki, 16
1978: Vida Blue, 18
1979: Vida Blue, 14

ERA

1970: Gaylord Perry, 3.20
1971: Gaylord Perry, 2.76
1972: Ron Bryant, 2.90
1973: Ron Bryant, 3.53
1974: Jim Barr, 2.74
1975: John Montefusco, 2.88
1976: John Montefusco, 2.84
1977: Ed Halicki, 3.32
1978: Bob Knepper, 2.63
1979: Bob Knepper, 4.64

1979 HIGHLIGHTS

Willie McCovey's 512th homer sets new career mark for NL lefties.

JOHN MONTEFUSCO
PITCHER GIANTS

From left: In 1979, Willie McCovey became the all-time home run leader among left-handed National Leaguers. John "The Count" Montefusco was a 25-year-old phenom and rookie sensation in 1975. *MVP Books Collection*

Strikeouts

1970: Gaylord Perry, 214
1971: Juan Marichal, 159
1972: Sam McDowell, 122
1973: Ron Bryant, 143
1974: John D'Acquisto, 167
1975: John Montefusco, 215
1976: John Montefusco, 172
1977: Ed Halicki, 168
1978: John Montefusco, 177
1979: Vida Blue, 138

Saves

1970: Don McMahon, 19
1971: Jerry Johnson, 18
1972: Jerry Johnson, 8
1973: Elias Sosa, 18
1974: Randy Moffitt, 15
1975: Randy Moffitt, 11
1976: Randy Moffitt, 14
1977: Gary Lavelle, 20
1978: Gary Lavelle, 14
1979: Gary Lavelle, 20

NL Awards

NL MVP Voting

1970: Willie McCovey, 9th
1971: Bobby Bonds, 4th
1973: Bobby Bonds, 3rd
1978: Jack Clark, 5th

NL Rookies of the Year

1973: Gary Matthews
1975: John Montefusco

NL Gold Glove Award Winners

1971: Bobby Bonds, OF
1973: Bobby Bonds, OF
1974: Bobby Bonds, OF

NL All-Stars

(*Italics* indicates starter)

1970: Dick Dietz, C
Willie Mays, OF
Willie McCovey, 1B
Gaylord Perry, P
1971: Bobby Bonds, OF
Juan Marichal, P
Mays, OF
McCovey, 1B
1972: Chris Speier, SS
1973: Bonds, OF
Speier, SS
1974: Speier, SS
1975: Bobby Murcer, OF
1976: John Montefusco, P
1977: Gary Lavelle, P
1978: *Vida Blue, P*
Jack Clark, OF
1979: Clark, OF

BOBBY
BONDS
All Star Game MVP &
Sporting News
Player of the Year

RON
BRYANT
Sporting News
Pitcher of the Year

GARY
MATTHEWS
Rookie of the
Year

GIANTS 1970–1979 All-Decade Team

1B	WILLIE McCOVEY
2B	TITO FUENTES
SS	CHRIS SPEIER
3B	DARRELL EVANS
C	MIKE SADEK
OF	BOBBY BONDS
OF	GARY MATTHEWS
OF	JACK CLARK
SP	JUAN MARICHAL
SP	JOHN MONTEFUSCO
RP	GARY LAVELLE

The 1974 roster featured the reigning *Sporting News* Player of the Year in Bobby Bonds, *Sporting News* Pitcher of the Year in Ron Bryant, and NL Rookie of the Year in Gary Matthews. *MVP Books Collection*

THE 1980s

EARTH-SHAKING DEVELOPMENTS

With a new lineup of mostly homegrown stars such as Will Clark and Robby Thompson, the Giants surge again, returning to the World Series for the first time in 27 years.

Although the Giants limped into the 1980s, finishing in last place with new manager Dave Bristol, owner Bob Lurie resurrected one of the franchise's tried-and-true models: Put a Hall of Famer in the dugout. Lurie made Frank Robinson the first African American manager in the National League. (Robinson had already been the first African American manager in the majors with Cleveland in 1975.)

In his stellar career on the field, Robinson had been a hard-nosed player, and he was no different as a manager. He had the team a shade over .500 in that first strike-shortened season, and the Giants contended in 1982. As in the fabled year of 1951, the Giants fell 13½ games behind, and they then stormed all the way to within one game of first place. Again as in 1951, it was a banner year for the Giants-Dodgers rivalry, only this time neither team made the playoffs. The Dodgers knocked the Giants out of the pennant race, winning two straight late-season contests at Candlestick, and the Giants returned the favor, with future Hall of Famer Joe Morgan knocking a game-winning home run on the season's final day to enable the Atlanta Braves to edge LA in the West.

Alas, such moments were in too-short supply, and Robinson was replaced in 1984. The next season's manager, Jim Davenport, a star on the Giants' 1962 pennant-winner, was replaced in the middle of 1985. His successor, Roger Craig—a veteran of the polar-opposite 1962 Mets—joined too late to prevent the Giants' first-ever 100-loss season.

But Craig brought "Humm Baby" enthusiasm to the Giants at just the right time. In 1986, he installed Will Clark at first base and Robby Thompson at second, even though neither had played an inning at Triple-A. By the following season, Clark had blossomed into an MVP candidate and the outfield of Jeffrey Leonard, Chili Davis, and Candy Maldonado combined for 63 home runs. During the season, general manager Al Rosen wheeled and dealed, trading for Kevin Mitchell and a host of veteran pitchers, including Rick "Big Daddy" Reuschel, Don "Caveman" Robinson, Dave Dravecky, and Craig Lefferts. The Giants won the West but lost the NLCS to the Cardinals. Leonard had a monster series and became the only player from the losing side to win MVP honors.

Adversity defined the Giants in 1988, with the death of the wife of shortstop Jose Uribe and the sidelining of Dravecky with a cancerous tumor in his left arm. His valiant comeback the next year was cut short when the arm broke. It was ultimately amputated, and Dravecky's courage made him an inspiration to baseball lovers everywhere. Such tragedies brought the players closer together, and by 1989 they were contenders again. Mitchell blasted 47 home runs and knocked in 125 runs in an MVP season, Clark—the MVP runner-up—hit .333, and San Francisco won the division. Clark keyed the defeat of the Cubs in the NLCS, but the A's—and Mother Nature—were too much for the Giants in the long-awaited all–Bay Area World Series.

Although Candlestick Park survived the 1989 Loma Prieta earthquake, owner Lurie was not sure how much longer he could survive Candlestick. He had already lost one ballot measure, an attempt to gain voter approval to build a downtown ballpark in 1987. Another measure went on the ballot in 1989, and appeared headed for passage, but the earthquake jostled voters' priorities, and it failed by roughly 2,000 votes out of 173,000 cast. Even as the Giants seemed ascendant on the playing field, the question of where that field would be located seemed increasingly uncertain.

Top: One hundred years after the founding of the franchise, Giants manager Frank Robinson does his Jim Mutrie impersonation on the cover of the team's 1983 yearbook. *MVP Books Collection*
Bottom: Despite a checkered career, Kevin Mitchell was spectacular in 1989, when he belted 47 home runs en route to the NL MVP Award. *Stephen Dunn/ Hulton Archive/Getty Images*

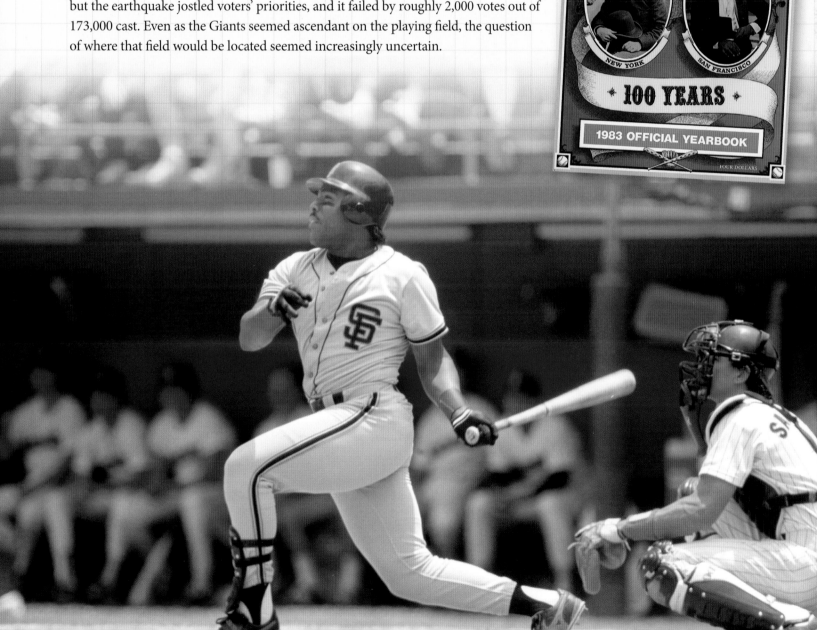

1980

▶ 75-86   5th ◀

Highlights

March 17: Giants coach Jim Lefebvre and Dodgers manager Tommy Lasorda get into a fistfight at an LA TV studio.

April 17: Prior to their home opener, the Giants are 1–6 and six games out in the NL West. They will remain six or more games out over the rest of the season.

May 7: After surrendering 31 runs in three games at St. Louis, San Francisco sits at 8–19.

June 6: Willie McCovey retires after hitting .204 in 48 games. His 521 home runs tie him with Ted Williams for eighth on the all-time list.

June 27: Jerry Reuss of the Dodgers no-hits the Giants at Candlestick. SF's only base runner reaches on an error.

July 14: A four-game sweep at Cincinnati gives the Giants seven straight wins and a .500 record.

December 9: The Giants fire manager Dave Bristol.

NOTES

Jack Clark (.284-22-82) and **Darrell Evans** (.264-20-78) are the team's heaviest hitters.

Vida Blue leads San Francisco in wins (14–10) and ranks fourth in the NL in ERA (2.97).

Ed Whitson (11–13, 3.10) finishes eighth in ERA.

BYE-BYE, WILLIE

McCovey Retires While Teammates Limp to Fifth-Place Finish

Catcher Mike Sadek blows a bubble and checks the weather while pitcher Greg Minton huddles under a blanket during a rain delay at Candlestick on April 15, 1980. *AP Images*

One of the greatest careers in baseball history came to an end on July 6, 1980. Longtime fan favorite Willie "Stretch" McCovey, playing in his fourth decade with the team, finally decided to hang it up. Even though he struggled to hit .204 in 48 games in his final season, McCovey left the game with a bang. In his last at-bat, at Dodger Stadium, McCovey lofted a pinch-hit sacrifice fly in the eighth inning off Rick Sutcliffe to bring home Jack Clark and secure a 4–3 Giants victory. It was an appropriate ending to a career littered with heroic feats. Upon his retirement, McCovey's 521 home runs tied him with Ted Williams for eighth on the all-time list.

While the Giants said farewell to one of their legends, there was still a season to play. And it wasn't pretty. Before the season even began, Giants coach Jim Lefebvre and Dodgers manager Tommy Lasorda got into a fistfight in an LA TV studio. Things weren't much better on the diamond. The Giants were already 1–6 and six games out in the NL West before they played their home opener. San Francisco would remain six or more games out the rest of the season.

Even though he had been ailing, McCovey's bat was sorely missed. The Giants offense finished last in the NL in hits, runs scored, and batting average—just .244. Jack Clark led the Giants with 22 home runs and 82 RBI. Bill North pilfered 45 bases, while fellow outfielder Terry Whitfield led the team with a .296 average.

Vida Blue was the only bright spot on the mound, as he went 14–10 and ranked fourth in the NL in ERA (2.97). The Giants finished in fifth place at 75–86, and after the season manager Dave Bristol was fired. It was definitely not the start to the decade that the Giants had hoped for.

158

BASEBALL STRIKES OUT

Robinson-Led Giants Finish Fifth, Third in Split Season

After bidding adieu to manager Dave Bristol in December 1980, the Giants looked for a leader who could bring a strong presence to the clubhouse. They found their man in proud, tough Frank Robinson, who thus became the first African American manager in the 105-year history of the National League.

While the signing of Robinson was noteworthy in San Francisco, the 1981 season would be remembered for something much more unfortunate. On June 11, Major League Baseball suffered a work stoppage for the fourth time in league history. The main issue at stake was that the owners demanded compensation for losing a free agent to another team. The players held the opinion that any form of compensation would weaken the concept of free agency. The strike went on for nearly two months before play resumed on August 10.

Further marring the national pastime, the season was split into two halves. Those teams in first place on June 11 would make the playoffs, and they'd face the second-half winners in division series. In the NL West, LA and Houston were the first- and second-half champs, respectively. The Giants finished fifth and then third, going 29–23 in the second half. Meanwhile, Cincinnati Reds fans were fuming. They had the best overall record in baseball that year but didn't make the playoffs.

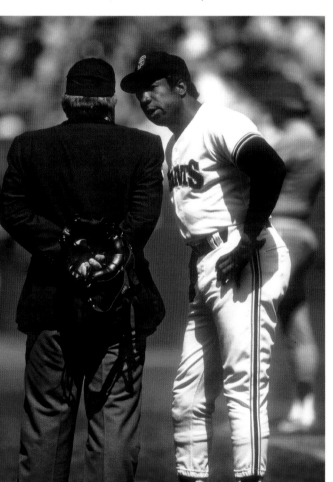

As for individual performances, Jack Clark finished sixth in the NL in home runs (17) and Milt May ranked seventh in batting (.310). Doyle Alexander emerged as the Giants' ace, going 11–7 with a 2.89 ERA. Vida Blue complemented Alexander by posting a 2.45 ERA. Greg Minton placed second in the league with 21 saves.

San Francisco finished with a winning record in Robinson's first season as manager, but their 56–55 mark was hardly anything to celebrate. On October 28, Giants fans watched squeamishly as the Dodgers won the World Series at Yankee Stadium. Outside of LA, it was a season that everyone wanted to forget.

On April 9, 1981, Frank Robinson became the first black manager in the 105-year history of the National League. *Focus on Sport/Getty Images*

Highlights

January 14: Frank Robinson becomes the Giants' manager—and the first African American manager in the National League.

March 9: Hall of Fame–bound second baseman Joe Morgan signs with the Giants.

May 10: Charlie Lea no-hits San Francisco in Montreal.

June 11: A fifth straight loss puts the Giants at 27–32, in fifth place.

June 12–August 9: A players strike, over the issue of compensation for teams that lose free agents, wipes out the heart of the season. MLB owners decide to split this season into two halves (pre-strike and post-strike). Division leaders from each half (eight teams in all) will compete in the postseason.

October 4: San Francisco finishes the second-half season at 29–23, 3½ games behind Houston. The Astros will face the first-half winning Dodgers in the playoffs.

NOTES

Catcher **Milt May** ranks seventh in the NL in batting (.310), while **Jack Clark** finishes sixth in homers (17).

Doyle Alexander (11–7, 2.89) is the star of the rotation.

Greg Minton places second in the NL with 21 saves.

1982

▶ **85-75   3rd** ◀

Highlights

March 30: The Giants trade pitching stars Vida Blue and Doyle Alexander to the Royals and Yankees, respectively.

July 30: San Francisco is 48–53, 13½ games out.

August 6: Facing Houston at Candlestick, SF's Jack Clark and Reggie Smith homer back to back twice, including in the ninth inning to tie the score at 6–6. A Darrell Evans ninth-inning single wins it for the Giants.

August 11: With a walk-off home run by Reggie Smith, the Giants win their 10th straight game and are now only four games out.

September 30: With a 7–6 triumph over Houston, the Giants are just one game behind first-place Atlanta.

October 1–3: San Francisco loses two out of three to LA and finishes the season two games back of the Braves.

NOTES

Jack Clark powers 27 home runs and ranks fifth in the NL in RBI (103).

Joe Morgan leads the Giants in batting (.289) and ranks second in the league in OBP (.400).

Bill Laskey (13–12, 3.14) paces the staff in wins, while **Greg Minton** (1.83 ERA) finishes second in the NL in saves (30).

CENTENNIAL CHEERS

Giants Nearly Win Division in 100th Season as Franchise

The Giants' 100th season started slowly, as the team christened its centennial anniversary by trading away its two best arms—Vida Blue and Doyle Alexander. By July 30, San Francisco was 48–53, 13½ games out of first place. Frank Robinson's first season as manager had been marked with an asterisk due to the players strike, but it looked like his second season by the Bay was quickly going down the drain. Then August happened.

San Francisco opened August by winning 11 out of 12, sling-shotting from 12 games out of first to just four. The streak was highlighted by Jack Clark and Reggie Smith hitting back-to-back home runs twice against Houston on August 6. Smith's walk-off home run against Atlanta on August 11 sewed up the Giants' 10-game winning streak. San Francisco continued to tear through the late summer months, posting a 17–12 overall record in August and a 20–7 mark in September.

Clark led the San Francisco attack with 27 home runs and 103 RBI. Second baseman Joe Morgan led the team in batting (.289) and was second in the league in OBP (.400), while outfielder Chili Davis stole 24 bases and paced the club in hits (167).

Filling the void left by the departed Blue and Alexander wasn't easy for San Francisco. Bill Laskey (13–12, 3.14 ERA) became the team's ace, while Greg Minton proved to be one of the best closers in baseball by posting a 1.83 ERA and finishing second in the NL in saves (30).

Despite giving up more runs than they scored during the year, the Giants found themselves just one game behind first-place Atlanta as the season entered its final weekend. Unfortunately for Robinson's team, its late-season charge was for nothing, as San Francisco dropped two out of three to the Dodgers to finish two games back of the Braves. At least the Giants had showed some heart under Robinson. In one-run games, they were 38–28.

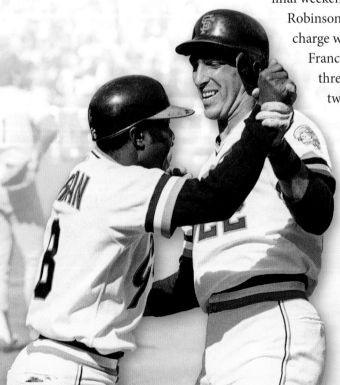

Jack Clark congratulates Joe Morgan, whose three-run homer helped beat LA 5–3 in the season finale. Atlanta won the NL West by one game over the Dodgers and two over the Giants. *AP Images*

Ho-Hum, Baby

The Giants Lose 83 in '83, as Fans Lose Interest

The Giants opened 1983 with one of the highest-scoring games in Opening Day history, a 16–13 loss to San Diego. That tumultuous game epitomized the roller coaster ride that was the season's first two months. By the end of April, the Giants were in last place at 7–14. By going 19–7 in May, they improved to 26–21. The rest of the season was more like an uneventful trolley ride, as the team

Darrell Evans high-fives Jeffrey Leonard after belting a home run against Houston. Evans knocked 30 homers in 1983, and Leonard chipped in with 21. *Bruce Bennett/ Hulton Archive/Getty Images*

hovered around .500 while fans gradually lost interest. In their final home series of the year, the Giants drew a total of just 12,121 fans over three games.

The oldest player in the Giants lineup proved to be the team's most valuable hitter. Darrell Evans, a lumbering 36-year-old first baseman, led San Francisco in doubles (29), home runs (30), and hits (145). (He would sign with Detroit after the season and help lead the Tigers to the 1984 world title.) Left fielder Jeffrey Leonard socked 21 home runs and compiled a team-high 87 RBI, while shortstop Johnnie LeMaster stole 39 bases. LeMaster, often the target of boo birds because of his anemic hitting, batted .240 on the year—his third highest average in 11 years with the team.

Offense wasn't a problem, as San Francisco finished fourth in the NL in runs. However, the team was fourth from the bottom in ERA. Lefty Atlee Hammaker led the league in that category (2.25) despite going just 10–9. Bill Laskey got much better support, finishing with a 13–10 mark despite a 4.19 ERA. San Francisco's dynamic bullpen duo of Greg Minton and Gary Lavelle combined for 42 saves.

The Giants wallowed in fifth place for almost the entire second half, but they played like world-beaters against the rival Dodgers. Even though Los Angeles would win the division, the Giants won the season series 13–5. San Francisco finished the year with a 79–83 record.

1983

▸ 79-83   5th ◂

Highlights

April 5: Bucking the baseball trend of low-scoring Opening Day games, the Giants lose the lid-lifter 16–13 to San Diego.

April 26: San Francisco is in the basement, nine games back, after a 5–13 start.

May 31: The Giants bounce back with a 19–7 record in May to improve to 26–21.

July 4: San Francisco enters the All-Star break at 39–40, 9½ games out. The team will not rise higher than fourth place in the second half.

July 31: Giants great Juan Marichal becomes the first Latino pitcher inducted into the Baseball Hall of Fame.

September 16–18: The Giants sweep rival Los Angeles at Candlestick. The Dodgers, who will win the division, will go 5–13 against SF.

NOTES

Darrell Evans (30 homers), outfielder Jeffrey Leonard (87 RBI), shortstop Johnnie LeMaster (39 steals), and infielder Joel Youngblood (.292) lead a balanced attack.

Bill Laskey leads the Giants in wins (13–10).

Left-hander Atlee Hammaker ranks fourth on the staff in wins (10–9) but leads the league in ERA (2.25).

Highlights

May 1: The Giants lose to the Dodgers 3–2 in 11 innings for their ninth straight defeat. They are 7–17 and 10 games out.

June 6: A fan falls out of Candlestick Park's upper deck and dies after the Giants' 11-inning loss to Atlanta.

June 7: A 14–5 shellacking by Houston drops San Francisco to 17–36. The Giants will spend the rest of the season in fifth or sixth place.

July 10: Candlestick Park is the stage for the MLB All-Star Game. Outfielder Chili Davis and catcher Bob Brenly represent the host team.

August 5: The Giants fire manager Frank Robinson. Danny Ozark will serve as interim manager.

October 30: Jim Davenport is hired to manage the Giants.

NOTES

Chili Davis (.315-21-81) ranks third in the NL in batting, while fellow outfielder Dan Gladden rips .351 in 342 at-bats.

Outfielder Jeffrey Leonard (.302-21-86) and catcher Bob Brenly (.291-20-80) are other big sticks.

Mike Krukow (11–12) is the staff's only double-digit winner, as the Giants finish last in the NL in ERA (4.39).

KILL THE CRAB

Fans Take Out Frustrations on "Anti-Mascot"

With their team mired in last place throughout the 1984 season, Giants fans had plenty of anger to vent. They took it out on the team's new "anti-mascot," Crazy Crab.

After the success of the truly hilarious San Diego Chicken, many MLB teams joined the mascot craze in the 1980s—for better or worse. With the club's prospects looking bleak for 1984, the Giants' marketing whizzes came up with the idea of a mascot parody—a sad-sack walking crab that fans would want to kick the bleep out of . . . while chuckling at the same time. In promotional commercials, manager Frank Robinson had to be restrained from attacking the pathetic sea creature.

Crazy Crab, played by actor Wayne Doba, ventured onto the field once a game, and fans showered him with boos, food, and beverages. Players Duane Kiper and Mike Krukow said they drilled him daily with resin bags. A Padres player tackled him so hard that Doba filed a lawsuit against the team. Prior to the last home game of the year, Doba reportedly told a Giants official, "I hope there's nobody up there with a gun." There wasn't, but the Giants laid Crazy Crab to rest after the season.

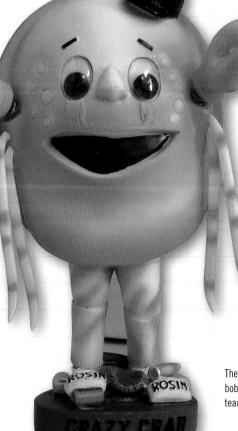

And what a crummy season it was. San Francisco was three games out after three games, and it was all downhill from there. A nine-game losing streak through May 1 left the Giants 10 games behind. With the team in last place in early August, Robinson was canned, replaced by 60-year-old Danny Ozark. The team finished in the basement at 66–96.

Though the Giants finished 11th in the NL in attendance, Candlestick was packed on July 10 for the MLB All-Star Game. Outfielder Chili Davis, who would finish the year with a .315 average, and catcher Brenly (.291) represented the host team. As it turned out, the best Giants hitter that season was a rookie outfielder. Dan Gladden arrived on June 26 and ripped .351 the rest of the way.

The Giants' Crazy Crab mascot, pictured here in bobblehead form, endured endless abuse during the team's 96-loss season. *MVP Books Collection*

Third baseman Chris Brown, who finished fourth in NL Rookie of the Year voting in 1985, drove trucks for Halliburton in Iraq during the first Gulf War and later died from fire-related injuries at his home in 2006. *Charles Bennett/AP Images*

Highlights

February 1: The Giants trade Jack Clark to St. Louis for five players.

May 12: SF pitcher Jim Gott belts two home runs as the Giants defeat the Cardinals 5–4 in 10 innings.

June 5–10: After scoring two runs total in five games, San Francisco falls into the basement for good.

June 11: A Bob Brenly RBI single in the 18th inning gives SF a 5–4 win at Atlanta.

June 20–30: A 10-game losing streak drops the Giants to 26–48.

June 27: Jeffrey Leonard hits for the cycle in a 7–6 loss to the Reds.

September 18: Roger Craig replaces Jim Davenport as Giants manager.

October 6: With an 8–7 loss to Atlanta on the season's last day, the Giants record their 100th defeat for the first time in franchise history.

NOTES

Third baseman **Chris Brown** (.271-16-61) falls a home run short of leading San Francisco in batting, homers, and RBI.

Reliever **Scott Garrelts** (9–6) paces the staff in wins.

The Giants are last in the NL in batting (.233) and runs per game (3.43).

ROCK BOTTOM

The Giants Drop 100 Games in Losingest Season Ever

In 1985, the best things to happen to the Giants occurred beneath the surface. On the field, the team was in the midst of its first 100-loss campaign in franchise history. But in June, San Francisco drafted a phenomenal young hitter with the second overall pick. First baseman Will "The Thrill" Clark had won the Golden Spikes Award at Mississippi State, and analysts predicted instant big-league stardom for the sweet-swinging slugger.

Down in Shreveport, Louisiana, second baseman Robby Thompson—a first-round pick in the 1983 draft—was en route to an All-Star campaign in the Texas League. Like Clark, he was primed to join the Giants' infield in '86. Then, in September, new GM Al Rosen hired Roger Craig as manager.

A tall, good-spirited former big-league pitcher with a thick Carolina drawl, Craig had turned around the Padres as their skipper in 1978. He was also one of the game's most revered pitching coaches, and he helped manager Sparky Anderson build a world championship club in Detroit. Though Craig would go only 6–12 in his three weeks with the Giants in 1985, the team would be in better hands with him than with Jim Davenport, who went 56–88 at the Giants helm in '85, his sole season as a major league manager.

Numerous Giants had subpar years in 1985. Catcher Bob Brenly followed his All-Star campaign with a .220 season. Dan Gladden saw his average plummet from .351 in 1984 to .243. First baseman David Green mustered just 20 RBI in 294 at-bats. Due to the most anemic offense in baseball, no Giants starter could muster more than eight wins. Poor Dave LaPoint was saddled with a 7–17 record despite a fine 3.57 ERA.

The team was so bad for so long, residing in last place for approximately 93 percent of the season, that only 818,697 loyalists came out to the Stick. In a four-game span during the season's last week, the Giants drew just 7,275 fans—or 1,819 per game.

‣ **83-79** **3rd** ◂

Highlights

April 8: In his first MLB at-bat, rookie first baseman Will Clark belts a home run off Houston's Nolan Ryan.

April 20: Vida Blue, who had re-signed with the Giants before the 1985 season, defeats San Diego for his 200th career victory.

June 22: In a Sunday doubleheader at Candlestick, in front of 47,030 fans, the Giants sweep Houston to move into first place.

June 23: San Francisco routs San Diego 18–1.

July 21–23: The Giants are swept in St. Louis and fall out of first place for good.

August 5: Steve Carlton, signed by SF a month earlier, becomes the second MLB pitcher to record 4,000 strikeouts.

September 14: Against Atlanta, catcher Bob Brenly fills in at third base and makes four errors in the fourth inning. He also belts two home runs, including a walk-off blast in the ninth.

September 25: Houston's Mike Scott no-hits the Giants.

NOTES

Outfielder **Candy Maldonado** paces the team in home runs (18) and RBI (85).

Chris Brown (.317) and **Will Clark** (.287) lead the Giants in batting.

Mike Krukow, has a career year, finishing second in the NL in wins (20–9).

YOU GOTTA LIKE 'EM

Clark, Thompson, and Other "Kids" Lead Resurgence

In 1984 and '85, the Giants had two of the lamest marketing slogans in baseball history. In 1984, it was "C'mon Giants, Hang in There." The next season: "Real Grass, Real Sunshine, Real Baseball." Real sunshine? Really?

Admittedly, the Giants did not have much to hang their hats on during those two abysmal seasons. But they did in 1986, and their slogan that year—"You Gotta Like These Kids"—had some resonance. That season, rookies Will Clark and Robby Thomson comprised the right side of the infield on Opening Day. Though Thompson that year became the first player in MLB history to be caught stealing four times in one game (June 27), he was runner-up for NL Rookie of the Year honors. The future Gold Glove–winning second sacker led the '86 Giants in hits (149) and runs (73).

Meanwhile, first baseman Will Clark lived up to his "Thrill" nickname immediately, belting a home run in his first major league at-bat—off the legendary Nolan Ryan, no less. While he batted .287 with 11 homers in 111 games, fans became enamored with the handsome young star. A year later, he'd become the toast of the town.

Other young stars shone in 1986. Third baseman Chris Brown rapped .317 and made the All-Star team. Candy Maldonado, a well-built slugger from Puerto Rico, drove in 85 runs despite just 102 hits. Closer Scott Garrelts went 13–9 with 18 saves.

Starting pitcher Mike Krukow (age 34) was no kid, but he did anchor the third best pitching staff in the league, going 20–9 with a 3.05 ERA. The towering right-hander became the team's first 20-game winner since 1973 when, pitching on three days' rest, he prevailed at Dodger Stadium in the season finale.

San Francisco hovered around first place until late July, when Houston began to pull away. Still, the Giants improved by 21 games in 1986 and finished above .500. Just as importantly, yearly attendance nearly doubled. Fans really did like those kids.

Opposite page: In spring of his rookie year, Will Clark was dubbed "The Thrill" by Giants catcher Bob Brenly. "It was just one of those things that seemed to roll off the tongue," Brenly said. *Ron Vesely/Hulton Archive/Getty Images*

Highlights

May 9: The Giants jump out to a 21–10 start.

July 4: San Francisco drops to 39–40, 5½ games back. In a seven-player swap with San Diego, the Giants land pitcher Dave Dravecky and third baseman Kevin Mitchell.

August 7–September 1: Thanks to an 18–7 stretch, the Giants go from five games out to 5½ up.

September 28: San Francisco edges San Diego 5–4 to clinch its first division title since 1971.

October 7: Dravecky shuts out St. Louis 5–0 in Game Two of the NLCS to even the Series.

October 10–11: The Giants take Games Four and Five at home, 4–2 and 6–3, to go up three games to two.

October 13–14: The Cardinals win Games Six and Seven in St. Louis, 1–0 and 6–0, to advance to the World Series. SF's Jeffrey Leonard, who homered in Games One through Four, is the NLCS MVP.

NOTES

Will Clark leads the charge at .308-35-91, while **Candy Maldonado** rips .292-20-85.

Mike LaCoss is the top winner at 13–10.

HUMM BABY!

Giants Thrive Thanks to Rosen's Trades, Leonard's HRs

For the New York Yankees and Houston Astros, Al Rosen was regarded as a conservative general manager. As the Giants' GM, Rosen shattered that reputation for good in the summer of 1987 with three gutsy trades—deals that propelled San Francisco to the NL West title.

Roger Craig's catch phrase of "Humm Baby!" represented the infectious enthusiasm that ran through this ball club in '87. The team opened at 5–0 and 21–10. When the club began a homestand on Memorial Day, with a three-game lead in the standings, more than 42,000 fans flocked to Candlestick.

Giants bats came alive in '87. Fan favorite Will Clark smashed .308-35-91, outfielder Chili Davis cracked .250-24-76, and Candy Maldonado bashed .292-20-85. Nevertheless, a 6–14 stretch left the Giants 5½ games back on the Fourth of July. That's when Rosen went to work.

The next day, Rosen traded four players, including Chris Brown, to San Diego for third baseman Kevin Mitchell and pitchers Dave Dravecky and Craig Lefferts. Mitchell would become a tremendous slugger for San Francisco, belting 143 homers in four and a half seasons. Rosen orchestrated two more trades over the next few weeks, as veteran pitchers Don Robinson and Rick Reuschel added depth to the staff.

Loaded with quality talent, the Giants went 36–19 in August and September and won the NL West by six games—their first division title in 16 years. Giants fever infected the Bay Area, as reflected in postseason attendance. In three NL Championship Series home games, more than 175,000 fans sardined themselves into Candlestick Park.

Jeffrey Leonard homered in each of the first four games of the NLCS, including here in Game three at St. Louis. *Sal Veder/AP Images*

Will "The Thrill"

Will Clark can thank the family dog for launching his career as a first baseman. When Will was a youngster in New Orleans, Flash returned not once but twice with left-handed first baseman mitts it had found in the neighborhood. Will put them to good use, becoming college baseball's best overall first baseman—and player—at Mississippi State.

Clark toiled for 15 years in the majors, hitting .303 with 284 home runs and 1,205 RBI. Mostly, he is remembered for his eight seasons with San Francisco, when he finished among the top five in NL MVP voting four times. His personal highs during that period include 35 homers in 1987, a .333 average in 1989, and 116 RBI in 1991, when he won a Gold Glove Award. At various times with San Francisco, he led the NL in runs, RBI, walks, slugging, and total bases.

Nicknamed "The Thrill" for his heroics (such as his .650-2-8 performance in the 1989 NLCS), Clark was also called "The Natural" for his smooth-as-honey swing. Ironically, he was known early in his career for his emotional outbursts when things didn't go his way. "But if he keeps hitting like this," teammate Bob Brenly said in 1987, "I'll keep supplying him with batting helmets to throw."

Clark kept hitting for San Francisco through the 1993 season, after which he signed with Texas as a free agent.

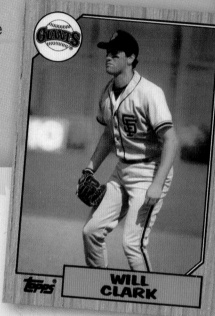

Will Clark thrilled San Francisco fans while averaging 22 homers and batting .299 in eight seasons with the Giants. *MVP Books Collection*

Facing the steal-crazy Cardinals, the Giants split the first two games in St. Louis, winning Game Two 5–0 on a Dravecky shutout. San Francisco's Jeffrey Leonard emerged as the Series storyline, as he homered in both games and agitated Cardinals fans with his "one flap down" home run trot (one arm down, the other extended). Davis's referral to St. Louis as a "cow town" didn't go over well, either.

Giants fans, though, loved Leonard's theatrics, especially when he went deep again in both Game Three and Game Four at the Stick. The teams split those games as well, but San Francisco prevailed in Game Five 6–3 thanks to a four-run fourth and five innings of one-hit relief by Joe Price. Sadly for Giants fans, that fourth-inning explosion would be the last runs their team would score in the Series. Though Dravecky was again brilliant in Game Six in St. Louis, pitchers John Tudor, Todd Worrell, and Ken Dayley shut out the Giants 1–0. The sole run came after outfielder Maldonado lost a ball in the lights.

Glued to their TV sets for Game Seven, Giants fans prayed for one more win—a single victory that would send their team to the World Series for the first time since the days of the Cuban Missile Crisis in 1962. Alas, it was not to be. Spirits sank in San Francisco when spindly Cardinal Jose Oquendo belted a three-run homer off Atlee Hammaker in the fourth inning, giving St. Louis a 4–0 lead. Danny Cox went the distance for a 6–0 shutout victory, sending the Cardinals to a Fall Classic matchup with the Minnesota Twins.

A quarter century later, while serving as the Cardinals' third base coach, Oquendo still got sour welcomes from Giants fans, who hadn't forgotten what he had done to their team in 1987. "I always get booed here," Oquendo told the *St. Louis Dispatch*, "and I always have somebody in the stands yelling at me, still whining about the old days."

1988

▸ **83-79   4th** ◂

Highlights

May 11: Kevin Mitchell homers in the top of the 16th to defeat St. Louis 5–4.

June 8: The Giants trade Jeffrey Leonard to Milwaukee for infielder Ernest Riles.

July 9: The Giants set a San Francisco record for runs in a 21–2 bombing of St. Louis, as Chris Speier hits for the cycle and adds an extra double. Riles belts what is believed to be the 10,000th home run in Giants history.

August 10–11: Back-to-back shutouts of Houston put San Francisco at 61–53, 2½ games out of first place.

August 23–September 7: With a 2–12 tailspin, the Giants fall out of the race.

September 23: LA's Orel Hershiser, in the midst of his MLB-record streak of 59 consecutive scoreless innings, shuts out SF 3–0.

NOTES

Will Clark belts 29 homers and tops the NL with 109 RBI and 100 walks.

Outfielder **Brett Butler** rips .287 with 43 steals and a league-high 109 runs scored.

Rick Reuschel (19–11, 3.12), **Kelly Downs** (13–9, 3.32), and **Don Robinson** (10–5, 2.45) shine on the hill.

A PAINFUL TWIST

Dravecky Battles Cancer While Team Falls Flat

On Opening Day in 1988, Dave Dravecky was on top of the world. After his NLCS heroics a year earlier, the left-hander went all the way in a 5–1 victory over the Dodgers. Little did anyone realize how dramatically the fortunes of the two teams would turn—and more tragically, how Dravecky's life would be turned upside-down.

It all started the very next day, when Dodgers pitcher Orel Hershiser shut out the Giants 5–0. Though San Francisco fans expected another playoff run after their team's fantastic 1987 season, the Giants lingered around .500 month after month. The problem was hitting. While Will Clark plated 109 runs, and newcomer Brett Butler—a speedy center fielder—scored 109, the rest of the lineup couldn't get it done.

The Giants finished in fourth place at 83–79, while LA rode the arm of Hershiser to the NL West title and eventually the world championship. The cerebral southpaw went 23–8 and pitched an MLB-record 59 consecutive scoreless innings.

While Hershiser lived the dream, Dravecky experienced a nightmare. He didn't pitch after May, and a biopsy revealed that he had a cancerous growth in his pitching arm. On October 7, doctors removed not only the tumor but half of his deltoid muscle, and they froze part of the humerus bone to kill any remaining cancer.

After months of rehab, Dravecky made an emotional return to the Giants on August 10, 1989. In front of 35,000 home fans on a Thursday afternoon, the miracle man shut out Cincinnati on one hit through seven innings before leaving to thunderous applause in the eighth, while up 4–3. "I was there when Don Larsen pitched that perfect game in the 1956 World Series," said manager Roger Craig, "[but] this was even more incredible."

Tragically, Dravecky's career ended just five days later, when the frozen bone in his arm snapped during a pitch. The pain that he suffered on the mound was felt throughout the baseball community. Doctors discovered that the cancer had returned, and they were forced to amputate his arm. Fortunately, Dravecky is alive and well today, traveling the country as a motivational speaker.

In October 1988, Giants left-hander Dave Dravecky underwent surgery for a cancerous tumor on his pitching arm. He would make a miraculous comeback in 1989 before breaking the arm and having it amputated. *Otto Gruele, Jr./Hulton Archive/Getty Images*

Highlights

June 20–21: Consecutive shutouts of Houston put the Giants up by four games in the NL West. They will remain in first place for the remainder of the season.

September 27: With a Padres loss, SF clinches the NL West title.

October 4: Will Clark goes 4-for-4 with a grand slam and another homer in an 11–3 win at Chicago in Game One of the NLCS.

October 7–9: The Giants win Games Three (5–4), Four (6–4), and Five (3–2) at home to win the NLCS.

October 14–15: Oakland wins Games One (5–0) and Two (5–1) of the World Series.

October 17: A massive earthquake just prior to Game Three at Candlestick results in a 10-day delay of the World Series.

October 27–28: Oakland wins Games Three (13–7) and Four (9–6) to sweep the Series.

NOTES

Kevin Mitchell wins the NL MVP Award after leading the league in homers (47) and RBI (125).

Will Clark (.333-23-111, league-high 104 runs) is NL MVP runner-up.

Robby Thompson tops the NL with 11 triples.

Rick Reuschel goes 17–8, while **Scott Garrelts** is 14–5 with an NL-best 2.28 ERA.

FROM MAGIC TO TRAGIC

Thrilling Seasons Ends with the "Earthquake" Series

The last time the Giants won the pennant, in 1962, the World Series ended in unimaginable heartbreak. This year, many fans believed, destiny was on their side. On October 9, in front of 62,000 fans at the Stick, Will "The Thrill" Clark cracked a two-run single in the eighth inning in a 3–2 win over Chicago—a triumph that clinched the NLCS. The Giants would square off against the Oakland A's in the first-ever Bay Area World Series.

All across San Francisco—on this sunny and unseasonably warm day—fans honked their horns, set off fireworks, and hooted and cheered in the streets. "It was a beautiful ending," David Gonsoroski told the *San Francisco Chronicle*. "The weather cooperated for a Columbus Day win. Hurray for North Beach!" Hurray for the Giants!

During the celebration, no one could have imagined the horrors that awaited in the days ahead.

In the midst of the World Series, in which Oakland would sweep the Giants with four lopsided wins, a massive earthquake rocked the Bay Area. People died. Property was destroyed. Lives were ruined. Giants baseball, which dominated headlines and conversations days earlier, now seemed utterly insignificant.

The season-ending events ruined what had been a magical year for the Giants. Most of the excitement happened at Candlestick, where the home team went 53–28 and where attendance topped 2 million for the first time in franchise history. After flirting with first place throughout the season, San Francisco took over the top spot for good during a 10–2 homestand in mid-June. San Diego and Houston would challenge but never catch the Giants, who finished 92–70 and won the division by three games.

Kevin Mitchell, who scored 100 runs and drove in 125 during the regular season, drives the ball in the clinching fifth game of the NLCS against Chicago. He batted .324 and drove in 9 runs in 9 postseason games. *Ronald C. Modra/Sports Imagery/Getty Images*

Four Giants players enjoyed remarkable campaigns in 1989. In his last hurrah, 40-year-old control artist Rick "Big Daddy" Reuschel went 17–8 with a 2.94 ERA. Scott Garrelts enjoyed the best season of his injury-shortened career, going 14–5 with a league-best 2.28 ERA. With a .333 average and 111 RBI, Will Clark finished runner-up for the NL MVP Award. Kevin Mitchell took that coveted honor after leading the league in home runs (47), RBI (125), slugging (.635), and total bases (345). Mitchell was the talk of baseball after bashing eight homers from June 2 through 9 and clubbing 31 long balls by the All-Star break—startling numbers in the pre-steroid era.

The Giants and the Cubs, who had gone 44 years since their last trip to the World Series, met in the NL Championship Series. This Series

Showing the Giants' mounting frustration, Robby Thompson tosses his bat after striking out in Game Two of the World Series against Oakland. *Eric Risberg/AP Images*

immediately became the Will Clark show. In a stunning display at Wrigley Field in Game One, Clark drove in six runs while going 4-for-4 with two doubles and two home runs. Mitchell also went deep in an 11–3 Giants cakewalk.

After a 9–5 Cubs win in Game Two, the Giants swept the Series with three wins in San Francisco. In Game Three, Robby Thompson's two-run homer in the seventh produced the final runs in a 5–4 Giants triumph. The next day, Matt Williams ended the scoring with a two-run, fifth-inning homer in a 6–4 Giants win.

With Game Five tied 1–1 with two outs in the eighth, Chicago pitcher Mike Bielecki—in true Cubs tradition—proceeded to walk the bases loaded. That set up a showdown between closer Mitch "Wild Thing" Williams and Clark, who capped off his NLCS MVP performance with a two-run single up the middle. The Giants hung on in the ninth for a 3–2 victory. In the on-field celebration, San Francisco pitcher Dave Dravecky rebroke his arm—an omen of things to come.

Most experts predicted the powerhouse Oakland A's, managed by Tony LaRussa, would win the World Series, and they were right. Oakland pitcher Dave Stewart, in the midst of four straight 20-win seasons, shut out the Giants 5–0 at the Coliseum in the opener. The A's breezed in Game Two as well, winning 5–1.

After a 10-day delay caused by the Loma Prieta earthquake, the A's swept the Series in San Francisco with 13–7 and 9–6 victories. Both games were over early, as Oakland amassed leads of 13–3 and 9–2. For San Franciscans, the World Series that they had dreamt about for so long couldn't have possibly turned out any worse.

The World Series Earthquake

On October 17, 1989, just after 5:00 P.M. Pacific time, ABC commentators Al Michaels and Tim McCarver were previewing Game Three of the World Series, scheduled to begin in a half hour. Showing highlights of the previous game, McCarver said, "Candy Maldonado with the hesitation, allowing Jose Canseco to score . . . and he fails to get Dave Parker . . . at second base, so the Oakland A's take . . . take . . ."

On millions of TVs across America, the picture began to fizz out.

"I tell ya what, we're having an earth . . ." Michaels said, and then the feed was lost.

Down on the field, Candlestick's backstop swayed back and forth. So did the light towers. San Francisco residents had experienced tremors before, but this one lasted longer—upwards of 15 seconds. Although no one was hurt in the ballpark, power was lost at Candlestick and telephones weren't getting a signal. People began to panic. Players from both teams spilled onto the field and then searched for their family members in the stands.

Above: Ticket stub from the fateful Game Three. *MVP Books Collection.* **Left:** The *San Francisco Chronicle* reports on the Loma Prieta earthquake. Initial reports from various media erroneously indicated that some 300 people had died. *MVP Books Collection*

Giants pitcher Kelly Downs carries his shaken nephew off the field amid the aftermath of the earthquake. *John Iacono/Sports Illustrated/Getty Images*

The Loma Prieta earthquake, nicknamed the World Series earthquake, was caused by a slip along the San Andreas Fault and measured a harrowing 6.9 on the Richter Scale. In a cruel twist of irony, the quake killed people in both San Francisco and Oakland—the two teams in the Series. The worst calamity occurred in Oakland, where an upper level of a double-deck portion of the Nimitz Freeway collapsed, crushing the cars on the lower deck. The San Francisco–Oakland Bay Bridge was damaged, too, and buildings in San Francisco's Marina District caught fire.

In all, the earthquake claimed 63 lives and injured more than 3,700 people, including 400 severely. The largest quake in San Francisco since the infamous 1906 calamity caused

In the aftermath, few players or fans were in the mood for baseball. "We just want to get this over with," said Giants outfielder Pat Sheridan, "and get home to our families and the offseason." However, the World Series would continue. As MLB Commissioner Fay Vincent said, "Churchill did not close the cinemas in London during the blitz. It's important for life to carry on."

The Series was rescheduled for October 27, and the A's breezed in Games Three and Four—both at Candlestick—to complete a sweep. The mood during both games was somber. Rescue workers threw out the ceremonial first pitches, and Oakland players did not indulge in a champagne-spraying celebration. As Oakland pitcher Dave Stewart, the Series MVP,

Team Leaders

(*Italics* indicates NL leader)

Batting Average

1980: Jack Clark, .284
1981: Milt May, .310
1982: Joe Morgan, .289
1983: Jeffrey Leonard, .279
1984: Jeffrey Leonard, .302
1985: Chili Davis, .270
1986: Chili Davis, .278
1987: Will Clark, .308
1988: Brett Butler, .287
1989: Will Clark, .333

Home Runs

1980: Jack Clark, 22
1981: Jack Clark, 17
1982: Jack Clark, 27
1983: Darrell Evans, 30
1984: Chili Davis, 21
  Jeffrey Leonard, 21
1985: Bob Brenly, 19
1986: Candy Maldonado, 18
1987: Will Clark, 35
1988: Will Clark, 29
1989: *Kevin Mitchell, 47*

RBI

1980: Jack Clark, 82
1981: Jack Clark, 53
1982: Jack Clark, 103
1983: Jeffrey Leonard, 87
1984: Jeffrey Leonard, 86
1985: Jeffrey Leonard, 62
1986: Candy Maldonado, 85
1987: Will Clark, 91
1988: *Will Clark, 109*
1989: *Kevin Mitchell, 125*

Runs

1980: Jack Clark, 77
1981: Jack Clark, 50
1982: Jack Clark, 90
1983: Darrell Evans, 94
1984: Chili Davis, 87
1985: Dan Gladden, 64
1986: Robby Thompson, 73
1987: Will Clark, 89
1988: *Brett Butler, 109*
1989: *Will Clark, 104*

Stolen Bases

1980: Bill North, 45
1981: Bill North, 26
1982: Chili Davis, 24
  Joe Morgan, 24
1983: Johnnie LeMaster, 39
1984: Dan Gladden, 31
1985: Dan Gladden, 32
1986: Dan Gladden, 27
1987: 3 tied at 16
1988: Brett Butler, 43
1989: Brett Butler, 31

Wins

1980: Vida Blue, 14
1981: Doyle Alexander, 11
1982: Bill Laskey, 13
1983: Bill Laskey, 13
1984: Mike Krukow, 11
1985: Scott Garrelts, 9
1986: Mike Krukow, 20
1987: Mike LaCoss, 13
1988: Rick Reuschel, 19
1989: Rick Reuschel, 17

ERA

1980: Vida Blue, 2.97
1981: Vida Blue, 2.45
1982: Bill Laskey, 3.14
1983: *Atlee Hammaker, 2.25*
1984: Bill Laskey, 4.33
1985: Mike Krukow, 3.38
1986: Mike Krukow, 3.05
1987: Atlee Hammaker, 3.58
1988: Don Robinson, 2.45
1989: *Scott Garrelts, 2.28*

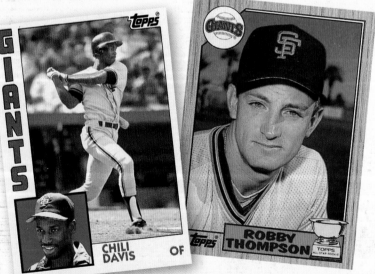

Left: Outfielder Chili Davis' best year as a Giant was 1984, when he went 21-81-.315. He earned All-Star honors in '84 and '86. *MVP Books Collection.* **Right:** Robby Thompson, who finished second in Rookie of the Year voting in 1986, spent his entire 11-year MLB career in a Giants uniform. *MVP Books Collection*

Strikeouts

1980: Vida Blue, 129
1981: Tom Griffin, 83
1982: Rich Gale, 102
Atlee Hammaker, 102
1983: Atlee Hammaker, 127
1984: Mike Krukow, 141
1985: Mike Krukow, 150
1986: Mike Krukow, 178
1987: Kelly Downs, 137
1988: Don Robinson, 122
1989: Scott Garrelts, 119

Saves

1980: Greg Minton, 19
1981: Greg Minton, 21
1982: Greg Minton, 30
1983: Greg Minton, 22
1984: Greg Minton, 19
1985: Scott Garrelts, 13
1986: Scott Garrelts, 10
1987: Scott Garrelts, 12
1988: Scott Garrelts, 13
1989: Craig Lefferts, 20

NL Awards

NL MVP Voting

1982: Jack Clark, 7th
Greg Minton, 8th
1987: Will Clark, 5th
1988: Will Clark, 5th
1989: *Kevin Mitchell, 1st*
Will Clark, 2nd

NL Gold Glove Award Winner

1987: Rick Reuschel, P

NL All-Stars

(*Italics* indicates starter)
1980: Ed Whitson, P
1981: Vida Blue, P
1982: Greg Minton, P
1983: Darrell Evans, 1B
Atlee Hammaker, P
Gary Lavelle, P
1984: Bob Brenly, C
Chili Davis, OF
1985: Scott Garrelts, P
1986: Chris Brown, 3B
Chili Davis, OF
Mike Krukow, P
1987: Jeffrey Leonard, OF
1988: *Will Clark, 1B*
Rick Reuschel, P
Robby Thompson, 2B
1989: *Will Clark, 1B*
Kevin Mitchell, OF
Rick Reuschel, P

Sports Illustrated hails Rick Reuschel as a "True Giant" due to his 240-plus pounds and enormous pitching success—36 wins in 1988–89. *MVP Books Collection*

GIANTS 1980–1990 All-Decade Team	
1B	WILL CLARK
2B	ROBBY THOMPSON
SS	JOSE URIBE
3B	KEVIN MITCHELL
C	BOB BRENLY
OF	JACK CLARK
OF	JEFFREY LEONARD
OF	CHILI DAVIS
SP	MIKE KRUKOW
SP	ATLEE HAMMAKER
RP	GREG MINTON

THE *1990s*

STAYING PUT, MOVING FORWARD

On the verge of moving to Florida, the Giants are saved once more, and the Barry Bonds era brings winning baseball back to San Francisco.

A fter their pennant-winning campaign of 1989, the Giants appeared poised for a long run of success. It came, but in typical Giants fashion, not before some hardships came first.

Although the nucleus of Will Clark, Robby Thompson, Matt Williams, and Kevin Mitchell was young and potent, older pitchers Rick Reuschel and Don Robinson could not repeat their past success. In 1991 and 1992, the Giants fell to fourth and fifth place. Even more demoralizing, owner Bob Lurie's attempts to replace old and cold Candlestick Park continued to meet with failure, as voters in San Jose and Santa Clara County rejected attempts to subsidize a new stadium in the South Bay.

In 1992, Lurie announced that he had sold the team to a group from Tampa Bay. (The Rays, Devil or otherwise, had not yet been born.) A mad scramble ensued, with echoes of 1976, when Lurie had saved the team from moving to Canada. This time, a broad coalition of Bay Area business people, led by Peter Magowan, stepped in and bought the Giants in the offseason.

Magowan, a Merrill Lynch scion and Safeway CEO, had grown up a Giants fan in New York, and his family moved to California at the same time as the Giants. He immediately moved to restore their winning ways, hiring manager Dusty Baker and signing free agent superstar Barry Bonds. Bonds, a two-time MVP with the Pirates, was Giants royalty; his father Bobby starred for the team in the 1970s, and his godfather was Willie Mays himself.

Bonds rewarded Magowan's faith with an MVP season in 1993, and Baker led the team to 103 wins. In those pre-wildcard days, it wasn't enough. The Giants needed to win the final four games in Los Angeles to have a chance to beat the Braves, and Magowan brought his two "good-luck charms" to the games—Mays and Bobby

This pin celebrates the Giants' sole division title of the decade. They finished second four times and never advanced past the League Division Series. *MVP Books Collection*

Thomson. "We won Thursday, we won Friday, and we won Saturday," Magowan recalled. But the Braves kept pace. "Now we've got to win a fourth time," he said.

On the season's final day—October 3, the anniversary of Thomson's home run—the Dodgers toyed with 21-year-old rookie Salomon Torres, winning 12–1. "My good luck charms ran out," Magowan said. The next year, the Braves moved to the National League East, and the wildcard was introduced into the playoff format, but both moves came too late for the Giants.

The Giants failed to play .500 ball the next three seasons, with the 1994 strike aborting Matt Williams's strong run at the then-MLB record of 61 home runs. But a vote in San Francisco gave them the necessary zoning change to build a privately financed ballpark in China Basin, and Candlestick Park's days were numbered.

Starting in 1997, the Giants embarked on one of their best historical runs, a stretch of eight years finishing either in first or second place. The 1997 season was all the sweeter because it followed a last-place finish in 1996. GM Brian Sabean gave the team a midseason boost, trading six minor-leaguers for pitchers Wilson Alvarez, Roberto Hernandez, and Danny Darwin. Locked into a tight pennant race with—who else?—the Dodgers, the Giants had actually fallen out of first place in September. But they swept a two-game series with LA at Candlestick Park, tying for the division lead by winning an epic extra-inning contest marked by Brian Johnson's walk-off home run. The Giants went 6–3 the rest of the year and won the division by two games.

The playoffs that year were another story. The format strangely had the wildcard Florida Marlins playing the first two games at home, and the Giants were swept.

Winning 89 and 86 games the next two seasons was not enough to put the Giants back into the playoffs before decade's end. They showed signs of contending, however. Jeff Kent and Bonds were forming a powerful middle-of-the-order threat. Sabean proved adept at bringing in aging sluggers such as Ellis Burks to provide support. Russ Ortiz and Kirk Rueter anchored the starting pitching, and Robb Nen dominated as a smoke-throwing closer.

In 1999, the Giants played their last game at Candlestick. "Tell it goodbye," the team declared, and fans did so gleefully. While San Francisco's high-tech industry girded for Y2K, the Giants prepared for great things in a new century, with a new ballpark rising downtown.

Slugger Barry Bonds and skipper Dusty Baker both joined the Giants in 1993. The team went on to enjoy a 103-win season but failed to earn a playoff spot.
Otto Greule Jr./Getty Images

Highlights

May 8: San Francisco is 11 games out of first place after opening at 9–18.

June 8: The Giants crack 27 hits in a 23–8 crushing of Atlanta, as Will Clark homers twice and drives in six.

June 13: Trevor Wilson tosses a one-hit shutout over San Diego after losing the no-hitter in the ninth.

June 18: The Giants win their ninth straight game, and 16th out of 17, to improve to 35–30.

July 29: Versus Cincinnati, Scott Garrelts loses a no-hitter with two outs in the ninth.

August 4: The Giants pull to within 3½ games of first place, but that's as close as they'll get.

August 15: Philadelphia's Terry Mulholland no-hits the Giants.

NOTES

Third baseman **Matt Williams** amasses 33 homers and an NL-high 122 RBI, while **Kevin Mitchell** tallies 35 big flys and 93 RBI.

Brett Butler bats .309 with 51 steals, 108 runs, and an NL-best 192 hits.

John Burkett leads the staff in wins (14–7), while **Jeff Brantley** records 19 saves and a 1.56 ERA.

CREEPY, STREAKY

Giants Can't Win at the Stick . . . Then Go on a Tear

It was as if the bad vibes from the Earthquake Series still lingered in Candlestick Park. The reigning NL champions got off to a fine start in 1990 by taking two out of three at Atlanta. But the trouble started in their home opener—on Friday the 13th. The Padres beat them 8–3 when aging sidearmer Dan Quisenberry—the AL's career saves leader at the time—blew the lead. "Quiz" gave up the winning runs the next day, too, and by April 26 San Francisco was 0–8 at Candlestick.

Finally, the Giants exorcised the tremoring demons with a 12–3 shellacking of St. Louis on April 27, but by that time they were seven games out of first. By May 28, the injury-wracked Giants resided in the basement at 17–28, 14½ games behind and apparently doomed.

But then came the streaks. From June 1 to 8, San Francisco won seven games in a row, capped by a 23–8 battering of the Braves. After a loss, nine straight victories followed. Young hurlers John Burkett and Trevor Wilson, who were a combined 10–1 at the time, as well as hot-hitting youngster Rick Parker, were credited with the turnaround.

"The kids came in and picked everybody up," manager Roger Craig said, "but I also think that our veterans never lost faith. We won in '87 and '89, and they knew in the back of their minds that we could play better, even with all of the injuries."

A power-laden lineup kept the Giants on the prowl. Will Clark (95 RBI), Kevin Mitchell (35 homers), and third baseman Matt Williams (33 homers, 122 RBI) flexed considerable muscle. By August 4, the Giants were in second place, 3½ games back; however, a subsequent 2–8 road trip did them in. They finished at 85–77, in third place, six games behind first-place Cincinnati.

Ironically, the final homestand included seven straight victories through September 30, the day that former Giant Vida Blue got married on Candlestick Park's pitcher's mound. What a year at the Stick.

Center fielder Brett Butler, who hit .309 with 51 steals and 90 walks in 1990, was a highly productive leadoff hitter and one of the best bunters in the game. *Mike Powell/ Hulton Archive/Getty Images*

"It Hurts"

Giants Dig a 12–29 Hole; Can't Crawl Out

It was enough to make the hardiest of Giants fans cry in their chowder.

San Francisco was supposed to make another pennant run in 1991, especially after signing three big-name free agents: starting pitcher Bud Black, closer Dave Righetti (who had saved 36 games a year earlier with the Yankees), and reigning NL batting champion Willie McGee. But on April 22, the day after Giants catcher Steve Decker defeated Houston 1–0 with a walk-off home run, the Giants began a stretch of futility that saw them drop from 6–6 to 12–29, the worst record in the majors.

What kept fans awake at night were the extra-inning defeats. San Francisco went 0–5 in extra frames during that ugly stretch, including a 15-inning heartbreaker at Montreal. "When you're going like we're going, everything happens against you," manager Roger Craig said after his team blew a lead against Cincinnati. "It hurts."

None of the free agents panned out like the Giants had hoped. Black led the NL with 16 losses. Righetti saved 24 games but lost seven. And McGee batted .312 but mustered only 67 runs and 43 RBI.

Like the season before, the Giants suddenly got hot when the weather warmed, going 32–19 in June and July. Yet even with their 11th straight win on August 1, the club was still only 49–51. A 4–16 stretch followed later in the summer, and the Giants finished at 75–87, 19 games behind Atlanta.

As for those Braves: With an outstanding starting rotation, which would be fortified in subsequent years by pitching ace Greg Maddux, the Braves in 1991 began a stretch of dominance never before seen in Major League Baseball. They would win 14 straight division titles. Fortunately for Giants fans, Atlanta would move to the NL East following the 1993 season.

Third baseman Matt Williams, who batted .268-34-98 in 1991, happened to average .267-34-98 from 1990 to '94 with the Giants.
Mitchell Layton/Getty Images

Highlights

April 21: Catcher Steve Decker belts a walk-off homer in the ninth in a 1–0 triumph over Houston.

April 22: Robby Thompson hits for the cycle in a 7–5 loss to San Diego.

May 24: The Giants lose their seventh straight game and plummet to 12–29.

June 15: Mike Remlinger shuts out Pittsburgh 4–0 in his first MLB game.

June 18: Dave Dravecky, who had made a courageous comeback in 1989 after having cancerous tumors removed from his pitching arm, has that arm amputated.

July 14: Will Clark goes 5-for-6 with seven RBI in a 17–5 rout of the Phillies.

August 1: The Giants whip Cincinnati 8–1 for their 11th straight victory, but they're still just 49–51, nine games back.

December 11: San Francisco trades Kevin Mitchell to Seattle in a five-player deal.

NOTES

Will Clark (.301-29-116) leads the league in slugging (.536) and total bases (303).

Matt Williams ranks second in the NL in homers (34), while newly acquired outfielder **Willie McGee** is fourth in batting (.312).

Southpaw **Trevor Wilson** (13–11, 3.56) is the staff's top winner.

Highlights

May 11–27: The Giants sit atop the NL West standings as they improve their record to 26–18.

June 4: With the Giants on the block, San Jose voters reject a plan to build a stadium there.

June 7: In the ninth inning of a 3–0 shutout over Houston, Trevor Wilson strikes out the side on nine pitches.

June 19: San Francisco drops to 8½ back after a 5–16 stretch.

June 21–25: After beating San Diego 1–0 in 11 innings, the Giants are shut out three straight games.

August 7: The Giants announce that the team has been sold and will move to St. Petersburg, Florida, but investors will block the move.

October 4: Greg Litton belts a pinch-hit grand slam to defeat Cincinnati 6–2 in the 13th inning of the season finale.

November 10: Baseball owners refuse to grant permission for the Giants to move to St. Petersburg.

December 8: The Giants sign outfielder Barry Bonds for six years, $43.75 million.

NOTES

Will Clark paces the Giants in batting (.300) and RBI (73).

John Burkett leads the staff in wins (13–9), while **Bill Swift** (10–4) tops the circuit in ERA (2.08).

STICKING AROUND

Magowan and Pals Buy Giants, Keep Them in SF

In 1992, everything interesting about the Giants happened in executive offices, from the near relocation of the team to a managerial change to the signing of an A-list free agent.

What happened on the field that year was utterly forgettable. The streaky team of the two previous years became *too* consistent in 1992. On July 16, they were 44–44, and then it was all downhill. A late-season nine-game losing streak contributed to 72–90 record, as San Francisco finished 26 games behind the first-place Braves.

A declining Kevin Mitchell had been traded before the 1992 season, and no Giants hitter picked up the slack. Matt Williams led the team with 20 homers while batting .227. Will Clark paced the team in RBI and runs, with just 73 and 69 respectively. While starter Bill Swift, acquired in the Mitchell trade, posted a sterling 10–4, 2.08 record, no Giants pitcher—due to the team's anemic offense—could muster more than 13 wins.

With so little to get excited about, many fans stopped coming to the park. The team drew just 1,560,998 fans, the second lowest figure in the league. Others stayed away because of Candlestick's crummy accommodations. Owner Bob Lurie had preferred to build a new ballpark in San Francisco, but in 1987 and '89 voters had rejected a new stadium built partly with tax dollars. Losing millions every year, Lurie turned to Silicon Valley, but San Jose and Santa Clara voters also said no.

Even if the Giants did move, it wouldn't have affected manager Roger Craig. The 62-year-old manager retired after the 1992 season. *Focus on Sport/Getty Images*

In August, Lurie shook Giants fans to the core when he announced that the team had been sold to Florida investors, and that the club would move to St. Petersburg for 1993. That move would be blocked in November by NL team owners. Local investors headed by businessman Peter Magowan purchased the Giants and vowed to keep them in San Francisco.

Magowan made his mark in December, replacing retiring manager Roger Craig with team hitting coach Dusty Baker and signing Pirates superstar Barry Bonds. To Giants fans, Peter Magowan was Santa Claus.

The One and Only Barry Bonds

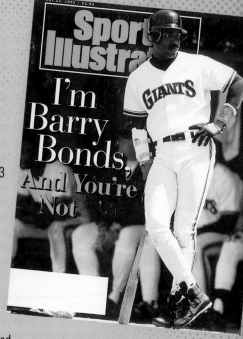

In December 1992, the Giants' new owners signed free agent Barry Bonds to a six-year, $43.75-million contract. "It is a lot of money," said new Managing General Partner Peter Magowan, "but there is only one Barry Bonds."

You can say that again.

The son of Giants star Bobby Bonds and godson of Bobby's legendary teammate Willie Mays, Barry benefitted from great genes and a steady stream of insider advice. Bobby taught his son to bat left-handed, since it's a shorter route to first and there are more righty pitchers, and to approach each pitch as if it's an 0-2 count. A football, track, and baseball star at Riverside Polytechnic High School in California, Barry wowed MLB scouts at Arizona State. He went sixth overall to the Pirates in 1985 and became a regular with Pittsburgh a year later, batting .223.

Like his dad and godfather, Bonds was a tremendous speed and power threat. By 1990, he put it all together, ripping .301-33-114 with 52 steals and winning his first of eight Gold Glove Awards for his outfield prowess. Bonds won the NL MVP Award in 1990 and '92 and finished second in the year in between.

Bonds was an immediate sensation with the Giants in 1993, setting then career highs in batting, homers, and RBI (.336-46-123) and winning his third league MVP crown. Bonds possessed a short, quick uppercut swing as well as extraordinary vision and pitch recognition. In 1996, the year he drew 151 walks, he became the second MLB player to amass 40 homers and 40 steals in a season. Along the way, he developed a reputation as an egotistical superstar who could be both charming and nasty to reporters.

Through his first 13 seasons, Bonds was in the midst of a Willie Mays-like career. But that wasn't quite good enough for Barry. According to the book *Game of Shadows*, authored by *San Francisco Chronicle* reporters Mark Fainaru-Wada and Lance Williams, Bonds began taking steroids after the 1998 season, the year in which juicer Mark McGwire belted 70 home runs.

From 2000 to 2004, Bonds belted 49, 73 (the all-time record), 46, 45, and 45 home runs. Due to his deadly power and improved hitting skills (he batted .370, .341, and .362 from 2002 to 2004), pitchers were afraid to pitch to him. His walk totals from 2001 to 2004 (he won the NL MVP Award each year) were 177, 198, 148, and an MLB-record 232. Bonds's .863 slugging average in 2001 and .609 on-base percentage in 2004 also set major league marks.

Early in 2004, it was reported that Bonds was among a number of athletes who had received illegal performance-enhancing drugs from personal trainer Greg Anderson. This information was obtained by federal agents in a sting that led to the indictment of Anderson and Victor Conte, president of the Bay Area Laboratory Co-Operative (BALCO). During grand jury testimony on December 4, 2003, Bonds said that he used a substance called "the clear," supplied by Anderson, but said he didn't realize it was a steroid.

Hounded by the media and fans for his steroid use, Bonds sometimes lashed back. "You wanted to bring me down, you've finally brought me and my family down," he told reporters in March 2005. "You've finally done it. So now go kick a different person. . . . I'm mentally drained. Tired of my kids crying."

In 2007, Bonds broke Hank Aaron's home run record of 755. That November, he was indicted on five felony counts of perjury and obstruction of justice for allegedly lying when he had testified that he never knowingly used performance-enhancing drugs. In 2011, a jury found him guilty of one count of obstruction of justice.

Bonds holds MLB career records for home runs (762), walks (2,558), and league MVP Awards (seven), but he left the game with more detractors than fans. He had bitten the steroid apple—and paid the price.

Above: Bonds vowed never to talk to *Sports Illustrated* again after the magazine portrayed him as a prima donna in this May 24, 1993, issue. *MVP Books Collection* **Below:** From 1993 to 2004 with the Giants, Bonds averaged .317 with 44 homers, 107 RBI, 21 steals, 141 walks, and a .479 OBP. *Lenny Ignelzi/ AP Images*

Highlights

January 12: A local group led by Peter Magowan buys the Giants and promises to keep them in San Francisco.

June 24: With a 17–2 rout of the expansion Colorado Rockies, the Giants improve to 49-24 and have a nine-game lead in the NL West.

August 22: The Giants are a stunning 83–41 and have a 7½-game lead.

September 17–October 2: Following an eight-game losing streak, San Francisco goes 14–2. On October 1, Barry Bonds drives in seven runs in an 8–7 win over the Dodgers.

October 3: The Giants finish one game behind the Braves after they lose 12–1 to LA and Atlanta wins its finale.

NOTES

Barry Bonds wins his third NL MVP Award in four years after batting .336 with 126 walks and league highs in homers (46) and RBI (123).

Matt Williams amasses 38 homers and 110 RBI.

Bill Swift (21–8) and **John Burkett** (22–7) shine, while **Rod Beck** smashes the team record for saves (48).

The Giants draw 2,606,354 to shatter the **franchise attendance record**.

BONDS TO THE RESCUE

Barry Leads SF to 103 Wins . . . But Not the Playoffs

From 1992 to 1993, the Giants saw their run production skyrocket from a paltry 574 to a whopping 808. Fans could credit the improvement to newcomer Barry Bonds, the former Pirates outfielder who had won two of the previous three NL MVP Awards. Bonds didn't create that 234-run improvement all by himself, but he came close. After all, he led the NL with 46 homers and 123 RBI, and his 129 runs scored ranked second in the league. On the day that Barry—the son of Giants legend Bobby Bonds—belted two home runs in a game against the Mets, New York manager Jeff Torborg proclaimed that "Bonds belongs in a higher league."

After frustrating starts the previous three seasons, the 1993 Giants were 31–15 on May 25, the day that Bonds was batting .401. The hot start was all it took to bring fans back to Candlestick—that and the fact that they knew the team was staying put. By May 25, the team had drawn more than 50,000 to a game four times.

Batting ahead of Bonds in the lineup, Matt Williams saw plenty of fat pitches, and he responded with a tremendous bounce-back season (38 homers, 110 RBI). The pitching corps also had a great one-two punch, as John Burkett led the NL in wins (22–7) while Bill Swift (21–8, 2.82) finished second in Cy Young Award balloting. Closer Rod Beck emerged with a franchise-record 48 saves.

Under new "player's manager" Dusty Baker, the Giants improved to 65–32 with a 10-game lead on July 22. Unfortunately, the hard-charging Braves swept them at the Stick in late August, cutting their advantage to 4½ games. September was a roller coaster ride, as the Giants lost eight straight to drop to 3½ back before going 13–3 to tie the Braves in the season's penultimate game. But on that final Sunday, Atlanta defeated Colorado 5–3 while San Francisco self-destructed at LA, losing 12–1.

The Giants had tied a franchise record with 103 wins, but they had needed 105.

John Burkett's league-leading 22 wins in 1993 were eight more than he had in any of his other 14 big-league seasons. *Michael Layton/Hulton Archive/Getty Images*

STRIKING OUT

Williams Flexes Muscle, but Season Ends Early

On June 23, 1994, Will Clark was batting .357 with 67 RBI. Unfortunately, he was playing for the Texas Rangers at the time.

With Will "The Thrill" lost to free agency, the 1994 Giants—like the 1990 to '92 teams—got off to an exasperating start in 1994. Barry Bonds and Matt Williams continued to pound the ball, but the rest of the lineup was downright pitiful. "We know we're going to start hitting," Giants closer Rod Beck said in late May, "but it's like, 'Come on, let's do it!'"

Most players never did. Robby Thompson, who had cracked .312 a year earlier, batted .209 in an injury-plagued 1994. Thompson, who had been beaned the previous September and again in March, said he thought about the beanings when he was in the batter's box. The team's woeful hitting led to a 6–19 record in June.

On August 11, the Giants were 55–60, yet they still had a chance to make the playoffs. That year, Major League Baseball broke into six divisions, including the East, Central, and West in both the AL and NL. The team with the next best record in each league would also make the playoffs, as a wildcard team. On August 10, San Francisco was in second place in the NL West, three games behind the Dodgers and ahead of the two other teams in the division, San Diego and the Colorado Rockies.

The only problem was that August 11 turned out to be the last day of the season. Refusing to accept the owners' demands for a salary cap for each team, the MLB Players Association went on strike. The two sides could not strike a deal, and the rest of the season—including the postseason—never happened.

Among big-league players, no one lost out as much as Matt Williams. He hammered 43 home runs through August 11, and he was on pace to break Roger Maris's major league record of 61. Scarily, besides Williams and Bonds, no other Giant tallied more than 32 RBI.

Baseball Weekly applauds Matt Williams, who was on pace for 60 home runs when the strike hit. Since 1962, no big-leaguer had belted more than 52 big flys. *MVP Books Collection*

1994

▸ **55-60**   **2nd** ◂

Highlights

April 3: The season opens with a major realignment, as MLB adds a Central Division to both the NL and AL. All six division winners plus two wildcard teams will make the playoffs. The Giants occupy the four-team NL West along with the Dodgers, Padres, and Rockies.

June 29: Matt Williams belts his 29th home run, breaking Willie Stargell's NL record for homers before July.

July 31: Williams becomes the first NL slugger to belt 40 home runs before August.

August 12: Major League players go on strike. The labor dispute centers around the owners' desire to institute a salary cap for each team. The strike will last until April 2, 1995.

NOTES

Matt Williams blasts an NL-high 43 home runs in the Giants' 115 games. At that pace, over a full slate of games, he would have tied Roger Maris's MLB record of 61 homers.

Barry Bonds swats 37 homers and steals 29 bases, and **Darren Lewis** leads the NL with nine triples.

Mark Portugal (10–8) is the team's only double-digit winner, and **Rod Beck** is second in the NL with 28 saves (in 28 chances).

1995

▶ 67-77   4th ◀

Highlights

April 26: Due to the players strike, the Giants' 144-game season doesn't begin until this day—and they get pounded 12–5 at Atlanta.

April 28: San Francisco plays its home opener at 3Com Park, the new name for Candlestick Park.

May 2: Down 3–0 in the 15th inning to the Dodgers, the Giants score four in the bottom of the frame, with Matt Williams doubling in the winning run.

May 28–June 7: An 8–2 stretch puts the Giants at 23–17 and in first place, but they will tumble out of first for good the next day.

June 14: Giants infielder Mike Benjamin goes 6-for-7 against the Cubs, giving him an MLB-record 14 hits over his last three games.

July 21: San Francisco acquires speed-burner and NFL superstar Deion Sanders in an eight-player trade with Cincinnati.

NOTES

Barry Bonds raps .294-33-104 with an NL-best .431 OBP.

Matt Williams cracks .336 in 76 games, while outfielder **Glenallen Hill** drives in 86 runs.

Mark Leiter is the staff's top winner at 10–12, while **Rod Beck** finishes third in the league with 33 saves.

PRIME TIME

"Neon" Deion Makes a Cameo with San Francisco

Officially timed at 4.27 seconds in the 40-yard dash, Deion Sanders stole 186 bases in the majors, including eight in his 52-game stint with San Francisco in 1995. *Ron Vesely/ Hulton Archive/Getty Images*

For some reason in the 1990s, Giants management believed that signing big-name stars—no matter their baseball ability—would help solve problems. The gambles never amounted to much. Legendary relievers Goose Gossage and Dan Quisenberry had little gas left in the tank, and former Mets slugger Darryl Strawberry mustered only four home runs in his stint with San Francisco in 1994. On July 21, 1995, in an eight-player trade with Cincinnati, the Giants acquired one of the greatest and flashiest athletes in American history: "Neon" Deion "Prime Time" Sanders.

Typifying the drama that always surrounded him, the legendary NFL defensive back was late in reporting to the Giants. He said at the time that he might retire from football or baseball; he wasn't sure which. In his 52 games with San Francisco in 1995, he batted .285 with five homers and five electrifying triples. Then he was gone.

Earlier in the year, it seemed as if the 1995 season itself might not happen. The 1994 players strike wasn't resolved until April 2, 1995. Following a rushed spring training, Opening Day didn't begin until April 26. Although the Giants got off to a nice start, holding first place until June 7, their lack of pitching talent finally caught up with them. On July 20, after giving up double digits in runs for the fifth time in seven games, the Giants fell into the basement, where they would finish.

It was a sour season all around for San Francisco. Manager Dusty Baker employed 25 pitchers, and only Mark Leiter (10–12) won more than six games. Although Matt Williams batted .336 with 23 homers, he played in only 76 games. Even Barry Bonds had a rather pedestrian season, batting .294 with 104 RBI. However, he did turn the 30-homer, 30-steals trick again, joining Ron Gant and former Giants Willie Mays and Bobby Bonds as those who had achieved the feat multiple times.

And remember, Barry did it during a shortened (144-game) season. A 40-40 campaign was certainly within his reach.

BONDS GOES 40/40

But His Team Goes Nowhere, Losing 94 Games

Highlights

March 26: San Francisco residents vote in favor of a new, privately funded ballpark.

April 27: Versus Florida, Barry Bonds cracks his 300th home run, becoming the fourth MLB player (including his father, Bobby Bonds) with 300 homers and 300 stolen bases.

May 28: The Giants and Expos play through a 4.8 earthquake at 3Com Park.

June 19: The Giants defeat the Marlins in 15 innings for the second day in a row, this one on a walk-off three-run homer by catcher Tom Lampkin. They improve to 36–33, 1½ games out.

June 21–30: San Francisco loses 10 straight games.

July 18: A 4–3 loss to the Dodgers concludes a woeful 4–21 stretch.

September 27: Against Colorado, Bonds steals his 40th base to become the second MLB player (following Jose Canseco) to tally 40 homers and 40 steals in a season.

November 13: The Giants trade injury-plagued star Matt Williams to Cleveland for four players, including second baseman Jeff Kent.

In a meaningless game at Colorado on September 27, 1996, Barry Bonds bolted for second in a stolen base attempt. After sliding in safely, giving him 40 steals along with 42 homers, he removed the base amid cheers and boos. Even before his involvement with steroids, Barry Bonds was a highly polarizing figure.

No one questioned Barry's extraordinary talent, output, or desire to win, and often he could dazzle you with his charming smile. But many also considered him a braggart and an egomaniac. Sportswriter Larry Stone recalled that "Barry remembered to tell me to wish [my daughter] a happy birthday when she turned 8 in 1994. But just when you thought you might have earned his confidence, he'd shoot you down the next day with a withering glance or a sharp put-down. Or, most often, he'd completely ignore you."

On the same day that Bonds became the second 40/40 player in MLB history, joining Jose Canseco, he won a court case against his ex-wife. Sun Bonds's $10,000-a-month spousal support payments would be cut off in about two years, instead of the six she had requested.

Rooting for Barry Bonds, or rooting against him, was about all that Giants fans could do in 1996—at least in the second half of the season. After back-to-back 15-inning victories on June 18 and 19, San Francisco was 36–33, 1½ games out. But a 10-game losing streak followed, and the Giants were doomed.

Bonds's numbers were astounding: 42 homers, 40 steals, 122 runs, 129 runs, and 151 walks. Yet outside of Matt Williams (.302-22-85), Barry had little support in the lineup. The pitching was atrocious (4.71 team ERA), as the starting staff consisted of Mark Gardner (12–7, 4.42) and four hurlers with losing records and ERAs between 4.60 and 5.40. Closer Rod Beck saved 35 games but went 0–9.

The Giants finished at 68–94, in last place, 23 games behind San Diego. Fortunately, new stars would emerge to turn this team around.

In 1996, Barry Bonds (far right) became the fourth member of the 300-homers/300-steals club, joining (left to right) his godfather Willie Mays, father Bobby Bonds, and Andre Dawson. *Susan Ragan/AP Images*

NOTES

Barry Bonds rips .308-42-129 with 40 steals, 122 runs, and an NL-record 151 walks.

Mark Gardner (12–7) leads the team in wins.

1997

▸ 90-72   1st ◂

Highlights

April 20: The Giants win their ninth straight game to improve to 13–3.

May 11–August 23: San Francisco sits atop the NL West.

June 12: The Giants play the first regular-season interleague game in MLB history, beating the Rangers 4–3 in Texas.

July 15: SF hitters erupt for 13 runs in the seventh in a 16–2 romp over the Padres.

September 18: The Giants tie the Dodgers for first place thanks to Brian Johnson's 12th-inning walk-off homer.

September 26–27: With 17–4 and 6–1 triumphs over San Diego, the Giants clinch the division.

September 30–October 1: Florida beats San Francisco 2–1 and 7–6 in Games One and Two of the NL Division Series, scoring both winning runs in the bottom of the ninth.

October 3: Jeff Kent knocks two homers in Game Three, but Florida breezes 6–2 to sweep the Series.

NOTES

Barry Bonds amasses 40 homers, 37 steals, 123 runs, 101 RBI, and 145 walks.

Jeff Kent and first baseman **J. T. Snow** tally 121 and 104 RBI, respectively.

Shawn Estes goes 19–5, 3.18.

WORST TO FIRST

Kent, Snow, Estes Help Revitalize the Giants

"It's Giants Baseball," proclaimed the team's slogan for 1997. "Anything Can Happen."

After consecutive last-place finishes, the new marketing catchphrase seemed like a desperate attempt to lure fans to the ballpark. Yet with this "Team of Destiny," amazing things really did happen.

Credit Nick Sabean for the turnaround. A former Yankees scout, Sabean spent several years in the Giants' front office before being promoted to general manager on September 30, 1996. Six weeks later, he incurred the wrath of fans when he traded slugger Matt Williams to Cleveland for four players, including second baseman Jeff Kent and shortstop Jose Vizcaino. Sabean responded to heavy criticism by declaring, "I am not an idiot."

Except for outfielders Barry Bonds and Glenallen Hill, the Giants had a completely different lineup in 1997. Most notable was the all-new double-play combination. Slick-fielding Vizcaino ranked fourth in the NL in assists that year. In his sixth big-league season, Kent suddenly emerged as a slugger, amassing 29 homers and 121 RBI. And first baseman J. T. Snow, acquired in a trade with the Angels for mediocre lefty Allen Watson, was sensational. After recovering from a scary beaning in spring training, Snow rapped .281-28-104 while working magic with his glove.

Bonds added 40 home runs, as the Giants finished fourth in the league in runs scored. Southpaw starter Shawn Estes was another difference-maker. In his first full season, he made the All-Star team and finished at 19–5.

With three tight victories over Florida in April, the Giants extended their winning streak to nine and boasted a 13–3 record. "We went 17–7 in April and everyone said we

Shawn Estes (second from left), who went 19–5 in 1997, sweats through Game Two of the NLDS. He yielded five runs in three innings, and Florida won 7–6. *Rhona Wise/AFP/Getty Images*

Johnson's Heroic Home Run

A playoff atmosphere gripped 3Com Park on September 18, 1997, as 52,000 fans fretted through 11 pressure-packed innings on a Thursday afternoon. The stakes were high, as the second-place Giants trailed the rival Dodgers by one game in the NL West. Through 11 frames, the score remained 5–5. Then the real drama began.

Giants closer Rod Beck, who had blown a save in his last outing, was cascaded with boos after loading the bases on singles to Mike Piazza, Eric Karros, and Raul Mondesi. However, Beck turned the jeers to cheers by striking out Todd Zeile and then inducing Eddie Murray to ground into a double play.

With the crowd still abuzz, Giants catcher Brian Johnson, a career-long backup, played the hero. On the first pitch of the bottom of the 12th, Johnson socked a Mark Guthrie offering deep to left field—but into the wind. "I thought, 'Oh, no, maybe the wind's going to knock it down," Johnson said. But the ball landed in the left field bleachers, prompting the catcher to thrust his arms in the air.

Johnson was mobbed at home plate, and Barry Bonds celebrated so hard that he temporarily popped his shoulder out of its socket. Amid the bedlam, Johnson emerged from the dugout to take a curtain call.

"That's classic right there," effused Dusty Baker afterward, "and the guys are on top of the world. . . . I've never seen anything like this before at a baseball game."

The Giants mob Brian Johnson (hidden in the photo) after his dramatic home run. *Otto Greule, Jr./Hulton Archive/Getty Images*

were playing the Mets and the Pirates," Baker would say in September. "Well, they've turned out to be two of the best teams in the league. Then we got to May and June and July and people started waiting for the fall."

A fall never came. While they played barely .500 ball over the next four months, the Giants held onto first place from May 11 to August 24—until the Dodgers claimed the top spot. Over the final six weeks, the two rivals fought for division supremacy, and when Giants catcher Brian Johnson beat LA with a 12th-inning, walk-off homer on September 18, the two teams were tied.

The Giants entered the final weekend leading by two games, and they immediately took care of business. Combining for six hits and seven RBI, Kent and Vizcaino powered San Francisco to a 17–4 rout of the Padres on Friday. The next day, lefty Wilson Alvarez tossed seven innings of shutout ball in a 6–1, division-clinching triumph. "I don't think anybody really expected this," Snow said after the game. "But as the season went on, we made believers of a lot of people."

Unfortunately, the dream died quickly in Florida, as the Marlins won the first two games of the NLDS in extra innings. The first walk-off heartbreak occurred in the bottom of the ninth of Game One, when Edgar Renteria snapped a 1–1 tie with a two-out, bases-loaded single off Roberto Hernandez. After the Giants scratched out a run in the top of the ninth to tie Game Two at 6–6, Florida's Moisés Alou singled in the winner in the bottom of the frame—again off Hernandez. In the sole game in San Francisco, the Marlins cruised 6–2 to sweep the mini series.

1998

▶ 89-74　2nd ◀

Highlights

May 8: Giants first baseman Charlie Hayes starts a triple play after catching a line drive against the Cubs.

May 24: The Giants win a 17th-inning marathon 9–6 at St. Louis.

May 28: Arizona intentionally walks Barry Bonds while the bases are loaded in the ninth inning of an 8–6 game. The Diamondbacks win 8–7.

June 9: A 7–6 home win over Seattle is the Giants' 11th straight victory. They are 41–24 with a one-game lead in the NL West.

August 23: At Florida, Bonds clubs his 400th career home run.

September 4: Bonds reaches base for an NL-record 15th straight time.

September 19: Jeff Kent and Jeff Mueller belt grand slams in an 18–4 blowout of the Dodgers.

September 27: Colorado scores a 9–8 walk-off win over San Francisco in the season finale. The Giants and Cubs tie for the NL wildcard.

September 28: The Cubs defeat the Giants 5–3 to advance to the NLDS.

NOTES

Barry Bonds cracks .303-37-122, and Jeff Kent slugs .297-31-128.

Lefty Kirk Rueter goes 16–9, while Robb Nen posts 40 saves.

WILD TIMES IN THE NL

Steroids Are Rampant; Giants Lose Wildcard Game

In a one-game playoff to determine the 1998 NL wildcard winner, Gary Gaetti slugged this two-run homer in the fifth to break a scoreless tie. The Cubs won 5–3. *Tom Hauck/Hulton Archive/Getty Images*

As in 1930, baseballs were flying out of ballparks in 1998. Only this time it wasn't the balls that were juiced.

The use of steroids and other performing-enhancing drugs became rampant in baseball in the 1990s. With homer totals and attendance skyrocketing, MLB officials turned a blind eye. In the National League, the "Great Home Run Chase" between nice guys and secret users Mark McGwire and Sammy Sosa was the feel-good story of the decade. "Big Mac" of the Cardinals smashed Roger Maris's major league record of 61 homers by crushing 70, and "Slammin' Sammy" of the Cubs launched 66.

In 1998, a clean Barry Bonds settled for his typical output: .303 average, 37 homers, 122 RBI. With Jeff Kent posting similar numbers and four other Giants batting over .290 (third baseman Bill Mueller and outfielders Darryl Hamilton, Stan Javier, and Marvin Benard), the Giants scored 845 runs, second most in the league. However, it was enough for only 89 wins and a second-place finish, as the Dodgers won the NL West with 98 triumphs.

Still, a 9–1 stretch in late September put the Giants in position for a wildcard bid. When 40-year-old legend Orel Hershiser, in his sole season with San Francisco, defeated Colorado in the penultimate game of the season, the Giants and Cubs were tied for the wildcard. San Francisco could have clinched on Sunday, but a Neifi Perez game-ending homer off Robb Nen in the ninth gave the Rockies a 9–8 victory.

That set up a wildcard-game playoff at Wrigley Field between the Cubs and Giants. SF's Mark Gardner (13–6 on the year) helped keep the game scoreless until the fifth, when 40-year-old Gary Gaetti put the Cubs up for good with a two-run homer. With Chicago leading 5–0 in the ninth, the Giants rallied for three runs, but the game ended when potential tying run Joe Carter popped out to first base.

According to the book *Game of Shadows*, it was after and because of the McGwire/Sosa homer race that Barry Bonds began juicing.

BYE-BYE, CANDLESTICK

A High-Scoring Season Ends With a Farewell Bash

For the San Francisco Giants, the 20th century ended with a bang. With steroid usage in full-flex in 1999, major league hitters produced 24,691 runs that year, setting an MLB record. San Francisco ranked third in the NL with a whopping 5.38 runs per game. In addition, the team played its final game ever at Candlestick Park, honoring it with a spectacular celebration.

Throughout the season, the Giants didn't have a weak link in the lineup. Infielders Jeff Kent and Bill Mueller and outfielder Marvin Benard all hit exactly .290. Catcher Brent Mayne rapped .301, and second baseman Rich Aurilia plated 80 runs. Outfielders Bonds and Ellis Burks topped 30 homers, and first baseman J. T. Snow drove in 98 runs. Unfortunately, the only reliable starter was Russ Ortiz, who went 18–9, 3.81.

The Giants spent about two-thirds of the first 100 games of the season in first place. But an August swoon (due largely to injuries) coupled with a Diamondbacks surge turned the tide. Though they bashed their way to an 86–76 record, the Giants finished 14 games behind first-place Arizona and 10½ out of the wildcard.

Though the game itself was meaningless, 61,389 fans would never forget the farewell festivities on September 30. Managing General Partner Peter Magowan paid tribute to the hardy souls who had weathered the cold winds of Candlestick over the years. "No fans were as loud, no fans stayed as late, no fans endured as much as you did," he said.

Broadcasters Lon Simmons and Jon Miller introduced dozens of former players on that Thursday afternoon, with the final tributes for Orlando Cepeda, Juan Marichal, Willie McCovey, and Willie Mays. After a 24-second countdown (in honor of his long-since retired number), Mays threw the last-ever pitch at Candlestick Park. As air cannons shot streamers through the air, and fans sang "Bye-Bay Baby" for the last time, home plate was dug up and loaded onto an orange-and-black helicopter, which transported it to its new home in China Basin.

Groundskeeper Neil Centranolo attempts to dislodge 3Com Park's pitching rubber after the Giants' last game ever at the ballpark.
John G. Mabanglo/AFP/Getty Images

Highlights

April 20: Barry Bonds undergoes arm surgery, which will sideline him for 10 weeks.

May 3: Jeff Kent hits for the cycle, but Pittsburgh scores four runs in the bottom of the ninth to defeat the Giants 9–8.

May 25: The Giants bomb the Cardinals 17–1. They are 26–19 and have been in first place virtually the whole season.

June 14: The Giants turn a 5–4–3 triple play in Colorado.

June 29: Ellis Burks belts two homers and knocks in seven runs in a 10–1 win over the Rockies.

July 15: Against Oakland, Bonds sets an MLB record with his 294th intentional walk.

July 23: The Giants have held first place the entire month so far, but they'll drop out for good the next day.

September 30: In the final game ever at 3Com/Candlestick Park, the Giants fall to the Dodgers 9–4.

NOTES

Barry Bonds clouts 34 home runs in his 102 games.

Other heavy hitters include outfielder **Ellis Burks** (.282-31-96), **J. T. Snow** (.274-24-98), and **Jeff Kent** (.290-23-101).

Russ Ortiz goes 18–9 in his first full season, while **Robb Nen** saves 37 games.

Team Leaders

(*Italics* indicates NL leader)

Batting Average
1990: Brett Butler, .309
1991: Willie McGee, .312
1992: Will Clark, .300
1993: Barry Bonds, .336
1994: Barry Bonds, .312
1995: Barry Bonds, .294
1996: Barry Bonds, .308
1997: Barry Bonds, .291
1998: Barry Bonds, .303
1999: Jeff Kent, .290

Home Runs
1990: Kevin Mitchell, 35
1991: Matt Williams, 34
1992: Matt Williams, 20
1993: *Barry Bonds, 46*
1994: *Matt Williams, 43*
1995: Barry Bonds, 33
1996: Barry Bonds, 42
1997: Barry Bonds, 40
1998: Barry Bonds, 37
1999: Barry Bonds, 34

RBI
1990: *Matt Williams, 122*
1991: Will Clark, 116
1992: Will Clark, 73
1993: *Barry Bonds, 123*
1994: Matt Williams, 96
1995: Barry Bonds, 104
1996: Barry Bonds, 129
1997: Jeff Kent, 121
1998: Jeff Kent, 128
1999: Jeff Kent, 101

Runs
1990: Brett Butler, 108
1991: Will Clark, 84
1992: Will Clark, 69
1993: Barry Bonds, 129
1994: Barry Bonds, 89
1995: Barry Bonds, 109
1996: Barry Bonds, 122
1997: Barry Bonds, 123
1998: Barry Bonds, 120
1999: Marvin Benard, 100

Wins
1990: John Burkett, 14
1991: Trevor Wilson, 13
1992: John Burkett, 13
1993: *John Burkett, 22*
1994: Mark Portugal, 10
1995: Mark Leiter, 10
1996: Mark Gardner, 12
1997: Shawn Estes, 19
1998: Kirk Rueter, 16
1999: Russ Ortiz, 18

ERA
1990: John Burkett, 3.79
1991: Trevor Wilson, 3.56
1992: *Bill Swift, 2.08*
1993: Bill Swift, 2.82
1994: John Burkett, 3.62
1995: Mark Leiter, 3.82
1996: Mark Gardner, 4.42
1997: Shawn Estes, 3.18
1998: Mark Gardner, 4.33
1999: Russ Ortiz, 3.81

Strikeouts
1990: John Burkett, 118
1991: Trevor Wilson, 139
1992: John Burkett, 107
1993: Bill Swift, 157
1994: Mark Portugal, 87
1995: Mark Leiter, 129
1996: Mark Gardner, 145
1997: Shawn Estes, 181
1998: Mark Gardner, 151
1999: Russ Ortiz, 164

Left: With his ten seasons as Giants skipper, Dusty Baker ranks second to only John McGraw in games managed (1,556) and won (840) in franchise history. *MVP Books Collection.* **Right:** Jack Thomas "J. T." Snow, shown on this Upper Deck card, won four straight Gold Gloves from 1997 to 2000 while also averaging 22 homers per year. *MVP Books Collection*

the Record Book

Saves

1990: Jeff Brantley, 19
1991: Dave Righetti, 24
1992: Rod Beck, 17
1993: Rod Beck, 48
1994: Rod Beck, 28
1995: Rod Beck, 33
1996: Rod Beck, 35
1997: Rod Beck, 37
1998: Robb Nen, 40
1999: Robb Nen, 37

NL Awards

NL MVP Voting

1990: Matt Williams, 6th
1991: Will Clark, 4th
1993: *Barry Bonds, 1st*
         Williams, 6th
1994: Williams, 2nd
         Bonds, 4th
1996: Bonds, 5th
1997: Bonds, 5th
         Jeff Kent, 8th
1998: Bonds, 8th,
         Kent, 9th

NL Gold Glove Award Winners

1991: Will Clark, 1B
         Matt Williams, 3B
1993: Kirt Manwaring, C
         Robby Thompson, 2B
         Matt Williams, 3B
         Barry Bonds, OF
1994: Matt Williams, 3B
         Barry Bonds, OF
         Darren Lewis, OF
1996: Barry Bonds, OF
1997: J. T. Snow, 1B
         Barry Bonds, OF
1998: J. T. Snow, 1B
         Barry Bonds, OF
1999: J. T. Snow, 1B

NL All-Stars

(*Italics* indicates starter)
1990: Jeff Brantley, P
         Will Clark, 1B
         Kevin Mitchell, OF
         Matt Williams, 3B
1991: *Clark, 1B*
1992: Clark, 1B
1993: Rod Beck, P
         Barry Bonds, OF
         John Burkett, P
         Robby Thompson, 2B

1994: Beck, P
         Bonds, OF
         Williams, 3B
1995: *Bonds, OF*
         Williams, 3B
1996: *Bonds, OF*
         Williams, 3B
1997: Beck, P
         Bonds, OF
         Shawn Estes, P
1998: *Bonds, OF*
         Robb Nen, P
1999: Jeff Kent, 2B
         Nen, P

GIANTS 1990–1999 All-Decade Team

1B	WILL CLARK
2B	JEFF KENT
SS	ROYCE CLAYTON
3B	MATT WILLIAMS
C	KIRT MANWARING
OF	BARRY BONDS
OF	WILLIE MCGEE
OF	DARREN LEWIS
SP	JOHN BURKETT
SP	MARK GARDNER
RP	ROD BECK

John Burkett, who is honored with a plaque on the "Wall of Fame" at AT&T Park, is the last Giants pitcher to win more than 20 games in a season, with 22 in 1993. *MVP Books Collection*

John Burkett

SAN FRANCISCO GIANTS: 1987, 1990-1994
SAN FRANCISCO GIANTS ALL-STAR: 1993

Sixth-round pick in 1983 Draft, "Burkey" combined with fellow right-handed starter Bill Swift to give Giants dual aces in early-'90s. Pennsylvania native had career year in 1993, leading NL pitchers in Wins (22-7), with 3.65 ERA. His .615 Winning Percentage, Career (67-42) ranks in San Francisco Giants All-Time Top Five (3rd).

SAN FRANCISCO GIANTS WALL OF FAME

CHAMPS AGAIN, AT LONG LAST

Barry Bonds almost takes the Giants to the promised land, but instead it is his successors, a lovable group of castoffs and misfits, who bring San Francisco not one but two unlikely world championships.

A funny thing happened to Barry Bonds as he hit his mid-30s, the age when baseball players start to decline. Bonds, already one of the best players in the game, got even better. Instead of comparisons to Ken Griffey Jr. and Mark McGwire, Bonds found his name mentioned alongside those of Babe Ruth, Ted Williams, and Hank Aaron.

Bonds belted 49 homers in 2000, but he finished second in MVP voting to teammate Jeff Kent. So he hit an otherworldly 73 in 2001, breaking McGwire's record set only three years earlier, and won the first of four straight NL MVP awards. In the first five years of the decade, Bonds batted .339, won two batting titles, hit 258 home runs, set records for walks (intentional and otherwise), and tallied a mind-boggling on-base percentage of .535.

Of course, the achievements came with an asterisk, as Bonds was implicated in the steroid scandal that engulfed Major League Baseball. He was eventually convicted of obstruction of justice for giving an evasive answer to a grand jury investigating steroids.

Although Bonds had never been a postseason star, the Giants made the playoffs as a wildcard team in 2002 and rode his bat to the World Series. Although he showed his dominating form, the Giants suffered a crushing defeat when—with champagne on ice and the locker room ready for a celebration—they blew Games Six and Seven to the Angels. San Francisco still hungered for its first World Series win.

Manager Dusty Baker was replaced the next season with one-time Giants star Felipe Alou. The Giants were wire-to-wire division champs, never trailing on their way to 100 victories. Yet once again, just as in 1997, the pesky wildcard Florida Marlins derailed the Giants' dreams.

Efforts to surround Bonds with aging stars no longer worked. Bruce Bochy came up from San Diego to manage the team. Bonds himself faded at last. He

The *San Francisco Chronicle* trumpets the Giants' second world title in 2012. *MVP Books Collection*

eclipsed Hank Aaron's career home run record in 2007, but the Giants didn't bring him back in 2008, and neither did anyone else. He finished with 762 home runs, and the Giants suffered through four straight losing seasons.

After so many years of relying on the long ball, the Giants, following general manager Brian Sabean's blueprint, began to assemble a team built for the spacious greenery of AT&T Park. Through careful drafting, they put together a spectacular starting rotation, led by Tim Lincecum, Matt Cain, and Madison Bumgarner. Lincecum—"The Freak"— won Cy Young Awards in 2008 and 2009, baffling hitters with an unorthodox delivery. A stellar bullpen, led by the eccentric Brian Wilson, held onto nearly every lead.

The rest of the team seemed assembled with rubber bands and duct tape, with a lineup known as "Bruce Bochy's Dirty Dozen" and more commonly as castoffs and misfits. (A popular shirt in San Francisco pointed out that the word *misfit* conveniently had the letters *SF* in the middle.) It was the perfect team for San Francisco. When Barry Zito nicknamed third baseman Pablo Sandoval "Kung Fu Panda" for his roly-poly athleticism, fans began wearing panda hats. When Wilson dyed his beard black as coal, fans donned their own black beards. When first baseman Aubrey Huff began strutting through the clubhouse in a rhinestone-studded "rally thong," fans even started waving similar undergarments at games.

The Giants players swarm the field after their championship-clinching victory in Game Five of the 2010 World Series. *Jose Luis Villegas/ Sacramento Bee/MCT/Getty Images*

The whole city turned orange in October 2010, as the Giants squeaked into the playoffs on the season's final day and beat the odds to win San Francisco's first-ever title. The Giants took the trophy on a tour, and long-suffering fans from throughout Northern California—and yes, all the way to New York City—could share in the redemptive power of the celebration.

A horrific injury to catcher Buster Posey derailed the 2011 season, but 2012 saw a rebuilt cast overcome all sorts of adversity—injuries, the suspension of Melky Cabrera, and deep deficits in playoff series—to bring home another championship.

Although 2013 turned out to be another year of injuries and transitions, and the Giants struggled to give their pitchers any run support, the good feelings from the two titles continued to bring fans to the ballpark in record numbers.

A wall outside AT&T Park commemorates all the Giants' World Series titles from the past. Finally, San Francisco is on the board. Even though 2010 and 2012 have been added to the wall, the Giants have left some white space for more.

Say hey!

2000

▶ **97-65   1st** ◀

Highlights

April 11: Pacific Bell Park opens to rave reviews, although the Giants lose the opener to the Dodgers 6–5.

May 24: Pitcher Shawn Estes belts a grand slam in an 18–0 win over Montreal.

July 31: The Giants settle into first place for good with a 4–3, 11-inning win at Milwaukee.

September 7: A ninth straight victory, 13–0 over San Diego, gives San Francisco an 8½-game lead.

September 21: The Giants clinch the division with an 8–7 home win over Arizona.

October 4: A three-run homer by Ellis Burks keys a 5–1 Giants home victory over the Mets in Game One of the NLDS.

October 5: New York takes Game Two 5–4 in 10 innings.

October 7: The Mets win Game Three 3–2 in 13 frames thanks to a Benny Agbayani walk-off homer.

October 8: New York's Bobby Jones throws a one-hit, 4–0 shutout in the Game Four clincher.

NOTES

Jeff Kent wins the NL MVP Award after bashing .334-33-125.

Barry Bonds belts 49 home runs, and **Ellis Burks** rips .344-24-96.

Livan Hernandez (17–11), **Shawn Estes** (15–6), and **Robb Nen** (41 saves) star on the hill.

Attendance skyrockets to 3,318,800.

REJUVENATION!

Giants Win 55 at New Park, Cruise to Division Title

It was January 21, 2000, and Barry Bonds was already launching home runs at Pacific Bell Park, the new home of the San Francisco Giants. In an offseason batting practice session, Bonds pulled one ball after the other over the 25-foot brick wall. "Right field does seem real close," he said with a smile.

Very close. Just 307 feet, in fact, making it the shortest right field fence in the National League. During the 2000 season, in which an all-time record 12,976 runs were scored in the NL, San Francisco ranked third with a head-spinning 925 (5.71 per game). But interestingly, Pac Bell was not a hitter's park. While the Giants outscored their foes 474–441 on the road, their home margin was 451–306.

As often happens when MLB teams move into a new ballpark, the Giants enjoyed a magical first season at home in 2000—thanks in part to a rabid, sellout crowd for every game. Though they lost their first six games at Pac Bell, the Giants went 55–20 there the rest of the way. Pac Bell games included 10 shutouts—all thrown by San Francisco pitchers. On May 24, the Giants blanked Montreal 18–0, as pitcher Shawn Estes went the distance and drove in five runs—four on a house-rocking grand slam.

Prior to the season, *Sports Illustrated* predicted that Bonds, Jeff Kent, and Ellis Burks—if healthy—would amass at least 100 homers and 300 RBI. Though Burks missed 40 games in 2000, he, Bonds, and Kent eclipsed *SI*'s prediction by tallying 106 homers and 327 RBI.

Kent, the NL MVP, had one of the greatest offensive seasons ever for a second baseman, smashing .334-33-125 with 41 doubles and 114 runs. Bonds set a career high with 49 homers—25 at home, 24 on the road. Burks cracked .344-24-96, and J. T. Snow joined the hit parade with a .284-19-96 season. Starter Livan Hernandez, who five years earlier was

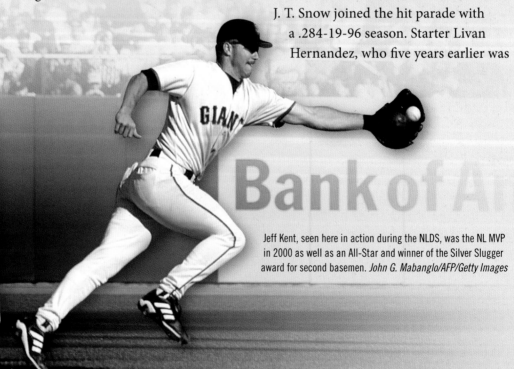

Jeff Kent, seen here in action during the NLDS, was the NL MVP in 2000 as well as an All-Star and winner of the Silver Slugger award for second basemen. *John G. Mabanglo/AFP/Getty Images*

earning $6 a month in Cuba, went 17–11, 3.75, and Estes finished at 15–6, 4.26. Closer Robb Nen, who once was clocked at 102 mph, slammed doors with 41 saves and a 1.50 ERA.

Though the Giants ended June at 38–38, 6½ games out, they went 59–27 the rest of the way—including a spirited 35–11 at home. San Francisco moved into first place on July 31 and never relinquished the top spot, winning the NL West by 11 games with a 97–65 record. While Dusty Baker was named NL Manager of the Year, Pac Bell deserved some sort of "good vibe" award.

The home-park magic continued in Game One of the NLDS, as a strong performance by Hernandez and a three-run homer by Burks led to a 5–1 victory over the Mets. The Giants seemed invincible the next day when Snow socked a dramatic three-run homer with two outs in the bottom of the ninth to tie the game at 4–4. However, the Mets scored in the 10th and Bonds struck out looking to end the game.

In New York, a nail-biting Game Three ended in the 13th inning on a Benny Agbayani homer. With a bitter twist of irony, the powerhouse Giants lineup mustered only one hit in Game Four, as Bobby Jones shut them out 4–0. The magical season was over.

The Giants' ballpark is nestled amid the downtown skyline, San Francisco Bay, Bay Bridge, and China Basin (a.k.a. "McCovey's Cove"). *MVP Books Collection*

Packin' Pac Bell

"Isn't it gorgeous!" exclaimed Dodgers shortstop Kevin Elster after the first game at Pacific Bell Park on April 11, 2000. "It's a fabulous place." Elster had reason to love the new ballpark, for he christened Pacific Bell with three home runs in the inaugural game.

Giants fans also had every reason to adore the gem that sits on the bay near downtown. China Basin is one of the warmest areas in the city, and the openness of the ballpark invited warm sunshine and spectacular views of the city, bay, and Bay Bridge. Sightlines in the fan-friendly ballpark were terrific, as was the food. And unlike decrepit Candlestick, the place was brand-spankin' new.

For these reasons, as well as the success of the team on the diamond, the Giants sold out every game in 2000, attracting 40,390 every contest and setting a franchise

record with an overall attendance of 3,315,330. That year, the price of the ticket almost guaranteed a victory, as San Francisco went 55–26 at home while pounding out 5.57 runs per game.

The sellout success continued into 2001. Not until a Monday game against the Montreal Expos on May 7 would attendance drop below 40,000. The Giants led the NL in attendance from 2001 through 2003 and topped 3 million fans each year through 2007.

Tickets were hard to come by in the first season of Pac Bell Park. *MVP Books Collection*

Highlights

April 17: At home against the Dodgers, Barry Bonds clouts his 500th home run.

May 19: In the midst of a nine-homers-in-six-games barrage, Bonds swats three against Atlanta.

May 29: Arizona tops San Francisco 1–0 in 18 innings.

July 25–August 3: After hovering around .500 all season, the Giants win nine straight games and move to within a half game of first place. It's as close as they'll get to the front-running Diamondbacks.

August 11: Bonds clubs homer No. 50.

September 9: Against Colorado, Bonds belts three more long balls for 63, most ever by a left-handed hitter.

October 5: At home against the Dodgers' Chan Ho Park, Bonds wallops his 71st home run to break Mark McGwire's MLB record.

NOTES

Barry Bonds, the NL MVP, finishes at .328-73-137 with 129 runs and MLB records for walks (177) and slugging (.863).

Jeff Kent sets a franchise record with 49 doubles, while All-Star shortstop **Rich Aurilia** bats .324 and leads the NL with 206 hits.

Shawn Estes (17–9, 3.29) is the team's pitching standout, though he will be traded after the season.

The Giants lead the league in attendance at 3,311,958.

TAINTED LOVE

In the Year of 9/11, Bonds Breaks MLB Homer Record

Barry Bonds watches the flight of his 73rd and last home run of the 2001 season on October 7, the season finale against the Dodgers. *Jed Jacobsohn/Getty Images*

In 2001, fans didn't realize that Barry Bonds was a steroid abuser. To the kids and grownups in "25" jerseys at Pac Bell Park, he was a heroic figure taking his game to new heights. Every home game that season, fans packed the park to see if Barry would splash another ball into McCovey Cove.

By May 16, Bonds had belted 15 home runs. By June 4, he had 30. That week, *Sports Illustrated*'s Tom Verducci credited Bonds's output to "an intense new off-season strength-training regimen" as well as a more aggressive mentality. "Barry is different now," teammate Jeff Kent told *SI*. "He's swinging at more pitches and being more aggressive."

The excitement peaked on September 9, 2001, when Barry bashed three home runs in the thin air at Colorado—including his longest of the year at 488 feet—to reach 63. After the 9/11 attacks, Americans were no longer interested in Bonds's personal achievements. At Pac Bell on October 5, Barry crushed No. 71—off the Dodgers' Chan Ho Park—to break Mark McGwire's MLB season record. As fireworks erupted, he was embraced by teammates and family. In a post-game ceremony, while at a podium marked "71," Barry said, "We've come a long way. We've had our ups and downs. Thank you." He then buried his face in his hands and burst into tears.

It's easy to be cynical about that evening. Bonds had achieved the feat with the help of performance-enhancing drugs. He basked in glory less than a month after 9/11. The ceremony came after the longest nine-inning game in major league history (4:27). And that night, the Giants were eliminated from playoff contention.

That season, the Giants' double-play combination of Jeff Kent and Rich Aurilia combined for 59 homers and 203 RBI. Shawn Estes went 17–9, and Rob Nenn saved 45 games. A nine-game winning streak through August 3 moved the Giants to a half game of first place. But in the end, it was all for naught. In San Francisco, the 2001 season will always be known as the year of 9/11 and Barry Bonds's steroid-tainted record.

SHOCKED BY THE MONKEY

Angels Mascot Sparks Rally, Kills Giants' Dream

For all intents and purposes, the Giants' 2002 season began on August 19. Sitting at 66–56 that day, Barry Bonds and Co. were 10½ games out of first place and well back in the wildcard chase. From there, they led their fans through a thrilling stretch run and won wild October. The Giants had the World Series in their grasp before a historic Game Six collapse to the Anaheim Angels, which was inspired by a nutty little monkey.

After his 73-homer barrage in 2001, Bonds cranked 46 in '02. Instead of Babe Ruth this year, he was Ted Williams, batting a career-high .370 while drawing an MLB-record 198 walks—68 intentional—and setting a major league mark with a .582 on-base percentage. Jeff Kent topped 100 RBI for the sixth consecutive season, and athletic outfielder Reggie Sanders drove in 85 runs.

Ultimately San Francisco's much improved pitching staff was the reason the team won 95 games. Giants pitchers finished second in the league (to the fabled Braves staff) with a 3.54 ERA. Kirk Rueter (14–8, 3.23), Jason Schmidt (13–8, 3.45), and Russ Ortiz (14–10, 3.61) led the way. SF hurlers helped the Giants go 29–10 down the stretch to clinch the wildcard over the Dodgers, and they were especially dominant over the season's last eight games: 8–0 with just eight total runs allowed.

The Giants clinched the wildcard with a 5–2 win over Houston in the season's penultimate game. In the locker room afterward, Bonds—who had belted a splash home run in the game—was noticeably reserved. "I've been here, done it—seven times," he said about making the playoffs. "I want to win the World Series."

So too did Giants manager Dusty Baker, who had overcome surgery for prostate cancer in the offseason, and San Francisco fans, who still hadn't experienced the ultimate glory. The Giants faced a seemingly invincible foe in the NLDS, as Atlanta had won its 11th consecutive division title, this time by a dominating 19-game margin. San Francisco banged out an 8–5 victory in Game One only to be crushed by a combined 20–5 score over the next two games.

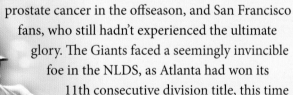

Kenny Lofton clinches the NLCS with a walk-off single in the bottom of the ninth against St. Louis in Game Five. Pitcher Steve Kline scored the winning run in the 2–1 victory. *Jeff Haynes/ AFP/Getty Images*

Highlights

August 9: Against Pittsburgh, Barry Bonds becomes the fourth MLB player to reach 600 home runs.

August 27: Bonds slugs three homers and a double against Colorado.

September 20–29: The Giants close with eight straight wins and clinch the wildcard on the 28th.

October 6–7: San Francisco tops Atlanta in Games Four and Five to win the NL Division Series.

October 14: The Giants defeat St. Louis 2–1 in Game Five of the NLCS, and clinch the Series, on a ninth-inning, walk-off single by Kenny Lofton.

October 26: Up three games to two over Anaheim in the World Series, the Giants blow a 5–0 lead in the seventh inning and lose 6–5.

October 27: The Angels cruise to a 4–1 home win in Game Seven to win the World Series.

NOTES

Barry Bonds wins his fifth NL MVP Award, this one unanimously. His numbers: 46 homers, 110 RBI, league highs in batting (.370) and slugging (.799), and MLB records for walks (198), intentional walks (68), and OBP (.582).

Jeff Kent belts .313-37-108 with 102 runs, ranking among the NL's top 10 in all four categories.

Starter **Kirk Rueter** goes 14–8, and reliever **Robb Nen** saves 43 games.

But these Giants wouldn't die, knocking postseason pitching legend Tom Glavine out of the box with seven early runs in Game Four and winning 8–3. Bonds played the hero in the decisive Game Five, homering and scoring twice to stake his team to a 3–1 lead. Rob Nen snuffed a ninth-inning Braves threat with a strikeout and double-play ball, sending the Giants to the NLCS.

Six early runs and four RBI by Benito Santiago led to a 9–6 Game One victory over St. Louis, and San Francisco won the next fray 4–1 behind the stout pitching of Jason Schmidt. The Giants followed a 5–4 loss with a 4–3 victory, putting them one win away from their first World Series in 13 years. Game Five was tied 1–1 in the bottom of the ninth before the Giants staged a two-out rally. David Bell, Shawon Dunston, and Kenny Lofton cracked consecutive singles for a dramatic pennant-clinching victory. Bonds, who led the charge out of the dugout, was going to his first World Series.

After the Giants blew a five-run, late-inning lead in Game Six of the World Series, Angels fans rubbed it in their faces the next day. *Timothy A. Clary/ AFP/Getty Images*

And did he deliver! Barry stroked .471 with four home runs in the Fall Classic against the Angels, giving him eight homers in the 2002 postseason. The first five games of this Series were action-packed: 4–3 Giants, 11–10 and 10–4 Angels, 4–3 Giants (on a Bell RBI single in the eighth), and 16–4 Giants (two homers by Kent). Three-year-old Darren Baker, Dusty's son, stole the spotlight in that game, as he ran toward home plate while two Giants runners were crossing it. But what everyone remembers most is Game Six.

With the Giants leading 5–0 in the seventh, and just eight outs away from their first world title, Baker pulled Russ Ortiz while the Angels' mascot—the "Rally Monkey" on the JumboTron—stirred Anaheim fans into a desperate frenzy. Sure enough, the Angels rallied for three in the seventh (all on a Scott Spiezio homer that barely cleared the right field wall) and three in the eighth for a 6–5 victory—the greatest in Angels history. John Lackey silenced the Giants' bats in Game Seven, winning 4–1.

In the corner of the dugout, a glum Barry Bonds watched the Angels celebrate their first-ever world title. "They outplayed us. They deserve it. They beat us," he said.

After the game, little Darren Baker wailed as his father carried him from the dugout. He wasn't the only Giants fan who was crying. Like the McCovey Series in '62, this was a heartbreaker.

WIRE TO WIRE

SF Wins 100 Games Before Falling to Marlins

Giants GM Brian Sabean could be proud of his MLB Executive of the Year Award in 2003. Sabean entered the new season with a new manager, Felipe Alou (Dusty Baker had signed a fat contract with the Cubs), and he had to replace free agent Jeff Kent and others. Even though a dozen members of the pennant-winning club didn't return for 2003, the new-look Giants won 100 games and became just the ninth MLB team ever to go wire to wire; i.e., maintain first place for the entire season.

Sabean replenished the lineup with leadoff-hitting second baseman Ray Durham, .300-hitting center fielder Marquis Grissom, and right fielder Jose Cruz, who won a Gold Glove Award in 2003. Bonds, at 38, continued to be the centerpiece of the offense, belting .341 with 45 homers and 148 walks.

Alou squeezed magic out of the pitching staff. Besides ace Jason Schmidt (17–5, 2.34 ERA), no starter had more than 10 victories, but all had winning records. With closer Robb Nen lost for the year to injury, Tim Worrell stepped in and saved 38 games.

The Giants, who started the season at 13–1, got clutch hitting and stellar relief pitching all year. Joe Nathan and Felix Rodriguez were a combined 20–6 out of the pen, and the club went 28–12 in one-run games. The Giants won the NL West by a whopping 15½ games over the Dodgers.

And yet, like the season prior, the year ended in bitter disappointment. Though Jason Schmidt shut out the wildcard Marlins in Game One of the NLDS, the tide turned in Game Two. Florida erupted for six runs in the fifth and sixth innings to key a 9–5 triumph. In the Series, the Giants hit no home runs, committed seven errors, and lost two one-run games.

In Game Three, the Giants went ahead 3–2 in the 11th when Edgardo Alfonzo singled in Rich Aurilia—only to lose on a two-out, two-run single by Florida's Ivan Rodriguez. The Marlins scored two runs in the bottom of the eighth of Game Four for a 7–6, Series-clinching victory.

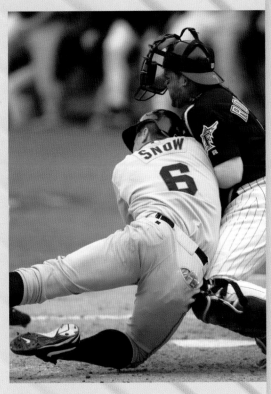

In Game Four of the NLDS, with Florida leading 7–6 in the top of the ninth, J. T. Snow tries to score on a Jeffrey Hammonds single to left field but is tagged out by Ivan Rodriguez to end the Series. *Eliot J. Schechter/Getty Images*

Highlights

May 9: Under new manager Felipe Alou, the Giants improve to 25–9. They have been and will be in first place the entire season.

June 23: Barry Bonds becomes the first MLB player with 500 homers and 500 steals.

September 17: The Giants beat San Diego at home to clinch the division title. Near the end of the game, a fan falls to his death.

September 30: Jason Schmidt shuts out Florida in Game One of the NLDS at Pac Bell. The Marlins will win the next game 9–5.

October 3: After an Edgar Alfonzo single gives SF a 2–1 lead in the 11th inning of Game Three, Florida prevails 3–2 on an Ivan Rodriguez two-run single.

October 4: Florida holds off the Giants 7–6 in Game Four to take the Series. J. T. Snow is thrown out at home to end the game.

NOTES

Barry Bonds wins his record sixth NL MVP Award after hitting .341-45-90 and leading the league in walks (148), OBP (.529), and slugging (.749).

Jason Schmidt goes 17–5 and leads the NL in ERA (2.34).

2004

▶ **91-71   2nd** ◀

Highlights

January 1: Pacific Bell Park is renamed SBC Park.

May 31: The Giants defeat Arizona 8–4 for their 10th straight victory.

June 20: Against Boston, Jason Schmidt throws his second one-hit shutout of the year.

June 22–July 4: San Francisco sits atop the NL West.

July 4: Bonds breaks Rickey Henderson's MLB record for walks with 2,191.

August 13: In a 16–6 rout of Philadelphia, J. T. Snow belts three home runs.

September 17: Versus San Diego, Bonds cracks his 700th career homer.

October 2: The Giants enter the penultimate game of the season two games back of the Dodgers. But LA clinches with a 7–3 win over SF, scoring all seven runs in the bottom of the ninth. Steve Finley triggers the celebration with a grand slam.

October 3: A Houston victory eliminates the Giants from the wildcard.

NOTES

Barry Bonds wins his seventh NL MVP Award. He sets MLB records for walks (232) and OBP (.609), leads in batting (.362) and slugging (.812), and tallies 45 homers and 129 runs.

Jason Schmidt goes 18–7 with a 3.20 ERA.

JUST WALK HIM

Bonds Gets 232 Free Passes as SF Falls a Game Short

On April 30, 2004, Giants rookie Brian Dallimore achieved an extraordinary feat. At 31 years old, in his first Major League start, Dallimore reached base five times against the hated Marlins and belted a grand slam. Yet that April, it was Barry Bonds—once again—who dominated the headlines.

After being embroiled in steroid controversy throughout the offseason, Bonds belted his 660th home run (into McCovey Cove) on April 12 to tie Willie Mays for third place on the MLB list. Mays, Barry's godfather, was on hand to pass a modified Olympic torch to him. The next night, Bonds passed Mays with another splash home run.

The more he homered, the more steroid attention he drew to himself, but Barry just kept hitting them. On April 20, he went deep for the seventh consecutive game, one short of the MLB record. Eventually, teams just started walking him.

The 40-year-old Bonds finished 2004 with 45 homers in just 373 official at-bats. He walked an unfathomable 232 times, including 120 intentionally. He became the oldest batting champion in history (.362), and his on-base percentage of .609 demolished his own MLB record of .582.

With a solid supporting cast that included J. T. Snow (.327) and Marquis Grissom (90 RBI), the Giants ranked second in the league with 850 runs. That production as well as ace Jason Schmidt (18–7) helped San Francisco overcome otherwise mediocre pitching. The Giants won 91 games in 2004 and darn near made the playoffs.

Just 60–55 on August 11, and 8½ games out of first place, the Giants went 31–16 down the stretch. On September 22, they trailed the first-place Dodgers by just a half game. However, a 5–5 finish wasn't good enough, as LA went 93–69 to best SF by two games. As for the wildcard chase, the suddenly red-hot Houston Astros won their last seven games to finish with 92 wins, one more than San Francisco.

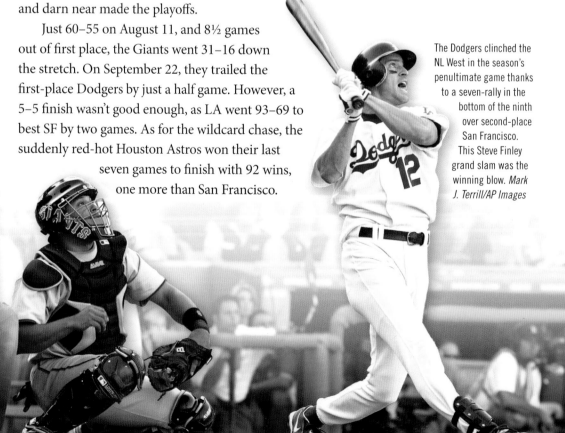

The Dodgers clinched the NL West in the season's penultimate game thanks to a seven-rally in the bottom of the ninth over second-place San Francisco. This Steve Finley grand slam was the winning blow. *Mark J. Terrill/AP Images*

SENIOR MOMENTS

Aging Giants Contend Despite a Losing Record

In 1983, the Philadelphia Phillies generated chuckles and Geritol jokes due to their old age. The "Wheeze Kids" lineup averaged 32 years old. But they were spring chickens compared to the grandpas that San Francisco put on the field in 2005. When 41-year-old Barry Bonds, who missed 148 games to injury, returned late in the season, the average age of the everyday lineup was nearly 36, making the Giants regulars the oldest group in MLB history.

Age truly was a problem for San Francisco in 2005. Bonds was breaking down, and though 39-year-old Moisés Alou could still get the job done (.321), 37-year-old J. T. Snow (40 RBI) and 38-year-old Marquis Grissom (.212) were nearly through. The DP combination of Ray Durham and Omar Vizquel (a legendary fielder at shortstop) averaged 36 years. Even the manager was old; Felipe Alou turned 70 on May 12.

In fact, as the Giants limped to a 25–37 start and managed just 71 wins against MLB's whipper-snappers, old age seemed to be a running theme. On July 9, the team presented retiring closer Robb Nen with a golf cart. On May 21, the club unveiled a statue of Juan Marichal, with his famous high leg kick, in Lefty O'Doul Plaza. And on July 23, Gaylord Perry's No. 36 was retired.

On July 30, the Giants stood at 45–58 but amazingly were just 5½ games out of first in the up-for-grabs NL West. Thinking they had a snowball's chance, management traded for solid-hitting outfielder Randy Winn. The 31-year-old youngster did all he could do, batting .359 for San Francisco, including .439 over his last 30 games.

On September 26, the Giants stood at 74–82 and yet still had a chance, as they trailed the first-place Padres by just three games. But in the last week, the SF hitters ran out of steam and dropped five straight. San Diego ended up taking the West with an 82–80 record, the worst ever by a division winner.

When outfielder Moisés Alou signed as a free agent with San Francisco in 2005, he got to play for his father, Felipe Alou. Both are pictured on this *Giants Magazine. MVP Books Collection*

Highlights

May 21: The Giants unveil a statue of Juan Marichal in the plaza outside the ballpark. It joins statues of Willie Mays and Willie McCovey.

May 26–June 14: The Giants endure a 2–15 tailspin and fall to 25–37, 10 games out.

June 17: Jason Schmidt throws eight shutout innings against Detroit but walks the first three batters in the ninth. Tyler Walker comes in and strikes out the side to preserve a 4–0 win.

July 14: The Giants record the franchise's 10,000th win, fittingly over the Dodgers.

August 15: Recent Giants acquisition Randy Winn hits for the cycle against Cincinnati.

August 16: Pedro Feliz and Deivi Cruz get five hits each for SF in a 10–8 win over the Reds.

NOTES

Outfielder **Pedro Feliz** leads a weak offense in homers (20) and RBI (81).

Outfielder **Moisés Alou**, the 38-year-old son of Giants manager **Felipe Alou**, raps .321.

Barry Bonds, who turns 41 during the season, plays just 14 games due to injury.

Southpaw **Noah Lowry** leads the Giants in wins (13–13) and ERA (3.78).

Every seat at AT&T Park offers a clear view of the diamond. *Eric Broder Van Dyke/Shutterstock.com*

The AT&T Park Experience

After years of shivering in homely, isolated Candlestick Park, veteran Giants broadcaster Lon Simmons took joy in Pacific Bell Park, which opened in April 2000. "Finally," Simmons said, "the Giants have a ballpark that looks like San Francisco."

Credit the architectural firm of HOK Sport, which, with Oriole Park at Camden Yards in Baltimore, had pioneered the construction of ballparks that reflected the character of their cities. In 2000, HOK unveiled three new gems: Comerica Park in Detroit, Enron Field in Houston, and Pacific Bell Park in San Francisco.

Renamed AT&T Park in 2006 (after two seasons as SBC Park in 2004–2005), San Francisco's new home was the most expensive of the three, costing $357 million, but it opened to rave reviews. For one thing, it was engineered to be only half as windy as Candlestick, thus minimizing the need for blankets and hot chocolate. As with Camden Yards, it reflects its environs. AT&T Park is so close to the city's most defining characteristic, the San Francisco Bay, that a powerful left-handed slugger can actually hit the ball into the water. From certain areas, fans can see the Bay Bridge. From the upper decks, patrons can view the Berkeley and Oakland hills. The stadium's brick exterior harkens the buildings of 19th century San Francisco, when the city boomed following the Gold Rush. Many fans reach the ballpark by walking across Lefty O'Doul Bridge over McCovey Cove.

Fans young and old enjoy the thrill of sliding through the "giant" Coke bottle. *Eric Broder Van Dyke/Shutterstock.com*

AT&T is much smaller than Candlestick, but the 41,000 fans who pack the park during frequent sellouts are treated to assorted pleasures. Every seat offers a clear view of the playing field. The anticipation of a splash hit into McCovey Cove is ever-present. The defining features in left field are outrageous—a giant (as in Giant) baseball mitt and an 80-foot-long Coke bottle with a special feature inside of it. Kids and young-at-heart adults "wheeeee" their way down the Coca-Cola Superslide.

To the right of the glove sculpture is Orlando's Caribbean BBQ, famous for its Cha Cha Bowl—grilled chicken marinated in a mild chili marinade over black beans, rice, and vegetables. Others opt for Gilroy's garlic fries; no ketchup needed. Right-center field features a San Francisco cable car with a label that reads "No Dodgers Fans Allowed."

In a review of all 30 major league parks—after touring each of them—ESPN's Eric Neel ranked Pac Bell No. 2 behind PNC Park in Pittsburgh. Neel gave the Giants' home park perfect scores of 5 for seat comfort, hot dogs, signature food, PA system, fun stuff, souvenirs, exterior, interior, access, ushers, and local scene. "Folks walk around the place with dopey grins on their faces," Neel wrote, "like they can't believe their good luck, like they know every minute they spend here is a lifetime they don't have to spend in the barren Candlestick wilderness."

The good vibes in the ballpark seemed to generate success on the field. In their first five seasons in Pac Bell Park, the Giants averaged 95 wins a year while making the playoffs three times. And in 2010 and '12, the team achieved what it never did in four decades at Candlestick. They won it all.

Splashin' in McCovey Cove

On the evening of May 1, 2000, Barry Bonds took a mighty uppercut swing against Mets pitcher Rich Rodriguez. As the Giants mascot and fellow fans threw their arms into the air, the ball skied deep to right field.

"He hits one high!" screamed Giants broadcaster Duane Kiper. "He hits one deep! McCovey Cove . . . outta here!"

As fans on the waterfront promenade high-fived each other, a man in a boat fished the ball out of the water with an enormous net. All had just been part of the first "splash hit" home run in Pac Bell history.

Fans had dreamt of this moment since the ballpark opened. If a player could blast one over the 24-foot wall in right field, and past the promenade (a wide walkway) behind it, the ball would splash into the China Basin, nicknamed McCovey Cove. On the fair side of the foul pole, a "Splash Hits" counter rests on the wall.

Splash hits are achievable but rare, which adds to their aura—as does the swarm of boaters who crowd the basin hoping to capture a wet souvenir. In the first 10 years of the ballpark, exactly 50 splash hits were launched, including 35 by Barry Bonds. Through the 2013 season, 62 "Splash Hits" have landed in McCovey Cove.

McCovey Cove. *Eric Broder Van Dyke/Shutterstock.com*

▶ 76-85   3rd ◀

Highlights

March: SBC Park is renamed AT&T Park.

May 20: Barry Bonds homers to tie Babe Ruth for second on the all-time homer list (714).

May 28: At home against Colorado, Bonds belts No. 715 to pass the Babe.

June 6: Jason Schmidt ties a franchise record with 16 strikeouts against Florida.

July 18–22: The Giants win five in a row and take over first place with a record of 51–47.

July 23–August 1: San Francisco drops nine straight games to plummet all the way to the division cellar.

September 14: After a 5–0 shutout of Colorado, the Giants are only three games out of first. However, they will go 2–12 the rest of the way.

September 23: At Milwaukee, Bonds clouts homer No. 734 to break Hank Aaron's NL record.

October 2: Felipe Alou is dismissed as manager. Bruce Bochy will replace him.

NOTES

Second baseman **Ray Durham** (.293-26-93), **Pedro Feliz** (.244-22-98), and **Moisés Alou** (.301-22-74) power the attack.

Barry Bonds hits .270-26-77 with 115 walks in 130 games.

Rookie **Matt Cain** leads the staff in victories (13–12).

HOW THE WEST WAS LOST

Aged Giants Can't Prevail in Winnable Division

In 2006, the National League was a bastion of mediocrity. Besides the Mets, no team won more than 88 games. The NL West was packed so tight that a team could drop from first place to last in the blink of an eye—like the Giants did in midseason.

On July 22, San Francisco held a half-game lead in the West. Ten days later, after losing nine straight games, they plummeted to fifth place in the five-team division. On August 1, Giants fans assaulted pitcher Armando Benitez with a chorus of boos. The SF closer, who had blown three straight games, responded with gestures to the crowd.

"That's definitely warranted," first baseman Mark Sweeney said of the fans' frustration. "Our fans are great fans and very smart. [But] you've got to understand, it's not like we're showing up and throwing our gloves out there."

Ray Durham emerged as the Giants' heaviest hitter, batting .293 with 26 homers and 93 RBI. Bonds hit a mortal .270-26-77 in 130 games while moving past Babe Ruth for No. 2 on the all-time home run list. The rise of young right-hander Matt Cain (13–12) offered a glimmer of hope for the future of this aged team.

Despite themselves, the Giants had a chance to win the NL West. On September 14, they were just three games out of first even though they boasted a 74–72 record. But after they gave up 52 runs over the next four games (that's 13 per game), the writing was on the wall. The Giants lost 13 of their last 15 and finished in third place, 11½ games behind the division-winning Padres.

At season's end, GM Brian Sabean made the "especially painful" decision to remove Felipe Alou as manager. Alou took it like a man. "Even though I will not be the Giants' manager next year, I will always be a Giant," he said. "I feel blessed that I was able to manage again, especially here in San Francisco."

In 2006, 6-foot-5 right-hander Jason Schmidt earned his third All-Star berth in a four-year span with the Giants. *Cameron Cross/Shutterstock.com*

Home Run King

Bonds Belts No. 756 to Break Aaron's Hallowed Record

On August 7, 2007, Barry Bonds launched a mammoth drive deep to right center off Washington's Mike Bacsik at AT&T Park. Bonds thrust his arms into the night air and clenched his fists. He had just broken the most hallowed record in sports. With No. 756, he had now usurped Hank Aaron as baseball's home run king.

"I knew I hit it," Bonds said. "I knew I got it. I was like, phew, finally."

At the time, it was widely accepted that Bonds's numbers were inflated by performance-enhancing drugs, including human growth hormone. Barry's new, larger cap, cried the accusers, was due to the bloating effects of HGH. Yet to reporters afterward, Bonds rejected that the achievement was tainted by steroids. "This record is not tainted at all. At all. Period," he said.

Bonds would finish the year, and his career, with 762 home runs, a record that baseball purists hoped would be toppled by a substance-free player. As for the Giants in 2007, they were in need of performance-enhancing play. With a lackluster offense ("defensive" catcher Bengie Molina led the team with 81 RBI), San Francisco won just 71 games.

Barry Bonds clouts home run No. 756 on August 7, breaking Hank Aaron's MLB record. Aaron congratulated Bonds in a videotaped message played on the scoreboard. *Ben Margot/AP Images*

In retrospect, the arrival of two men was much more important to the Giants than Bonds's record-breaking feat. Prior to the season, the team signed Bruce Bochy, a four-time division winner as San Diego's skipper, to manage the team. "He's the calming influence," said Larry Baer, president and CEO of the Giants. "He fits the combination of a strong hand while staying under the radar."

Bochy, a former major league catcher, would become a rock-steady leader of the Giants as well as a mentor to the team's many young players in upcoming seasons. One of the youngsters was rookie pitcher Tim Lincecum, who made his big-league debut on May 6. The undersized fireballer known as "The Freak" went just 7–7 with a 4.00 ERA in 2007, but he—like the Giants themselves—were on the verge of greatness.

Highlights

April 26: The Giants edge the Dodgers 5–4 for their eighth straight win. They are 12–8 and in first place for the only day of the year.

May 7: In a 9–4 win over the Mets, catcher Bengie Molina belts two-run and three-run homers in the fifth inning.

May 13: Rookie Fred Lewis hits for the cycle and adds another single in a 15–2 rout of Colorado.

June 22: The Giants lose their eighth straight to fall to 30–42, in last place, 11½ games out. They will remain in the cellar for the rest of the season.

August 4: Barry Bonds ties Hank Aaron's MLB home run record when he belts No. 755 off Clay Hensley at San Diego.

August 7: Bonds becomes MLB's home run king when he launches No. 756 over AT&T Park's center field fence off Washington's Mike Bascik.

NOTES

In his final season, **Barry Bonds** hits .278-26-66 with league highs in walks (132) and OBP (.480).

Randy Winn strokes .300, and **Bengie Molina** leads the team with 81 RBI.

Noah Lowry is the Giants' winningest pitcher (14–8).

▸ 72-90   4th ◂

Highlights

April 8: Bengie Molina belts a walk-off home run in the 11th inning to beat San Diego 3–2.

May 16: Peter Magowan announces he will be stepping down as the managing partner of the Giants.

May 19: A sixth straight loss puts the Giants at 17–29, 12 games out.

May 25: Omar Vizquel sets a Major League record by playing his 2,584th game at shortstop.

July 5: Despite a 39–49 mark, the Giants are only four games out, as every NL West team has a losing record. However, San Francisco will lose the next six games to fall out of contention for good.

NOTES

Bengie Molina leads a weak-hitting Giants team in homers (16) and RBI (95).

Randy Winn steals 25 bases and leads all Giants regulars with a .306 average.

Tim Lincecum emerges with an 18–5 record, a 2.62 ERA, and an NL-high 265 strikeouts. He wins the Cy Young Award.

Brian Wilson logs 41 saves.

Attendance drops below 3 million for the first time in the new ballpark.

GET YOUR FREAK ON

Lincecum Shines Brightest on Young, Talented Staff

Could the Giants survive without Barry Bonds? By their play in spring training in 2008, after the team decided not to resign the controversial home run king, it sure didn't look like it. San Francisco went 9–23–2, finishing last in the Cactus League in batting, ERA, and fielding percentage.

That performance carried over to the regular season, as the Giants got shut out on Opening Day, dropped six of their first seven, and on May 19 sat at 17–29, 12 games out of first place. Bruce Bochy's crew cut the deficit to four games by July 5, but this was no playoff contender. The Giants were 39–49 that day, and they would finish in fourth place at 72–90.

The team employed a franchise-record 16 rookies in 2008, yet this was not exactly a rebuilding season—at least not with position players. Graybeards Ray Durham and Omar Vizquel still manned the keystone positions, and catcher Bengie Molina and outfielders Randy Winn and Aaron Rowand were all in their 30s. The younger players who filled the other positions were more stop-gaps than cornerstones. Who among us remembers first baseman John Bowker, third baseman Jose Castillo, and outfielder Fred Lewis? With Bonds gone, Molina led this team in homers with a paltry 16.

Though the lineup was still in need of a major overhaul, pitching coach Dave Righetti was excited about the young arms on his staff. Nicknamed "The Horse," 23-year-old Matt Cain logged a 3.76 ERA in 34 starts. Southpaw Jonathan Sanchez, 25, fanned 157 batters in 158 innings. And free-spirited, 26-year-old reliever Brian Wilson arrived with 41 saves.

But the ace in the loaded deck was 24-year-old Tim Lincecum, the svelte, super-flexible righty who generated 100-mph fastballs from his exaggerated windup. Even though the Giants had the second-worst offense in the league in 2008, Lincecum led the NL in winning percentage (18–5, .783) as well as strikeouts (265) while logging a 2.62 ERA. "The Freak" won the Cy Young Award and, more importantly, gave Giants fans hope for a brighter future.

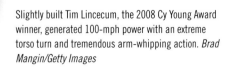

Slightly built Tim Lincecum, the 2008 Cy Young Award winner, generated 100-mph power with an extreme torso turn and tremendous arm-whipping action. *Brad Mangin/Getty Images*

BREAKOUT STARS

Sandoval, Cain Emerge as Big-Time Talents

If you throw enough spaghetti at the wall, some of it will stick. Pablo Sandoval, a 240-pound third baseman who would never say no to a bowl of pasta, was the spaghetti that stuck in 2009.

On Opening Day, the Giants started three players 25 and under in the infield. Travis Ishikawa, a 21st-round pick out of high school, manned first base. Emmanuel Burriss, a former first-round selection, replaced Ray Durham at second. And Sandoval, a 22-year-old out of Venezuela, took over at the hot corner. While Ishikawa and Burriss wouldn't hit enough to last in the majors, Sandoval was clearly a star in the making.

A gregarious, bubblegum-blowing slugger, Sandoval had bashed .345 in his 41-game trial with San Francisco in 2008. This year, he was the star of the show, leading the Giants in batting (.330), doubles (44), homers (25), RBI (90), and runs (79). Known as "Kung Fu Panda," Sandoval would become a fan favorite, inspiring the wearing of panda hats on chilly nights at AT&T Park.

Pablo Sandoval, who finished second in the NL batting race at .330 in 2009, has accumulated several nicknames, including the "Round Mound of Pound." *Photo Works/Shutterstock.com*

The Giants were still near the bottom of the NL in offense in 2009, but their pitching staff ranked second in the league with a 3.55 ERA. Despite just 15 victories (15–7), Tim Lincecum repeated as the Cy Young winner, as he logged a 2.48 ERA and won his second strikeout crown (261). Jonathan Sanchez suffered from control issues but was extremely hard to hit. In fact, he fired a no-hitter at home against San Diego on July 10.

Just as exciting was the breakout season of Matt Cain, who joined Lincecum on the NL All-Star team. Displaying more poise and throwing his breaking balls for strikes, Cain was able to lower both his walk and hit totals in 2009. The result was a 14–8 record and 2.89 ERA.

Though the Giants were 11 games out on September 26, they showed enough heart to win six of their last seven games. That never-say-die attitude would bode well during their historic run in 2010.

Highlights

May 22: A 2–1, 12-inning loss to Seattle drops the Giants to 19–21. They are nine games out of first place.

June 4: Randy Johnson, age 45 and in his sole season with the Giants, defeats Washington for his 300th career victory.

July 10: Jonathan Sanchez no-hits San Diego 8–0, walking none and striking out 11. The only base runner reaches on an error in the eighth inning.

July 14: Tim Lincecum is the NL's starting pitcher in the All-Star Game.

July 19: Giants majority owner Sue Burns dies of lung cancer.

September 27–October 4: The Giants win six of their last seven games, but they finish four games behind Colorado in the wildcard chase.

NOTES

Third baseman **Pablo Sandoval** is third in the league in batting (.330) and second in doubles (44). He leads a lackluster lineup in home runs (25) and RBI (90).

Tim Lincecum repeats as the NL's Cy Young Award winner after going 15–7, 2.48 with a league-leading 261 strikeouts.

Matt Cain goes 14–8, 2.89, while **Brian Wilson** finishes third in the NL with 38 saves.

2010

Highlights

September 10: A 1–0 win over the Padres catapults San Francisco into first place.

October 3: After steady improvement throughout the season, the Giants clinch the NL West on the last game of the season, 3–0 over San Diego.

October 11: The Giants defeat Atlanta in four games in the NLDS, as each contest is decided by one run.

October 20: Juan Uribe's sacrifice fly in the bottom of the ninth gives SF a 6–5 win over Philadelphia in Game Four of the NLCS.

October 23: Uribe's eighth-inning homer is the winner in the Giants' 3–2, NLCS-clinching triumph in Game Six.

October 31: Behind rookie pitcher Madison Bumgarner, San Francisco defeats Texas 4–0 in Game Four of the World Series to take a three-games-to-one lead.

November 1: Tim Lincecum shuts down Texas 3–1 in Game Five for the Giants' first world title in San Francisco.

NOTES

Catcher **Buster Posey** (.305) is the NL Rookie of the Year.

Tim Lincecum (16–10, league-best 231 strikeouts) and **Brian Wilson** (NL-high 48 saves) lead the best staff in baseball (3.26 ERA).

WORLD CHAMPS, AT LAST!

Misfits and Castoffs Bring Glory to San Francisco

After the Giants' 15-inning ordeal in Colorado on July 4, 2010, you might have expected them to just throw in the towel. Surely, many of their fans did. During extra innings of this five-hour, 24-minute torture test, the Rockies loaded the bases in the 10th, 13th, 14th, and 15th, finally winning 4–3. In San Francisco, fans blew off fireworks and went to bed, pondering if 49ers quarterback Alex Smith could bring the city at least one playoff team in 2010.

After the July 4 defat, the Giants owned a record of 41–40. They had lost eight of their last nine and were mired in fourth place, 7½ games out of first. And they had to hop onto a plane and play in Milwaukee the next day, for an afternoon game.

Saying he was "playing on fumes," Giants outfielder Aubrey Huff mustered three hits in the matinee affair as his team prevailed 6–1. You could call it the season's turnaround game. "After all the losses we had and especially the game we had last night, it's pretty tough to keep battling," said winning pitcher Jonathan Sanchez. "We battled the whole game, and finally we got the win."

The Giants picked up a game on the first-place Padres that day, sparking optimism that the team might chip away at the lead. "One game a week," Huff said. "That way it doesn't seem so overwhelming."

Manager Bruce Bochy referred to his 2010 Giants as a "bunch of misfits." The lineup was loaded with castoffs, such as bounceback-player Huff (.290-26-86) and shortstop Juan Uribe (.248-24-85). The pitching staff was largely homegrown, but it featured such characters as closer Brian "The Beard" Wilson, who dyed his fuzzy monstrosity inky black, and ace Tim "The Freak" Lincecum, whose long, shiny hair would attract derisive hey-good-lookin' whistles in enemy ballparks.

Rookie sensation Buster Posey (right) celebrates his home run with Cody Ross in the division-clinching game against San Diego in the 2010 season finale. *Ezra Shaw/Getty Images*

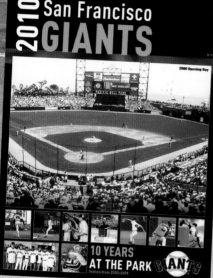

While the misfits and castoffs inspired little more than eye rolls and yawns in the season's first half, they began to captivate their fans from July on. For a number of reasons, this team got a whole lot better in the second half. Super-prospect Buster Posey, who made his season debut on May 29, ripped off a 21-game hitting streak in July, which raised his average to .355. He'd finish the year with a .305 mark and win the NL Rookie of the Year Award.

Veteran Pat Burrell, whom the Giants signed as a free agent on May 29, cracked 18 homers in just 96 games. Outfielder Cody Ross, a Marlins castoff who was claimed on waivers in August, ripped .288 down the stretch and would come up big in the postseason. General manager Brian Sabean pulled off midseason deals for relievers Javier Lopez and Ramon Ramirez, who combined to yield just five runs in 52 appearances. And starter Madison Bumgarner, a 20-year-old southpaw, debuted on June 26 and went 7–6, 3.00 the rest of the way.

In the second half, these odd-shaped pieces formed a perfect puzzle. After the season's nadir on July 4, the Giants went 19–5 over the rest of the month. And while they swooned in August (13–15), they were spectacular in September (18–8)— particularly the pitching staff. San Francisco's ERA for the month was 1.78, the lowest by any major league team in any calendar month since MLB lowered the pitching mound in 1969. Over one stretch of 18 games, the Giants never gave up more than three runs. Bumgarner was untouchable in September (1.13 ERA in five starts), and Lincecum went 5–1, 1.94 that month.

Pundits across the country said to "beware of the Giants" in the postseason, but first they had to get there. While simultaneously battling Atlanta for the wildcard, the Giants entered the final weekend up three games on San Diego—whom they would host over the final three games. Stunningly, the Padres erupted for 6–4 and 4–2 triumphs, putting San Francisco up by just one game entering the season finale.

Juan Uribe trots to the dugout after cracking a solo homer in the eighth inning of Game Six in Philadelphia. The shot broke a 2–2 tie, and the Giants hung on for a 3–2, NLCS-clinching win. *Rich Pilling/MLB Photos/Getty Images;*

The Giants responded with a 3–0 victory. Pitcher Jonathan Sanchez tripled and scored the first run before leaving after five innings. That's when Bochy marched in a parade of standout relievers: Santiago Casilla (1.95 ERA in 2010 for the Giants), Ramon Ramirez (0.67), Javier Lopez (1.42), top set-up man Sergio Romo (2.18), and Brian Wilson (1.81 with an NL-high 48 saves).

As players doused each other with champagne in the clubhouse, GM Brian Sabean compared this team to the old days with Barry Bonds. "Versus the past when we lived and died with one superstar player, there aren't any superstars on this team," Sabean said. "There might be a couple rising stars. Our organization is built on pitching. It's old-school baseball."

Giants pitchers took the Braves to school in the NL Division Series. Lincecum electrified AT&T Park with a 1–0 shutout in Game One, as he scattered two hits and a walk while striking out 14. Atlanta managed a 5–4 win in Game Two on a Rick Ankiel homer in the top of the 11th. The Braves almost stole the next game, scoring twice in the bottom of the eighth to take a 2–1 lead. But the Giants scored twice in the ninth, the latter coming on a two-out error by second baseman Brooks Conrad, and prevailed 3–2. In Game Four, Cody Ross singled in the winning run in the seventh, and the Giants won another one-run game, 3–2.

They won three more single-run affairs in the NLCS against Philadelphia, the two-time defending league champion. In a battle of Cy Young Award winners, Lincecum topped Roy Halladay in Game One 4–3, as Ross cracked two home runs. He homered the next night in Philadelphia, but the Phillies cruised 6–1. Back in San Francisco, Matt Cain pitched seven innings of a 3–0 shutout. In Game Four, Juan Uribe drove in Aubrey Huff with a sac fly in the bottom of the ninth for a walk-off 6–5 victory.

Though Halladay conquered Lincecum in Game Five, the Giants wrapped it up in Philly. Uribe's homer in the eighth inning of Game Six put SF up 3–2, and Wilson struck out Ryan Howard to end the game and send the Giants to the World Series. "It seems like the better teams we've played, the more we rose to the occasion," Sabean said.

As in 2002, the World Series pitted two teams that had never won a World Series: the San Francisco Giants versus the Texas Rangers. It could also be called the PC World Series, as San Francisco Mayor Gavin Newsom and Arlington Mayor Robert Cluck agreed that the losing city's mayor would go to the winning team's city and join that mayor "in a day of support for local youth and community service initiatives." After Game One, it looked like Cluck would be servicing in San Francisco, as a Juan Uribe three-run homer was the focal point in an 11–7 Giants victory. They continued to pile it on in Game Two, winning 9–0, as Matt Cain shined into the eighth.

While the Rangers came back with a 4–2 win in their home park, they subsequently bowed to the Giants' relentlessly strong pitching. In Game Four, the 21-year-old Bumgarner was unfazed by the pressure, pitching eight shutout innings of a 4–0 win. "He had it all working," Bochy said.

In Game Five in Texas, Lincecum and Cliff Lee posted goose eggs for six innings before veteran Giants shortstop Edgar Renteria delivered the killer blow. With two on and two out in the seventh, Renteria (the Series MVP) launched a Lee pitch just over the Geico sign in left-center for a 3–0 Giants lead. It was all the offense San Francisco needed, as Wilson preserved a 3–1 Lincecum victory with a perfect ninth inning. After punching out Nelson Cruz to end the game, Wilson was mobbed by catcher Posey and the entire Giants team.

"I dreamed it to happen, and then it happened," Wilson said amid the on-field celebration.

After 52 years in San Francisco, the Giants were finally world champions. "This buried a lot of bones—'62, '89, 2002," Sabean said. "We're proud and humbled by the achievement."

Upon returning to San Francisco, the Giants were treated to a parade that was dubbed the largest in city history. Hundreds of thousands of fans—along with float drivers, marching bands, and costumed mascots—lauded their heroes. Fans in "Fear the Beard" T-shirts chanted "Let's go Giants" as the players were driven through downtown.

It was a feeling that Juan Marichal, who had debuted in the Giants system in 1958, never had the chance to experience. "I don't mind," he said. "I don't care. We couldn't do it in those days. But I knew these kids could do it. That's baseball, you know? That's baseball."

The streets of San Francisco were awash in orange and black for the first baseball-championship parade the city had ever held.
Justin Sullivan/Getty Images

2011

▸ **86-76   2nd** ◂

Highlights

May 16–August 10: The Giants are either in first place or a half game out every day throughout this stretch.

May 25: Catcher Buster Posey breaks his ankle after a Marlins runner plows over him at home plate. Posey will miss the rest of the season.

July 6: The Giants beat the Padres 6–5 in 14 innings in a game that features 36 strikeouts.

August 14: When Cody Ross hits a two-run homer, it breaks San Francisco's streak of 21 consecutive solo home runs—an MLB record.

September 11–18: The Giants win eight in a row, but they are not within striking distance of first-place Arizona.

September 15: Pablo Sandoval hits for the cycle at Colorado.

NOTES

Pablo Sandoval leads SF in batting (.315), homers (23), and RBI (70).

Four Giants starters rank in the NL's top 10 in ERA: **Ryan Vogelsong** (2.71), **Tim Lincecum** (2.74), **Matt Cain** (2.88), and **Madison Bumgarner** (3.21). They all win 13 or 12 games.

San Francisco is last in the NL in scoring (570 runs) and second best in runs allowed (578).

The Giants set a **franchise attendance record** with 3,387,303 fans.

BUSTED!

Posey Injury Is a Back-Breaker for Limp-Hitting Giants

For the 2011 Giants, the highlight of the season—visiting the White House on July 25 as reigning world champions—couldn't make up for the lowlight on May 25.

It was the top of the 12th inning at AT&T Park, and the Marlins and Giants were tied 6–6. With runners on the corners, Florida's Emilio Bonifacio lofted a lazy fly ball to short right field, setting the stage for a play at the plate. Rocket-armed right fielder Nate Schierholtz caught the ball and rifled a strike to catcher Buster Posey. As Posey turned to block the plate, the hard-charging Scott Cousins freight-trained into his left side—a violent collision in which Posey suffered a fractured fibula and torn ligaments in his ankle.

Cousins, who showed genuine concern for the fallen warrior, would nonetheless be threatened by Giants fans. As for Posey, the reigning NL MVP was done for the season. The Giants, who were 27–20 and in first place at the time, hung tough without their heart and soul. They held onto first place, or were within a game of it, continuously until August 10, when the Diamondbacks began to pull away. San Francisco finished at 86–76, eight games behind.

Runs were scarce in Giants games in 2011, as San Francisco was last in the league with 570 runs scored and second with a 3.20 ERA. The lineup was so ravaged by injuries that only first baseman Aubrey Huff (who was out of shape) played more than 121 games. In Posey's absence, catcher Eli Whiteside batted .197 with 17 RBI in 82 games.

The Giants sent four pitchers to the All-Star Game: closer Brian Wilson and starters Tim Lincecum, Matt Cain, and Ryan Vogelsong (who had spent the previous four years in Japan and the minors). All three of SF's All-Star starting pitchers had ERAs in the 2.00s in 2011, but none could muster more than 13 wins. Needless to say, bolstering the lineup would need to be a priority if the Giants were to contend in 2012—let alone win a World Series.

After posting a 10–22 record in the majors, and then pitching three seasons in Japan, Ryan Vogelsong returned to the bigs in 2011 and earned All-Star status by going 13–7 and 2.71. *Doug Pensinger/Getty Images*

THE COMEBACK CHAMPS

Giants Win Six Elimination Games before Sweeping World Series

A year after losing Buster Posey to injury, which pretty much ruined their season, the Giants suffered another potentially deadly blow on August 15, 2012. Outfielder Melky Cabrera, the league's leading hitter at .346 and the All-Star Game's MVP, was suspended for 50 games after testing positive for testosterone. "It happened, and now we move on," said fellow Giants outfielder Hunter Pence. "Now we play with what we've got."

At the time, fans wondered if what they had was enough. When Tim Lincecum lost to Washington that day, dropping his record to 6–13, San Francisco stood at 64–54, a game behind the first-place Dodgers. The Giants were pretty good with Cabrera but seemingly mediocre without him. With Melky out, Lincecum struggling, and star closer Brian Wilson lost for the season, other players would have to step up big-time for the Giants to contend. And did they ever!

"The Freak" notwithstanding, the starting pitching was outstanding. Matt Cain and young Madison Bumgarner each won 16 games, while veterans Barry Zito and Ryan Vogelsong earned 15 and 14 victories, respectively. In the bullpen, Sergio Romo (14 saves, 1.79 ERA) and Santiago Casilla (25 saves, 2.84) filled in nobly for Wilson. Romo even boasted a Wilson-like black beard.

Offensively, league MVP Buster Posey smashed .336-24-103 and became the first NL catcher in 70 years to win the batting title. With Cabera's season cut short and Pablo Sandoval limited to 108 games due to injuries, no other Giant drove in more than 63 runs. However, center fielder and leadoff man Angel Pagan laced 38 doubles and 15 triples. And as in 2010, midseason pickups sparked the team down the stretch. Hunter Pence, a wild-eyed outfielder with knee-high socks, drove in 45 runs in 59 games for San Francisco. Meanwhile, second baseman Marco Scutaro cracked .362 in his 61 games with the Giants.

Following Cabrera's suspension and Lincecum's loss on August 15, the Giants responded like champions. They won seven of their next eight games to take a three-game lead in the NL West, and then went 19–8 in September. Bruce Bochy's boys finished at 94–68, eight games ahead of the second-place Dodgers.

Outfielder Gregor Blanco beams with excitement after scoring in a six-run fifth inning in Game Five of the NLDS. The Giants eliminated the Reds after losing the first two game of the Series. *Andy Lyons/Getty Images*

Highlights

June 13: Matt Cain authors a perfect game against Houston.

July 10: Cain starts the All-Star Game, while Pablo Sandoval hits a bases-loaded triple, and game MVP Melky Cabrera belts a home run.

August 15: Outfielder Cabrera, batting .346, is suspended for 50 games after testing positive for testosterone.

September 22: The Giants clinch the NL West with an 8–4 win over San Diego.

October 9–11: Down two games to none in the NLDS, the Giants defeat Cincinnati in Games Three, Four, and Five.

October 19–22: San Francisco wins three more elimination games, defeating St. Louis in Games Five, Six, and Seven of the NLCS. Marco Scutaro goes 14-for-28.

October 24: Pablo Sandoval belts three home runs in an 8–3 win over the Tigers in Game One of the World Series.

October 28: After a pair of 2–0, multi-pitcher shutouts, the Giants complete the sweep in Detroit with a 4–3, 10-inning win, as Scutaro singles in the winning run.

NOTES

Buster Posey (.336-24-103) wins the NL batting crown and MVP Award.

Angel Pagan knocks an NL-best 15 triples.

Matt Cain (16–5, 2.79) leads a strong staff.

Above: In the fifth inning of Game One of the World Series, Pablo Sandoval enjoys his third home run trot. His three blows were the equivalent of a first-round knockout; the Tigers never recovered. *Marcio Jose Sanchez/AP Images* **Below:** The Giants beat Detroit 8–3, 2–0, 2–0, and 4–3 (10 innings) to sweep the World Series. *MVP Books Collection*

Despite closing the season with a 30–14 run, the Giants flopped in the first two games of their NLDS with the Reds, losing 5–2 and 9–0 at home. No NL team had ever come back from an 0–2 deficit in a Division Series, and the Giants would have to win three in a row in front of the red-clad, towel-waving zanies in Cincinnati. Bochy gave a pep talk before Game Three, but it was Hunter Pence who stole the show.

"He's a fired-up guy, an amped guy," said reliever Jeremy Affeldt, "and when he started talking and pacing and getting louder and louder and louder, it was like, 'This is going to get loud. And it's going to be awesome.' It was one of those, 'Don't look him in the eye or he'll head-butt you.' He started slamming into stuff and yelling at us. I'm not a rah-rah guy, but I was high-fiving him too."

Affeldt was one of four Giants pitchers who limited the Reds to just one run that day. With the score 1–1 in the 10th, MVP Posey and emotional leader Pence opened the inning with singles. After two strikeouts and a passed ball, Posey scored the winning run on a rare error by third baseman Scott Rolen. From that point on, the Giants seemed unstoppable. They cruised 8–3 in Game Four and won Game Five 6–4, thanks to a fifth-inning grand slam by Posey.

"This team is so close," Pagan said after the emotional finale. "We're like brothers. We play for each other. We lift each other. And that's why we were able to do this."

In the NLCS, the Giants dug themselves into another hole, trailing three games to one to the Cardinals. But again they came roaring back. In Game Five in St. Louis, Zito pitched all but four outs of a 5–0 whitewash. In Game Six at a rocking AT&T Park, Scutaro—who would bat .500 for the Series—drove in two runs and Vogelsong pitched seven strong innings in 6–1 triumph. And in Game Seven, Pence busted opened the game with a three-run double in the third inning. Behind Matt Cain and four trusted relievers, the Giants won 9–0 to storm into the World Series.

The Detroit Tigers' starting pitchers had been virtually unhittable in their first two playoff series, particularly Justin Verlander, the reigning AL MVP. But the Giants were on an electrifying, seemingly unstoppable run, and they teed off on Verlander in Game One of the World Series at AT&T Park. This time, Sandoval played the hero, homering off the world's greatest pitcher in the first and third innings—then going deep off Al Albuquerque in the fifth. "Kung Fu Panda" thus joined Babe Ruth (twice), Reggie Jackson, and Albert Pujols as the only sluggers to go deep thrice in a World Series game.

The Giants followed the 8–3 thrashing with a pair of 2–0 shutouts. In Game Two, Bumgarner yielded just two hits in seven innings, while Casilla and Romo—both of whom were dynamic in the postseason—got the last six outs. In Detroit, Vogelsong, Lincecum, and Romo shut out the suddenly impotent Tiger bats on five hits.

Detroit finally showed some fight in Game Four, as the game went to extra innings tied at 3–3. But with two outs in the top of the 10th, Scutaro drove in Ryan Theriot with a single to center to break the tie. Romo punctuated the victory by striking out the side, including AL Triple Crown winner Miguel Cabrera on a called strike three to end the game. An ecstatic Romo punched the air three times before Posey and pals and joined the on-field celebration.

The Giants, who had treated their fans to five elimination-game wins, won their last seven postseason games by a combined score of 36–7. They thus became the first team since the 1998–2000 Yankees to win two World Series within three years. "I don't know if it's a dynasty," said Affeldt. "I just know we've been part of something amazing."

The Giants returned to a tickertape parade in San Francisco, this one drawing an estimated one million people. The parade took place on Halloween, meaning it was especially appropriate to dress in orange and black and other costumed attire, such as black beards and panda hats. Willie Mays rode in the parade, and Tony Bennett sang "I Left My Heart in San Francisco"—exactly 50 years after the song became a hit.

It was a perfect day to be a Giants fan.

Giants fans who trekked to Detroit for Game Four were on hand to celebrate the team's second world championship in three years. *Leon Halip/Getty Images*

Cain's Perfect Game

"I just love watching him pitch," Tim Lincecum once told the *Sporting News* about his buddy, Matt Cain. "Cain's that guy who doesn't give up any hits. You're looking at the board, you're like, 'They've only got two hits.' He just sneaky-dominates you."

An unassuming redhead from small-town Alabama, Cain "sneaky-dominated" the Houston Astros at AT&T Park on June 13, 2012. In a sense, it was one of the two greatest games anyone has every pitched. He not only threw a perfect game—the 22nd in MLB history and the first ever by a Giant—but he tied Sandy Koufax for the most strikeouts in a perfecto: 14. From the first inning on, he said, "I felt like I knew what I was doing with my fastball." He also threw his breaking balls for strikes—although he did need 125 pitches to get the deal done.

Of course, Cain had some help. Outfielder Melky Cabrera made a running catch at the wall in left field in the sixth inning. In the next frame, Gregor Blanco made a diving catch in right-center at the warning track. The last out came on a Jason Castro ground out to third, which triggered a world-title-like mob scene at the mound.

Matt Cain, June 13, 2010. *Missy Mikulecky/MLB Photos/Getty Images*

Highlights

March 29: The Giants announce that they have signed Buster Posey to a nine-year, $167-million contract.

May 25: Angel Pagan cracks a two-run, walk-off, inside-the-park home run to defeat Colorado 6–5.

May 26: San Francisco (28–22) holds first place for the last time.

July 10: The Giants lose to the Mets for their 14th loss in 16 games.

July 13: Tim Lincecum no-hits San Diego despite throwing a career-high 148 pitches.

July 16: Posey, Madison Bumgarner, Sergio Romo, and Marco Scutaro represent the Giants at the All-Star Game.

September 6: Yusmeiro Petit comes within one strike of throwing a perfect game against Arizona. Eric Chavez breaks it up with a single, and Petit finishes with a one-hit shutout.

September 14: Brandon Belt goes 5-for-6 with six RBI, and Hunter Pence drives in seven in a 19–3 win at LA.

September 28: The Giants sign Hunter Pence to a five-year, $90-million contract extension.

NOTES

Hunter Pence leads the team in homers (27) and RBI (99).

Madison Bumgarner paces the Giants' starting staff in wins (13–9), ERA (2.77), and strikeouts (199).

Sergio Romo saves 38 games.

Despite the team's losing record, the Giants finish third in the NL in attendance (3,369,106).

BUBBLE BURST

Pitching Woes, Mild Hitting Doom the Reigning Champs

With San Francisco trailing Colorado 5–4 in the 10th inning on May 25, 2013, on a sun-splashed Saturday afternoon at AT&T Park, Giants outfielder Angel Pagan blasted a ball into the deep recesses of right-center field. Brandon Crawford scored to tie it and Pagan flew all the way around the bases, diving headfirst into home with a walk-off, inside-the-park home run.

Unfortunately for Giants fans, Pagan's blast was one of the few highlights of the season. San Francisco's 2013 season ranked somewhere between disappointment and disaster. After storming through the previous World Series like an F5 tornado, the Giants were expected to make another championship run. Unfortunately, pitching calamities coupled with the team's genuine lack of offensive punch resulted in the Giants' playoff elimination on the ominous day of September 11, 2013, when they became the 13th consecutive MLB team not to repeat as world champion.

While the Giants finished fifth in the NL in batting, they placed 11th in runs scored, as they lacked both home run punch and timely hitting. Witness the numbers of their premier hitters: Buster Posey (.294-15-72), Brandon Belt (.289-17-67), Marco Scutaro (.297-2-31), and Pablo Sandoval (.278-14-79). Outfielder Hunter Pence (.283-27-99) was the only player on the team to top 20 homers, 90 RBI, or 20 stolen bases.

The season began well enough. Pagan's walk-off winner on May 25 put

Outfielders Gregor Blanco, Hunter Pence, and Angel Pagan celebrate a September 17 win over the Mets. Of this trio, only Pence provided offensive punch. *Al Bello/Getty Images*

The Rock Behind the Plate

Baseball people talk about Buster Posey like they do Derek Jeter. Dependable. Unflappable. Respectful of the game. A centerpiece of the team and its community. "Buster's work ethic, leadership, and extraordinary talent represent all that's great about our game and what it means to be a San Francisco Giant," team president Larry Baer told *Newsday*.

At Lee County High School in Georgia, Posey was every parent's dream child. Handsome and well-mannered, he graduated fourth in his class of 302 (3.94 GPA) while earning All-American honors in baseball—as a shortstop and pitcher. After converting to catcher at Florida State, he won the 2008 Golden Spikes Award as the nation's best amateur player.

Drafted fifth overall that year, Posey scored a Giants-record $6.2 million signing bonus and reached the majors

a year later. The rest is well documented: NL Rookie of the Year Award in 2010, season-ending injury in a home-plate collision in '11, and the NL batting crown, MVP Award, and second World Series title in '12.

The Giants, who consider Posey the cornerstone of the franchise, cemented him in place in 2013. Prior to spring training, he signed a one-year, $8 million contract. Then on March 29, he agreed to an eight-year extension worth $167 million—the largest contract in franchise history.

Buster Posey. *Photo Works/Shutterstock.com*

them at 27–22 and in a first-place tie in the NL West. However, San Francisco tanked in June (10–17) and July (8–17), and with the Dodgers in the midst of a 53–13 stretch (with rookie sensation Yasiel Puig the talk of California), the Giants were toast. They finished the season at 76–86 in third place, 16 games behind first-place LA.

Clearly, the collapse of the starting pitching staff was the biggest factor in the team's demise. Ryan Vogelsong, a dominant force the two previous seasons, owned an 8.06 ERA through his first eight starts. "I'm just off, man . . . ," he said in late April. "I just can't get anything consistent going with my delivery." In his next start, he broke his finger.

Matt Cain, 55–35, 2.93 over his previous four seasons, finished at 8–10, 4.00. He was a victim of the big inning in the first half of the season and lack of run support in the second. Tim Lincecum no-hit the Padres on July 13 but recorded his second straight disappointing season (10–14, 4.37). Barry Zito followed his comeback 15–8 campaign with the worst performance (5–11, 5.74) of his career. Young left-hander Madison Bumgarner—13–9, 2.77 as a first-time All-Star—was the only reliable arm in the starting rotation.

A weak offensive attack and an error-prone defense made it difficult for pitchers to prevail. In September, manager Bruce Bochy said "I'm working on ways we can make the ballclub better, including being more demanding on fundamentals, the things that have gone wrong this year, offensively and defensively."

By season's end, the Giants' sellout streak had eclipsed 240 games. But that fan support would undoubtedly dwindle in 2014 unless Bochy could somehow turn the club around.

2004: Jason Schmidt, 251
2005: Noah Lowry, 172
2006: Jason Schmidt, 180
2007: Matt Cain, 163
2008: *Tim Lincecum, 265*
2009: *Tim Lincecum, 261*
2010: *Tim Lincecum, 231*
2011: Tim Lincecum, 220
2012: Matt Cain, 193
2013: Madison Bumgarner, 199

Saves

2000: Robb Nen, 41
2001: *Robb Nen, 45*
2002: Robb Nen, 43
2003: Tim Worrell, 38
2004: Matt Herges, 23
2005: Tyler Walker, 23
2006: Armando Benitez, 17
2007: Brad Hennessey, 19
2008: Brian Wilson, 41
2009: Brian Wilson, 38
2010: *Brian Wilson, 48*
2011: Brian Wilson, 36
2012: Santiago Casilla, 25
2013: Sergio Romo, 38

NL Awards

NL MVP Voting

2000: *Jeff Kent, 1st*
        Barry Bonds, 2nd
2001: *Bonds, 1st*
2002: *Bonds, 1st*
        Kent, 6th
2003: *Bonds, 1st*
2004: *Bonds, 1st*
2009: Pablo Sandoval, 7th
2010: Aubrey Huff, 7th
2012: *Buster Posey, 1st*

NL Cy Young Award Winners

2008: Tim Lincecum
2009: Tim Lincecum

NL Rookie of the Year

2010: Buster Posey

NL Gold Glove Award Winners

2000: J. T. Snow, 1B
2003: Jose Cruz, Jr., OF
2005: Mike Matheny, C
        Omar Vizquel, SS
2006: Omar Vizquel, SS

NL All-Stars

(*Italics* indicates starter)
2000: Barry Bonds, OF
        Jeff Kent, 2B
2001: *Rich Aurilia, SS*
        Bonds, OF
        Kent, 2B
2002: *Bonds, OF*
        Robb Nen, P
        Benito Santiago, C
2003: *Bonds, OF*
        Jason Schmidt, P

2004: *Bonds, OF*
        Schmidt, P
2005: Moisés Alou, OF
2006: Schmidt, P
2007: *Bonds, OF*
2008: Tim Lincecum, P
        Brian Wilson, P
2009: *Lincecum, P*
        Matt Cain, P
2010: Lincecum, P
        Wilson, P
2011: Cain, P
        Lincecum, P
        Ryan Vogelsong, P
        Wilson, P
        Pablo Sandoval, 3B
2012: *Cain, P*
        Buster Posey, C
        Melky Cabrera, OF
        Sandoval, 3B
2013: Marco Scutaro, 2B
        Buster Posey, C
        Madison Bumgarner, P
        Sergio Romo, P

GIANTS 2000–2013 All-Decade Team

1B	J. T. SNOW
2B	JEFF KENT
SS	RICH AURILIA
3B	PABLO SANDOVAL
C	BUSTER POSEY
OF	BARRY BONDS
OF	RANDY WINN
OF	HUNTER PENCE
SP	TIM LINCECUM
SP	MATT CAIN
RP	BRIAN WILSON

A North Carolina boy, lefty Madison Bumgarner led or shared the team lead in wins every year from 2011 to 2013. *MVP Books Collection*

INDEX

Aaron, Hank, 85, 181, 192, 193, 204, 205
Adams, Ace Townsend, 89
Adcock, Joe, 113
Affeldt, Jeremy, 214, 215
Agbayani, Benny, 194, 195
Albuquerque, Al, 214
Aldridge, Vic, 62
Alexander, Doyle, 159, 160
Alfonzo, Edgardo, 199
Ali, Muhammad, 105
Allen, Johnny, 89
Alou, Felipe, 130, 192, 199, 201, 204
Alou, Jesus, 130, 131
Alou, Matty, 119, 127, 130
Alou, Moisés, 187, 201, 204
Altobelli, Joe, 141, 150, 151, 153
Alvarez, Wilson, 177, 187
Anderson, Greg, 181
Anderson, Sparky, 143, 163
Ankiel, Rick, 210
Antonelli, Johnny, 108, 109, 112, 113, 114, 120,
    122, 123
Arnold, Chris, 147
Aurilia, Rich, 189, 196, 199

Bacsik, Mike, 205
Baer, Larry, 205, 217
Baker, Darren, 198
Baker, Dusty, 4, 176, 177, 180, 182, 184,
    186–187, 190, 192, 195, 197, 199
Baker, Frank, 33, 38
Baker, Newton D., 44
Bancroft, Dave, 48, 50, 52
Barber, Red, 93
Barnes, Jesse, 45, 50
Barnes, Virgil, 58, 59
Barr, Jim, 146, 150
Bartell, Dick, 76, 80, 82, 84, 87
Beck, Clyde, 62
Beck, Rod, 182, 183, 184, 185, 187
Becker, Beals, 32
Bell, David, 198
Belt, Brandon, 216
Benard, Marvin, 188, 189
Bench, Johnny, 147
Bender, Chief, 21
Benitez, Armando, 204
Benjamin, Mike, 184
Bennett, James Gordon, Jr., 8
Bennett, Tony, 215

Bentley, Jack, 58
Benton, Larry, 62
Benton, Rube, 31, 41, 42, 43, 45
Bessent, Don, 120
Bielecki, Mike, 171
Black, Bud, 179
Blanco, Gregor, 213, 215, 216
Blue, Vida, 152, 153, 158, 159, 160, 164, 178
Bochy, Bruce, 5, 192, 204, 205, 206, 208, 210,
    213, 214, 217
Bonds, Barry, 4, 85, 143, 145, 176, 177, 180,
    181, 182, 183, 184, 185, 186, 187, 188,
    189, 192–193, 194, 195, 196, 197, 198,
    199, 200, 201, 203, 204, 205, 206, 210
Bonds, Bobby, 136, 137, 140, 141, 142, 144,
    145, 146, 147, 148, 149, 155, 176, 181,
    182, 184, 185
Bonifacio, Emilio, 212
Bonura, Zeke, 81
Bowerman, Frank, 17, 18
Bowker, John, 206
Boyer, Clete, 127
Branca, Ralph, 101, 105
Brantley, Jeff, 178
Brenly, Bob, 162, 163, 164, 167
Bresnahan, Roger, 12, 16, 17, 23
Bridwell, Al, 13, 24, 25
Bristol, Dave, 153, 156, 158, 159
Brown, Charlie, 127
Brown, Chris, 163, 164, 166
Brown, Walter, 80
Browne, George, 18, 21
Brush, John T., 12, 16, 19, 34, 42, 45
Bryant, Ron, 146, 147, 148, 155
Bumgarner, Madison, 193, 208, 209, 210, 212,
    213, 214, 216, 217, 218
Burdette, Lew, 123
Burkett, John, 178, 180, 182, 191
Burks, Ellis, 177, 189, 194, 195
Burns, George, 39, 41, 42, 43, 44, 45, 50, 64
Burns, Sue, 207
Burrell, Pat, 209
Burriss, Emmanuel, 207
Bush, Joe, 56
Butler, Brett, 168, 178
Byron, Bill, 42, 43

Cabrera, Melky, 193, 213, 215
Cabrera, Miguel, 215

Cain, Matt, 11, 193, 204, 206, 207, 210, 212,
    213, 214, 215, 217
Caldwell, Mike, 147, 148
Camilli, Dolph, 89
Cammeyer, Bill, 6–7
Cannon, Jimmy, 110
Canseco, Jose, 172, 185
Carlton, Steve, 164
Carrick, Bill, 14
Casilla, Santiago, 210, 213, 214
Castillo, Jose, 206
Castro, Jason, 215
Centranolo, Neil, 189
Cepeda, Orlando, 118, 119, 120, 121, 122, 123,
    125, 126, 127, 130, 131, 132, 134, 189
Chance, Frank, 22
Chapman, Ray, 48
Chase, Hal, 31, 45
Chavez, Eric, 216
Christopher, George, 124
Cicotte, Eddie, 43
Clapp, John, 8
Clark, Jack, 152, 153, 158, 159, 160
Clark, Will, 156, 157, 163, 164, 166, 167, 168,
    170, 171, 176, 178, 179, 180, 183
Clarke, Fred, 17
Cluck, Robert, 210
Coakley, Andy, 23
Cobb, Ty, 26, 42, 74
Cohen, Andy, 62
Collins, Eddie, 31, 38
Comiskey, Charles, 39
Conlon, Jocko, 87
Conn, Billy, 87
Conniff, Frank, 118
Connor, Roger, 7, 8, 9, 10
Conrad, Brooks, 210
Conte, Victor, 181
Coolidge, Calvin, 58
Cooper, Mort, 93, 94
Cooper, Walker, 85, 93, 94, 96, 97
Cousins, Scott, 212
Cox, Danny, 167
Craig, Roger, 156, 163, 166, 168, 178, 179, 180
Crandall, Doc, 32
Crawford, Brandon, 216
Creamer, Joseph, 26
Cronin, Jack, 16
Cronin, Joe, 66, 74
Cruz, Deivi, 201

Cruz, Jose, Jr., 4, 199
Cruz, Nelson, 211
Cunningham, Bill, 49
Curtis, John, 153

Dahlen, Bill, 13, 17, 18
Daley, Arthur, 103
Dallimore, Brian, 200
Danning, Harry, 81, 86, 89
Dark, Alvin, 85, 102, 103, 105, 106, 107, 108, 117, 123, 131
Darwin, Danny, 177
Davenport, Jim, 125, 127, 134, 135, 138, 156, 162, 163
Davis, Chili, 156, 160, 162, 166, 167, 174
Davis, George, 11, 14
Dawson, Andre, 185
Day, John B., 7–9, 10
Dayley, Ken, 167
Dean, Dizzy, 75
Dean, Paul, 75
Decker, Steve, 179
Delahanty, Ed, 17
Demaree, Frank, 80, 81
Dempsey, Jack, 91
Dent, Bucky, 4
Devlin, Art, 22, 29, 32
Devore, Josh, 33
Dickey, Bill, 67
Dietz, Dick, 142, 145
DiMaggio, Joe, 67, 77, 118
Doba, Wayne, 162
Doby, Larry, 108, 109
Donlin, Mike, 13, 20, 21, 24–25
Doolan, Mickey, 41
Dooley, Michael, 133
Douglas, Phil, 50, 52, 53, 54, 55
Downs, Kelly, 168, 173
Doyle, Bernard, 102
Doyle, Jack, 11, 14
Doyle, Larry, 26, 30, 33, 36, 38, 40, 41, 42
Dravecky, Dave, 157, 166, 167, 168, 171, 179
Dressen, Chuck, 107
Dreyfuss, Barney, 20
Drysdale, Don, 119, 120
Dunston, Shawon, 198
Durham, Ray, 199, 201, 204, 206, 207
Durocher, Leo, 81, 84, 85, 93, 95, 96, 97, 100–101, 102, 103–104, 107, 109, 112

Easterly, Jamie, 152
Ebbets, Charles, 95
Elster, Kevin, 195
Emslie, Bob, 14, 25

Engel, Clyde, 37
Erskine, Carl, 95
Estes, Shawn, 186, 194, 194–195, 196
Evans, Darrell, 150, 158, 161
Evers, Johnny, 13, 22, 25
Ewing, Buck, 7, 8, 9, 10, 14

Faber, Red, 43
Facone, Pete, 149
Fainaru-Wada, Mark, 181
Fairly, Ron, 126
Faust, Charlie, 30
Feliz, Pedro, 201, 204
Feller, Bob, 109
Finley, Steve, 200
Fitzsimmons, Freddie, 60, 62, 65, 66–67, 68, 70, 76
Fletcher, Art, 38, 39, 47, 50
Fogel, Horace, 16
Foster, George, 140
Fox, Charlie, 140, 142, 145, 148
Foxx, Jimmie, 74, 94
France, Joseph, 16
Franks, Herman, 119, 131, 136
Freedman, Andrew, 10, 11, 12, 15, 16
Frisch, Frankie, 31, 48, 49, 50, 52, 56, 58, 59, 60, 61
Fuentes, Tito, 144, 145
Fullerton, Hugh, 27
Furillo, Carl, 107

Gaetti, Gary, 188
Gaffney, John, 10
Gant, Ron, 184
Gardella, Danny, 90, 92, 93
Gardner, Larry, 31, 37
Gardner, Mark, 185, 188
Garrelts, Scott, 163, 164, 170, 171, 178
Gee, Johnny, 90
Gehrig, Lou, 67, 74, 77
Gibson, Bob, 136, 143
Giel, Paul, 109
Gilbert, Billy, 21
Gladden, Dan, 162, 163
Glavine, Tom, 198
Gleason, Kid, 14
Gomez, Ruben, 107, 109, 113, 114, 120
Gonsoroski, David, 170
Goodson, Ed, 148
Gordon, Sid, 93, 95, 96, 97
Gossage, Goose, 184
Gott, Jim, 163
Grady, Mike, 14
Graham, Billy, 119

Grant, Eddie, 44, 49, 52, 101
Grant, Ulysses S., 9
Green, David, 163
Greenberg, Hank, 94
Griffey, Ken, Jr., 192
Grimes, Burleigh, 61, 62
Grissom, Marquis, 199, 200, 201
Grissom, Marv, 109
Groat, Dick, 135
Gumbert, Harry, 80, 81, 86
Guthrie, Mark, 187

Halicki, Ed, 149, 151
Halladay, Roy, 210
Haller, Tom, 134, 135, 136
Hamaura, Toru, 146
Hamilton, Darryl, 188
Hammaker, Atlee, 161, 167
Hanno, Arnold, 109
Harney, Charles, 124
Hart, Jim Ray, 132, 134, 135, 136, 142
Hartnett, Gabby, 62
Hausmann, George, 93
Hayes, Charlie, 188
Hearn, Jim, 102, 106, 112
Heiber, Hank, 76
Henderson, Rickey, 200
Hensley, Clay, 205
Hernandez, Livan, 194–195
Hernandez, Roberto, 177, 187
Herndon, Larry, 150
Herseth, Bud, 150
Hershiser, Orel, 168, 188
Herzog, Buck, 41, 42
Hiatt, Jack, 136, 137
Hickman, Charlie, 14
Hildebrand, Ernie, 54
Hill, Glenallen, 184, 186
Hiller, Chuck, 127
Hodges, Russ, 101, 105
Hoey, Fred, 11
Hofman, Solly, 25
Hogan, John, 66, 68
Hogan, Shanty, 62
Hornsby, Rogers, 49, 60, 61, 62, 69
Howard, Ryan, 210
Hubbell, Bill, 50
Hubbell, Carl, 5, 62, 63, 66, 67, 68, 70, 71, 72, 73, 74, 75, 76, 77, 78, 80, 84, 86, 88, 89, 128, 135
Huff, Aubrey, 193, 208, 210, 212
Huggins, Miller, 48
Hulbert, William, 6–7
Hunt, Ron, 136

Hunter, Herb, 41
Huston, Cap, 55
Hynd, Noel, 84

Irvin, Monte, 97, 101, 103, 104, 106, 107, 113, 116
Ishikawa, Travis, 207
Ivie, Mike, 152, 153

Jackson, Reggie, 214
Jackson, Travis, 49, 60, 63, 68, 72, 75
Jansen, Larry, 94, 96, 97, 98, 102, 103, 104, 106
Javier, Stan, 188
Jennings, Hughie, 59
Jeter, Derek, 217
Johnson, Ban, 19
Johnson, Brian, 177, 186, 187
Johnson, Frank, 146
Johnson, Randy, 207
Johnson, Walter, 27, 58
Johnstone, James, 22
Jones, Bobby, 194, 195
Jones, Sam, 122, 123
Jones, Sheldon, 96, 97, 122
Joshua, Von, 149
Joyce, Robert, 80
Jurges, Billy, 80, 81, 86, 99

Karros, Eric, 187
Kasheta, Frank, 136
Keefe, Tim, 7, 8, 9, 10, 11, 20
Kelly, George, 48, 50, 52, 54, 55, 56, 58, 61
Kennedy, Monte, 97
Kennedy, Robert F., 136
Kent, Jeff, 177, 185, 186, 187, 188, 189, 192, 194, 196, 197, 199
Kerr, Buddy, 93, 94, 97
Khrushchev, Nikita, 118
Kieran, John, 73
Killefer, Red, 41
King, Clyde, 136, 140, 142
Kingman, Dave, 140, 146, 149
Kiper, Duane, 162, 203
Klein, Chuck, 63
Klem, Bill, 31, 54
Kline, Steve, 197
Knepper, Bob, 152
Koslo, Dave, 89, 93, 94, 97
Koufax, Sandy, 119, 130, 133, 215
Krug, Frank, 80
Krukow, Mike, 162, 164
Kuiper, Duane, 5

Lackey, John, 198
LaCoss, Mike, 166
Lampkin, Tom, 185
Landis, Kenesaw Mountain, 48
LaPoint, Dave, 163
Lardner, Ring, 31
Larsen, Don, 168
LaRussa, Tony, 171
Laskey, Bill, 160, 161
Lasorda, Tommy, 158
Latham, Arlie, 12
Lavelle, Gary, 151, 161
Lavender, Jimmy, 40
Lea, Charlie, 159
Leach, Freddy, 70
Lee, Cliff, 211
Lefebvre, Jim, 158
Lefferts, Craig, 157, 166
Leiber, Hank, 80, 88
Leiter, Mark, 184
LeMaster, Johnnie, 141, 149, 161
Lemon, Bob, 109
Leonard, Jeffrey, 156, 161, 162, 163, 166, 167, 168
Lewis, Darren, 183
Lewis, Fred, 205, 206
Lincecum, Tim, 11, 193, 205, 206, 207, 208, 210, 211, 212, 213, 214, 215, 216, 217
Lindstrom, Freddie, 49, 58, 62, 68
Linzy, Frank, 132, 134, 135
Liston, Sonny, 105
Littlefield, Dick, 113
Litton, Greg, 180
Lobert, Hans, 40
Lockman, Whitey, 92, 105, 106
Lofton, Kenny, 197, 198
Lohrman, Bill, 88
Lombardi, Ernie, 89, 92, 99
Lopez, Javier, 209, 210
Louis, Joe, 87, 91
Lowitt, Bruce, 95
Lowry, Noah, 201, 205
Luque, Dolf, 73
Lurie, Bob, 141, 150, 156, 157, 176, 180

Mack, Connie, 30, 33, 38, 51
Maddox, Garry, 141, 147
Maddux, Greg, 179
Madlock, Bill, 151, 152, 153
Magerkurth, George, 81, 95
Maglie, Sal, 93, 95, 102, 103, 104, 106, 107, 109, 112, 113, 135
Magowan, Peter, 176–177, 180, 181, 182, 189, 206

Maldonado, Candy, 156, 164, 166, 172
Mancuso, Gus, 73, 80, 89
Mann, Leslie, 54
Mantle, Mickey, 95, 127
Marberry, Firpo, 76
Marichal, Juan, 5, 119, 123, 126, 127, 128, 130, 131, 132, 133, 134, 135, 136, 137, 138, 140, 142, 144, 145, 147, 161, 189, 201, 211
Maris, Roger, 127, 183, 188
Marquard, Rube, 13, 30, 33, 36, 38, 39, 40, 46
Marshall, Mike, 147, 148
Marshall, Willard, 85, 94, 96, 97
Mathewson, Christy, 11, 12, 13, 14, 15, 16, 17, 18, 20–21, 22, 23, 24–25, 26, 27, 29, 30, 31, 32, 33, 36, 38, 39, 40, 41, 42, 45, 47, 50, 77, 135
Mathewson, Henry, 22
Matsui, Hideki, 131
Matthews, Gary, 141, 147, 148, 150, 155
May, Milt, 159
Mayne, Brent, 189
Mays, Carl, 53, 55
Mays, Willie, 5, 35, 79, 85, 95, 100, 101, 103, 103–104, 106, 108, 109, 110–111, 112, 113, 114, 118, 119, 120–121, 122, 123, 125, 126, 127, 130, 131, 132, 134, 135, 136, 137, 139, 140, 141, 142, 143, 144, 146, 147, 153, 176, 181, 184, 185, 189, 200, 201, 215
McCarthy, Joe, 77
McCarty, Lew, 41
McCarver, Tim, 172
McCormick, Mike, 119, 122, 123, 135
McCormick, Moose, 25
McCovey, Willie, 5, 118, 119, 122, 123, 126, 127, 130, 131, 132, 134, 135, 136, 137, 140, 142, 143, 144, 145, 146, 147, 151, 152, 153, 154, 158, 189, 201
McDaniel, Lindy, 134
McDougald, Gil, 104
McDowell, Sam, 140, 146
McGann, Dan, 16, 23, 32
McGee, Willie, 179
McGinnity, Joe, 11, 12, 13, 16, 17, 18, 20, 21, 24, 25
McGraw, John, 5, 12–13, 16, 17, 18, 19, 20, 22, 23, 30, 31, 33, 38, 39, 40, 41, 42–43, 44, 45, 48, 49, 50, 51, 52–53, 54, 55, 58, 59, 60, 61, 62, 63, 66, 67, 68, 69, 70, 71, 72–73, 74, 75, 76, 77, 78, 79, 94, 95, 115, 190
McGwire, Mark, 181, 188, 192, 196

McKechnie, Bill, 41
McNeely, Earl, 58
McQuade, Francis X., 45, 63
McQuillan, Hugh, 55, 60
Medwick, Joe, 90
Melon, Cliff, 78, 88, 89
Merkle, Fred, 13, 24, 25, 30, 33, 41, 42, 58
Mertes, Sam, 17, 18, 20, 28
Meusel, Bob, 54
Meusel, Irish, 49, 54, 56, 58, 59
Meyers, John "Chief," 30, 36, 46
Michaels, Al, 172
Miller, Jon, 189
Miller, Stu, 124, 125
Minton, Greg, 158, 159, 160, 161
Mitchell, Kevin, 157, 166, 168, 170, 171, 176,
    178, 179, 180
Mize, Johnny, 84, 85, 87, 88, 89, 93, 94, 96,
    97, 112
Molina, Bengie, 205, 206
Mondesi, Raul, 187
Montanez, Willie, 150
Montefusco, John, 141, 148, 149, 150, 151,
    152, 154
Mooney, Jim, 70
Moore, Joe "Jo-Jo," 71, 75, 76, 78, 80, 81, 86
Morgan, Joe, 147, 156, 159, 160
Moscone, George, 150
Mueller, Bill, 188, 189
Mueller, Don, 105, 107, 108, 112
Mueller, Jeff, 188
Mueller, Ray, 97
Mulholland, Terry, 178
Mungo, Van, 92
Murakami, Masanori, 131
Murcer, Bobby, 141, 148, 149, 150, 151
Murray, Eddie, 187
Murray, Red, 26, 32, 33, 36
Musial, Stan, 79, 144
Mutrie, Jim, 7, 8, 9, 10, 157
Myer, Buddy, 72

Nash, Ogden, 27
Nathan, Joe, 199
Neel, Eric, 203
Nehf, Art, 50, 52, 53, 54, 56, 58
Nen, Robb, 177, 188, 194, 195, 196, 197, 198,
    199, 201, 218
Newcombe, Don, 104–105
Newson, Gavin, 210
Nixon, Richard, 124
Noble, Ray, 107
Nomo, Hideo, 131

North, Bill, 153, 158
Nottebart, Don, 132

Obama, Barack, 111
O'Brien, Tom, 15
O'Connell, Jimmy, 58
O'Day, Hank, 25
O'Dea, Ken, 80
O'Dell, Billy, 126
O'Doul, Lefty, 63, 72, 201
Oliver, Nate, 136
O'Malley, Walter, 101
Ontiveros, Steve, 151
Oquendo, Jose, 4, 167
Orengo, Joe, 84, 89
O'Rourke, Jim, 9, 10
Ortiz, Russ, 177, 189, 197, 198
Ott, Melvin Thomas "Mel," 5, 49, 60, 62, 63, 67,
    68, 70, 71, 72, 73, 75, 76, 77, 78, 79, 80,
    81, 84, 85, 86, 87, 88, 89, 90, 92, 93, 94,
    95, 96, 97, 134, 153
Ozark, Danny, 162

Pagan, Angel, 213, 214, 216
Park, Chan Ho, 196
Parker, Dave, 172
Parker, Rick, 178
Pasquel, Bernardo, 93
Pasquel, Jorge, 93
Patterson, Floyd, 91
Peckinpaugh, Roger, 58
Pegler, Westbrook, 55
Pence, Hunter, 213, 214, 216
Perez, Marty, 150
Perez, Neifi, 188
Perritt, Pol, 41, 44
Perry, Gaylord, 119, 127, 131, 134, 135, 136,
    140, 142, 144, 145, 201
Petit, Yusmeiro, 216
Pezzullo, John, 76
Pfiester, Jack, 25
Piazza, Mike, 187
Pierce, Billy, 126, 127
Plank, Eddie, 21, 31
Portugal, Mark, 183
Posey, Buster, 5, 193, 208, 209, 211, 212, 213,
    214, 215, 216, 217
Price, Joe, 167
Puig, Yasiel, 217
Pujols, Albert, 214
Pulliam, Henry Clay, 15, 24, 25
Purdin, Juan, 136

Quisenberry, Dan, 178, 184

Rader, Dave, 148
Ramirez, Ramon, 209, 210
Raymond, Bugs, 32, 36
Reese, Andy, 62
Remlinger, Mike, 179
Renteria, Edgar, 187, 211
Reuschel, Rick, 157, 166, 168, 170, 171, 175, 176
Reuss, Jerry, 158
Reyes, Nap, 92
Rhodes, Dusty, 101, 106, 107, 108, 109, 115
Richardson, Bobby, 5, 119, 126, 127, 143
Righetti, Dave, 179, 206
Rigney, Billy, 101, 112, 113, 123, 141, 149, 150
Riles, Ernest, 168
Ring, Jimmy, 60, 61
Ripple, Jimmy, 78
Roberts, Robin, 112
Robertson, David, 41, 42
Robinson, Don, 157, 166, 168, 176
Robinson, Frank, 156, 157, 159, 160, 162
Robinson, Jackie, 94, 95, 97, 98, 113
Rodriguez, Felix, 199
Rodriguez, Ivan, 199
Rodriguez, Rich, 203
Rolen, Scott, 214
Romo, Sergio, 210, 213, 214–215, 216
Roosevelt, Franklin, 77, 87
Rose, Pete, 146
Roseboro, John, 132, 133
Rosen, Al, 156–157, 163, 166
Ross, Cody, 208, 209, 210, 212
Roush, Edd, 41, 61, 63
Rowand, Aaron, 206
Rucker, Johnny, 90
Rueter, Kirk, 177, 188, 197
Ruppert, Jacob, 55
Rusie, Amos, 10, 11, 12, 20
Russell, Jack, 73
Ruth, George Herman "Babe," 7, 40, 48, 50, 51,
    52, 53, 54, 55, 67, 74, 76, 86, 94, 192, 197,
    204, 214
Ryan, Bill, 54, 56
Ryan, Blondy, 76
Ryan, Nolan, 164

Sabean, Brian, 177, 193, 199, 204, 209, 210, 211
Sabean, Nick, 186
Sadecki, Ray, 119, 121, 134, 135
Sadek, Mike, 158
Sallee, Slim, 43
Sanchez, Jonathan, 206, 207, 208, 210

Sanders, Deion, 184
Sanders, Reggie, 197
Sandoval, Pablo, 193, 207, 212, 213, 214, 216
Sanford, Jack, 123, 126, 127, 130
Santiago, Benito, 198
Sauer, Hank, 114
Schang, Wally, 38
Schierholtz, Nate, 212
Schmidt, Jason, 197, 198, 199, 200, 201, 204
Schoendienst, Red, 113
Schumacher, Garry, 115
Schumacher, Hal, 66, 67, 72, 73, 76, 83, 86, 87, 89
Schupp, Ferdie, 42, 43
Scott, Jack, 54, 55, 56
Scott, Mike, 164
Scutaro, Marco, 213, 214, 216
Sears, Ziggy, 92
Seaver, Tom, 147
Seeds, Bob, 80
Selbach, Kip, 14
Seymour, Cy, 22, 23
Sheehan, Tom, 123
Sheridan, Pat, 173
Simmons, Al, 74
Simmons, Lou, 105, 189, 202
Smith, Alex, 208
Smith, Earl, 52
Smith, George, 16
Smith, Reggie, 133, 160
Snider, Duke, 95
Snodgrass, Fred, 30–31, 32, 33, 36, 37, 39, 40, 58
Snow, Jack Thomas "J. T.," 4, 186, 189, 190, 194, 195, 199, 200, 201
Snyder, Frank, 54
Sosa, Sammy, 188
Spahn, Warren, 110, 123, 130, 132
Spalding, Albert, 15
Speaker, Tris, 31, 37
Speier, Chris, 144, 145, 148, 168
Spencer, Daryl, 113, 119
Sperring, Rod, 151
Spiezio, Scott, 198
Stanky, Eddie, 85, 102, 106
Stargell, Willie, 183
Stengel, Casey, 49, 52, 54, 56
Stewart, Dave, 171, 173
Stone, Larry, 185
Stoneham, Charles A., 45, 60, 62, 71, 77
Stoneham, Horace, 77, 84–85, 96, 97, 101, 113, 115, 119, 120, 124, 150

Stow, Bryan, 133
Strang, Sammy, 15
Strawberry, Darryl, 184
Suhr, Gus, 78
Sutcliffe, Rick, 158
Suzuki, Ichiro, 131
Sweeney, Mark, 204
Swift, Bill, 180, 182

Taft, William, 26
Takahashi, Hiroshi, 131
Talcott, Edward, 10
Tanaka, Tatsuhico, 131
Taylor, Luther, 15, 16, 66
Terry, Bill, 5, 49, 61, 62, 63, 66, 67, 68, 69, 70, 71, 72, 72–73, 75, 76, 77, 78, 84–85, 87, 88, 89, 95
Terry, Ralph, 127
Tesreau, Jeff, 30, 36, 38, 39, 40, 41, 44, 47
Theriot, Ryan, 214
Thomas, Derrel, 149, 152
Thomasson, Gary, 151
Thompson, Hank, 97, 102, 107, 108
Thompson, Robby, 156, 163, 164, 170, 171, 174, 176, 179, 183
Thomson, Bobby, 5, 85, 94, 96, 97, 100–101, 102, 103, 104, 105, 106, 107, 108, 110, 119, 176–177
Thorpe, Jim, 38, 39, 44
Tinker, Joe, 22, 25
Toney, Fred, 44, 50
Torborg, Jeff, 182
Torres, Salomon, 177
Tudor, John, 167

Uribe, Jose, 157
Uribe, Juan, 208, 210

Van Haltren, George, 15
Verducci, Tom, 196
Vergez, Johnny, 76
Verlander, Justin, 214
Vila, Joe, 56
Vincent, Fay, 173
Vizcaino, Jose, 186, 187
Vizquel, Omar, 201, 206
Vogelsong, Ryan, 212, 213, 214, 217
Voiselle, Bill, 90, 92

Wagner, Honus, 24, 26
Wagner, Leon, 124

Wagner, Robert, 114
Walker, Bill, 68, 70
Walker, Tyler, 201
Ward, John Montgomery, 9, 11
Watkins, George, 76
Watson, Allen, 186
Watson, Bob, 149
Weintraub, Phil, 90
Welch, Mickey, 7, 8, 9, 11
Welsh, Jimmy, 62
Werber, Bill, 84
Wertz, Vic, 108, 109
Westrum, Wes, 109, 113, 148, 149
White, Bill, 113
Whitehill, Earl, 73
Whiteside, Eli, 212
Whitfield, Terry, 158
Whitson, Ed, 158
Wilhelm, Hoyt, 106, 109
Williams, Charlie, 146
Williams, Harry, 79
Williams, Joe, 78
Williams, Lance, 181
Williams, Matt, 171, 176, 177, 178, 179, 180, 182, 183, 184, 185, 186
Williams, Mitch, 171
Williams, Peter, 69
Williams, Ted, 51, 69, 158, 192, 197
Willis, Maury, 126
Wilson, Brian, 193, 206, 207, 208, 210, 211, 212, 213
Wilson, Hack, 59, 68, 94
Wilson, Trevor, 178, 179, 180
Wiltse, Hooks, 24
Winn, Randy, 201, 205, 206
Witek, Mickey, 89
Wood, Joe, 36
Worrell, Todd, 167, 199
Worthington, Al, 119
Wynn, Early, 109

Young, Cy, 27, 33
Young, Norman Robert, 86, 87
Youngblood, Joel, 161
Youngs, Ross, 45, 48, 49, 50, 52, 56, 58, 61
Yvars, Sal, 103

Zeile, Todd, 187
Zimmerman, Heinie, 5, 31, 41, 42, 43, 44
Zimmerman, Roy, 93
Zito, Barry, 193, 213, 214, 217